The Look of Russian Literature

The Look of Russian Literature

Avant-Garde

Visual

Experiments,

1900-1930

Gerald Janecek

PRINCETON UNIVERSITY PRESS

Princeton, New Jersey

Copyright © 1984 by Princeton University
Press

Published by Princeton University Press,
41 William Street, Princeton, New Jersey
08540
In the United Kingdom: Princeton
University Press, Guildford, Surrey

Library of Congress Cataloging in
Publication Data will be found on the last
printed page of this book

ISBN 0-691-06604-3

This book has been composed in Linotron
Trump

Publication of this book was made possible
(in part) by a grant from the Publications
Program of the National Endowment for the
Humanities, an independent Federal agency

Clothbound editions of Princeton University
Press books are printed on acid-free paper,
and binding materials are chosen for
strength and durability. Paperbacks,
although satisfactory for personal
collections, are not usually suitable for
library rebinding

Printed in the United States of America by
Princeton University Press, Princeton,
New Jersey

For **MOM**
who gave me eyes

and for **SUE AND SARAH**
who keep them bright

One must demand of the writer that he actually pay attention to typeface. After all, his thoughts reach us by means of the eye and not the ears. Therefore expressive typographic plasticity ought by its optic action to produce the same effect as both the voice and gestures of an orator.

El Lissitzky, 1925
(Lissitzky-Küppers 1968, p. 357)

SOCRATES: I quite agree with you that words should as far as possible resemble things; but I fear that this dragging in of resemblance . . . is a kind of hunger, which has to be supplemented by the mechanical aid of convention with a view to correctness; for I believe that if we could always, or almost always, use expressions which are similar, and therefore appropriate, this would be the most perfect state of language; as the opposite is the most imperfect.

Plato, *Cratylus*, p. 100

Contents

Illustrations
and Portraits

PORTRAITS

Transliteration System

The transliteration system is designed to guide the non-Russian-speaking person toward a simple but reasonably close approximation of Russian phonetics rather than toward a precise duplication of the Russian spelling, for which diacritical marks would be required. The resolution for problem letters is as follows:

e = e	й = y (omitted in nominative adjectival endings)	ч = ch
ё = yo (o after sibilants)		ш = sh
ж = zh	x = kh	щ = shch
и = i(-ский = -sky)	ц = ts	ы = y

э = e
ъ, ь omitted
ю = yu
я = ya

Abbreviations

IMLI—Institut mirovoy literatury imeni Gorkogo, Moscow
PSS—V. Mayakovsky, *Polnoe sobranie sochineniy*, 1955-61
TsGALI—Tsentralny gosudarstvenny arkhiv literatury
       i iskusstva, Moscow

Preface

Faced with what at first seemed a reasonably well-defined and manageable topic, the visual effects in Russian literature of 1900-1930, I soon discovered that it was rather hydralike in its complexity. It seems that during this period everyone was doing a little of everything. That was, of course, in the spirit of the times. But such a situation aggravates problems every researcher faces in deciding where to stop, what not to include. Every aspect of the visual and verbal arts is relevant to some extent, and one room explored leads inevitably to several others going off in different directions. Thus, in order to keep the project in check, I had to consider many rooms off-limits; subjects such as book design separated from authorship, text as part of a painting, and transrational language (*zaum*) are left unexplored. Sometimes the boundary between a literary work and a graphic work or painting becomes hard to define, but generally it is possible to decide whether a given work is basically a text or a picture. Since this is a literary investigation, I have excluded from detailed consideration works that are pictures—for example, a Cubist painting with fragments of text in the collage. Excluded also are editions or works whose graphic interest is the product of a designer, rather than the author himself, and therefore is not part of the original conception; for example, the book *For The Voice* (1923), a collection of Mayakovsky's poems brilliantly designed by El Lissitzky, and Filonov's lithographed manuscript of part of Khlebnikov's *Selected Poems* (1914) fall into this category.

In recent years the same rooms have been traversed in many sources, since the study of the Russian Avant Garde of the early twentieth century has become a blossoming field. Yet the rooms I have chosen still remain uninspected, even though a few scholars have glimpsed at them in passing, some more intently than others. Of the available sources, Vladimir Markov's definitive *Russian Futurism: A History* (1968) is the cornerstone of the entire field, and without it this book could not have been written. Susan Compton's *The World Backwards* (1978) is the one work that comes closest to the area I have investigated, although her study is oriented toward the art side of the intersection of the two media, while mine is oriented toward the literary side. Another difference is her basically chronological design, while mine is device- and author-oriented.

My main focus here is the interpenetration of the literary medium by features usually associated only with visual, nonverbal media. To have been considered a subject for study, a work must basically be a *text* to which have been added, as a somewhat subsidiary element, innovative visual properties that are bound directly to the text in some way. Five major figures in this trend—Bely, Kruchonykh, Kamensky, Zdanevich, and Mayakovsky—are the focus of the study, but only insofar as their work relates to this topic. It will not be a complete survey of these writers' entire *oeuvre*.

The first chapter attempts to place the subject in its context. Its emphasis is on the historical, tracing those features of book culture that preceded and are perhaps seminal for the rise of interest in visual effects in Russia during the period 1900-1930. Following this introduction are five chapters, each of which is devoted to one of the key figures in the vanguard of Russian visual literature whom I have identified as the creator of a particular style or set of devices that made the look of a literary work dynamic. Thus Bely was chosen as the earliest experimenter with layout in both verse and prose; Kruchonykh as the key figure in the production of manuscript books; Kamensky as the creator of the unique "ferroconcrete" poems; Zdanevich as a master of elaborately typeset books; and Mayakovsky as the proponent of the stepladder line that continues to be used to this day in Russian verse.

The result is a survey that is, in retrospect, more extensive than intensive, though individual key examples have been analyzed in some depth. Yet further in-depth investigation remains to be done. In particular, the links between graphics and text in the Kruchonykh chapter remain sketchy because preliminary work on the nature of *zaum* is not yet done. But as an extensive survey, this book is relatively complete and ought to demonstrate, I think, the richness and strength of the Russian achievement in the European-American context.

I hope that the reader is already familiar with the books by Markov and Compton mentioned earlier, as well as with Camilla Gray's *The Russian Experiment in Art: 1863-1922*, and perhaps with John Bowlt's *Russian Art of the Avant-Garde: Theory and Criticism, 1902-1934*. Little space will therefore be given to general information that can be found in these sources unless the information is essential to the discussion. I trust that the readers who are picking up this book without a knowledge of the others will find that enough connective tissue has been provided to make the argument comprehensible.

Translations of Futurist titles generally follow V. Markov's rendering. All other translations are mine unless otherwise indicated.

August 26, 1983

Acknowledgments

An important part of the research for this project was conducted in Moscow and Leningrad in 1979 under the exchange program administered by the International Research and Exchanges Board between the American Council of Learned Societies and the Soviet Academy of Sciences. Of particular value were the materials provided by the Institute of Russian Literature (Pushkin House) in Leningrad, with significant contributions made by the Lenin Library, the Saltykov-Schedrin Library, the Gorky Institute of World Literature, the Central Government Archive of Literature and Art (TsGALI), and the Mayakovsky Museum. To these institutions and their staffs I hereby express my gratitude.

A number of individuals supplied me with copies of otherwise unavailable books and sections of books. Most important of these is Vladimir Markov, whose generosity toward me has been unstinting. To him I would like to offer a special word of thanks. Others are Edward Możejko, Mme. Helène Zdanevitch-ILIAZD, V. A. Katanyan (now deceased), and the directors of the Marvin and Ruth Sackner Archive.

I am grateful to have had the suggestions and criticism of a number of respected people who were willing to read the manuscript or parts of it, namely, Robert L. Jackson, James Bailey, Gay Reading, Vladimir Bubrin, and my colleague Boris Sorokin.

The onerous burden of preparing clean drafts of the manuscript fell to Sharon Artis, who did the job with consummate skill and a smile. A special thanks goes to her.

The Look of Russian Literature

1. Introduction

A Historical

Perspective

THE AGE OF THE AVANT GARDE

Visual experimentation in Russian literature coincides with the age of the Avant Garde, which flourished during the first three decades of the twentieth century. These three decades witnessed an astonishing flowering of Russian arts in all spheres; their richness and level of achievement are unprecedented in Russia's history. The Golden Age of Pushkin relinquished its place to an even greater age—one that cannot be relegated to a Silver Age except in chronological terms.

The period of visual experimentation can be fixed with more preciseness than is usual in such cases. It began with the appearance on the literary scene of Andrey Bely in 1902 and can be said to have ended with the death of Mayakovsky in 1930. Russian Symbolism, the first Modernist movement, arose somewhat earlier, at the end of the 1880s, and a few artists continued to survive and work to the best of their abilities into the 1930s, but all the important events that concern us within the scope of this book fall into the three decades indicated. While some Symbolist writings of significance existed before 1900, they are traditional in appearance, if Modernist in other respects. By 1930 the age of avant-garde experimentation was over in Russia, if only for political reasons. In 1928 Lunacharsky was replaced as minister of culture and the Avant Garde lost perhaps its only defender in the government.

The first successful gambit of the Russian Avant Garde was the manifesto "A Slap in the Face of Public Taste" (December 1912), which declared, among other things, that "the Academy and Pushkin are more incomprehensible than hieroglyphics," and that poets had the right to create new words and "to feel an insurmountable hatred for the language existing before them" (Markov 1968, 46). It was signed by David Burliuk, Kruchonykh, Mayakovsky, and Khlebnikov and attracted significant public attention. Individually or collectively, these poets had already been publishing for several years, but their works went largely unnoticed: they were not sufficiently different from prevailing norms or simply failed to catch the critical and public eye for lack of distribution, publicity, or notoriety.

"A Slap," however, had the necessary shock value to command the desired attention.

The year 1913, perhaps the key year in the history of Russian Futurism, brought with it a bumper crop of publications (books, manifestoes, and miscellanies), many of which will be discussed in the succeeding chapters. The term *zaum* (transrational, beyond-mind language) was introduced—a concept unique to the Russian context that had paler analogues in the Avant Gardes of other literatures. The independence of the word from meaning and its value for its own sake were declared in Kruchonykh and Khlebnikov's manifesto, "The Word as Such." The year ended with the initiation of a tour of the provinces by Burliuk, Kamensky, and Mayakovsky that continued through March 1914. If the tour was not a financial success, it was at least great publicity, and with this, "everyone talked about Futurism in the fall of 1913 and the winter of 1913-14. The Futurists were lionized in literary circles" in the capitals (Markov 1968, 138). The three were also warmly received in Georgia, and this may have been an important factor in the relocation of Kruchonykh and others to Tiflis in 1919-21.

In the postrevolutionary period the Avant Garde, never too tightly knit to begin with, underwent a continuous process of disintegration, occasional regrouping, and scattering. David Burliuk, the most cohesive figure, was in Japan by 1920; in 1922 he moved to the United States, leaving Mayakovsky, the most visible and active member of the original group, at the helm in Moscow. The early 1920s also saw a move by some artists and writers, who called themselves Constructivists, away from art for its own sake toward an art that would be utilitarian: in times of material austerity, they felt, art must serve to improve the daily life of the masses and not be merely a decorative item for the aesthetic pleasure of the upper classes. The designs that resulted were clearly an outgrowth of the foregoing emphasis on purification of media and the trend toward abstract simplification, yet with a practical purpose. Constructivism in book production found its best theoretician and practitioner in El Lissitzky, and its most interesting creative writer in A. N. Chicherin.

But by the mid-1920s a crackdown on liberal trends in the arts was already underway; a policy of artistic political subservience was being formulated. The Avant Garde was soon wiped out.

The period had begun with escalated attempts to produce a synthesis of the arts, comparable to Wagner's *Gesamtkunstwerk*, but on a level more profound than cooperation or coexistence in the framework of a single artistic enterprise. Rather, a genuine synesthesia was sought on the basis of associations of the senses on the deepest psychological or spiritual level. This attempt at synthesis was combined with an investigation of the essence of the various art media, a "back-to-basics" approach. A characteristic declaration of the time is this passage from N. Kulbin's "Cubism":

In our great time when in official physics the absoluteness of time and space has been
     abolished,
When a new life is being built in new higher dimensions,
Cheerfulness has overfilled and spun the heads of harlequins.
Experiments, one more multicolored than another, stage designs, one more ragged than
     another.
What remains of the holiday hullabaloo?
Every "ism" brings use to the techniques of art.
Let everything be—genuine.
For music—sound.
For sculpture—form in the narrow sense.
For the word—values of expression [*narechiya*].
In the new synthesis of art we know where the kernel is and where the shell.
Painterly painting—that is the slogan of the painter.
And everything else—freedom.   (Belenson 1915, 216)

Thus painting as a matter of plane, color, and form was reanalyzed and
purified; verbal structure was freed from conservative grammatical restraints;
new harmonies, rhythms, and melodic shapes were explored in music. Malevich
wrote: "Architecture begins where there are no practical aims. Architecture for
its own sake" (Kovtun 1974, 46). Nineteenth-century canons were questioned
and rejected as academic, artificial, and unidiomatic. In this context, an "un-
idiomatic" canon can be understood as one which places restrictions (such as the
requirement to be representational in painting) that are not of the essence of the
art or medium itself. Once the basics of an art were defined, new relationships
between arts could be intuitively felt and possibilities for new combinations could
be perceived and developed.

A hallmark of the period was Scriabin's *Prometheus Symphony* (No. 5) with
its "color organ" that attempted to produce color effects corresponding to the
musical effects by a very carefully worked-out system of relationships. Scriabin's
unfinished *Mysterium* was to have been even more elaborate and monumental.
Other efforts at synesthesia were Kandinsky's "musical" style of painting (Stuck-
enschmidt) and his painterly literary efforts, the drama *Der gelbe Klang*, and the
book of prose poems, *Klänge*; Meyerhold's theatrical productions, which, while
laying bare theater conventions, introduced balletic, musical, and painterly tech-
niques in innovative ways (Marshall 1977, 125-44); and perhaps most exten-
sively, Diaghilev's Ballets Russes, which brought together some of the most
advanced minds of the time in all the arts: painters (Bakst, Benois, Larionov,
Goncharova, Matisse, Picasso) for set designs and costumes; composers (Stravin-
sky, Prokofiev, Ravel, Debussy) for ballet scores; and dancers and choreographers
(Fokin, Nijinsky, Pavlova, Karsavina) to produce brilliant, often shocking and
controversial, but nearly always innovative, productions.

Russian Symbolism had regarded music as the highest art, and one which literature should emulate. With the Futurists, however, music receded into the background. The majority of Futurists had begun as painters, and some of them continued to paint and draw even after establishing their writing careers. It is therefore not surprising that they considered the possibilities offered by literature as a visual medium. This study focuses on their efforts by glancing both backward and forward at their important predecessors and successors.

Since Russian Futurism was an avant-garde movement par excellence in almost prototypical form, I will focus briefly on one point in Renato Poggioli's *The Theory of the Avant Garde* that to me expresses the tenor of the avant-garde spirit in general. He draws a clear distinction between the classical and avant-garde attitudes toward art:

The tacitly enunciated task of classic art was the splendid repetition of the eternal maxims of ancient wisdom; impossible, then, for it to conceive of the commonplace pejoratively. But since the triumph of the romantic cult of originality and novelty, the aesthetic equivalent of the commonplace has come to be more and more pejoratively considered. (Poggioli 1968, 80)

In classical thinking about art, there was either beauty or ugliness, but there was no concept of cliché or "a not-new beauty, a familiar or well-known beauty, a beauty grown old, an overrepeated or common beauty" (p. 81). In contrast, Poggioli notes, "For modern art in general, and for avant-garde in particular, the only irremediable and absolute aesthetic error is a traditional artistic creation, an art that imitates and repeats itself" (p. 82).

Classical art seeks an eternal beauty that is stable and permanent, while avant-garde art is in constant ferment: art must change, progress, look to the future, avoid the past. Newness becomes a value in itself and ceaseless experimentation is the way to achieve it. A restless, frenetic, youthful, revolutionary mood predominates and finds artists changing their views, styles, and techniques seemingly from day to day. This attitude toward art is still prevalent today in many circles in the West, whereby an artist who produces a work similar to the preceding one is immediately accused of stagnation. Yet we must remember that such an attitude is an entirely modern one, less than one hundred years old.[1] In the Russia of the early twentieth century, this avant-garde mood was the main propellant for the development of the visual effects discussed here.

MANUSCRIPT CULTURE

In two areas of historical interest that are relevant to this study—manuscript culture and Baroque figure poetry—Russia shared the history of Europe, though

[1] The term "Avant Garde" in its metaphoric use is older, however—even older than Poggioli thought it was. See Calinescu 1977, 97.

on a somewhat delayed basis. The Gutenberg revolution was slower to reach Russia and slower to take a firm hold. The first dated printed Russian book, an *Acts of the Apostles*, appeared in 1564 (fig. 1) and bore the name of the typographer Ivan Fyodorov (d. 1583), who was eventually given the title of Father of Russian Printing. It is notable how much the first printed book resembled a manuscript, as was true of early European printing in general (Zemtsov 1964, 16). It was not, however, until Peter the Great's printing enterprise that books were printed in large enough quantities to challenge the hegemony of the manuscript (Kalder 1969-70), though manuscript culture itself managed to continue well into the nineteenth century, at least in ecclesiastical and Old Believer spheres. The nineteenth-century Romantic movement stimulated an interest in native antiquities in Russia as in the rest of Europe; by the end of the century the process of collecting and studying old manuscript books resulted in the flowering of paleographic science and the appearance of manuals by renowned Russian scholars such as Sreznevsky (1882), Sobolevsky (1906), Shchepkin (1920), and Karsky (1928). The first decades of this century were particularly rich in scientific literature and scholarly editions of old books, largely directed at the academic community but certainly available to others interested in antiquities.

Fig. 1. A page from the first dated printed Russian book, *The Acts of the Apostles*, by Ivan Fyodorov, 1564.

Fig. 2. Poem by Simeon Polotsky in the form of a star from the "Greeting" to Tsar Aleksey Mikhaylovich on the birth of his son Simeon; manuscript, second half of seventeenth century.

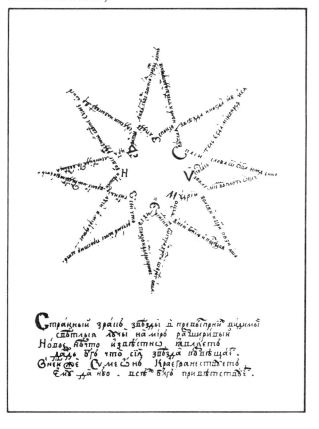

THE FIGURE POEM

Figure poems, in which the text has the outlines of an object central to the poem, were apparently the invention of Greek poets. Simias of Rhodes (fl. ca. 300 B.C.) evidently was the earliest practitioner (Higgins 1977), but only three of his poems, in the shape of an axe, an egg, and wings, survive. The best-known practitioner, however, was Publilius Optatianus Porfirius (fourth century A.D), who produced a range of cryptograms and figure poems (Mueller 1877, 69; also Doria 1979, 82-85). In the period of European Baroque this exotic genre was revived and used by a number of prominent poets.

Whether or not Russia can be said to have had a "genuine" Baroque period in literature, one can safely point to Simeon Polotsky (1628-80) as having practiced *figura poesis* on Russian soil during this period. Belorussian by birth, Kievan by scholastic training, he became the official poet to the Muscovite royal court, bringing to that post a knowledge of the Baroque practices of Europe, chiefly from Polish and Latin. His output includes a variety of figure poems (star [fig. 2], heart, cross) and cryptograms (Eryomin 1966; Hippisley 1971, 1977). These are, it seems, a purely imported product without a native Russian source, and, as was also the case in Europe, the figure poem did not develop an extensive tradition in Russia. Polotsky has never been held in high regard for his literary achievements. If his name was known at all by Russian writers of 1900-1930, it is unlikely that this knowledge went much beyond the cursory, and there is no evidence that he served as a model for anyone. In that period, only one noteworthy publication appeared about him—an edition of *Oryol rossiysky* (*The Russian Eagle*, 1915), which contained, among others, the illustrated poem.

Fig. 3. I. Rukavishnikov, poem in the form of a star (n.a. "Figurnye stikhi," source and date not given).

Fig. 4. Erl. Martov, "Rhombus," *Russkie simvolisty*, II, 1894.

Fig. 5. V. Bryusov, "Triangle," 1918.

```
                 И
                КТО
               ПРИДЯ
              В ТВОИ
            ЗАПРЕТНЫЕ
      ГДЕ НЕ БЫЛ ДО ТОГО НИКТО
     НАЙДЕТ БЕЗМОЛВНЫЕ ТВОИ
        И ТАЙНЫ СВЕТА НИЗВЕДЯ
          В ТЬМЫ БЕЗОТВЕТНЫЕ
           РОДИТ ТЕБЕ МЕЧТЫ
            ТОТ СВЕТЛЫЙ ТЫ
          ТВОЯ ЗВЕЗДА ЖИВАЯ
          ТВОЙ ГЕНИЙ ДВОЙНИКА
        ЕГО СМИРЕННО ПРИЗЫВАЯ
      СМУТЯСЬ МОЛИСЬ ИЗДАЛЕКА
    А ТЫ А ТЫ ВЕЧЕРНЯЯ ЗВЕЗДА
            ТЕБЕ ТУДА
             ГЛЯДЕТЬ
              ГДЕ Я
               ГДЕ
                Я
```

```
            II.

          Ромбъ.


            Мы —
        Среди тьмы
      Глазъ отдыхаетъ.
     Сумракъ ночи живой.
    Сердце жадно вдыхаетъ.
  Шопотъ звѣздъ долетаетъ порой,
 И лазурныя чувства тѣснятся толпой.
  Все забылося въ блескѣ росистомъ.
     Поцѣлуемъ душистымъ
       Поскорѣе блесни!
        — Снова шепни
         Какъ тогда—
          ...Да!»

          Эрл. Март въ
```

```
        ТРЕУГОЛЬНІКЪ.

             Я
            сле
           качая
          веревки,
         въ синели
        не  различая
       синихъ  тоновъ
      и милой  головки,
     летаю  въ  просторѣ
    крылатый  какъ  птица
   межь лиловыхъ  кустовъ!
  но въ заманчивомъ  взорѣ,
 знаю, блещетъ алѣя зарница!
и я счастливъ ею безъ словъ!
```

In the eighteenth century, figure poems were written by A. Rzhevsky (Gukovsky 1927, 181); eventually, around the turn of the twentieth century, the genre was adopted by I. Rukavishnikov (fig. 3), Erl. Martov (fig. 4), and Valery Bryusov. Bryusov's single figure poem, "Triangle" (fig. 5), from his book, *Experiments* (1918, 160), was part of a survey of verse form with illustrations by the author.[2] Bryusov also wrote a cryptogram (fig. 6) in answer to one written to him by Vadim Shershenevich (fig. 7) (Bryusov 1973-75, 3:627; Shershenevich 1916, 33).

The genre of the figure poem never caught on and is therefore of minor concern here, to be mentioned only briefly hereafter (see also Kuzminsky 1980).

THE *LUBOK*

Much more relevant and influential is the Russian broadside, or *lubok*. The oldest surviving example dates from between 1619 and 1624, and *luboks* were produced continuously into the early twentieth century. These "comic books" from the realm of pop literature typically combined a text with illustrative pictures in a variety of ways. Some had a block of text placed either above or below the illustration (fig. 8), while others had only a text that served, iconlike, to identify the characters and scene without narration. Still others had a narrative text distributed within the frame of the illustration (fig. 9), or combined a variety of layouts. Subjects ranged over the religious, historical, adventurous, and amorous, the text typically being a popularization of some already-existing literary

---

[2] See also Bryusov (1973-75), 3:544 and 524, respectively, and pp. 626-27 for further background.

Fig. 6. V. Bryusov, "Belated Answer. To Vadim Shershenevich," 1913.

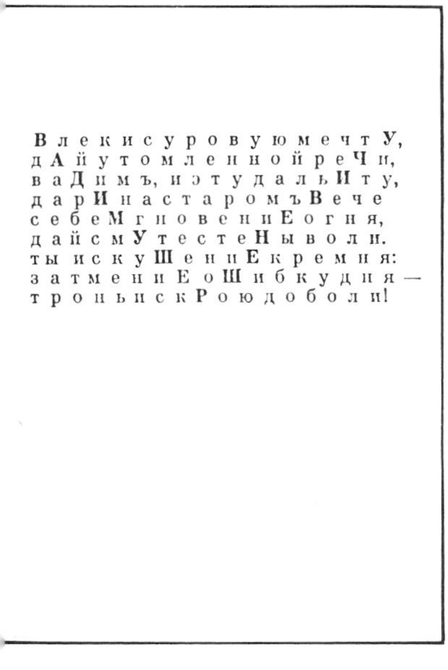

Fig. 7. V. Shershenevich, "To Valery Bryusov from the Author," published 1916, written prior to fig. 6.

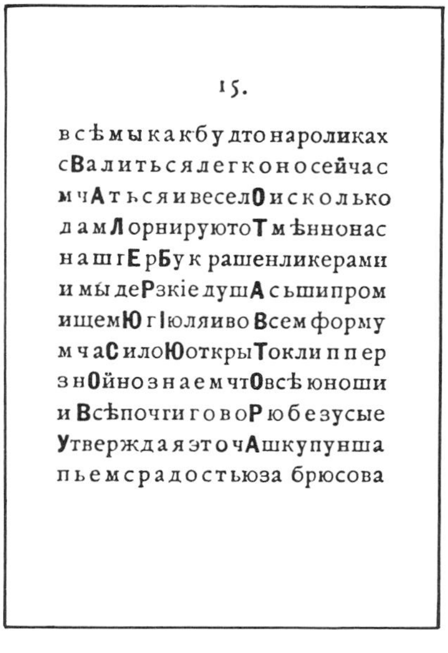

work. The illustrations were what we might call "primitive" in style but lustily drawn and brightly colored, with a freedom from academic canons of perspective, anatomy, and composition. These characteristics held great appeal for twentieth-century artists such as Nataliya Goncharova, Mikhail Larionov, David Burliuk, Kazimir Malevich, and Olga Rozanova (Bowlt 1974; 1980, 10, 13; Chamot 1973, 495), who were looking for ways to escape the restrictions of realism and were finding new vitality in folk creativity. Larionov and Goncharova, in particular, extensively collected and exhibited examples of the art of the *lubok*, and used them as "domestic stimuli" in their search for "the virtues of traditional Russian art forms" (Bowlt 1974, 137). This interest even grew briefly into a commercial-patriotic enterprise to aid the war effort:

In August-September, 1914, a special corporation called the Modern Broadside was established in Moscow for the production and publication of "lubok" posters and postcards. Some of the avant-garde artists, including Vasilii Chekrygin, Larionov, Lentulov, Maia-kovsky and Malevich were active in this enterprise, although the employment of professional studio artists in "lubok" production, however sincere their admiration of primitive art forms, was, of course, contrary to the very basis of the "lubok" industry. The new "lubok" was at its most powerful before the reversal of Russia's military fortunes. But when the consistent defeats of the Russian army began in 1915, the "lubok" "petrified . . . and grew silent." (Bowlt 1980, 15)

Some of these artists contributed visual material to the early publications of Kruchonykh and others and will be discussed in chapter 3.

Fig. 8. Old-time Hospitality; woodcut, first half of eighteenth century.

Fig. 9. Picture Bible; wooduct by Vasili Koren, 1696.

SYMBOLISM

The followers of Russian Symbolism, the literary movement immediately preceding and overlapping with the period of greatest visual experimentation, were not particularly interested in tampering with the look of their texts. Andrey Bely was the obvious exception and will be studied in detail in chapter 2. The others were more conservative, which is not to say that they were entirely indifferent to the printed appearance of their works. In fact, they were important precursors to the experimentation that was to follow, because they wanted the look of their books to contribute to a general mood. But they preferred an elegance and luxuriousness of book design that was rather traditional, though in consonance with their neo-romantic orientation. The Petersburg journal *Mir iskusstva* (*The World of Art*, 1898-1904), with its large format, many illustrations, rich decorations, fine paper, and exquisite typographical design, introduced an aesthetic refinement that was absent in the journals of the late nineteenth century and spawned a series of descendants of similar elegance, such as the major journals *The Balance, The Golden Fleece, Apollo, Works and Days*, and *Dreamers' Notes*, plus a variety of shorter-lived journals and almanacs (Lapshina 1977, 72-76, 82; Chamot 1973, 494).

The Symbolists' striving for unity of mood, involving even the visual level, is expressed in this previously unpublished fragment of an unfinished novel on the life of the decadents by Valery Bryusov:

"Now let's talk about the title," said L-in.

D-ov, standing opposite him, slowly opened his eyes. His pale face lit up. He began to speak quietly and not right away . . .

"The title . . . They didn't understand that earlier . . . There is a mysterious bond among all the parts of a book . . .

There are mysterious, caressing bonds
Between the aroma and the contour of a flower.

And the paper, and the typeface . . . O, Baudelaire understood that. . . ."[3]

Another statement by a major Symbolist is contained in a letter, recently come to light, from Aleksandr Blok to Bryusov, dated April 18, 1906, having to do with the publication of Blok's second volume of poems *Unexpected Joy*:

May I ask you that it be printed in the normal "Skorpion" typeface, as in the first issues of *Northern Flowers* (1901-1903); I think that the typeface of *Urbi et orbi* and *Stephanos* [two books by Bryusov] is too classical for my poetry; in addition, I would like each verse to begin with a capital letter. I have long pictured the format, cover and even the paper as being like that in *Letters by Pushkin and to Pushkin*; this is because there is a conservative bookishness in me: I have always felt a particular affection for covers with simple

[3] Lenin Library, ms. div., fond 386, Bryusov, k.3, e. kh. 17, January 1898.

lettering or in an old book border, but have felt that complex lines and everything which exceeds vignetteness [*vinetochnost*] soon becomes tiresome. To this day I love the edition of *Pan* in its entirety: the format, and the paper and the four simple green letters on gray; nevertheless I do have in mind red letters on gray or grayish blue. But everything concerning the cover, format and paper is secondary; the main thing I ask for is the typeface and capitals.[4]

This relatively conservative position is reasonably representative of the general Symbolist attitude in matters of printing. Symbolist books as a result often have a somewhat neutral, if not old-fashioned look. Innovation in sound was of more concern to them than newness of visual appearance. Music was the perfect art form.

Yet even a great verbal artist such as Blok cast an occasional envious glance in the direction of the visual arts, as in his short article "Colors and Words" (1905):

The art of colors and lines permits one always to remember the closeness of real nature and never allows a submersion into a schematism from which a writer has no strength to remove himself. Painting teaches one to look and to see (these are different things and rarely coincide). Thanks to that, painting preserves alive and untouched the kind of feeling which is notable in children.

Verbal impressions are more foreign to children than visual ones. Children enjoy drawing everything possible; and what is impossible to draw—that isn't needed. In children words are subordinate to drawing, they play a secondary role. (Blok 1960-63, 5:20-21; see also West 1975)

This childlike orientation toward the visual is what would be brought to the fore by the Futurists, but would be condemned by many as childish and primitive.

THE ORTHOGRAPHIC REFORMS

Unique to Russia (and other parts of the eventual Soviet Union) during the period of the Avant Garde was the enactment of reforms in the orthography by the Bolshevik government immediately following the October Revolution. These reforms in some sense did more than anything else to change the appearance of the Russian text, affecting all written materials—literary and nonliterary, avant-garde and conservative. Only the émigré publishing houses held off for a time in capitulating to this symbol of the new Soviet power.

Slavists are quite familiar with the essential features of the reform since most of them deal regularly with materials printed in periods both before and after the reform, yet few of them, probably, have ever looked into the matter more than

---

[4] The title *Pan* in the Russian old orthography would have a "hard sign" added to it, making it four letters; in Suvorova (1978), 89.

cursorily. Although extensive discussion is not needed for our purposes, the story itself is interesting and it casts a valuable light on certain features of some of the texts we will be dealing with.

When a given language evolves, spelling that once closely approximated pronunciation becomes outmoded as the sound structure changes. With time the discrepancy between spelling and pronunciation increases and spelling becomes a burdensome matter of learning rules that seem arbitrary because they no longer have observable foundations in speech. But changing the orthography often becomes an inefficient solution: either all materials written in the old orthography must be replaced, which is too monumental a task to be considered seriously, or two or more orthographies must exist side by side, which has its problems as well. Some authority must decide when a given sound change is clear enough, permanent enough, and universal enough to be enshrined in official spelling— not an easy decision, given regional and personal variations. It is interesting to note, moreover, that spoken language evolves slowly yet inevitably (Sapir's "linguistic drift" [Sapir 1949, 147-70]), but is beyond the control of anyone, while written language usually does not evolve gradually and produces permanent, timeless documents, yet is amenable to legislation.

Russian orthography had been a topic of discussion in learned circles for more than two centuries, ever since the Petrine reforms opened up the subject of orthographic questions by introducing changes in the orthography beginning in 1710. Concepts of the sacredness of traditional spelling were swept out in the face of the practical considerations of printing government documents and technical treatises in large numbers for the first time. Precision and efficiency were more valued than tradition. This reform eliminated some unnecessary letters and many variant letter shapes, added й, and brought the remaining letters closer to Latin forms (Eskova 1966, 58-59). Nonetheless, several redundant letters were allowed to remain, as was the silent ъ. The result was called the "civil script" (*grazhdansky shrift*). As a half-measure it remained a subject of controversy in which leading literary figures such as Trediakovsky, Lomonosov, and Karamzin added their views and proposed solutions.

As was true elsewhere in the eighteenth and early nineteenth centuries, spelling rules were not as rigid in Russia as they have become in more recent times. Finally, in 1885, Ya. K. Grot, in his practical manual *Russian Orthography* (*Russkoe pravopisanie*) set up standards that received wide acceptance. Ironically, Grot, as a prominent linguist who knew all the inadequacies of the civil script and had written about them critically, was instrumental in canonizing the civil script as the norm. His manual, which went through at least twenty editions (the twentieth appeared in 1912), became the standard reference source for typesetters, proofreaders, writers, and teachers for more than thirty years. Grot's contribution was positive in that with his scientific erudition and authoritativeness he eliminated some of the many orthographic problems plaguing the language and brought a uniformity to spelling that cleared the way for the more complete and decisive reforms that were to follow.

The first move was made by those who were most able to appreciate the hardships visited upon the innocent by orthographic problems—the teachers of Russian.[5] They knew at firsthand how much classroom time was spent teaching students to know when to write ѣ, і, and Ѳ and when to write е, и, and ф In 1901 the Moscow Pedagogical Society began a study of the question. They were followed by similar groups in Kazan and Odessa. Finally, in 1904 the Academy of Sciences formed a commission to study the matter. The chairman of this commission was the president of the Academy of Sciences, Grand Duke Konstantin Romanov. The commission, at its one and only meeting, voted that it was appropriate to reform the orthography and that all unnecessary letters should be dropped. The remaining issues were to be dealt with by a subcommission of experts which included F. F. Fortunatov (chairman), I. A. Baudouin de Courtenay, F. E. Korsh, and A. A. Shakhmatov—some of the most illustrious linguists of the day. Soon their recommendations were formulated and published, but the war and the 1905 Revolution intervened to cause the matter to be tabled indefinitely.

In 1912 the discussion was reopened by the publication of the *Resolutions of the Orthographic Subcommission*, which was a somewhat less radical version of the 1904 plan.

The last stage took another five years. The debate was quite heated. On one side stood most of the teachers and linguists, and on the other stood the traditionalists, some of whom claimed that the orthographic reforms would drive a wedge between the people and their heritage. Among the opponents of the reform stood some major literary figures, such as the Symbolists Vyacheslav Ivanov, Bryusov, and Blok. Their objections are particularly relevant to our study as they focus on the look of words. The opinion of Vyacheslav Ivanov (1905): "The danger that threatens on this path is graphic amorphousness or formlessness which not only, as a consequence of the weakening of the *hieroglyphic* [emphasis added] element, is aesthetically unpleasant and psychologically unnatural, but also can facilitate general apathy toward language" (Eskova 1966, 87). Bryusov: "However, both ѣ and ъ play one important role that is ordinarily forgotten about: an aesthetic role. By means of some sort of 'natural selection' Russian words have acquired in their shapes the most beautiful of attainable forms. The word вѣсть printed with a simple 'e' (instead of вѣсть) loses its beauty of shape, as will be the case with words printed without ъ" (Eskova 1966, 87). This despite the fact that the letters ѣ and e were no longer distinguished phonetically, and ъ, indicating the hardness of the preceding consonant, was in most cases entirely superfluous.[6]

---

[5] The account of the orthographic reforms from this point on is based chiefly on Chernyshov (1947).
[6] On a similar graphic distinction in Lermontov see Lotman (1972), 73; trans., p. 72.

Blok's opinion was that the works written in the old orthography should be reprinted that way, and only those written with the new system in mind should be printed in the reformed orthography. This view had its merits: as Bryusov pointed out, in the works of some poets of the nineteenth century and earlier, such as Pushkin, the use of ѣ and e does seem to reflect a phonetic distinction still made (Bryusov 1973-75, 7:108). Yet it is striking that three of the leading Symbolists—Russia's first group of avant-garde Modernists—should oppose modernization of the orthography; it is even more striking that they, as sonically oriented writers, should do so because it would change nothing but the way a word looks. Among them only Bely had shown any interest in the graphic side of literature beyond a certain aestheticism, and he was among the first to accept the orthographic reforms when they were finally implemented. John Malmstad notes: "Unlike Blok, who remained loyal to the old orthography to the end of his life, Bely showed no preference for the old. He began almost immediately to publish his verse in the new orthography and in his own personal writing after the changes employed the new orthography" (Malmstad 1968, xci).

Lev Tolstoy was against the reform because, although it might simplify writing, it would "lengthen the process of reading: after all we only write by letters, but we read . . . by the general look of words. We take in a word all at once with a glance, not breaking it into syllables; . . . every word had its special physiognomy . . ." (Chernyshov 1947, 218). It is true that modern studies of reading agree entirely with this view of the reading process, although they would add that word recognition depends also on what you are used to seeing and is not tied to any specific "look" for a given word.

Other voices in opposition were more extreme. *Apollo*, the Acmeist journal, published an article by Valerian Chudovsky, "In Favor of the Letter ѣ ," in which the author made the threatened letter a "symbol of mortally wounded philological tradition, of linguistic heritage." The reform, a product of "rotten politics," threatened to undermine Russian culture and children's faith in their elders: "Language is a religion: orthography is its sacred liturgy. Like the heavens above the earth, there must be given to children in their education a feeling of spiritual expanses not created by us." He went so far as to say that "there is no path to Pushkin without ѣ , for he lives on the Olympus of the accumulation through the ages, of the unbrokenness of heritage whose symbol and key is the letter ѣ " (Chudovsky 1917, v-viii).

The matter indeed was seen to have profound political implications. Korney Chukovsky relates the following about an abortive attempt to publish an early collection of Mayakovsky's poems:

The censorship reacted to it fiercely and did not even permit Mayakovsky as microscopic a liberty as writing words without hard signs, having seen in this free orthography virtually a shock to the foundations of the country. The book had already been typeset when the censor demanded that Mayakovsky put hard signs at the ends of all words ending in a consonant. Therefore on one of the proofs which I have kept are crowded whole phalanxes of these letters written in Mayakovsky's hand. Why the book did not come into print I don't remember. (Chukovsky 1967, 337)

Another figure of note was also against the reform. The philosopher Nikolay Fyodorov, in a posthumously published article "On Characters," pointed out that

letters are merely the graphic depiction of the progress of that creature who is gifted with the word. . . . These forms of letters say much more than words, speak more sincerely than words do; the forms of letters are less bribable than words; cursive writing, for example, speaks in words of progress, but the letter forms themselves . . . are a witness to regression. . . . Letters merely note the changes taking place in the soul of a society which is passing from a life loyal to the strict uncial script to a life of vain and feverish activity. (Fyodorov 1904, 2-4)

The old, slowly written script showed a care for words and life and the high quality of both; the Petrine rapid style demonstrates a substitution of quantity and speed for quality in modern society.[7] This view has relevance for the rise of the manuscript book, which will be considered in chapter 3. Nikolay Burliuk, in his essay "Poetic Sources" (1914) written with his brother David, refers to Fyodorov, evidently having in mind precisely the above-quoted article. Paraphrasing a number of Fyodorov's thoughts contained therein, he even uses for "letters" Fyodorov's archaic term *pismena* instead of the modern *bukvy*. In the "Supplementum to Poetic Counterpoint" at the end of "Poetic Sources," Nikolay Burliuk calls "for the creation of a new alphabet, for new sounds." After all, "many ideas can be conveyed only by ideographic script. Many words will come alive in new written forms." While agreeing with Baudouin de Courtenay that "our alphabet . . . [was] created historically, and not according to the laws of inner necessity," he nevertheless felt that the ideas of the orthographic subcommission were worthwhile. Yet for him they were too mechanistic and pedantic and did not show a proper understanding of living, creative language.

In defense of the reform, Baudouin de Courtenay wrote the monograph "On the Relationship of Russian Writing to the Russian Language" (1912). One of its main points, made repeatedly by the linguists in the discussion, is that language (*langue, yazyk*) as living speech is independent of a writing system. The latter is merely a means of conveying the former and is entirely arbitrary. Thus linguistic heritage and orthography are distinct and separate entities, which is a point not noticed by Chudovsky and other opponents of the reform, but which had been

---

[7] Kovtun (1974), 38, comments on Fyodorov: "The Russian Futurists thought very highly of his works." See also Kovtun 1976, 183, where he points to the influence of Fyodorov on N. Burliuk and V. Chekrygin. The link to the latter was noted earlier in Khardzhiev and Trenin (1970), 120.

made as early as 1904 by the proponents of the reform (Chernyshov 1947, 178). In fact, the critics often did not realize that what was thought to be the heritage of Pushkin in orthographic terms was actually the heritage of Grot, since the typesetters were following not Pushkin's personal spelling, nor even the spelling of the first editions that may have "corrected" his spelling according to the then prevailing practices, but Grot's rules (Eskova 1966, 85).

P. N. Sakulin, another member of the 1904 subcommission and longtime defender of the reform, wrote in 1917:

A literate person naturally develops definite associations with the graphic appearance of words and since very many people are not capable of clearly distinguishing the boundary between writing and language, the characteristics of speech itself are not uncommonly attributed to the letter shapes. (Chernyshov 1947, 245)

Finally, in early 1917, the teachers took the initiative again and asked the Academy of Sciences to implement the reform. The academy appointed another committee, headed by Shakhmatov, and on May 11, 1917, it passed thirteen resolutions. The letter ъ was dropped at the ends of words but retained as a separating sign in the middle of words. The letters ѣ, Ѳ, and i were dropped and replaced by е, ф, and и, respectively. Use of the letter ё was considered desirable but not obligatory. Prefixes ending in з replaced the з with с when followed by a voiceless consonant. Adjective endings -аго, -яго, and -ыя, ия were replaced by -ого, -его, and -ые, -ие respectively. Онѣ became они, однѣ, однѣх and so on became одни, одних, and the pronoun ея became её. A rule for hyphenation was advanced, and the separation or joining of prepositions in phrases used as adverbs was allowed. An appended note indicated that the proposals made by the Moscow teachers and the earlier subcommissions, concerning the dropping of ь after sibilants (мыш, знаеш, береч) and writing о instead of е after sibilants when the stress falls there (чорный, лжот, шол), were not included in the thirteen points because they had for some reason been voted down by the new commission. (See appendix 1 for complete text.)

The Ministry of Education of the Provisional Government immediately acted on this plan by directing its schools to begin implementation of the reform by the beginning of the new school year (the fall of 1917). Despite vocal opposition of the sort already discussed, the ministry held to this position.

It remained for the Bolshevik government, however, to adopt the reform on a broad scale. The decree of December 23, 1917, ordered the implementation of the May 11 plan (word for word, it might be added) in "all, without exception, national and government agencies and schools in the soonest possible time." A decree of October 10, 1918, reconfirmed the earlier decree, broadening the implementation to include not only all periodical and nonperiodical publications, but also documents and papers. However, it omitted points 5 and 13 from the plan, wisely judging that definiteness, and not suggestions for alternatives, was needed.

One aspect of orthographic reform involves its economics. Aside from time and labor previously wasted on learning spelling rules, proofreading and correction, there was the matter of wasted paper. It had been calculated that one of every seventeen letters was an unnecessary ъ. Thus the reform saved 5 to 6 percent of the paper that would have been used to print the same material in the old orthography. In a copy of *War and Peace* this would be about 70 pages, or in a printing of 3,000 copies a total of 210,000 pages would be saved (L. Uspensky 1973, 226-27). Considering the shortage of paper after the Revolution, the reform was most timely.

Another upshot of the reforms was somewhat amusing. Evidently some overly zealous revolutionary sailors went into various printing offices and destroyed the supplies of the now obsolete letters, including all the ъs, not having noticed that they were still needed in some words as separators (see point 3 in appendix 1). As a result, for more than a decade until the ъs could be resupplied, many printers were obliged to substitute apostrophes for them (Eskova 1966, 92). When the ъs were reintroduced, there was a brief outcry of "counterrevolution" because that letter had become a symbol of the old regime. In this context Gleb Struve has pointed out that émigré publishers could use the old orthography only for books not intended for the Soviet market, otherwise their bourgeois, tsarist origin would be immediately obvious and their products would be rejected (Struve 1978, 22).

Although the orthographic reforms are only one part of the total avant-garde picture and cannot be said to have generated experimentation with visual effects, the heated and prolonged discussions preceding the reforms certainly contributed to a nationwide awareness of the way written and printed Russian looked. However different their origins and purposes may have been, the orthographic reforms and the experiments of the Futurists and other members of the Avant Garde doubtless seemed to many to be part of the same unsettling picture. Thus when *A Trap for Judges* (1910) appeared, for all its various *épatage*, the most upsetting feature to the conservative critics was, according to Kamensky, its revisionist orthography: "O, of course, there was subversiveness: for the destruction of the sacred letter *'yat'* alone they branded us with the shame of illiteracy and charlatanism" (Kamensky 1931, 117). Kamensky preferred to see "yat" (ѣ) not as a cruciform symbol but as a "skeleton" (p. 113).

Nevertheless, the reform had its minor costs even to the Avant Garde. Jakobson and Waugh (1979, 240) point out that Mayakovsky's pun on миръ = peace and міръ = world was lost in his poem *Voyna i mir* (War and the World, 1916) when the graphic distinction disappeared a year later.

EUROPEAN PARALLELS

In the first decades of the twentieth century Russian contacts with Europe were probably more frequent than at any previous time. This was especially true of the Avant Garde. I will not attempt to establish the influence of parallel developments in Europe on the Russians much more specifically than to say that it existed. However, it is useful to survey briefly the most obvious parallel activities in Europe so that we can sense what was unique about the Russian achievement.

Perhaps the best beginning point for visual literature in our century is Stéphane Mallarmé's *Un Coup de Dés* with its word clusters and double-page diagonal layouts. The poem was not published in this original dramatic form until 1914, though it was written much earlier. It utilizes a variety of typefaces, and therefore is midway between Bely's later layouts and the works by Terentev. The page space is often used as a true spatial surface and the layout is poised between having a direct visual value and being a signal for recitation (such as pausing and intonation). At the same time, typefaces are used to create a certain polyphonic simultaneity, since the full title (*Un Coup de Dés Jamais n'Abolira le Hazard*) is scattered in segments throughout the rest of the text. This key sentence is easy to pick out because the given segments are all in the same typeface of a size much larger than any other words. Other similar counterpoints based on typeface are found throughout the poem. Mallarmé's masterpiece was the ultimate illustration of a profoundly hermetical philosophy of typography in verbal art according to the Symbolist orientation (Bruns 1969) to which there is nothing to correspond among the Russian Symbolists, or even in Bely. None of the Russian Avant Garde of the period took this approach, and only in Voznesensky's "Oza" (1961) is there a comparable, though much less developed, example (Janecek 1980b).

Apollinaire was a figure well known among the Russian Avant Garde as a proponent of Cubism. His calligrams, originally handwritten on postcards sent to friends, were later (1918) set in type. The typesetting was done with some difficulty but with reasonable accuracy, and preserved as well as possible the original designs, such as rain falling, a fountain, and smoke from a cigar. Most of the calligrams qualify as traditional figure poems, while others create geometrical patterns not unlike those quoted in Khudakov's article (see chapter 4). Stefan Themerson, in a sympathetic and profusely illustrated study of Apollinaire's calligrams, remarks on the different perceptual process involved in reading a figure poem:

The calligrammes can be read aloud. Though it is a sort of reversed process. In a "normal" poem, its sonorities build the image of the poem gradually, and it is not complete until the poem has been read. The image of the poem is its end-product. With a calligramme it is different. Here you start with the image. Your eye sees it. And only then, when your eye has already seen it, your ear is allowed to decipher the elements that have created it. (Themerson 1968, 30)

As Themerson points out, Apollinaire expected the reader to be surprised to discover that the poem out of which the figure was built was no different from the author's usual poems. In order to be successful, however, such a poem would have to have added significantly to the meaning of the whole.

The Russians, however, generally avoided figure poetry. Zhovtis provides a good explanation justifying this rebuff:

The configuration of the text is meaningful only when it pursues the goal of accenting statements, words, groups of words, or of establishing new (thanks to typography) relationships between units of the text. Figure poetry reveals its shallowness and even enmity to verbal art not in the force of whimsically shaped layouts, but because a similar goal was not being pursued by figure poetry: the expressiveness of the drawing and the expressiveness of the verses are as if on different planes. The pre-ordained "figure" remains only an external, purely visual form; the graphic and sonic, existing in a written verse as two hypostases of one phenomenon, are torn apart from each other—and to unite them in this instance turns out to be impossible. (Zhovtis 1968b, 152)

The Russians used visual devices to supplement, rather than to duplicate, the verbal level or to give it greater precision. Folejewski is therefore on target when he remarks, "The device of special typographical arrangement in Mayakovsky is more natural than the obviously superficial experiments of this kind by Marinetti or Apollinaire" (Folejewski 1963, 75). And, we might add, it is more purposeful.

Another work of interest from France at this time, Blaise Cendrars' *La prose du Transsibérien et de la petite Jehanne de France* (Paris, 1913) (1966) reached Petersburg right away. By the end of the year it was being discussed at the Wandering Dog Café of the Futurists (Khardzhiev and Trenin 1970, 313-14). This evocation of Cendrars' trip on the Transsiberian railroad was printed in a variety of typefaces with coloring in the blank spaces and paralleled by an entirely painted strip done in an abstract simultanist style. It was designed by Sonia Delaunay-Terk and printed in a vertical column on a folding strip of paper 1.5 meters long, as an illustration of the new "simultaneous" book. Both margins were used alternately to line up the sections of the poem (Delaunay 1980, 31-35, 137).

One A. A. Smirnov brought back a copy of the work from Paris and gave a lecture on it and simultanism on December 22, 1913.[8] Livshits, who was not sympathetic to this type of visual orientation, comments:

[8] *Apollon* 1-2 (1914):134.

Just as in painting, one wanted to perceive all elements of the picture simultaneously instead of sequentially, so in poetry, one tried to displace the sequential by the simultaneous. This was distinct from the simplified solution of the problem which people like Barzun had reached by reducing the whole thing to a simultaneous reading of the work by several voices (i.e., he had substituted relative simultaneity for poetic simultaneity). Cendrars, together with Delaunay's wife, had tried to attain the required effect by isolating individual words by means of variously coloured letters and a coloured background.

Guillaume Apollinaire was publishing his Simultanist poems at the same time. He strewed syllables and fragments of sentences all over the page on the theory that the geometric figure formed by the scattered typographical signs would be apprehended by the eye simultaneously. This was not very different from the visual shape which Marinetti and Pallazzeschi gave their Futurist poems. (Livshits 1977, 175-76)

It is noteworthy in this context that the Russians, for all their radicalness in other respects, never thought to depart, as did Cendrars and Sonia Delaunay, from the folio format of the traditional book. Only Lissitzky created some Jewish scrolls. Everyone else stuck to the standard book.

The most obviously parallel phenomenon to the Russians was the Italian Futurist movement led by F. T. Marinetti. His initial statement, "The Founding and Manifesto of Futurism," published in the February 20, 1909, issue of *Le Figaro* (Paris), came at a time when the Russian Avant Garde was just beginning to group itself independently. By the time of Marinetti's visit to Russia in January 1914 as the self-proclaimed leader of a worldwide movement, the reaction of many Russian Futurists was an unwillingness to acknowledge that he had anything to do with what was happening in Russia (Markov 1968, 147-68). His influence was greater, however, than many Russians were willing to admit. Some difference existed, of course, such as the Russians' development of *zaum*, which Marinette could not understand, and their rejection of his emphasis on onomatopoetic effects, and these were used as a basis for declaring complete independence from the Italians. Roughly the same thing happened with the Vorticists on Marinetti's visits to London in 1913-14.

It is safe to say, though, that many, if not most, of the typographical "innovations" of the Russians were preceded, if only immediately, by comparable Italian examples. The Italian writers made great advances in the use of typesetting under the program of *parole in libertà* (words in freedom) beginning in late 1913 to early 1914, and they were evidently not interested in the possibilities of lithography. Perhaps economic constraints were not important to the wealthy Marinetti, but print was also more modernistic than the primitivistic effect of a lithographically produced manuscript.

The involvement of Marinetti and other Futurists in Papini and Soffici's semimonthly newspaper *Lacerba* in March 1913 soon led to experimental typography. In November the masthead was changed from a normal, "restrained" one, to one featuring dramatically massive, black six-inch-high lettering. The contents soon contained sophisticated avant-garde typographical effects, "sometimes of an intricacy that would make any printer blench" (Tisdall and Bozzolla 1978, 168). Some of the effects did not go much beyond display typography customary for posters and newspaper advertisements (used now in manifestoes and literary works), but others used every imaginable typeface and layout, including diagonal, vertical, upside-down, and curved placement of words, often decreasing, increasing, or alternating letter size within one word. Here Zdanevich and 41° added nothing new, except perhaps the formation of letters from printers' decorations such as crowns and squares in *lidantYU*. The Russians were, if anything, more conservative, since they did not generally use experimental typography for their manifestoes. However, although lines are used in some of the Italian compositions of early 1914, there is really nothing comparable to Kamensky's ferroconcrete poems to be found prior to their publication.

Surprisingly, within the confines of *Lacerba* it is not Marinetti who is most radical, but others such as Cangiullo, Carrà, and even Soffici, though Marinetti is not far behind them. Where Marinetti shines, however, is in the books he published separately, most notably *Zang tumb tumb* (1914). Featured in this volume was a form of typographic collage that was full of onomatopoetic effects. The impression is of superimposed layers of activity and sound recreated on paper by intersecting or layered typographical masses (Tisdall and Bozzolla 1978, 97). Virtually identical effects were created by painters such as Balla and Severini, but these were executed on drawing paper and canvas rather than within the confines of a book designed by a typographer.

In this technique only the two typographical compositions by Zdanevich (see figs. 135 and 136 in chapter 5) are comparable. The Russians tended to avoid onomatopoeia, and, although isolated words and phrases appeared in the easel art of Russian painters as with other Cubists and Cubist-influenced artists, the textual component never reached the level it did with the Italians.

One can also point among the Italians to occasional figure poems such as Marinetti's "Turkish Captive Balloon" (1914) and Govoni's "The Sea" (1915) (Tisdall and Bozzolla 1978, 94, 100), doubtless inspired by Apollinaire's similar efforts. The Russians generally avoided this as well.

It should be mentioned that Marinetti combined two basic orientations of visual devices, the musical score and the painting-icon (Finter 1980, 167ff).[9] The immediately independent visual impression of Words-in-Freedom is obvious, but the existence of an onomatopoetic feature in the collage effects and elsewhere points to a recitational orientation that Marinetti indicates in the manifesto,

[9] For another interesting application of semiotic theory to Italian Futurist typography, see White (1976).

"Geometric and Mechanical Splendour and the Numerical Sensibility" (March-April 1914):

Free expressive orthography and typography also serve to express the facial mimicry and the gesticulation of the narrator. . . . This energy of accent, voice, and mimicry that has shown up hitherto only in moving tenors and brilliant talkers finds its natural expression in the disproportions of typographic characters that reproduce the facial grimaces and the chiseling, sculptural force of gestures. (Apollonio 1973, 137)

Marinetti was, of course, famous as a reciter, able to invoke single-handedly the sounds of an entire battlefield.

The English Vorticists' main achievement during their heyday (1912-15) was the publication of *Blast*, nos. 1 and 2 (1914, 1915). The Russian Avant Garde was soon apprised of the Vorticists' activities in one of their own publications, *The Archer I* (1915), in an article by Zinaida Vengerova called "The English Futurists" (Belenson 1915, 93-105). The article was informative and insightful, but rather negative. *Blast* does not seem to have played much of a role in Russia and may not have been known directly. By Russian standards it was not particularly innovative in typography, but the sans-serif boldface type laid out in columns and blocks was more in consonance with the Constructivist book designs of the 1920s (Lissitzky, Gan) than the Russian experiments of its own decade. Russian contacts with England were much less developed at this time than contacts with the continent.

Dadaism (1915-24) was a Germanic-French outgrowth of Italian Futurism that, under the influence of World War I, took artists and writers in several new directions where Russian Futurism had already been and where Italian Futurism was just going. The war experience, with its technologically wrought horrors, turned the Dadaists against the machine and social organization and toward primitivism, nihilism, rejection of accepted conventions, anarchy, and art as play; these actions were perceived as ways of reinstating the human element in culture. In the words of Ribemont-Dessaignes (1931): "The activity of Dada was a permanent revolt of the individual against art, against morality, against society. . . . It was necessary to replace submission to reality by the creation of a *superior reality* . . . to pursue the work of God without taking it seriously" (Motherwell 1951, 102). If "normal" ways of living and thinking inevitably led, as it seemed, to war, social decay, dehumanization, and mediocrity, then the inverse, the Dadaists reasoned, may be the only salvation. In addition to "found art" and the role of chance, Dadaism gave prominence to simultaneous recitation of poetry and short plays, to the "static poem" (Motherwell 1951, 132), and to opto-phonetic or abstract poetry (akin to *zaum*). Typographical invention did not advance noticeably, though handwritten materials took on a somewhat greater role.

The prominent Dada, Hans Richter, in his history of the movement, assigns the Russians precedence in turning to Dadaism: "Curiously enough, Dada tendencies seem to have made their first appearance in Russia, where the Futurist influence was still very strong" (Richter 1965, 198); but even he does not know much about the movement in Russia. Dadaism indeed did not add much to what the Russians were already doing; when Zdanevich moved to Paris, he found a congenial group of Dadas and easily became one of its more radical members.

Of interest vis-à-vis our comments on *zaum* and Zdanevich, and indeed for the theory of visual effects in general, is Kurt Schwitters' statement on late-Dadaism in *G*, No. 3, 1924:

The basic material of poetry is not the word but the letter. . . . The sequence of letters in a word is unequivocal, the same for everyone. It is independent of the personal attitude of the beholder. Sound is only unequivocal in the spoken word. In the written word, the sound depends on the capacity of the beholder to imagine it. Therefore sound can only be material for the reciting of poetry and not for the writing of poetry. (Richter 1965, 147-48)

The Dadas were inclined on occasion to claim too much originality for themselves; but if we construe "Futurist" to include the broadest possible membership, including the Dadaists, then the following statement by Hans Richter serves well in ending this discussion:

They created inflammatory book-jackets and a new typography which gave to the individual letter, word or sentence a freedom it had never possessed (outside the Futurist and Zurich Dada movements) since Gutenberg. An inspired dip into the compositor's type-case, and school orthography was replaced by heterography. Large and small letters joined in new combinations and danced up and down; vertical and horizontal words arranged themselves to carry the meaning, and gave new life to the printed page, so that it not only described the new freedom to the reader, but allowed him to see and feel it for himself. (Richter 1965, 116)

Indeed the term heterography, were it to include, as it easily could, manuscript productions and new layouts for poetry, describes perfectly the entire range of visual experimentation we will study, even including matters of orthographic variation.

I have covered here only the most prominent European literary figures and movements during the time of the Russian Avant Garde, although roughly similar activities did take place elsewhere—for instance, in America and among the Slavs in Czechoslovakia, Poland, and the Ukraine (Folejewski 1978, 1980; Ciszkewycz 1980).

2. Andrey Bely

The modern history of Russian typographical experimentation can be said to have begun with the appearance in print of the first literary works by Andrey Bely (1880-1934). Though he remained conservative, or rather stayed within certain bounds, while others soon tried more radical things—thus relieving him of his avantgarde preeminence—he was nevertheless the first of the line and, in certain areas, the best. The year 1902, the date of the appearance of *Symphony*, Bely's first published work (actually his second work in the series of four "symphonies"), can be considered the chronological starting point of this survey on visual experimentation.

As we shall see, Bely was in theory an adherent of the view that the text is a musical score. His visual devices were intended to show how the text should be recited, though this principle is not very clear in the early works. He is the only writer of note to initiate such devices in prose.

Although Bely himself made no hard-and-fast distinction between prose and verse, I shall, for the sake of convenience, separate the two by discussing first, in chronological order, the typographical innovations in his prose works, and then in his verse. Once this history is clear, I shall turn to Bely's theoretical statements and principles. Analysis of the texts will accompany the chronological survey rather than follow Bely's theories, but I will reserve some general evaluative comments for the very end.

THE PROSE WORKS

The fact that written verbal art is at least partially a visual experience is something that is not usually taken into consideration in connection with prose.[1] Bely, however, thoroughly utilized all aspects of the word, including the visual. A rapid glance at a page of one of Bely's more experimental prose works will suffice to show, even before any of the words have been taken in, that something other than normal prose is before you. The zenith of his course of experimentation

[1] Significant theoretical work on the subject of literary media and their effects on human culture has been done by McLuhan and others; what is meant here is a study by literary critics and commentators of specific works of verbal art.

with prose is *Kotik Letaev*,[2] but his interest in visual effects spans his whole creative career from the *Symphonies* to the Moscow novels.

The text of the *First Symphony* (1904a),[3] a fairy tale in which a princess in a tower is courted by a sensuous knight, consists of series of short paragraphs, consecutively numbered like the verses in the Bible (fig. 10). A given "verse" often contains more than one sentence but rarely runs to longer than five lines of type. Occasionally it is composed of a single word. The consecutive numbers continue until there is a space between "verses," after which the numbering begins again at "1." This larger division will hereafter be called a "stanza." Stanzas contain from one to as many as fifty "verses" (the introduction has fifty "verses"). This arrangement constitutes the only typographical abnormality of the text; however, it is an abnormality that is uniformly and unfailingly observed throughout and is thus constantly before the reader's eyes.

Such a numbering system serves mainly to emphasize the independence of

[2] The core of this chapter, the part on *Kotik Letaev*, is based on my dissertation (Janecek 1971), which includes a more extended discussion of Bely's punctuation practices than what is found here.
[3] Though published after the *Second*, the *First* was, of course, written before it (December 1900).

Fig. 10. Andrey Bely, page from *First Symphony*, 1904.

бедь, лебедь печали, грустно покрикивая въ тишину, ластясь.

10. Отовсюду падали ночныя тѣни.

1. Почившій король приподнялъ мраморную крышку гробницы и вышелъ на лунный свѣтъ.

2. Сидѣлъ на гробницѣ въ красной одеждѣ, отороченной золотомъ и въ зубчатой коронѣ.

3. Увидѣлъ грусть, разлитую по городу, и лицо его потемнѣло отъ огорченія.

4. Онъ понялъ, что его сынъ бросилъ эту страну.

5. И онъ пригрозилъ убѣжавшему сыну мертвой рукой и долго сидѣлъ на гробницѣ, подперевъ усталой рукой старую голову.

1. А молодой король съ королевой бѣжалъ въ одинокихъ поляхъ. Ихъ окачивало луннымъ свѣтомъ.

2. Луна стояла надъ кучкой чахлыхъ, сѣверныхъ березъ и они вздохнули въ безысходныхъ пустотахъ.

3. Король плакалъ.

4. Слезы его, какъ жемчугъ, катились по блѣднымъ щекамъ.

5. Катились по блѣднымъ щекамъ.

Fig. 11. Andrey Bely, p. 25 from *Third Symphony (The Return)*, 1905.

Она не могла удушить ребенка и вотъ перетащила на спинѣ черезъ необъятный океанъ убійцу, способнаго на все...

Ребенокъ. Старикъ, кто это реветъ такъ протяжно, такъ грустно въ океанѣ?... Я никогда еще не слышалъ такого голоса...

Старикъ. Это морской гражданинъ вынырнулъ изъ глубины... Теперь онъ отрясаетъ отъ воды свою зеленую бороду и пробуетъ голосъ, потому что считаетъ себя пѣвцомъ...

Ребенокъ. Я знаю голоса морскихъ гражданъ, и они не звучатъ такъ протяжно, такъ странно.

Но старикъ молчалъ. Дрожалъ отъ нехорошаго холодка, обвѣвавшаго ихъ. Бормоталъ про себя: „нѣтъ, его не спасешь... Онъ долженъ повториться... Случится одно изъ непужнихъ повтореній его"... „Наступаетъ день Великаго Заката".

Отдаленное прошлое хлынуло на нихъ отъ сверкающихъ въ небѣ созвѣздій...

На песчаномъ мысѣ происходило поганое совѣщаніе. Змій, свернувшись въ мерзкій клубокъ, вытягивалъ свою шею и тупо мычалъ, а привезенный изъ-за туманнаго океана негодникъ покорно выслушивалъ приказанія повелителя...

Пощипывалъ волчью бородку, сверкалъ зелеными глазками, мялъ въ рукѣ войлочный колпакъ, не

the individual "verses" (or, according to Bely [1902, p. i], "musical phrases"). Assigning a number to a sentence gives it a separateness, a status of its own, a place superior to the normal sentence. Normal sentences do not have the visual definition of a line of verse, and Bely is here trying to give his sentence this kind of visual definition. One does indeed perceive the "verses" as independent units, beads on a string, placed in series to form a larger unit, the stanza.

But the need for numbers is questionable. Indentation alone would give the "verses" visual independence, and the divisions between stanzas are redundantly marked by both a blank space and the return to #1. The numbers seem a super-fluous and even distracting intrusion of arithmetic into the narrative, forcing the reader to unnecessary counting off as he goes along. A rationale for the numbering system as a means of identification similar to Biblical practice is weakened by the fact that numbers are not also assigned to the stanzas, and so no absolute means of identification is provided.

In my attempt to discover other possible motivations for numbering, such as some arrangement in the text based on the numbers, I find noteworthy only the fact that parts 1 and 2 both have the same number of "verses," 235, and the same number of stanzas, 44. This observation led me to hope that further investigation would reveal more of a pattern, but I uncovered none. The coincidental totals in parts 1 and 2 might have been due to mere chance; or Bely, the mathematician's son, might have employed a more deeply hidden formula; but if so, it is unlikely that such a formula would have much impact on even the most astute of readers.

The possibility of Ruskin's influence on Bely at this time is established by Maslenikov (1956), and the fact that Ruskin numbered his paragraphs may have encouraged Bely to do the same. But Bely's most likely model may have been Nietzsche's *Also sprach Zarathustra*—his favorite book at this time. Szilard has studied the influence of Nietzsche's style on Bely's *Second Symphony* (1902), a parody of Moscow mystical groups, and the impact of *Zarathustra* was no doubt quite strong. If this is the case, Bely did not provide titles for the sections, as did Nietzsche. In Nietzsche the effect is to give a series of aphoristic statements subsumed under a subject heading; in Bely such a setup is inappropriate to the narrative content. What we are ultimately dealing with is a poorly thought-out technique. Bely went too far to achieve the independence of his sentences, and he soon realized this. He had used a similar numbering system in the *Second Symphony*, but abandoned it thereafter and never used it again.

Typographical practice is otherwise much the same in Bely's *Third* and *Fourth* (1905 and 1908), but he did add a few other dimensions. For example, in the *Third*, in which a chemistry graduate student goes mad and drowns himself, he presents a dialogue as if it were a play script (fig. 11), which gives it an important effect: if the passage had been written as a normal novelistic dialogue (*Starik*

skazal, "*Glaza tvoi . . .*" [The old man said, "Your eyes . . ."]), the recurrence of
the dialogue as a dialogue between the hero and Dr. Orlov in part 3 (pp. 109-10),
with the same scriptlike arrangement, would not have been nearly so obvious a
replay of the dialogue in part 1. In other words, the unusual typographical practice
is a device for emphasizing the circularity of structure referred to in the sym-
phony's title, "The Return." At the same time, the reiteration of the dialogue is
not a literal one. Although the points of similarity between the two are quite
evident, what was simply a fantasy in part 1 has taken on the flesh of real persons
and actual events, a "nightmare come true." Both dialogues occur in the fifth
chapter of their respective parts.

In the *Fourth Symphony* ("A Goblet of Blizzards"), which deals with Solov-
yovian mystical love, several innovations are introduced that further emphasize
the fact that Bely's paragraph is more than a logical subdivision of thought. Let
me give an example (from p. 19):

Inogda prezhde rydal ot vechno strannykh, uskolzayushchikh dum.
Neizmennykh . . .
Kak vo sne . . . net, ne vo sne . . .

Sometimes he first sobbed from eternally strange fleeting thoughts.
Unchanging ones . . .
As in a dream . . . no, not in a dream . . .

Here we have what is actually a single sentence broken up into three verses. The
principles upon which this is based are possibly rhythmic (line end = pause),
and assuredly visual (the second and third verses are given more prominence by
being raised typographically to verse status), but certainly not logical, according
to the usual norms for punctuation. The second and third verses are fragments
syntactically bound to the first. In this example the ends of the lines are given
a form of final punctuation and the first word in each is capitalized, but what of
the case of fig. 12b, where neither is true? As shown in fig. 12, Bely has begun
to use indentation and other typographical means for visual and rhythmic pur-
poses beyond the function of creating verselike lines or melodic phrases, as had
heretofore been the case. The reader's attention is called to a word or phrase
because of its unusual visual isolation. This same device can be used to spotlight
various aspects of the word or phrase (meaning, sound, rhythm) and, if the ty-
pographical arrangement is repeated with the same or similar words, the very
fact of repetition can be emphasized. Thus the passage in fig. 12a precedes fig.
12b by almost a page. The repetition of "Nevolno" (involuntarily) in figs. 12a
and 12b stands out because of the fragmentation of a sentence; but why should
Bely want that word to stand out? Probably because he wants the reader to notice
the rhyme with "Dovolno" (enough), the word in an equivalent (though this time

normal) typographical situation not too far above it. I doubt that anyone would have heard or noticed the rhyme between two such common words if Bely had not singled them out visually. Indeed, the typography makes it difficult to miss the relationship between this entire passage (fig. 12a) and its repetition (fig. 12b).

Several other cases of radical fragmentation are noteworthy in the *Fourth.* Some sentences are split up into as many as nine lines (pp. 133-34), and in others a single word or even a single syllable is stretched out over several lines. The latter is particularly amusing (fig. 13). Examples such as these are not especially frequent in the *Fourth,* but they are a sign of things to come in later works.

In the *Silver Dove* (1910b), Bely eschews the typographical experimentation that was observed in the *Symphonies.* This was perhaps dictated by the change in genre from the experimental "symphonic" form to the novel, but whatever the reason, there are no peculiarities of typographical usage.

Petersburg (1916) introduces a new and more permanent set of typographical devices, but their use is sporadic and not especially systematic. In roughly five hundred pages of text (depending on the edition), only about thirty instances of visual effects of interest occur. All of these involve deep indentation of a segment

Fig. 12. Andrey Bely, pages from *Fourth Symphony (A Goblet of Blizzards),* 1908.

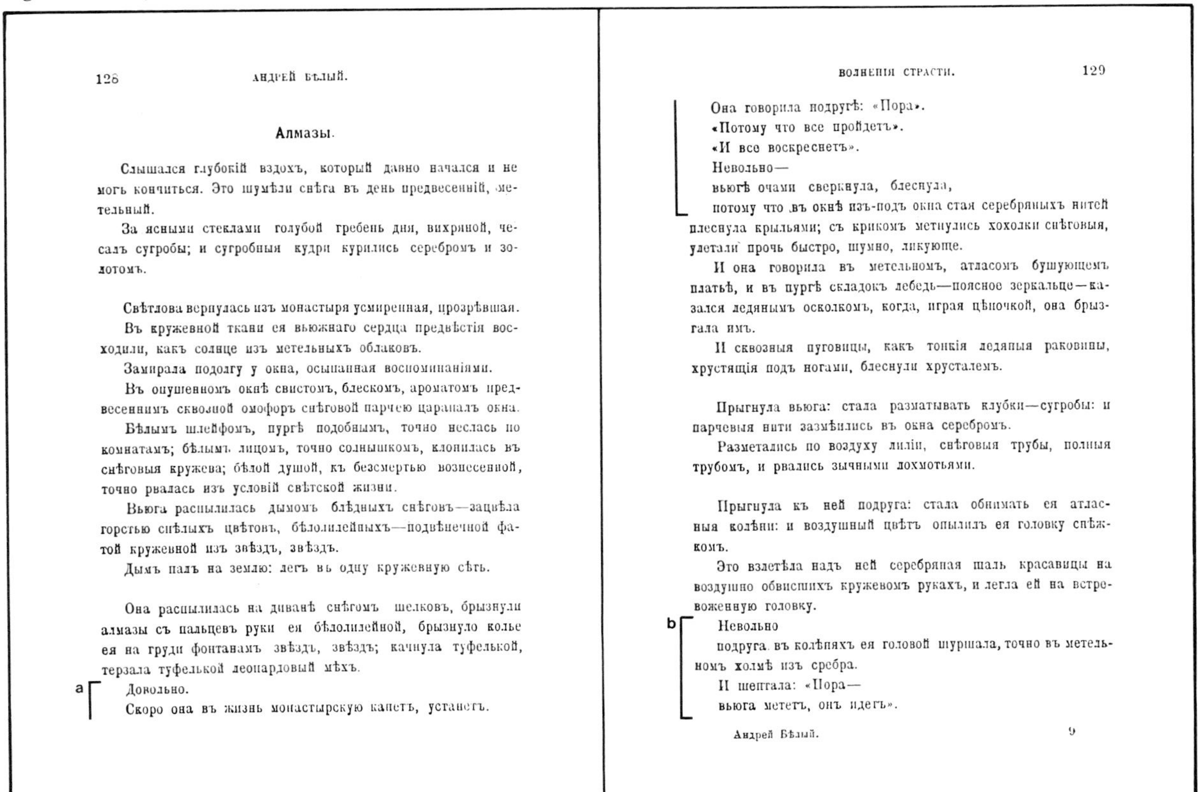
128 АНДРЕЙ БѢЛЫЙ.

Алмазы.

Слышался глубокій вздохъ, который давно начался и не могъ кончиться. Это шумѣли снѣга въ день предвесенній, метельный.

За ясными стеклами голубой гребень дня, вихряной, чесалъ сугробы; и сугробныя кудри курились серебромъ и золотомъ.

Свѣтлова вернулась изъ монастыря усмиренная, прозрѣвшая.

Въ кружевной ткани ея вьюжнаго сердца предвѣстія восходили, какъ солнце изъ метельныхъ облаковъ.

Замирала подолгу у окна, осыпанная воспоминаніями.

Въ опушенномъ окнѣ свистомъ, блескомъ, ароматомъ предвесеннимъ скволиой омофоръ снѣговой парчею царапалъ окна.

Бѣлымъ шлейфомъ, пургѣ подобнымъ, точно неслась по комнатамъ; бѣлымъ лицомъ, точно солнышкомъ, клонилась въ снѣговыя кружева; бѣлой душой, къ безсмертью вознесенной, точно рвалась изъ условій свѣтской жизни.

Вьюга распылилась дымомъ блѣдныхъ снѣговъ—зацвѣла горстью снѣлыхъ цвѣтовъ, бѣлолилейныхъ—подвѣнечной фатой кружевной изъ звѣздъ, звѣздъ.

Дымъ палъ на землю: легъ въ одну кружевную сѣть.

Она распылилась на диванѣ снѣгомъ шелковъ, брызнули алмазы съ пальцевъ руки ея бѣлолилейной, брызнуло колье ея на груди фонтанамъ звѣздъ, звѣздъ; качнула туфелькой, терзала туфелькой леопардовый мѣхъ.

a Довольно.
Скоро она въ жизнь монастырскую канетъ, устанетъ.

ВОЛНЕНІЯ СТРАСТИ. 129

Она говорила подругѣ: «Пора».
«Потому что все пройдетъ».
«И все воскреснетъ».
Невольно—
вьюгѣ очами сверкнула, блеснула,
потому что въ окнѣ изъ-подъ окна стая серебряныхъ нитей плеснула крыльями; съ крикомъ метнулись хохолки снѣговыя, улетали прочь быстро, шумно, ликующе.

И она говорила въ метельномъ, атласомъ бушующемъ платьѣ, и въ пургѣ складокъ лебедь—поясное зеркальце—казался ледянымъ осколкомъ, когда, играя цѣпочкой, она брызгала имъ.

И сквозныя пуговицы, какъ тонкія ледяныя раковины, хрустящія подъ ногами, блеснули хрусталемъ.

Прыгнула вьюга: стала разматывать клубки—сугробы: и парчевыя нити замѣнились въ окна серебромъ.

Разметались по воздуху лиліи, снѣговыя трубы, полныя трубомъ, и рвались зычными лохмотьями.

Прыгнула къ ней подруга: стала обнимать ея атласныя колѣни: и воздушный цвѣтъ опылилъ ея головку снѣжкомъ.

Это взлетѣла надъ ней серебряная шаль красавицы на воздушно обвисшихъ кружевомъ рукахъ, и легла ей на встревоженную головку.

b Невольно
подруга въ колѣняхъ ея головой шуршала, точно въ метельномъ холмѣ изъ сребра.
И шептала: «Пора—
вьюга мететъ, онъ идетъ».

Андрей Бѣлый. 9

or segments of text and some form of linking punctuation between the main paragraph and the indented segment, most often a double dash, that is, a dash ending the main paragraph and another introducing the indented segment. This typographical arrangement subsequently became Bely's main device for visual impact. In *Petersburg* these instances have no notable pictorial or representational suggestiveness;[4] they are used for emphasis, mostly at dramatic moments, particularly when a shift to another level of consciousness is involved. Compared with *Kotik Letaev*, the visual devices in *Petersburg* may not seem to be obviously organized, but an intriguing rationale for these indentations has been presented recently by V. Alexandrov: "In addition to representing the narrator/author's intrusive relationship to his text, the indented passages also depict graphically the intrusive role of the transcendent in the narrator/author's own life (and art), as well as in the lives of his characters." They therefore show "a strong positive correlation with the novel's most portentous symbols and symbol clusters" (Alexandrov 1983, 89). Thus about half of the indentations relate to the bomb. Many of the remaining instances can be related to the appearance of some mysterious

---

[4] With the possible exception of p. 438 (1916), in which the increasing indentation might represent the withdrawal or disappearance of the "little figure."

Fig. 13. Andrey Bely, pages from *Fourth Symphony*, 1908.

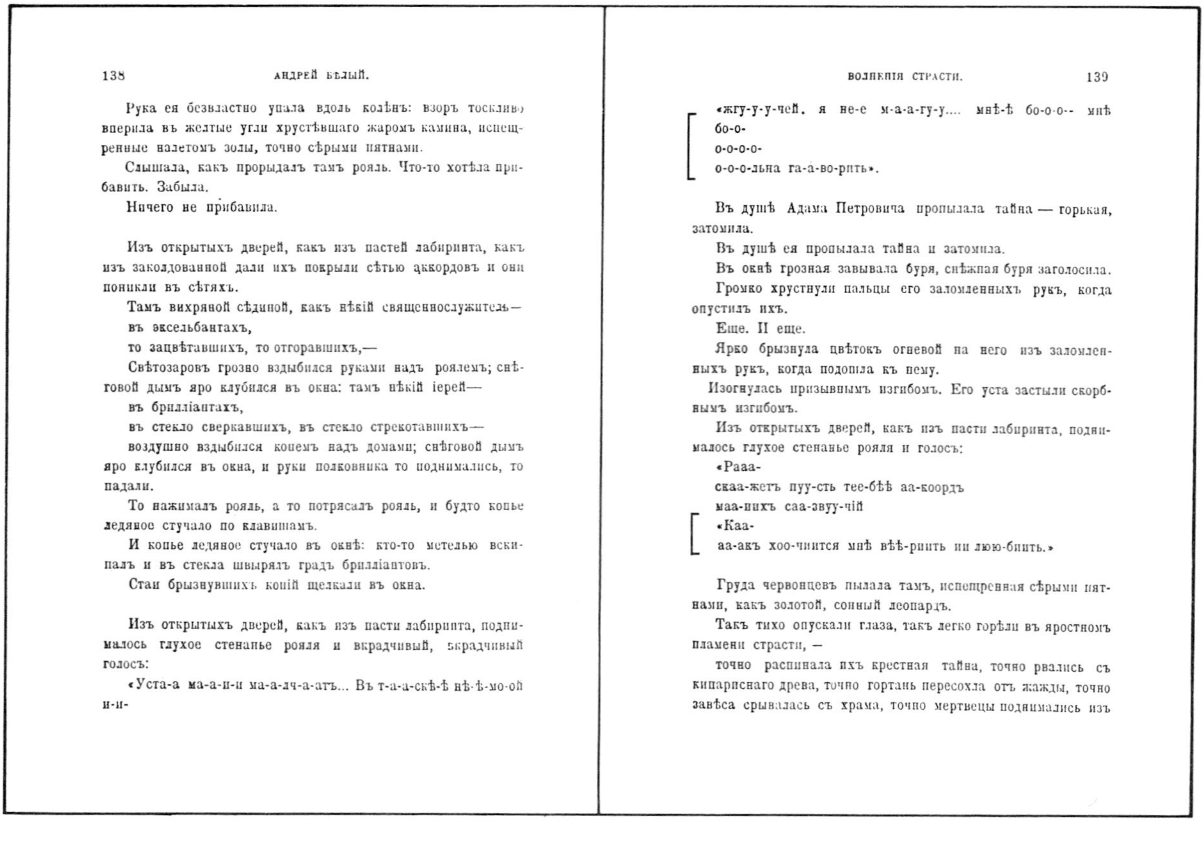

Рука ея безвластно упала вдоль колѣнъ: взоръ тоскливо вперила въ желтые угли хрустѣвшаго жаромъ камина, испещренные налетомъ золы, точно сѣрыми пятнами.

Слышала, какъ прорыдалъ тамъ рояль. Что-то хотѣла прибавить. Забыла.

Ничего не прибавила.

Изъ открытыхъ дверей, какъ изъ пастей лабиринта, какъ изъ заколдованной дали ихъ покрыли сѣтью аккордовъ и они поникли въ сѣтяхъ.

Тамъ вихряной сѣдиной, какъ нѣкій священнослужитель—

въ эксельбантахъ,

то зацвѣтавшихъ, то отгоравшихъ,—

Свѣтозаровъ грозно вздыбился руками надъ роялемъ; снѣговой дымъ яро клубился въ окна: тамъ нѣкій іерей—

въ бриліантахъ,

въ стекло сверкавшихъ, въ стекло стрекотавшихъ—

воздушно вздыбился конемъ надъ домами; снѣговой дымъ яро клубился въ окна, и руки полковника то поднимались, то падали.

То нажималъ рояль, а то потрясалъ рояль, и будто копье ледяное стучало по клавишамъ.

И копье ледяное стучало въ окнѣ: кто-то метелью вскипалъ и въ стекла швырялъ градъ бриліантовъ.

Стаи брызнувшихъ копій щелкали въ окна.

Изъ открытыхъ дверей, какъ изъ пасти лабиринта, поднималось глухое стенанье рояля и вкрадчивый, вкрадчивый голосъ:

«Уста-а ма-а-и-и ма-а-лч-а-атъ... Въ т-а-а-скѣ-ѣ нѣ-ѣ-мо-ой и-и-

«жгу-у-у-чей, я не-е м-а-а-гу-у.... мнѣ-ѣ бо-о-о-- мнѣ бо-о-

о-о-о-о-

о-о-о-льна га-а-во-рить».

Въ душѣ Адама Петровича пропылала тайна — горькая, затомила.

Въ душѣ ея пропылала тайна и затомила.

Въ окнѣ грозная завывала буря, снѣжная буря заголосила.

Громко хрустнули пальцы его заломленныхъ рукъ, когда опустилъ ихъ.

Еще. И еще.

Ярко брызнула цвѣтокъ огневой на него изъ заломленныхъ рукъ, когда подошла къ нему.

Изогнулась призывнымъ изгибомъ. Его уста застыли скорбнымъ изгибомъ.

Изъ открытыхъ дверей, какъ изъ пасти лабиринта, поднималось глухое стенанье рояля и голосъ:

«Рааа-

скаа-жетъ пуу-сть тее-бѣ аа-коордъ

маа-нихъ саа-эвуу-чій

«Каа-

аа-акъ хоо-чнится мнѣ вѣ-рить ни люю-бить.»

Груда червонцевъ пылала тамъ, испещренная сѣрыми пятнами, какъ золотой, сонный леопардъ.

Такъ тихо опускали глаза, такъ легко горѣли въ яростномъ пламени страсти, —

точно распинала ихъ крестная тайна, точно рвались съ кипариснаго древа, точно гортань пересохла отъ жажды, точно завѣса срывалась съ храма, точно мертвецы поднимались изъ

figure (for example, the "white domino"). The others relate to Apollon Apollonovich and his wife.

Since the use of the double dash, with its usually neat positioning of one dash below the other, is such a regular feature of many of Bely's later novels, it is worthwhile to note that in the published texts of *Petersburg*, such neatness is missing in a number of places. The manuscript of the novel,[5] from which the Sirin edition (1913-14) was set, confirms that from the beginning Bely intended the dashes to be placed one directly below the other. However, no doubt due to his absence from Petersburg at the time of publication, Bely's intentions were not carried out, possibly because of an editorial misunderstanding. The very first instance of the use of double dashes in the manuscript illustrates well how the mistake occurred (page 13 is reproduced in fig. 14; trans. Bely 1978, 10). Note that the two dashes are heavily drawn and lined up, and that the indented position is meant to line up below the first word after the second dash. Note also the editor's direction to the typesetter "Otstupit na 2 kvadrata" (indent by two squares). The amount of indentation is made independent of the position of the first dash

[5] It can be seen in the archives of Pushkinsky dom, Leningrad, fond 79 (Ivanov-Razumnik), op. 3, no. 235.

Fig. 14. Andrey Bely, page of manuscript for *Petersburg*, Sirin edition, 1913-14.

Fig. 15. Andrey Bely, page of published text of *Petersburg*, Sirin edition, vol. 1, 1913.

чили четыре перпендикулярныя стѣнки; такъ онъ былъ отдѣленъ отъ протекающихъ людскихъ толпъ, отъ тоскливо мокнущихъ красныхъ обертокъ журнальчиковъ, продаваемыхъ вонъ съ того перекрестка.

Планомѣрность и симметрія успокоили нервы сенатора, возбужденные и неровностью жизни домашней, и безпомощнымъ кругомъ вращенія нашего государственнаго колеса.

Гармонической простотой отличалися его вкусы.

Болѣе всего онъ любилъ прямолинейный проспектъ; этотъ проспектъ напоминалъ ему о теченіи времени между двухъ жизненныхъ точекъ; и еще объ одномъ: иные всѣ города представляютъ собой деревянную кучу домишекъ, и разительно отъ нихъ всѣхъ отличается Петербургъ.

Мокрый, скользкій проспектъ: тамъ дома сливалися кубами въ планомѣрный, пятиэтажный рядъ; этотъ рядъ отличался отъ линіи жизненной лишь въ одномъ отношеніи: не было у этого ряда ни конца, ни начала; здѣсь средина жизненныхъ странствій носителя брилліантовыхъ знаковъ оказалась для скольнихъ сановниковъ окончаніемъ жизненнаго пути.

Всякій разъ вдохновеніе овладѣвало душою сенатора, какъ стрѣлою линію Невскаго разрѣзалъ его лакированный кубъ: тамъ, за окнами, виднѣлась домовая нумерація; и шла циркуляція; тамъ, оттуда — въ ясные дни, издалека-далёка, сверкали слѣпительно: золотая игла, облака, лучъ багровый заката; тамъ, оттуда, въ туманные дни,—ничего, никого.

А тамъ были—линіи: Нева, острова. Вѣрно въ тѣ далекіе дни, какъ вставали изъ мшистыхъ болотъ и высокія крыши, и мачты, и шпицы, проницая зубцами своими промозглый, зеленоватый туманъ —

— на тѣневыхъ своихъ парусахъ полетѣлъ къ Петербургу оттуда Летучій Голландецъ изъ свинцовыхъ пространствъ балтійскихъ и нѣмецкихъ морей, чтобы здѣсь воздвигнуть обманомъ свои туманныя земли, и назвать островами волну

2*

19

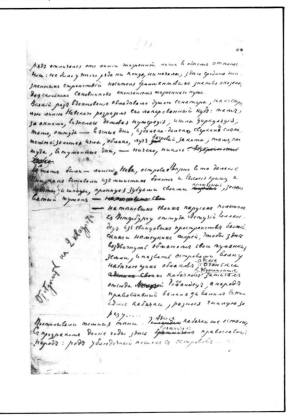

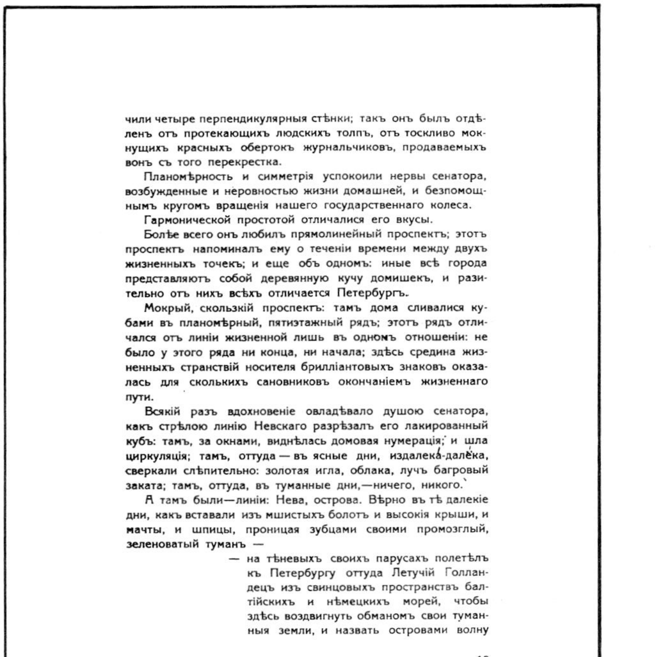

by being specified as an absolute quantity. Only by pure chance would the dashes have lined up correctly in the typeset version, since the position of "tuman—" would probably vary from manuscript to printed text. Bely's systematic lining up of the double dashes leads one to believe that they, rather than the amount of indentation, are the essential factors in styling his prose—a fact the editor did not appreciate. The result is shown in fig. 15.

The following example illustrates how the solution to a typesetter's problem requires the author's participation. In the manuscript (see fig. 16; trans. Bely 1978, 138) all is fine; the dashes occur in mid-page. However, when the passage is typeset, the first dash occurs toward the end of the line, leaving only seven spaces (fig. 17). If the rather large indented portion had been set with the dashes and the indention aligned as the author intended, the result would be a ridiculous-looking narrow column several pages long. In this instance, the editor's standard 2-square indentation actually follows the manuscript more closely than would have been the case of the author's rules had been followed. But a subsequent instance leaves the printed text with the first dash at the very end of the line, with absolutely no room for indented text if the second dash were to come below it (1913-14, 3:265).

Fig. 16. Andrey Bely, page of manuscript for *Petersburg*, Sirin edition.

Fig. 17. Andrey Bely, page of published text of *Petersburg*, Sirin edition, vol. 2, 1913.

Такъ пѣлъ голосъ.

Дверь захлопнулась. Въ обывателѣ Аполлонъ Аполлоновичъ подозрѣвалъ что-то мелкое, пролетающее за стекломъ каретныхъ отверстій (разстояніе, вѣдь, между ближайшей стѣною и дверцей кареты исчислялось Аполлономъ Аполлоновичемъ многими милліардами верстъ). И вотъ передъ нимъ всѣ пространства смѣстились: жизнь обывателя вдругъ обстала его подворотнями, стѣнами, а самъ обыватель предсталъ предъ нимъ голосомъ.

Голосъ же пѣлъ:

„Духомъ мы къ Тебѣ, Отецъ.
„Въ небо мыслію паримъ
„И за пищу отъ сердецъ
„Мы Тебя благодаримъ".

Вотъ какой обыватель? Къ обывателю Аполлонъ Аполлоновичъ восчувствовалъ интересъ, и былъ мигъ, когда онъ хотѣлъ постучаться въ первую дверь, чтобъ найти обывателя; тутъ онъ вспомнилъ, что обыватель его собирается казнить позорною смертью: набокъ съѣхалъ цилиндръ, дрябло такъ опустились надъ грудью изможденныя плечи:—

—да, да, да: они его разорвали на части: не его, Аполлона Аполлоновича, а другого, лучшаго друга, только разъ посланнаго судьбой; одинъ мигъ Аполлонъ Аполлоновичъ вспоминалъ тѣ сѣдые усы, зеленоватую глубину на него устремленныхъ глазъ, когда они оба склонялись надъ географической картой имперіи, и пылала мечтами молодая такая ихъ старость (это было ровно за день до того, какъ)... Но они разорвали даже лучшаго друга, перваго между первыми... Говорятъ, это длится секунду; и потомъ—какъ есть ничего... Что-жъ такое? Всякій государственный человѣкъ есть герой, но—брр-брр...—

10* 147

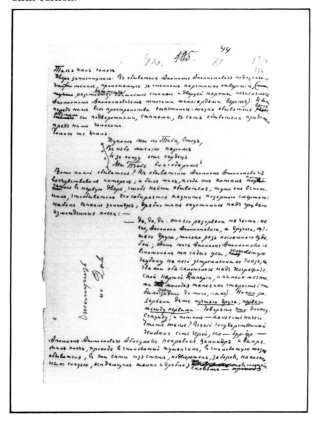

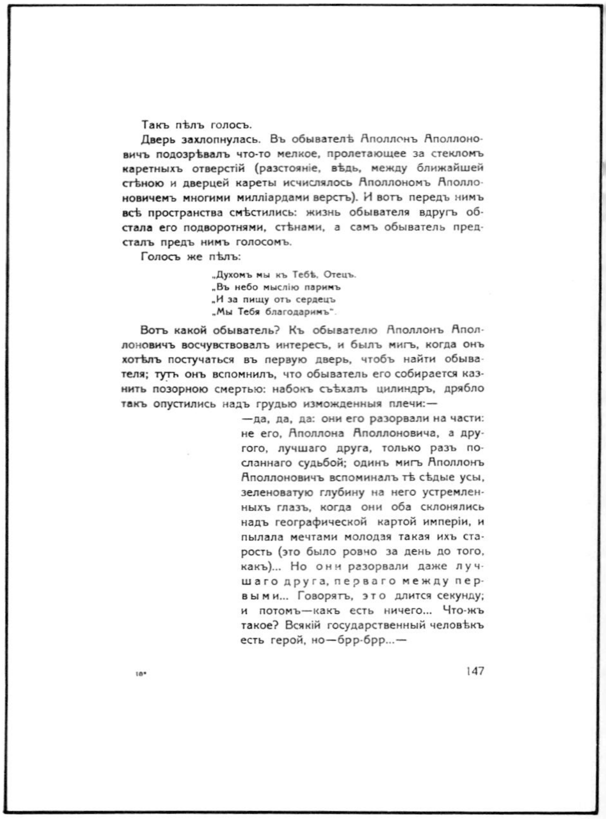

The most attractive example in the manuscript, showing how the indenting device was meant to work, is reproduced in fig. 18 (trans. Bely 1978, 163-64). A beautifully symmetrical indentation within an indentation seems visually to depict the series of mental shifts to the deepest level of Nikolay's consciousness and back out again at the point in which he sets the time bomb in motion. Each of the sections of text is balanced spatially on the page, and the whole is perfectly centered. This arrangement would seem to represent the original conception, though Bely himself crossed out the bottom eight lines that balanced the top portion, thus somewhat upsetting the symmetry. But if Bely intended this page to look the same in print, he was disappointed. In none of the editions did this whole passage end up on the same page, and much of the visual expressiveness of the dramatic sinking in and coming out again was lost when a page had to be turned at an inopportune moment, as in the Sirin version (fig. 19a, b). In the 1922 and 1928 editions, Bely eliminated the deepest indentation, bringing it out to the level of the other two, perhaps because he felt the content of the middle passage was not sufficiently different from the others to warrant its further indentation.

Bely did not take the opportunity to correct these discrepancies, since the later editions (1922a, 1928) present substantially the same picture as the Sirin text, with allowances made for the effects of different page and type size, authorial abbreviation (1922), and introduction of the new orthography (1928). However, the more recent reprint of the Sirin text (1967), although in the new orthography, comes close to duplicating the visual picture of the original manuscript. But the fact remains that none of the published editions of *Petersburg* accurately reflect the systematic way Bely aligned his double dashes in the manuscript and how he used indentation; therefore they cannot serve as a firm basis for discussing the visual expressiveness of the text.

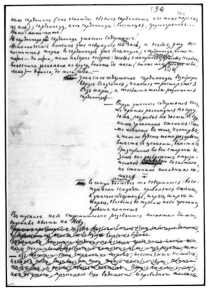

Fig. 18. Andrey Bely, page of manuscript for *Petersburg,* Sirin edition.

Fig. 19. Andrey Bely, two consecutive pages of the published text of *Petersburg,* Sirin edition, vol. 2, 1913.

лическій ключикъ межъ пальцевъ; оттого ли, что дрогнули пальцы, оттого ли, что Николай Аполлоновичъ, почувствовавъ головокруженіе, свалился въ ту самую бездну, которую онъ хотѣлъ всею силой души избѣжать—только, только: ключикъ медленно повернулся на часъ, потомъ повернулся на два часа, а Николай Аполлоновичъ... сдѣлалъ невольное антраша: отлетѣлъ какъ-то въ сторону; отлетѣвъ какъ-то въ сторону, онъ опять покосился на столикъ: такъ же все на столѣ продолжала стоять жестяная коробочка изъ-подъ жирныхъ сардинокъ (онъ однажды объѣлся сардинками и съ тѣхъ поръ ихъ не ѣлъ); сардинница, какъ сардинница: блестящая, круглогранная....

Нѣтъ—нѣтъ—нѣтъ!

Не сардинница, а сардинница ужаснаго содержанія!

Металлическій ключикъ уже повернулся на два часа, и особая, уму непостижная жизнь въ сардинницѣ уже вспыхнула; и сардинница хоть и та-жъ — да не та; тамъ навѣрно ползутъ: часовая и минутная стрѣлки; суетливая секундная волосинка заскакала по кругу, вплоть до мига (этотъ мигъ теперь недалекъ)—до мига, до мига, когда...—

— ужасное содержанье сардинницы безобразно вдругъ вспучится; кинется—расшириться безъ мѣры; и тогда и тогда: разлетится сардинница....

— струи ужаснаго содержанія какъ-то прытко раскинутся по кругамъ, разрывая на части съ бурнымъ грохотомъ столикъ: что-то лопнетъ въ немъ, хлопнувъ, и тѣло—будетъ тоже разорвано; вмѣстѣ съ щепками, вмѣстѣ съ брызнувшимъ во всѣ стороны газомъ оно разбросается омерзительной кровавою слякотью на стѣнныхъ холодныхъ камняхъ...—

199

— въ сотую долю секунды все то совершится: въ сотую долю секунды провалятся стѣны, а ужасное содержаніе, ширясь, ширясь и ширясь, свиснетъ въ тусклое небо щепками, кровью и камнемъ.

Въ тусклое небо стремительно разовьются косматые дымы, впустивъ хвосты на Неву.

Что̀-жъ онъ сдѣлалъ, что̀ сдѣлалъ онъ?

На столѣ, вѣдь, пока еще все стояла коробочка; разъ онъ ключъ повернулъ, надо было немедленно схватить ту коробочку, положить ее на должное мѣсто (напримѣръ—въ бѣлой спаленкѣ подъ подушку); или тотчасъ же раздавить подъ пятою. Но упрятать ее въ должномъ мѣстѣ, подъ взбитой отцовской подушкою, чтобы старая, лысая голова, утомленная только-что бывшимъ, упала съ размаху на бомбу,—нѣтъ, нѣтъ, нѣтъ: на это онъ неспособенъ; предательство это.

Раздавить подъ пятой?

Но при этой мысли ощутилъ онъ нѣчто такое, отъ чего его уши положительно дернулись: онъ испытывалъ столь огромную тошноту (отъ семи выпитыхъ рюмокъ), точно бомбу онъ проглотилъ, какъ пилюлю; и теперь подъ ложечкой что-то вспучилось: не то — изъ резины, не то — изъ матеріи очень странныхъ міровъ...

Никогда не раздавитъ онъ, никогда.

Остается бросить въ Неву, но на это есть время: стоитъ только разъ двадцать повернуть еще ключикъ; и п о к а все отсрочится; разъ онъ ключъ повернулъ, надо было немедленно растянуть то п о к а; но онъ медлилъ, въ совершенномъ безсиліи опустившись въ кресло; тошнота, странная слабость, дремота одолѣвали ужасно; а ослабшая мысль, отрываясь отъ тѣла, рисовала безсмысленно Николаю Аполлоновичу все какія-то дрянныя, праздныя, безсильныя арабески... погружаясь въ дремоту.

. . . .

Николай Аполлоновичъ былъ человѣкъ просвѣщенный; Николай Аполлоновичъ не безсмысленно посвятилъ филосо-

200

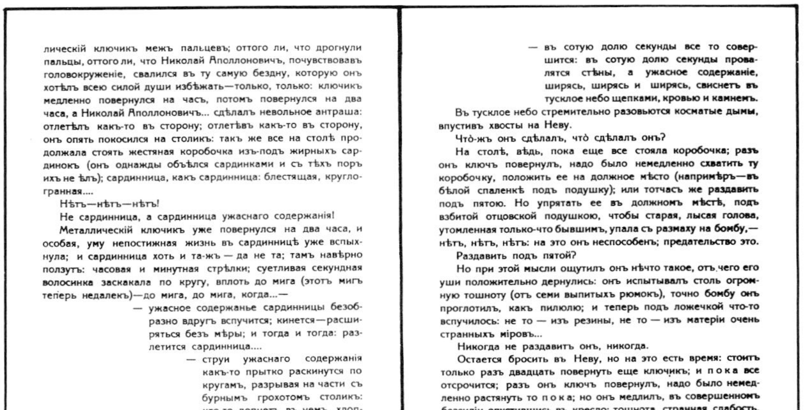

Even though in most cases the printed text simply does not look the way it was intended to, it is not clear why Bely did not insist on correcting this situation. The complex and difficult life he led during these years must have played a role in preventing him from giving the matter the needed attention, and perhaps the limited scope of the device as it impinged on this novel (about thirty instances) did not warrant greater concern for precision. Then, too, Bely was constantly changing his mind about such things, with punctuation in particular being a most unstable element in his writing. Certainly, as we shall see, it was not because he was indifferent to the result.

Kotik Letaev (1917-18; 1922c), the autobiographical story recounting how the three- to five-year-old narrator Kotik achieves self-consciousness, brings the visual devices with which Bely had toyed in the *Symphonies* and *Petersburg* into full and regular use. Nearly every page carries some visual effect—mostly the double dash and indentations. In the published text, the dashes (with few exceptions) are now placed precisely one below the other. Unfortunately, the original manuscript is incomplete, with only eight pages surviving.[6] Among these pages

[6] Pushkinsky dom, fond 79 (Ivanov-Razumnik), op. 3, no. 13, 1917. For a history of this fond, see Keyes (1978).

Fig. 20. Andrey Bely, page of manuscript for *Kotik Letaev*, 1917.

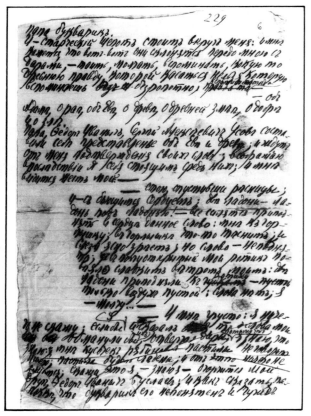

Fig. 21. Andrey Bely, page of typescript for *Kotik Letaev*, 1921-22.

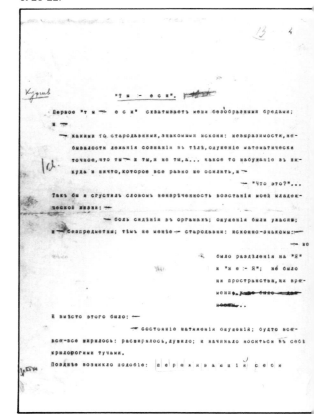

(fig. 20) are several containing double dashes, which are neatly aligned, as in *Petersburg* (Bely 1922c; 1971b, 217-18). The typescript from which the novel was set[7] is also incomplete, consisting of only fifty-eight pages (about one-third of the work) with missing pages in between and without the ending. Comparison of this typescript with the printed text shows that the latter fairly well conforms to the former, as, for example, in figs. 21 and 22, although Bely does not use paragraph indentation while the printed text does. This changes the visual impression somewhat. Occasionally the typesetter slips up (as in fig. 23 compared to fig. 24) by not aligning the dashes or observing the proper indentation, but basically he does his job conscientiously; only if two dashes are not aligned could one reasonably suspect a slip-up. Unfortunately, some of the more interesting pages of text discussed below are missing from the surviving typescript and cannot be validated by comparison; and perhaps even more unfortunate is the fact that no corrected author's page proofs have survived. Thus we must remain cautious about how to interpret some of the resulting configurations. We may, however, compare the two printed versions (1917-18, 1922) for discrepancies; if they agree, we are probably on solid ground. The 1922 edition, the last version, will serve

[7] "Mashinopis nabornaya izdatelstva Epokha s neznachiteln. avtorskoy pravkoy," fond 79 (Ivanov-Razumnik), op. 3, no. 14, 1921-22.

Fig. 22. Andrey Bely, pages of published text of *Kotik Letaev*, 1922.

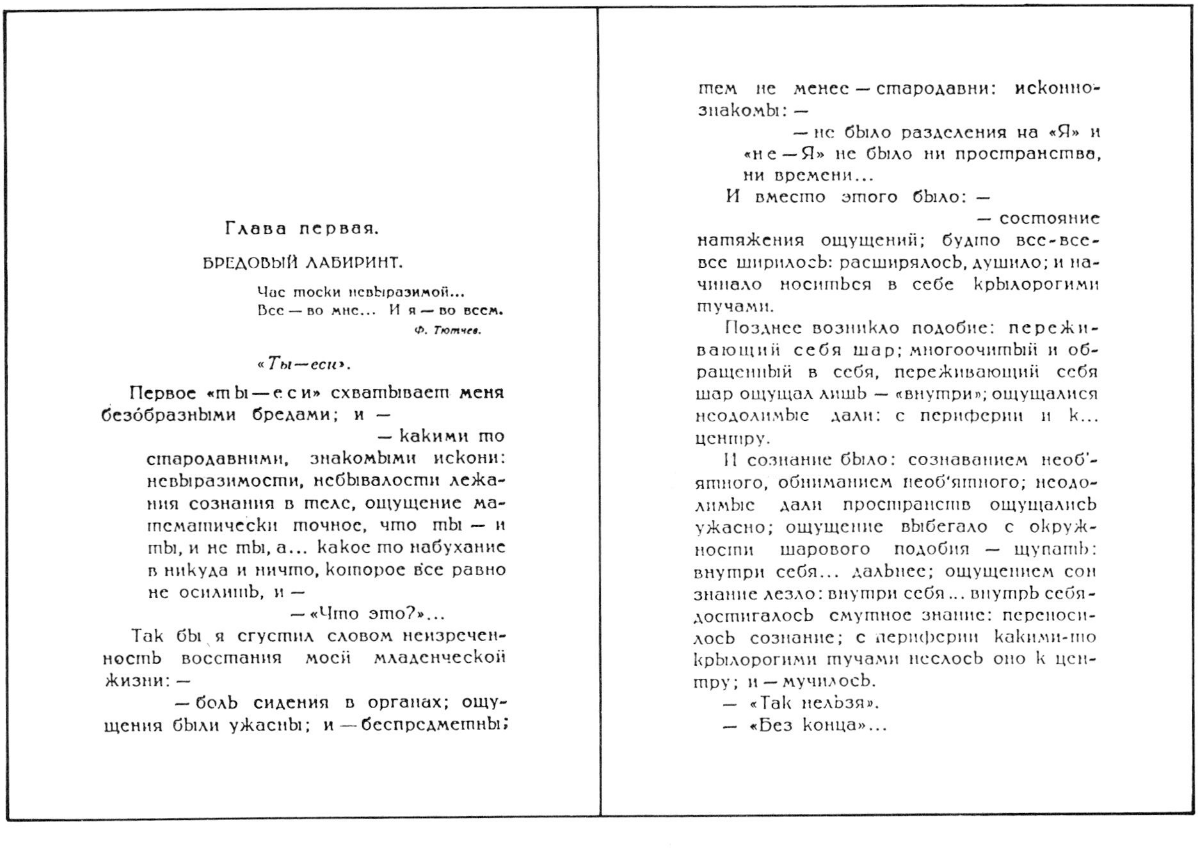

Глава первая.

БРЕДОВЫЙ ЛАБИРИНТ.

Час тоски невыразимой...
Все — во мне... И я — во всем.
Ф. Тютчев.

«*Ты — еси*».

Первое «ты — еси» схватывает меня безобразными бредами; и —
— какими то стародавними, знакомыми искони: невыразимости, небывалости лежания сознания в теле, ощущение математически точное, что ты — и ты, и не ты, а... какое то набухание в никуда и ничто, которое всё равно не осилить, и —
— «Что это?»...

Так бы я сгустил словом неизреченность восстания моей младенческой жизни: —
— боль сидения в органах; ощущения были ужасны; и — беспредметны;

тем не менее — стародавни: исконно-знакомы: —
— не было разделения на «Я» и «не — Я» не было ни пространства, ни времени...

И вместо этого было: —
— состояние натяжения ощущений; будто все-все-все ширилось: расширялось, душило; и начинало носиться в себе крылорогими тучами.

Позднее возникло подобие: переживающий себя шар; многоочитый и обращенный в себя, переживающий себя шар ощущал лишь — «внутри»; ощущалися неодолимые дали: с периферии и к... центру.

И сознание было: сознаванием необ'ятного, обниманием необ'ятного; неодолимые дали пространств ощущались ужасно; ощущение выбегало с окружности шарового подобия — щупать: внутри себя... дальнее; ощущением сознание лезло: внутри себя... внутрь себя — достигалось смутное знание: переносилось сознание; с периферии какими-то крылорогими тучами неслось оно к центру; и — мучилось.

— «Так нельзя».
— «Без конца»...

as the basis for our discussion. Because of Bely's frequent use of visual devices in *Kotik*, with double dashes and indentations occurring everywhere, on almost every page, I will select examples that best illustrate the various functions of the devices.

Though used in an unorthodox manner by Bely, indentations and dashes fall under the rubric of punctuation. Their function is to create unusual emphasis. A piece of text, whether a single word or a paragraph, draws attention to itself by being set apart from the rest of the text by the use of these devices. Bely has found a means above and beyond the usual means available to prose—and to some extent even to verse—to heighten emphasis. But to what purpose? Let us study a number of examples and attempt to discern the goal of the effect.

The double dash, wherever it occurs, automatically causes a pause of considerable length, probably as strong or nearly as strong as that between paragraphs. The eye must pass through at least two items of punctuation and move down a line before coming to the next word. Often the first dash is preceded by some other cadential punctuation, such as a colon, semicolon, comma, or three dots. If the double dash is accompanied by indentation of the text, it is set apart from the body of the text, and one's natural inclination is to change intonation, pitch, or expression when reading, either mentally or aloud. (As we shall see in the theoretical section, Bely definitely has this in mind.) A comparable effect in speaking would be a similar change in voice for an aside, a parenthetical remark, or a digression.

In more than half the instances, the double dashes occur in what would in any case be a cadential position where a pause would be expected, such as at the end of a clause. There are many instances, however, where they are in an "un-

Fig. 23. Andrey Bely, page of typescript for *Kotik Letaev*, 1921-22.

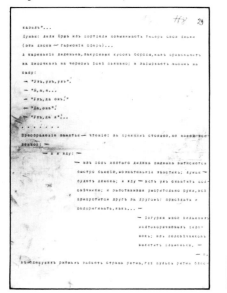

Fig. 24. Andrey Bely, page of published text of *Kotik Letaev*, 1922.

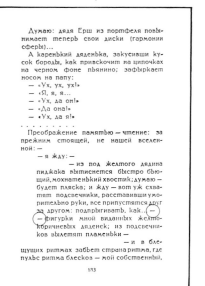

Fig. 25. Andrey Bely, *Kotik Letaev*.

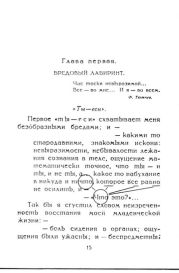

natural" position—a noncadential position—and the shift is a surprise. The very first instance in chapter 1 is such a case (fig. 25). The shift occurs suddenly in mid-thought and therefore with particular force. Here we begin with the view of the time-focused adult narrator ("Pervoe 'ty—esi' skhvatyvaet menya" [the first *thou—art* grips me]), who is able to characterize the given experience by a negative reference; then we move to the concept, "bezobraznymi," developed later (the child cannot, of course, have a concept of "imagelessness" without having first experienced an image); then on to the direct, nearly unarticulated, experience of the child as described in the indented portion. We exit by means of another set of dashes and an analytical question, "What is it?" and return to the viewpoint of the adult narrator.

Shifts of this sort usually involve one or more of the following elements:

1. Adult narrative to child's experience;
2. Temporal change (fig. 26);
3. Child's experience to adult interpretation (fig. 27);
4. Change of level of consciousness or perception.

The last category is a catchall for a variety of shifts, such as from the literal to the metaphoric, from the specific to the general, from delirium to clarity, from concrete sense impressions to mystical experiences. As an example of the use to

Fig. 26. Andrey Bely, *Kotik Letaev.*

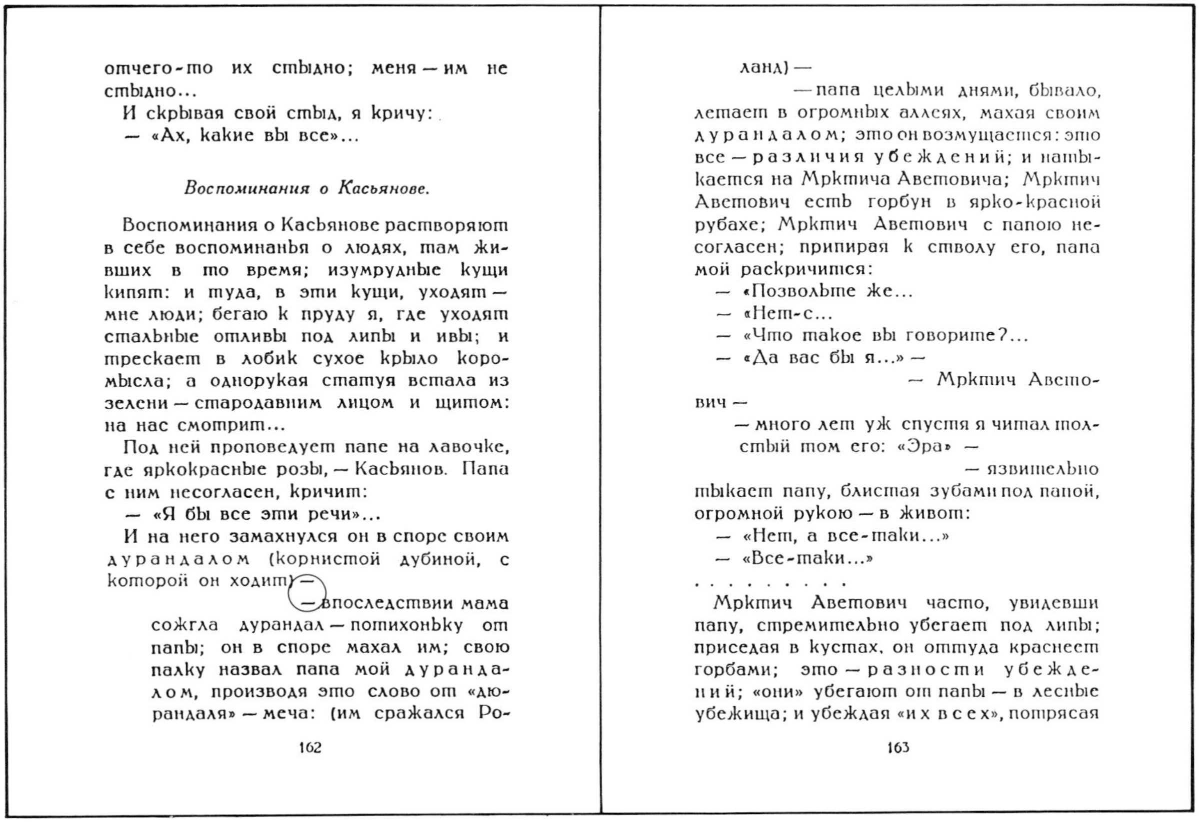

отчего-то их стыдно; меня — им не стыдно...

И скрывая свой стыд, я кричу:
— «Ах, какие вы все»...

Воспоминания о Касьянове.

Воспоминания о Касьянове растворяют в себе воспоминанья о людях, там живших в то время; изумрудные кущи кипят: и туда, в эти кущи, уходят мне люди; бегаю к пруду я, где уходят стальные отливы под липы и ивы; и трескает в лобик сухое крыло коромысла; а однорукая статуя встала из зелени — стародавним лицом и щитом: на нас смотрит...

Под ней проповедует папе на лавочке, где яркокрасные розы, — Касьянов. Папа с ним несогласен, кричит:
— «Я бы все эти речи»...

И на него замахнулся он в споре своим дурандалом (корнистой дубиной, с которой он ходит)—

—впоследствии мама сожгла дурандал — потихоньку от папы; он в споре махал им; свою палку назвал папа мой дурандалом, производя это слово от «дюрандаля» — меча: (им сражался Ро-

162

ланд) —

— папа целыми днями, бывало, летает в огромных аллеях, махая своим дурандалом; это он возмущается: это все — различия убеждений; и натыкается на Мрктича Аветовича; Мрктич Аветович есть горбун в ярко-красной рубахе; Мрктич Аветович с папою несогласен; припирая к стволу его, папа мой раскричится:
— «Позвольте же...
— «Нет-с...
— «Что такое вы говорите?...
— «Да вас бы я...» —
— Мрктич Аветович —

— много лет уж спустя я читал толстый том его: «Эра» —

— язвительно тыкает папу, блистая зубами под папой, огромной рукою — в живот:
— «Нет, а все-таки...»
— «Все-таки...»
. . . .

Мрктич Аветович часто, увидевши папу, стремительно убегает, под липы; приседая в кустах, он оттуда краснеет горбами; это — разности убеждений; «они» убегают от папы — в лесные убежища; и убеждая «их всех», потрясая

163

which Bely puts typography to express a complex series of shifts or overlay of levels of perception, see fig. 28.

The general framework of the example is an episode in which Raisa Ivanovna, the maid, tells fairy tales to Kotik. The episode begins in normal narrative manner with a statement of this fact (A). Thereupon B indicates an immediate intensification of enthusiasm at the mention of "incomprehensible" kings and swans; this passage is indented. A return to the margin at C reflects a settling down to the story and describes a series of metaphoric connections between concrete objects and items in the story—for example, the lamp is a swan, and the chair back is a cliff. At D a transition is made from a metaphoric cliff to a cliff largely within the fairyland and having little connection now with the concrete object. It is a cliff from which a king summons a swan. Indentation has come to mean here "within the dreamlike fairyland." At E the boy becomes a participant in the action of the story: he and the swan fly over the waves. A voice is heard (F), but instead of a voice from within the story, the absence of which is expressed by a row of dots, it is a song (G) that filters into dreamland from the concrete world (as stated parenthetically and unindented at H). D' returns us briefly to the level of D in order to restore briefly our logical focus. But we immediately return to fairyland (I) and from there to an amalgamation of the external song with elements

Fig. 27. Andrey Bely, *Kotik Letaev.*

тем не менее — стародавни: исконно-знакомы;— не было разделения на «Я» и «не — Я» не было ни пространства, ни времени...

И вместо этого было: — — состояние натяжения ощущений; будто все-все-все ширилось: расширялось, душило; и начинало носиться в себе крылорогими тучами.

Позднее возникло подобие: переживающий себя шар; многоочитый и обращенный в себя, переживающий себя шар ощущал лишь — «внутри»; ощущалися неодолимые дали: с периферии и к... центру.

И сознание было: сознаванием необ'ятного, обниманием необ'ятного; неодолимые дали пространств ощущались ужасно; ощущение выбегало с окружности шарового подобия — щупать: внутри себя... дальнее; ощущением сознание лезло: внутри себя... внутрь себя-достигалось смутное знание: переносилось с периферии какими-то крылорогими тучами неслось оно к центру; и — мучилось.

— «Так нельзя».
— «Без конца»...

16

— «Перетягиваюсь»...
— «Помогите»...
Центр — вспыхивал: —
— «Я — один в не-об'ятном».
— «Ничеговнутри: все — во вне»...
И опять угасал. Сознание, расширяясь, бежало обратно.
— «Так нельзя, так нельзя: Помогите»...
«Я — ширюсь»... — так сказал бы младенец, если бы мог он сказать, если б мог он понять; и — сказать он не мог; и — понять он не мог; и — младенец кричал: отчего, — не понимали, не поняли.

. . . .

Образованье сознания.

В то далекое время «Я» не был... —
— Было хилое тело; и сознание, обнимая его, переживало себя в непроницаемой необ'ятности; тем не менее, проницаясь сознанием, тело мучилось ростом, будто грецкая губка, вобравшая в себя воду; сознание было вне тела; в месте тела же ощущался громадный провал: сознания в нашем смысле, где еще мысли не

17

of the fairy tale: "I wept without you . . . You returned to me—my swan queen"
(*J*). *J* occurs within the transition from *I* to *F'* as indicated by the parentheses.
We again shift to an awareness of the song in progress at *G'*, and from there by
steps to *A'*, passing through a retrograde series of levels of consciousness. At least
three levels are well defined typographically by margin, indentation, and paren-
theses within indentation, representing, respectively, full consciousness, fairy
tale dreamland, and a subconscious mixture of the two in which, as it turns out,
the boy is prescient of things to come (Raisa Ivanovna does depart before the end
of the novel and Kotik is bereaved). The intricate concatenations of consciousness
are expressed visually with a clarity that would be hard to imagine without such
typographical arrangements.

Visual effects are often used to emphasize certain words or phrases, such as
the word *milaya* (dearest) in reference to Raisa Ivanovna (fig. 29). This word often
occurs between two sets of double dashes, underscoring Kotik's positive attitude
toward her. The word also contains the important sounds *m-l*, about which there
is a discussion on p. 116 (1971b, 85) of the novel. Many other important phrases
are given a visual configuration that is repeated. The visual component adds to
the memorability of such passages and aids the reader in following the extremely
important aspect of passage repetition in the narration. Some instances are non-
recurring but underline a dramatic moment, such as the discovery of bugs in a
piece of bread (fig. 30).

A beautiful example of visual expressiveness successfully combined with
sonic expression is the following chain of instances. Kotik's Auntie Dotty (Tyotya
Dotya) is associated with the piano as she sits down to play while the child
watches with rapt attention. In a classic exemplification of childish *ostranenie*
(defamiliarization), the event is described in the following way:

g. 28. Andrey Bely, *Kotik Letaev.*

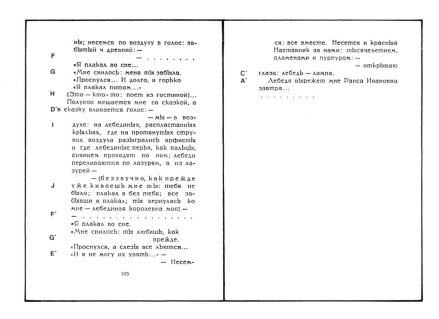

> All becomes very strange, but Auntie Dotty
> sits down at a massive black chest; she opens the
> lid and with one finger she taps melodically
> along the sonorous white row of coldish
> little sticks—
>   —"it is"—
>   —something Aun-tie Dot-ty-ish . . . (1922c, 69; 1971b, 48)

The very syllables of her name reflect the do-re-mi of the scale, while the physical action of fingers moving in a straight line across the keyboard is reflected in the straight line of the syllables on the page. The musical imagery leading to broad philosophical vistas is developed in an extremely compact passage following this section and recurs later in the story, when, beginning on page 242 (1971b, 182), the dark cloud of disaster gathers and results in the dismissal of Kotik's only secure haven, the warm, loving servant Raisa Ivanovna. Auntie Dotty becomes part of the forces fomenting dismissal, and "something Auntie Dottyish appears." The confrontation occurs and Kotik is overwhelmed with sadness at the impending departure of his beloved friend, and the Auntie Dotty phrase becomes:

> —Some—
>   —thing—
>   —Aun—
>   —tie—
>   —Dot—
>   —ty—
>   —ish!—
> the droplets fall in the washbasin. (p. 245; 1971b, 184)

Fig. 29. Andrey Bely, *Kotik Letaev.*   Fig. 30. Andrey Bely, *Kotik Letaev.*   Fig. 31. Andrey Bely, *Kotik Letaev.*

каркуны сквозь суки пропорхнули ей вслед.

Рассыпаются снеговые вьюны; рассыпаются неосыпные свисты; пахнет трубами в воздухе; золотою ниточкой фонарей многоочитое время уже побежало по улицам: предвечерним дозором; все на небе расколото; кто то блистает оттуда, из-за багровых расколов; желтеет, мрачнеет; и — переходит во тьму.

Мы — домой.

. . . .

Вечером: —

— на летящих спиралях, с обои, кружевеют, горя, косяки красных зорь: бледнорозовым роем, а —

— Раиса Ивановна мягким, агатовым взглядом таинственно переводит мой взгляд: переводит туда, где —

— багровая голова, со стены хохоча, огрызнулась оскалом.

Не успею я вскрикнуть: Раиса Ивановна —

— милая! —

— шаловливо уж клонит свой локон в мой локон; и — начинает смеяться.

103

— раз принесли мне кусочек черствого хлебика... из него делать грешника, то есть, обмакивать в чай; разломили кусочек, а там то—

— в кусочке - то! —

— мурашки: —

— красные! —

— ползают! —

— папа придвинул свой нос и подпирая очки двумя пальцами, лицом и воскликнул:

— «Ай! Какая гадость:-мурашки!»

Сам же он поразвел на дому всяких функций на листиках (до функций Лагранжа включительно), и существа иных жизней во всем: и в буфетных щелях, и в паутине под шторой —

— видел я там брюхоногую функцию: —

— папа пестрит своей функцией белые листики; функции с листиков располагаются по дому; листики бросит в корзиночку; я же листики вытащу; и — Раиса Ивановна мне из них нарежет ворон; все вороны мои не простые, а — пестрые; и — на себе оне носят: многое множество ра-

107

стельку к себе; я не сплю; я — молчу: чуть дышу; мне —

— и мило и древне, и жарко, и грозно, и грустно:—

— ужасно —

сжимая мне грудку, ужасные сжатия в грудку опустятся чувствами: пухнуть... И все начинает опять мне кричать в очень громких рассказах; сквозь милое, древнее, крестное древо прорежется:—

— ясно:—

— уже не Раиса Ивановна дышет со мною тут рядом, а пламя тут пышет:—

— оно! —

— ужасаюсь и чувствую: произрастание, набуханье «его» — в никуда и ничто, которое все равно не осилить; и —

— что это? —

«Оно» — не было мною; но было мне, как... во мне, хоть — «во вне:—

— Почему «это?..» Где? Не «оно» ли уж Котик Летаев? «Где я»? Как же так? И почему это так, что у «него» не «я» — «я»?—

— «Ты не ты, потому

220

Sliding down the page diagonally, the syllables depict an eloquent gesture of sadness, decline, a descending musical scale, and the morose, empty sounds of drips of water in the sink.

All of the preceding effects are absolute—that is, they come off properly regardless of the exact position of the dashes in the line so long as the typesetter has followed the basic ground rules, as he has in nearly all cases. There are other situations in which one is tempted to apply interpretations, but where the layout is not "absolute," and perhaps merely the product of chance. Here, lacking an authoritative manuscript, typescript, or author's proofs, we must compare printed versions for some semblance of verification.

The use of double dashes and indentation has the effect of opening up the visual space on the page, particularly if there are several instances in close proximity. Certain words are isolated, that is, they are surrounded by white space. They—their content, their sound, their look—are more noticeable than if they were buried in the lines of a paragraph. The reader is encouraged thereby to notice their relationships to other words that are similarly prominent in the visual space. Sonic links become evident, in the same way as end-rhyme is more perceptible in poetry than is internal rhyme. Perhaps because of the configuration on the page, words whose relationship would have been masked under normal circumstances are indeed perceived to be related. For example, would we be likely to notice the relationships (t-o) marked in fig. 25 without the typographical arrangement? Or the distantly placed rhyme between *uzhasno* and *yasno* in fig. 31, a later development of fig. 25? When we compare fig. 25 with the 1917-18 version in fig. 32, we see that because of the wider margins, the "related" words are farther apart and their "relationship" is less palpable. Fig. 31 is, however, less relative than fig. 25, since the emphasized words would be prominent regardless of how they were typeset. *Kotik Letaev* is so packed with sonic expressiveness that any configuration is likely to "reveal" some sonic relationship or other, but this is a result of the richness of the sound texture rather than of the visual emphasis provided.

Most tempting, however, are those passages in which the visual patterning seems to take on an expressiveness of its own, when it conveys an additional meaning. For instance, when the child first becomes aware that beyond the nursery in the apartment it is "all rooms, rooms, rooms!" this passage in the Epokha edition is lumped together in a confusing block (fig. 33a; 1971b, 18). Later, as the child's understanding of the nature of the apartment becomes clearer, the configuration changes to a more orderly sequence of chambers, one leading to another (fig. 33b; 1971b, 25).

Unfortunately, in the 1917-18 text the first occurrence of this passage places the words in a line just like the later occurrence, which suggests that the two cases were not meant to be differentiated. Bely had the chance to influence the appearance of the page in the 1922 edition if he was dissatisfied with the earlier outcome, and he appears to have intervened. A close look at fig. 33a makes one doubt that the new layout was accidental. The second *komnaty* is hyphenated in a place that would leave just enough room for a double dash and syllable to continue the text below it. There would be no reason to break the word at that point if the series was meant to be in a straight line—as later—extending to the left margin on the next line. For that matter, one wonders why, in fig. 33b, the first *komnaty* was not placed directly after the *vsyo* and hyphenated,

i komnaty—
—vsyo kom -
naty, komnaty, komnaty!—
—v kotorom

as would be natural, unless the idea was to line up the two double dashes vertically, as it turned out, visually reflecting a geometrical rigor that was suggestive of Kotik's insight into the order of his home. Only by leaving an otherwise unnecessary space after *vsyo* was this accomplished. An accident? Unlikely.

Another example of the use of clever visual effects involves Nanny Aleksandra, who represents rigid order, structure, and regulation to the child. In passages related to her, a certain visual symmetry is evident (fig. 34). In fact, following the material in fig. 34 the section "A Stroll" is entirely encompassed in a symmetrical pattern similar to this example. In fig. 35 are reproduced the equivalent passages of the 1917-18 version, where page divisions and margins influence the impression of symmetry. The passage marked in fig. 34 is divided between pages 42 and 43 in the 1917-18 version, and because of wider margins the double dashes

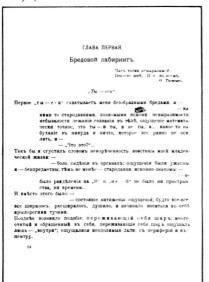

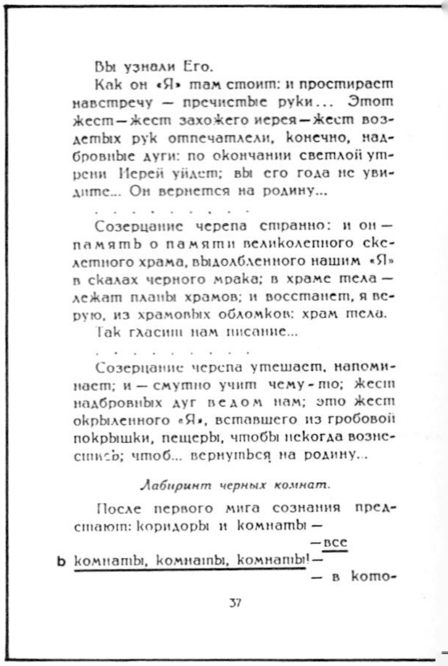

Fig. 32. Andrey Bely, *Kotik Letaev*, Skify I, 1917.

ГЛАВА ПЕРВАЯ.

Бредовой лабиринтъ.

Часъ тоски невыразимой...
Все—во мнѣ... И я—во всемъ.
Ө. Тютчевъ.

„Ты—еси".

Первое „ты—еси" схватываетъ меня безобразными бредами; и—
—ка-
кими то стародавними, знакомыми искони: невыразимости небывалости лежанія сознанія въ тѣлѣ, ощущеніе математически точное, что ты—и ты, и не ты, а... какое то набуханіе въ никуда и ничто, которое все равно не осилить, и—
—„Что это?"...

Такъ бы я сгустилъ словомъ неизрѣченность возстанія моей младенческой жизни:—
—боль сидѣнія въ органахъ; ощущенія были ужасны, и—безпредметны; тѣмъ не менѣе—стародавни: исконно-знакомы:—
—не
было раздѣленія на „Я" и „не—Я" не было ни пространства, ни времени...

И вмѣсто этого было:—
—состояніе натяженія ощущеній; будто все-все все ширилось: расширялось, душило; и начинало носиться въ себѣ крылорогими тучами.

Позднѣе возникло подобіе: переживающій себя шаръ; многоочитый и обращенный въ себя, переживающій себя шаръ ощущалъ лишь—„внутри"; ощущалися неодолимыя дали: съ периферіи и къ центру.

14

Fig. 33. Andrey Bely, *Kotik Letaev*, 1922.

щемся на стене—из табачного дыма; и капот, и лысина в слабых мерцаниях свечки мне не кажутся добрыми. Знаю я,—скверновато: даже совсем скверновато; а почему,—этого не могу я понять; потому ли, что открыто мне неприличие бабушки (вместо чепчика с лиловыми лентами вовсе голая голова), потому ли, что целая половина стены отсутствует вовсе: не четыре стены—три стены; четвертая—распахнулась своим темнодонным оскалом со множеством комнат—

a
—все комнаты, ком-
наты, комнаты!—
—в ко-

торые, если вступишь, то—не вернешься обратно, а будешь охвачен предметами, еще не ясно какими, но, кажется, креслами в сероватых, суровых чехлах, вытарчивающих в глухонемой темноте; суть же не в креслах, а так сказать в протяжениях материи воздуха и в открытой возможности ощутить холодноватый бег сквознячка из комнаты в комнату, увидать прыжок в зеркало... кресла. Словом—скверные комнаты!

Между тем: сознавая немыслимость там водиться, кто то все же наперекор всему там завелся; и—безалаберно

29

Вы узнали Его.

Как он «Я» там стоит: и простирает навстречу—пречистые руки... Этот жест—жест захожего иерея—жест воздетых рук отпечатлели, конечно, надбровные дуги: по окончании светлой утрени Иерей уйдет; вы его года не увидите... Он вернется на родину...

. . . .

Созерцание черепа странно: и он—память о памяти великолепного скелетного храма, выдолбленного нашим «Я» в скалах черного мрака; в храме тела—лежат планы храмов; и восстанет, я верую, из храмовых обломков: храм тела.

Так гласит нам писание...

. . . .

Созерцание черепа утешает, напоминает; и—смутно учит чему-то; жест надбровных дуг ведом нам; это жест окрыленного «Я», вставшего из гробовой покрышки, пещеры, чтобы некогда вознестись; чтоб... вернуться на родину...

Лабиринт черных комнат.

После первого мига сознания предстают: коридоры и комнаты—
—все
b комнаты, комнаты, комнаты!—
—в кото-

37

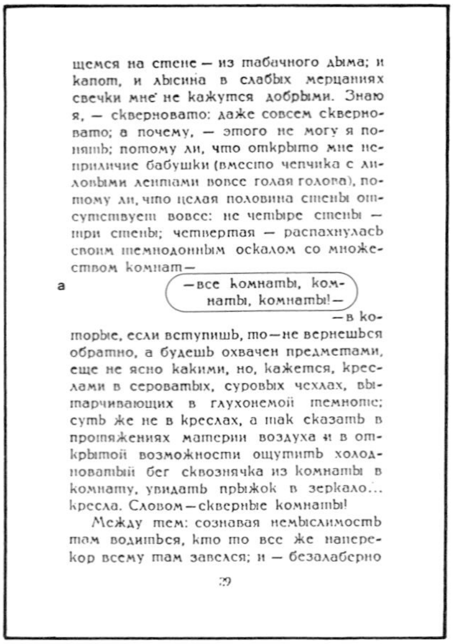

do not line up in a neat diagonal as in fig. 34. On the other hand, because the "A Stroll" section fits on one page (p. 43) in the 1917-18 version, the symmetry is more evident there than in the 1922 version, where it is spread over three pages (pp. 71-73, not shown). Such examples of visual symmetry, large and small, can be found throughout the work; indeed, the whole novel is symmetrically organized (Janecek 1971).

One can see even from these selected examples that the visual aspects of the text of *Kotik Letaev* are often multifunctional and complex and relate intimately to the various other stylistic and thematic aspects of the work. The visual configurations are not a sporadic experiment as was true in *Petersburg;* but they are a well-worked-out system that contributes successfully to the whole and is thoroughly integrated with such other devices as soundplay, thematic repetition, and architectonics into an elaborate but carefully ordered overall structure (Janecek 1971).

The double dash fits well into this structure precisely because of its multiplicity of uses. It relates to rhythm as a pause indicator, it relates to passage repetition as a "molecular" bond (copula), and it gives to Bely's page a unique typographical appearance, not found anywhere else in prose or poetry except among his few imitators (Remizov, Pilnyak, Artem Vesyoly). It is the symbol of the bonding process that is the essence of *Kotik Letaev:* bonding by sound linkage, by repeated juxtaposition, by rhythmic impulse, by syntactic linkage. It represents the core of Bely's prose: a prose founded on poetic association.

Most of Bely's later prose works follow the same principles for visual effects as *Kotik Letaev.* Exceptions are the first two volumes of the Moscow trilogy, *A*

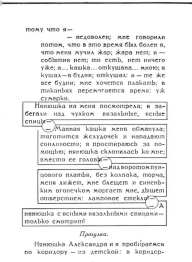

Fig. 34. Andrey Bely, *Kotik Letaev.*

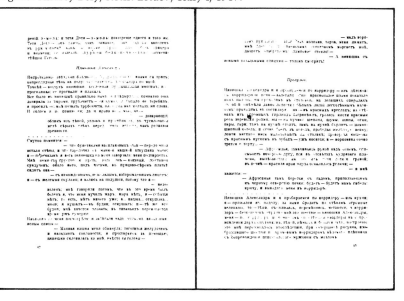

Fig. 35. Andrey Bely, *Kotik Letaev*, Skify I, 1917.

Moscow Eccentric and *Moscow under Stress* (1926), which contain no visual effects of the sort I have discussed. However, *The Baptized Chinaman* (1927), a sequel to *Kotik Letaev*, is a bit more radical than the latter: to my knowledge it has the only example of a genuine pictogram in which phallic symbolism is unmistakable, given the content of the passage (fig. 36). Interesting here are the two parallel blocks of text that seem to be simultaneous in time and direction. The earlier serialized publication of this work shows the same layout (1921, 154). Bely was the editor of the journal in which it appeared, thus relieving us of any doubt about whether the results corresponded with the author's intentions.

Notes of an Eccentric (1922d) deserves mention for its even more radical configurations, such as those seen in fig. 37, which visually depict the confusion and excitement of the narrator. These, however, occur erratically at moments of emotional stress and are not well integrated into the text as a whole.

Finally, *Masks* (1932), the last volume of the Moscow trilogy, is not homogeneous with the first two volumes: unlike the latter, it follows the visual devices of *Kotik Letaev*. However, as is true of other aspects of Bely's final, peculiar novel, the visual effects seem at times to be less frequent, more arbitrary, and less open to rational analysis than those in *Kotik Letaev*.

THE POETRY

The conventions for layouts in poetry of course differ from those for prose. Modern poetry is always printed with spaces to mark line ends and stanza divisions; line lengths, stanza patterns, or any combination of these virtually ran a gamut of possibilities by the beginning of this century. Yet Bely is credited

Fig. 36. Andrey Bely, *The Baptized Chinaman*, 1927.

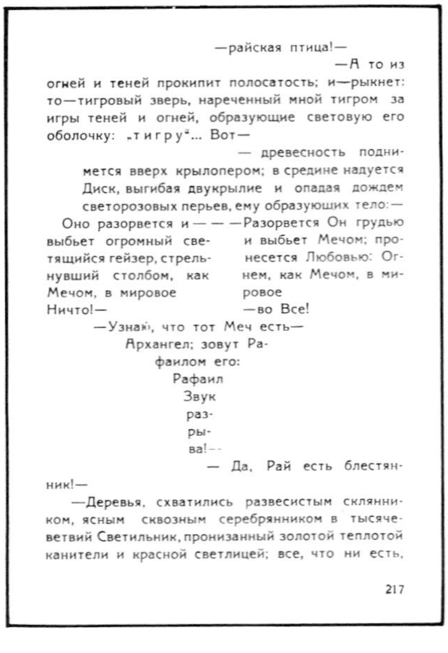

—райская птица!—
—А то из
огней и теней прокипит полосатость; и—рыкнет:
то—тигровый зверь, нареченный мной тигром за
игры теней и огней, образующие световую его
оболочку: „тигру"... Вот—
— древесность подни-
мется вверх крылопером; в средине надуется
Диск, выгибая двукрылие и опадая дождем
светорозовых перьев, ему образующих тело:—
Оно разорвется и — — —Разорвется Он грудью
выбьет огромный све- и выбьет Мечом; про-
тящийся гейзер, стрель- несется Любовью: Ог-
нувший столбом, как нем, как Мечом, в ми-
Мечом, в мировое ровое
Ничто!— —во Все!
—Узнай, что тот Меч есть—
Архангел; зовут Ра-
фаилом его:
Рафаил
Звук
раз-
ры-
ва!—
— Да, Рай есть блестян-
ник!—
—Деревья, схватились развесистым склянни-
ком, ясным сквозным серебрянником в тысяче-
ветвий Светильник, пронизанный золотой теплотой
канители и красной светлицей; все, что ни есть,

217

Fig. 37. Andrey Bely, *Notes of an Eccentric*, 1922.

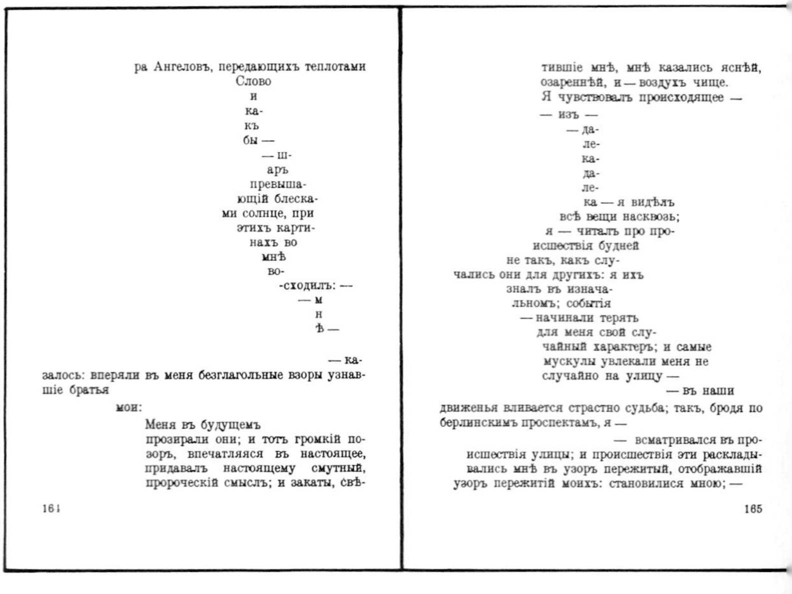

ра Ангеловъ, передающихъ теплотами
Слово
и
ка-
къ
бы —
— ш-
аръ
превыша-
ющій блеска-
ми солнце, при
этихъ карти-
нахъ во
мнѣ
во-
-сходилъ: —
— м
н
ѣ —
— ка-
залось: вперяли въ меня безглагольные взоры узнав-
шіе братья
мои:
Меня въ будущемъ
прозирали они; и тотъ громкій по-
зоръ, впечатляяся въ настоящее,
придавалъ настоящему смутный,
пророческій смыслъ; и закаты, свѣ-

164

тившіе мнѣ, мнѣ казались яснѣй,
озареннѣй, и — воздухъ чище.
Я чувствовалъ происходящее —
— изъ —
— да-
ле-
ка-
да-
ле-
ка — я видѣлъ
всѣ вещи насквозь;
я — читалъ про про-
исшествія будней
не такъ, какъ слу-
чались они для другихъ: я ихъ
зналъ въ изнача-
льномъ; событія
— начинали терять
для меня свой слу-
чайный характеръ; и самые
мускулы увлекали меня не
случайно на улицу —
— въ наши
движенья вливается страстно судьба; такъ, бродя по
берлинскимъ проспектамъ, я —
— всматривался въ про-
исшествія улицы; и происшествія эти раскладывались мнѣ въ узоръ пережитый, отображавшій
узоръ пережитій моихъ: становилися мною; —

165

with introducing still another variant, the *stolbik* or "column," in his first book of verse, *Gold in Azure* (1904b; Zhovtis 1968a, 126), which employed an innovative use of short lines. Short lines had been used earlier in Russian poetry, most notably by A. M. Koltsov (1809-42), so this in itself was nothing new. Short lines in tandem with long lines had long been part of the typical verse fable (*basnya*), which occasionally had one-word lines, and from time to time many poets have used such mixed line lengths. Both of these usages were within the bounds of classical prosody and involved short or varying line lengths of a traditional meter.

Bely's innovation consisted of taking the traditional metrical line, breaking it into pieces, and arranging the pieces vertically. In some instances, the result was indistinguishable from the style of the *basnya*, except for the vertical alignment at the left margin and the use of capital letters only for those lines that begin a sentence. The *basnya* would typically be aligned to a vertical page-center axis and would begin each line with a capital letter. Here is an example of Bely's new practice:

Teper ne nastignut ikh nochke.
Sapfiry vsyo rezhe, a krasnye yakhonty chashche.
Koronoy ikh v vozdukhe stary korol sobiraet
i dochke
struyoyu goryashchey
k nogam vysypaet. ("Vechernyaya progulka," 1903 [1904b, 41])

Now night cannot overtake them.
Sapphires more rarely, but red rubies more often.
A crown in the air the king gathers them
and for his daughter
in a burning stream
he sprinkles them out at her feet.

Each line is both the continuation of the amphibrachic meter of the preceding line and the correct beginning of a new amphibrach line.

However, there are instances in the same poem where the line break occurs in a place that, when the meter is continued unbroken as it is, results in a nonamphibrachic opening line. For example,

I v vózdukhe yásnom blistáya,   And in the clear air shining
delfín   a dolphin
poletél . . . (p. 41)   flew . . .

Scanned, we get:

ˇ / ˇ ˇ / ˇ ˇ / ˇ
ˇ /
ˇ ˇ /   .

The last word fits metrically into the preceding line, but does not properly begin a new line. The conflicts between the ongoing metrical pulse and the line arrangement might pass unnoticed in this example, because the meter is unbroken; but in a soon-to-follow extended example, the tension that develops is likely to force the reader to notice the unorthodox layout.

V izyáshchnoy koróne	In an elegant crown
v serébryano-blédnom, rosístom	in a pale silver, dewy
khitóne,	chiton,
oná—	she—
5 igráet sedóy	plays with the gray
borodóy	beard
korolyá	of the sorcerer-
charodéya.	king.
Kak mnogo izyáshchestva v néy! . .	How much elegance there is in it! . .
10 Blestyá	Sparkling
ognevéya,	fiery,
vozdúshnye tkáni atlásistykh, rýzhykh kudréy	the airy fabric of satiny, auburn curls
nesútsya	is flowing
za néyu po vétru i rvútsya . . .	behind her in the wind and bursting . . .
15 Delfín	The dolphin
zolotóyu	like a golden
ladyóyu	skiff
nyryáet	is diving
sred óblachnykh vzdútykh vershín,	amid cloudlike, puffy peaks,
20 s luchóm	with a ray
zakhodyáshchego sólntsa igráet,	of the setting sun it plays,
plesnúvshi po vózdukhu rýbim khvostóm.	swashing the air with its fishy tail.

Metrically, lines 6, 7, 8, 11, 16, and 21 have "incorrect" line beginnings, all anapests. But if run into the preceding lines, they are metrically correct, thus: ĭgráeĭ sĕdóy bŏrŏdóy kŏrŏlyá chărŏdéyă. Nevertheless, the layout is likely to throw the reader off, since a natural pause at line end would interrupt the pulse, and the anacrusis of the next line would be a surprise. Furthermore, each of the line-end words, even if the line consists of only one word, is rhymed with another in an unpredictable pattern. This fact reinforces the independence of each line and militates against the tendency to restore the "misplaced" words to their preceding lines, as done above. What we have is a layout in conflict with the meter, the conflict being supported by the unpredictable but all-pervasive rhyme scheme. The look of the poem is not per se an innovation, but its conflict with the meter is new. There are two advantages to this device: (1) It highlights many more words than would have been the case if the lines were not so divided and the existing rhymes became internal; and (2) it breaks the monotony of the meter, which is a problem in particular for ternary meters.

Another case is represented by the poem "World Soul" (pp. 57-59), which is a pure *stolbik* with only one long line out of forty-seven, thus giving the visual appearance of a true column (fig. 38a, b, c).[8] What is different here is the absence of a meter. It is free verse whose only organizing feature, except for the columnar appearance, is the thorough but unschematic rhyming. The poem is, in fact, composed of almost nothing but rhymed words!

At this stage of his career, however, most of Bely's poems used traditional stanza layouts, and the above examples were exceptions.

The next two collections of poems, *Ashes* (1909a) and *The Urn* (1909b) are generally no more innovative in layout than the first. In all three, the most frequently used stanza pattern is the quatrain. Yet there are at least a few new elements. In *Ashes*, most notable is the introduction of the dash as a form of end punctuation and a form of indentation in mid-stanza. Both of these can be seen in the poem "In Open Space" (fig. 39), where the first stanza is also a *stolbik*.

The Urn is, if anything, more conservative than the preceding volumes; only three of the sixty-six poems have unusual layouts (Malmstad 1968, nos. 276, 285, and 310). Of these, only "To Enemies" is innovative (fig. 40). The new feature is the pronouncedly divided page with its left and right halves. The poem is not quite a *paramoeon*, in which the two halves are to be read independently, but it comes very close. Each half is almost a syntactically complete poem in itself, and, while there are some strong sonic links between the halves, each has its own independent sonic structure. The links between the halves are somewhat

[8] The most authoritative source of Bely's poetry, superseding even the original editions themselves in some instances, is Malmstad (1968). Poems quoted from this source will be cited as "Malmstad, no." Malmstad capitalized the beginning of all lines, however.

Fig. 38. Andrey Bely, "World Soul," *Gold in Azure*, 1904.

57

ДУША МІРА.

Вѣчной
тучкой несется,
улыбкой
безпечной,
улыбкой зыбкой
смѣется.
Грядой серебристой
летитъ надъ водою—
—лучисто—
волнистой
грядою.

Чистая,
словно міръ,
вся лучистая—
золотая заря,
міровая душа.
За тобой бѣжишь,
весь
горя,
какъ на пиръ,

58

какъ на пиръ
спѣша.
Травой шелестишь:
«Я здѣсь,
«гдѣ цвѣты...
«Миръ
«вамъ»...

И бѣжишь,
какъ на пиръ,
но ты—
Тамъ...

Пронесясь
вѣтеркомъ,
ты зелень чуть тронешь,
ты пахнешь
холодкомъ,
и смѣясь
вмигъ
въ лазури утонешь,
улетишь на крыльяхъ стрекозовыхъ.

59

Съ гвоздикъ
малиновыхъ,
съ блѣднорозовыхъ
кашекъ—
ты рубиновыхъ
гонишь
букашекъ.
1902

haphazard; for example, the end words in the first half-lines of stanzas 1 and 2, *prostor* (space) and *kloki* (shreds), become internal in the second half of the respective lines. In stanza 3 this turns into an actual internal rhyme, *zvon—son* (sound—dream), only to disappear thereafter as a pattern. In stanza 5 the same end word of the first half-line rhymes instead externally with its second half, *vas—glaz* (you—eye), while in stanza 6 it rhymes with the end of the second line. Yet stanzas 4 and 7 have no links of this sort of all. On the other hand, the sound structure of each of the halves is quite strict when independently considered. The tristichs on the right have end rhymes of the A × A type, wherein the middle line usually does not rhyme with anything (exception: stanzas 5 and 6 *gromnye—tomnye* [thunder—languid]). The left half of the poem is marked by a recurrence of the last two words of the stanza in the succeeding stanza. A rhyme is even developed eventually between the first hemistichs *verolomnye—tomnye—verolomnye* (treacherous—languid—treacherous). The spatial separation of the hemistichs inclines the eye to read not only across the page, but down each of the halves, and the poem's structure supports this inclination.

With *The Princess and the Knights* (1919), we enter a decidedly new stage where traditional layout takes a back seat to innovation. Of the fifteen poems,

Fig. 39. Andrey Bely, "In Open Space," *Ashes*, 1909.

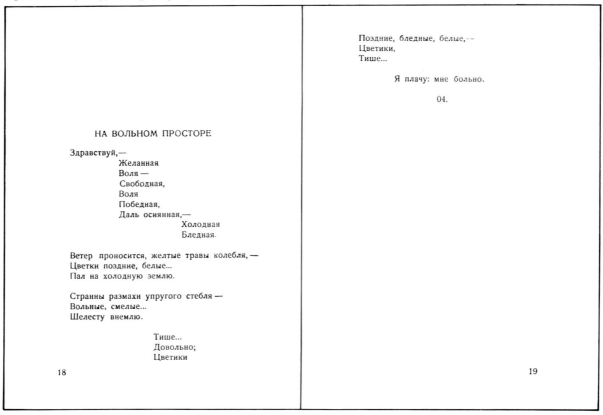

only two are in quatrains, one in couplets; the rest are *stolbiki* or some mixture. Of interest vis-à-vis the previous discussion of Bely's prose is the first appearance of the double dash in verse, in the poem "Rodina" ("Homeland") (Malmstad 1968, no. 338), dated 1909, Moscow, with one instance of the practice:

V usta eti, vleysya—   Into these lips, pour—
        —O, nektar!—   —O, nectar!—

This, then, is Bely's first use of the device, unless he made the addition later.

Other poems in the collection, but dated later, use double dashes and other forms of spacing more extensively. Of particular variety and richness is the third section of "Shut, Ballada" (The Jester, A Ballad, 1911) (Malmstad 1968, no. 330; see also fig. 41a,b,c). We have here a high degree of visual fragmentation; of the 102 words, a majority (53) are spatially isolated and distributed across the width of the page. It is important to note, however, that Bely does not scatter his words haphazardly but makes it quite clear in what order they are to be read. He is careful, in his configurations, to provide signs indicating where the eye should go next. Even if on occasion two paths—a "fork in the road"—might be suggested

Fig. 40. Andrey Bely, "To Enemies," *The Urn*, 1909.

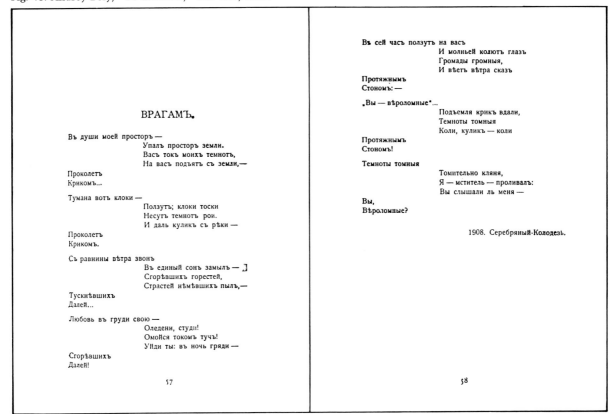

(for example, "Shut: Plamen" or "Shut Nad ney" [Jester: A Flame, or Jester Above It]), they are definitely paths, and usually one path is the correct one. Bely does not envision a random wandering over the field of the page. In this he differs from the practices of some Futurists, Dadaists, and Concrete poets who encourage just such a visual wandering.

Bely, as we shall see, was highly concerned with oral delivery, which called for a clear, correct path to guide the reciter. Recently a recording was released of Bely's own recitation of one of the poems from *The Princess and the Knights*, "Golos proshlogo" (Voice of the Past) (Malmstad 1968, no. 334). This recording affords one a marvelous opportunity to hear just how he intended the layout and punctuation to be interpreted orally (see Janecek 1980a for detailed comments). Suffice it to say here that the crosslike and swordlike visual configurations in *The Princess*, based on the major cross-sword symbol in the poem, have given it the quality of a figure poem. Bely's recitation of the poem corresponds more closely to this version than it does to the quatrain layout of the poem's somewhat earlier first version.[9]

The *poèma*, *Christ is Risen* (1918), uses the *stolbik* heavily, but without further innovations. Bely's next collection, *The Star* (1922e), regardless of its innovations in other areas, represents a return to conservative typographical layouts; nearly all its poems are in traditional stanza forms, mainly quatrains. One poem in the collection is of particular interest to us here—the only *stolbik*, entitled, appropriately, "Shutka" (Joke) (Malmstad 1968, no. 359). The only novelty here is a verse line of "no syllables," possible in Russian because the enclitic preposition *v* is without a vowel. The poem opens with the stanza,

[9] *Apollon*, no. 6 (1911), 30.

Fig. 41. Andrey Bely, "The Jester, a Ballad," fragment, *The Princess and the Knights*, 1919.

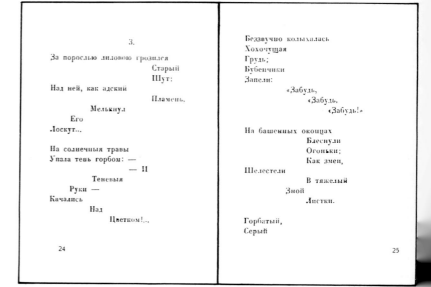

V	In
Doline	The Valley
Kogda-to	Once
Mechtatelno	Dreamily

and contains the amusingly bizarre stanza visually torn into small pieces:

V	In
Lokhmotyakh	Tatters
I	And
V	In
Krovi	Blood

If the reader wonders if he should pause between the enclitic "nonsyllable" *v*, as seems to be necessitated by the line end, he is ultimately assured to do so by the final stanza:

V—	In—
—Zodiak.	—the Zodiac.

With this example, the intrusion of the pause into the syntax of the sentence reaches its maximum.

    After Parting (1922f) is, as the title suggests, in part a response to Bely's excited discovery of Marina Tsvetaeva's *Parting* (1922). The creative relationship between the two poets and the rhythmic developments that grew out of this contact are well worth a detailed study, but the matter of visual devices is easily covered in brief. Both books of poetry demonstrate their authors' fondness for

g. 41 (*continued*)

Замок
Над лугом в белый день.
Крылом — нетопырииым
Развеял
Злую
Тень.

Очнулась королевна:
Всему —
    — Конец,
    Конец!...
    Разбейся же, —
          — О, сердце! —
Трескучий
Бубенец...

Ты, —
    — Одуванчик —
          Счастье:
      Пушинкой облетай!

26

Пошла,
    Роняя
        Слезы,
          На белый горностай.

Отмахиваясь веткой
От блещущих стрекоз, —
За ней
Седой
Насмешник —
        Тяжелый
        Шлейф
        Понес.

Качались
Стебелечки
Пленительных
Вербаи
      Между атласных,
      Черных,

27

      Обтянутых
      Колен.

          4.

Поток
Рыдает
Пеной,
    Клокочет
    Бездной
    Дней...
В решетчатыи окна
Влетает сноп огней.

Расплачется в воротах
Заржавленный засов:
          Пернатый,
          Ясный
          Рыцарь

28

the dash as a form of punctuation. Tsvetaeva traces her use of the dash to the standard practice in the vocal musical notation of putting dashes between word syllables when the vocal line takes up more space than the printed text below the staff:

Later, when I was forced by the rhythmic structure to break words, to tear the words apart by means of the dividing dash unfamiliar in verse, and everyone scolded me for this while a few praised (in both cases for "modernity"), I was not able to say anything except "it has to be." Suddenly I saw once with my eyes those song texts of my infancy, shot through with completely legal dashes—and I felt myself washed clean by all of Music from my charge of "modernity": washed clean, supported, confirmed and legalized. . . . (Karlinsky 1966, 163)

Tsvetaeva used the dash innovatively to indicate a break in the interior or polysyllabic words, a practice Bely was not generally inclined to follow (Karlinsky 1966, 161). For example,

Mu—zhaysya zhe serdtse!	Take cour—age heart!
Mu—zhaysya i chay!	Take cour—age and hope!
Ne—besny zarverzsya	The hea—venly vault has
Svod! V trepete stay (1927)	Opened! In the trembling of flocks

And even,

Kacha—"zhivyot s sestroy"—	Rock—"lives with his sister"—
yutsya—"ubil otsa!"— (1928)[10]	ing—"killed his father"—

But this is a later radical development. There is no word splitting in *Parting*. Rather, the dash is used to indicate a pause where there would ordinarily not be one, or at least not a long one. For example,

ne Muza, ne Muza,
Ne brennye uzy
rodstva,—ne tvoi puty,
O Druzhba!—Ne zhenskoy rukoy,—lyutoy
Zatyanut na mne
Uzel.

Not the Muse, not the Muse
Not the transient bonds
Of kinship,—not your fetters,
O Friendship!—Not by woman's hand,—fierce
Will tighten on me
The knot.

[10] Zhovtis (1968a, 124) points to these particular lines as an example of an "unnormative" effect made possible by layout. Only because of the vertical alignment of the two halves of the word can they be perceived as a unit.

In this she followed Bely's practice, in which he is her predecessor by a decade or more. For both Tsvetaeva and Bely the *single* dash, aside from its standard use as a copula in the present tense, is a pause-producing divider. On the other hand, Bely's *double* dash, which Tsvetaeva never adopted, is a linking device that produces a pause like the single dash but also conjoins words on two successive lines. *After Parting* in this respect represents a new departure in layout for Bely, as the first poem will dramatically illustrate (fig. 42).

The frequent double dashes produce a diagonal composition with knots of words in small columns linked like beads on a chain of double dashes slanting down to the right and even across pages. Though it has obvious differences, this practice is akin to Mayakovsky's *lesenka* (stepladder). Suffice it to note here that the existence of "knots" of words on each step of the ladder changes the rhythmic, syntactic, and linear picture considerably from that used by Mayakovsky. Bely's configurations are frequently more complex than is possible with a simple stepladder, as demonstrated in fig. 42.

One reviewer of *After Parting*, P. Zhurov (and, I might add, one of the few to comment on Bely's layout), criticized this breaking-up of the line as deadening. "What is the result? Reading is made difficult" (Zhurov 1923, 279). He also noticed the isolation of a preposition-consonant ("V" [Bely 1922f, 72]) on a line by itself, as I have noted in an earlier instance. Zhurov concludes his review with the following:

Almost all [the stanzas] are taken in with great difficulty: it is necessary to musicalize oneself, it is necessary to follow the poet into his mimetic-sound-making laboratory. As an experiment and a school, pursuing these attempts is interesting and instructive, but to accept them as ready for people to read—is impossible, painful. (Zhurov 1923, 280)

Fig. 42. Andrey Bely, "Spring Melody," *After Parting*, 1922.

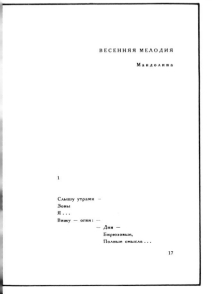
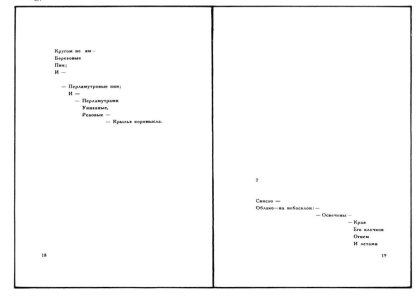

But he adds that such a bizarre, tortured form corresponds to the psychological content of the poetry.

We may add, on the other hand, that as with a stepladder, the vertical alignment of pieces of the line—"steps" if you will—inclines the eye to notice sonic and syntactic relationships in similarly positioned steps. Thus, reading down the page we note the repetition of *Pronizyvaet* (Pierces) as the word farthest to the left after the first step, and we link to this pattern the word *obryzgivayut* (splash) because of its comparable position, similar sound, and form. We also notice the rhyme *Beryozovuyu—rozovuyu* (Birch—rosy) and *Rozu* (Rose) in parallel positions. Then there are *Vzvizgi/Vetrov* (Whistling of Winds) and *Vzbryzgi/Strof* (Splashes of Stanzas), and *Zovami—Rosami* (Calls—Dews), and so on. Syntactic parallelism goes hand in hand with layout configuration and sound play to heighten the elaborately organized relationships of extensive periodic constructions. At the same time, the open look of the page relieves, even eliminates, a sense of ponderousness and clottedness that might result from a compact layout. The prose of *Petersburg* (1916) is typically described as having "a certain heaviness" (Bely 1967, 1) yet the present example would more likely be described as "airy," despite a similarity in style.

Bely's attempt in *Kotik Letaev* to do something comparable with his prose leads to some uncertainty as to whether juxtapositions that bring out word relationships are accidental or intentional. But in verse such as we have here, the juxtapositions and parallelisms are absolute, not subject to fate in the hands of the typesetter. The layout and resultant configurations are automatic, so long as the author's obvious intentions are followed (which is not the case with the Soviet edition [Bely 1966]).

One can perhaps argue that the double dashes are excess punctuation and

Fig. 42 (*continued*)

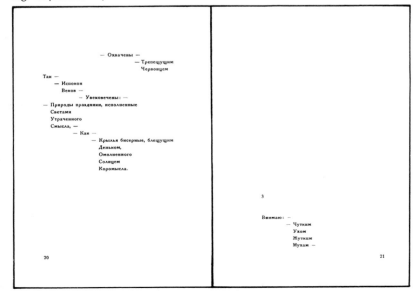

that a step down without them would have the same effect, but there is a difference. The empty space after the first word is suggestive of isolation. One can feel that the words look scattered down the page. But when the first word is followed by a normal punctuation mark that leads downward to another dash, the two form what looks like an equal sign, or nearly the *gestalt* of a quadrilateral. There is attraction, a sense of bonding, and a visual continuity linking the two "steps." This is purely a product of the visual medium and would not be audible at all in recitation, where intonation must be substituted.

More than half of the fifteeen poems in *After Parting* use double dashes extensively, and the device takes on primary significance for Bely's later poetry, or more precisely, for his later revisions of his earlier poetry. Thus his 1931 revision of *Gold in Azure* has many of the old poems laid out in stepladders with double dashes.

In essence, we have reached the end of Bely's career of innovation in verse layout. A fine discussion by Herbert Eagle (1978) of Bely's revisionary practices, specifically in regard to a poem from *Gold* reworked for the later republication *Poems* (1923), has already been published and need not be repeated here. Extensive study of his later poetry, revised and new, would be a valuable task, but it would not add much on visual effects to the present study.

THEORY

The Symbolists saw in language primarily its similarity to music. They strove to "overcome Gutenberg" by increasing the musical features of their poetry (Szilard 1973, 294). Bely, for all his experimentation with visual effects, never con-

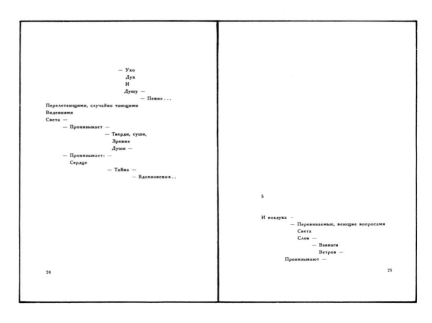

Fig. 42 (*continued*)

sciously departed from this basic Symbolist orientation. The essays in his earlier collections of articles (1910-11) contain numerous statements linking poetry to music and, despite his sporadic interest in the graphic side of the word, Bely's main orientation throughout his career was toward its sonic properties: "Language is first of all sound symbolism" (Bely 1910a, 527). Following Schopenhauer's hierarchy of art forms, like a true Symbolist he placed music at the summit—as the expression of "pure will," pure movement, pure form, pure energy. "Music is the soul of all the arts," because it is the least materially bound, the closest to a direct expression of the spiritual. He quotes Schopenhauer: "Our self-consciousness has as its form not space but only time" (ibid., 152). Thus music is the best reflection of the human consciousness or spirit. (See also Hughes 1978.)

Poetry is not as pure as music, but is rather a nexus of time and space. "Poetry is a bridge thrown across from space to time" (Bely 1910a, 154). It is more materially bound than music, but shares some of its exalted properties by being a succession of images, that is, images that are oriented toward concrete reality but ordered in time (ibid., 161). Poetry, of course, also has a temporal element in its rhythmical or metrical pulse.

Poetry combines the formal conditions of temporal and spatial forms of art *by medium of* the word: *The word depicts medially;* in this is poetry's weakness. But the word depicts not only the *form* of an image, but also the *change* of images. In this is poetry's strength. Poetry is medial, but the diapason of its depictive sphere is broad; poetry dissolves spatial traits into temporal traits; and vice versa.   (Ibid., 178)

That Bely became a poet rather than a musician seems unexpected, given the higher status of music in his hierarchy of the arts—that is, until we read his article, "The Magic of Words," where the theurgical power of the word raises it to heights that are evidently above pure music.

Fig. 42 *(continued)*

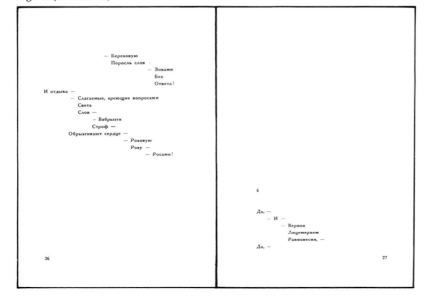

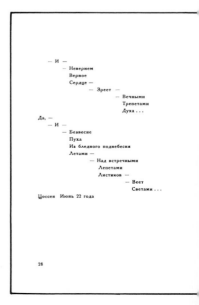

The word creates a new, third world—the world of sound symbols . . . in the word and only in the word do I create for myself what surrounds me on the outside and on the inside, for I am the *word* and only the *word*. . . . In *sound*, space and time come into contact and therefore sound is the root of all causality. . . . It is not without reason that magic recognizes the power of the word. Living speech itself is an uninterrupted magic; by means of a successfully created word I penetrate deeper into the essence of phenomena than in the process of analytical thinking; by thinking I differentiate a phenomenon; by the *word* I control it, subdue it. . . .

And therefore living speech is a condition for the existence of humanity itself; it is— the quintessence of humanity itself; and therefore originally poetry, the gaining of knowledge, music and speech were a unity; and therefore living speech was magic, and people who were live-speaking were beings on which lay the stamp of communication with the divinity itself. (Ibid., 430-31)

With this theoretic position in mind, one can easily see that Bely would have been disinclined to a preoccupation with visual effects, considering them a form of backsliding into a lower, more materially bound art form divorced from living speech and sound. Nowhere in his theories does Bely give independent value to the visual component of the text. It is always a facilitative feature, a means of conveying the sound. This does not, however, prevent him from in fact taking some theoretical interest in graphics.

Bely was familiar with the hermetic and cabalistic primary and secondary sources available and discusses them in the notes to *Symbolism* (1910a), where he describes the mystical interpretation of the Hebrew IEVE (usually YHWH [Yahweh]) in three places (pp. 493, 499, 622-23). He also surveys the matter of the "sacred language" of magic connected with the hermetic tradition in which "every letter corresponds with a number and an image" (p. 620). Continuing the quote from "The Magic of Words" begun above, he notes:

It is not by accident that each of the sacred hieroglyphics of Egypt had a triple meaning: the first meaning was joined with the word's sound which gave a name to the hieroglyphic image (time); the second meaning is joined with the spatial configuration of the sound (image), i.e., with the hieroglyph; the third meaning was included in the sacred number which was symbolized by the word. (Ibid., 432)

On the less mystical and more technical side, he insists in regard to literary criticism that "description must begin with a sequential description of everything that strikes our eye in a poetic work; in opening a book of poems I first of all see lines joined into stanzas; so I must begin the description with the natural sequence in which elements composing the whole are presented to my consciousness" (p. 612). He does not, however, pursue this first element impinging on our consciousness as an initially visual impression. Elsewhere, he discusses the effect of punctuation marks, which "have a huge, often elusive, logical meaning," by using the illustration of two nominal phrases separated by various punctuation marks; their value, however, is sonic (pause length, intonation) and logical, not visual (pp. 589-90). Nevertheless, he on occasion toys with letters as emblems, as in line 24 from *The First Encounter* (1921):

"Ха" с "I" в "Же"—"Жизнь": Христос Iисус—

"X" and "I" into "Ж" is "Life." Christ Jesus—   (Bely 1979, 3)

Occasionally the layout of a poem or prose passage has an emblematic significance, as noted above. But this is a rarity in his work.

Both of the major theoretic works written in 1917, "Aaron's Rod" and *Glossolalia*, maintain the same sound-oriented viewpoint as *Symbolism*.[11] *Glossolalia* (published in 1922), as the subtitle "A Poem about Sound" indicates, continues Bely's focus on language as a sonic phenomenon. An odd, idiosyncratic document, heavily influenced by anthroposophy, it parallels *Kotik Letaev* many ways in design. Instead of chronicling the rise of childhood self-consciousness as *Kotik* does, it chronicles the development of language; but, like *Kotik*, to do this it uses the physiology of the mouth cavity, world mythology, the Biblical creation of the world, Steinerian cosmology, and Indo-European etymologies, plus a personal frame of reference. Many of the images and passages resonate strongly with places in *Kotik*, often to the point of being nearly verbatim correspondences and leading to an actual quote (Bely 1922b, 119; 1922c, 16; 1971b, 8). Out of articulatory relationships emerges a whole cosmogony of sound. He supplies numerous diagrams to illustrate the various relationships. There is no denying that these are often intended to have a true spatial focus, such as the line drawing to illustrate *strast* (passion) (fig. 43). As Bely comments: "We can note down sound in lines, we can dance in it, we can build images in it" (1922b, 125). This is because Bely is keenly aware of the articulatory "gestures" of the vocal apparatus and gives them an elaborate, if questionable, symbolic interpretation. Sound takes on concrete, observable spatial dimensions in the human mouth: "The gestures of sound are composed: by the contact of the tongue and the spiral of the [air] stream (the broadening, narrowing, compression of its flow)" (ibid., 125-26).

[11] "Zhezl Aarona" was written in January 1917, and *Glossaloliya* in September-October 1917; see Nivat (1974), 76. Bely consistently misspelled the word *Glossolalia*.

Fig. 43. Andrey Bely, illustration from *Glossolalia*, 1922, page 124.

СТРАСТЬ

Despite the occasional use of the word "letter" *bukva*, which he does not keep entirely distinct from the "sound" *zvuk* for which the letter stands, Bely never passes over into a consideration of the symbolic shapes of the letters, though this might seem to be an attractive possibility. The closest he comes to this is in a passage where he says: "Concepts are models of processes; processes are mobile; concepts are frozen letters" (ibid., 90). Soon after, he elaborates: "But they [concepts] are categories (letters)" (p. 91). It must be kept in mind that a "concept" is a negative term in Bely's philosophy of language and thought, representing a dead leaf on the living branch of language, a word which once had the life of a true symbol but has become automatized by overuse and has lost its vital force (Bely 1910a, 434). Letters seem to be identified with "concepts," perhaps because they are fixed, immobile, dead on the page, as opposed to the living, moving dimension of sound, so they are of little interest to Bely.

To his collection of poems *After Parting* (1922f) Bely attached a preface that proclaimed a needed new direction in poetry that he called "melodism," with "melody" in a poem being "the predominance of intonational mimicry" (Bely 1966, 546). This predominance of intonation becomes a slogan in Bely's theories for the remainder of his career, though he drops the label of "melodism" immediately. Punctuation, of course, plays an important role in conveying intonation and he discusses this briefly, pointing out individual preferences: "The period is the sign of Pushkin's prose, the semi-colon—of Tolstoy's; the colon is my sign; the dash is the beloved sign of the modernists" (ibid., 547)—and of Bely, too, we might add. He also illustrates the importance of layout by taking a famous line of Gogol's prose and laying it out in two variants with indentations and dashes. "We can express one and the same page in various intonational architectonics; each places its mark on the whole" (p. 548). Since "melody" is becoming an increasingly more important factor, according to the author, modern writers are trying in their individual ways to come up with a design (*nachertanie*) that will convey the proper intonation to the reader (p. 548). Nevertheless, he does not here go into the specifics of how he is trying to accomplish this himself with indentation. The Gogol layouts are given but not explained. Bely does, however, give an illustration of the use of line-internal dashes to force the reader to make rhythmically necessary pauses in the manner of Tsvetaeva (p. 547).

Only in his later years did Bely finally turn his attention in written form to an explanation of his layout practices. Everywhere he emphasized that

I do not think of my artistic prose without the pronouncing voice and in every way I try by means of spacing and all sorts of fragile methods of the printer's art to insert the intonation of a certain speaker who is reciting the text to the readers. In an eye reading, which I consider barbarism, for artistic reading is internal pronunciation and primarily *intonation*, in eye reading I am meaningless; but on the other hand the reader who flits over the line with his eye is not my concern. (Bely 1930, 16)

The conveying of intonation was his main goal, whether in prose or in verse.

In two significant statements, which did not come to light until 1971, Bely spells out in more detail the principles that guided his later typographical compositions. In his foreword (February 1931) to the unpublished edition of poems *Zovy vremyon* (The Calls of Times), he concentrates on the question in connection with verse. The traditional verse line, say iambic tetrameter, is for Bely a "metrical corset" that "reminds me of a unilaterally developed biceps: in it the intonation is predetermined" (Bely 1971a, 96). But he foresees that "the concept of the line and stanza in the future will be replaced by the concept of an intonational whole of qualitatively sounding words: the line and stanza are like an aria (in the Italian sense): a euphonic whole—an uninterrupted melody like a Wagnerian one where the role of a closed unit (melody) is replaced by a ligature of leitmotifs" (ibid., 94-95). Thus "the line in a structure which I call an uninterrupted melody is subordinated only to the intonational whole of rhythm and not, let's say, to tetrametric measurement: the whole unit of rhythm is the ear of the lyricist upon whom depends the distribution of words in the line" (p. 96). Bely is reasserting the dominance of the artist over the form by locating the determining role of unification in him or her rather than in a predetermined formal arrangement. He asserts this dominance by taking a "canonical" form and changing its look as a means of conveying the artist's personal implementation. "I try at times to replace the canonical meaning—the horizontal position of the line—with a perpendicular chain of words distributed in intonational breaks which correspond to the accents and pauses I hear" (p. 94).

In this connection, Bely also discusses end rhyme. If end rhyme is the dominant bearer of sonic expressiveness, all is well and good; the line can stay as it is. But if the poet wishes to heighten sonic expressiveness by having frequent internal rhymes or semirhymes, the line falls apart anyway, so why not reflect this in the layout: "The sonic whole (instrumentation, abundance of internal rhymes) annuls end rhyme, replacing it with the rhythmic fabric of the whole" (p. 94). These ideas were illustrated and discussed in connection with examples of the poetry quoted earlier.

More valuable, however, is Bely's discussion of specific examples.

One and the same complex of words laid out differently will reveal different breathing: in each distribution is its own intonation: intonation in lyric poetry is everything: it is like the expression of a face, gesticulation: intonation, gesticulation—change the meaning of a word: the conjunction *i* [and] can be extended to *iii*, can be effaced to a proclitic: *I ya* [And I], can sound like either *I ya* or *Iiii—ya*. *I* can be emphasized to the point of being a line: prosody does not recognize an intonationally stressed "i": in prosody "i" is always unstressed. The metric canon partially forces lyrical expressiveness into a corset of conventionality. (p. 95).

One poem is singled out for a one-and-a-half-page discussion. Since this is the fullest available instance of Bely's discussion of the matter in concrete terms, I find it worth quoting in its entirety:

I present the following example: the poem "Motylyok" (Butterfly), a *tanka* (speaking metrically), i.e.: it is a five-line poem in which the first half gives the image and the two last lines develop the thought contained in the image. The line layout is:

1. Nad travoy motylyok—	Above the grass a butterfly—
2. Samolyotny tsvetok . . .	An autoflying flower . . .
3. Tak i ya: v veter—smert—	So am I: into the wind—death—
4. Nad soboy stebelkom	Above myself, a stem,
5. Prolechu motylkom.[12]	I'll fly past, a butterfly.

Lines 1 and 2 give the image, and 4 and 5 develop it. But the same poem can have a different intonation given by me below in the following layout:

Nad travoy
Motylyok

Samolyotny
Tsvetok . . .—

    —Tak
      I ya:—

        V veter—
        Smert—

Nad soboy
Stebelkom—

Prolechu
Motylkom.[13]

What is the difference in intonation of the second and the first layout? Moving the third line of the tanka layout out to a new perpendicular column, and breaking it into two couplets not only doubles, it quadruples the accent on the third line, i.e. "Tak i ya": by this means the accent of the tanka is transferred from the end to the middle: the tanka stops being a tanka: the disintegration of the first two lines into two couplets (1) emphasizes the antinomy "butterfly-flower", (2) emphasizes the paradoxicalness of the flower: "a flying flower": and the disintegration of the two last lines emphasizes the antinomy between the "stem"—of the body and the "blossom"—butterfly-spirit. But the two antinomies "butterfly-flower" and "stem-blossom" correspond to each other, which is expressed by the fact that both antinomies have fallen into the same line of the perpendicular. To both is opposed "Tak i ya." The layout forms an intonational angle.

In the tanka layout the meaningful intonation is obliterated: in it the flighty lightness

[12] This poem was first published in *The Star* (1922), and is included in Bely (1966, 375). It is dated June 1916.
[13] The poem is reproduced here following the layout and punctuation in Malmstad, no. 586. The layout given in *Novy zhurnal* is clearly inaccurate.

is emphasized: in the second layout the cover is ripped from this lightness: in the first layout I observe the flight of the butterfly: in the second I observe the philosophical profundity of the flight: the first layout is "allegretto"; the second—"andante." In thinking about the layout I considered what was more important for me to emphasize; and I saw: it was more important to emphasize the thought and not the image (sometimes it is the opposite: it is more important to submerge the thought in the image); in laying out words the poet is a composer of rhythm; he composes a melody; rather he seeks by this external ear to express his internal hearing. (Bely 1971a, 97-98)

It is frustrating that while Bely here discusses the layout in terms of intonation, he does not indicate *what* intonation is desired and therefore how the indicated "intonational angle" that is so graphically clear to the eye on the page can be made equally clear to the ear without the page to look at.

A third example, "Letni lepet" (Summer Murmur, 1922) is discussed without presenting the poem, which is as follows:

Letni lepet

Kak—
    —Rasplesk
      Vetrov—

      V zov
      Leta—

      Taet
      Oblakom perlovym—
                  —V biryuzovom
               Nebe,—

  Tak—
    —Blesk
      Strof—

      Pitaet
      Serdtse—
           —Rozovuyu
          Rozu—
              —Rosami—
                  —Ot
                Sveta
                Slov!   Zossen.   (Malmstad, no. 598)

Summer Murmur

As—
    —The splash
      Of winds—

      Into the call
      Of summer—

Melts
Like a pearly cloud—
                    —In the turquoise
                Sky,—

So—
  —The sparkle
  Of stanzas—

  The heart
  Feeds on—
              —The roseate
              Rose—
                    —Like dews—
                                —From
                                The light
                                Of words!

Bely says that this poem is

a single indivisible recitative phrase; if you read it "by lines" the poem is nonsense; the phrase is taken in one recitative breath in which the intonation rises like the ripple of waves intercepting each other, the two downbeats, *Kak* [As] and *Tak* [So] each raise their own wave, inside which I hear the rising and splashing of a beat of cadence (on the words *nebo* [sky] and *Ot sveta slov* [From the light of words]); in the second wave, like a curl of foam, a trill-like combination—the assonance *rozovuyu rozu—rosami* [roseate rose—like dews] is heard as a tongue-twister [*skorogovorka*]. (1971a, 98)

Here at least a certain suggestion is made, though by simile, of how the intonation might be read into or from the layout: there are to be two phases to a single intonational arch with cadences on the last words to the far right of each phase. But what of the pauses? Does the more diagonal layout of the second phase indicate something? Bely does not say.

Bely admits his lack of a final solution to the problem: "I do not say that— I have found a method of expressing the particulars of intonation: *I am seeking them*: in every poem after its metrical formation one must see its rhythmical accent: and—reflect it in the layout" (ibid., 96). In a brief memoir published in 1971 by Klavdiya Nikolaevna Bugaeva, Bely's second wife, she recalls his complaints about the inadequacy of punctuation for his needs, and also his envy of the composer's advantages in notation. The period, for instance, is an incognito, an "x" that could be a quarter note, eighth note, whole note, or several of these. He praises the dash, however: "The best is the dash. It is a cut into the depths and at the same time a step on the road to intonation. It is a sign: pay attention, stop: something is happening here" (Bugaeva 1971, 106). As John Malmstad comments:

Realizing the inadequacies of punctuation Belyj turned instead to the arrangement and rearrangement of lines and stanzas. As early as *Gold in Azure* [1904] one finds poems in regular syllabo-tonic meters but written in lines of extremely varied feet. This variation in line length in turn affects the meters themselves. If one pauses at the end of lines the effect becomes one of accentual verse rather than syllabo-tonic. It was such a practice which impressed the young Majakovskij, and Belyj continued to develop it as his poetic career progressed. The arrangement of lines became his primary method for indicating pauses and intonation.   (Malmstad 1968, part 1, lxxxiv)

Klavdiya Nikolaevna, in her memoir, provides a unique glimpse of the poet working on the layout of his poems:

In his search for an intonational layout which would reveal the rhythmically mean-ingful accent, B. N. [Boris Nikolaevich, Bely's given name] would write out more than one page. He said that until the poem was written down and the eye passed over the lines like a kind of musical notation, one could yet say nothing. First it was necessary to *see* them [italics here and below K. N.] and then check by ear how the voice would fit itself into them. He patiently copied out one and the same poem in various line arrangements and brought them to *show*. And first he did not read, but spread them out before me on the table and said: *"Have a look!* Which will *sound* better?"

He waited silently while I examined them all. And only then did he pick up the page on which the positioning of the lines seemed most successful to him. After this he read through the other line versions as well, changing the intonation correspondingly. He wanted once again to ascertain the correctness of his choice and then "with a clear conscience" put aside what hadn't sounded right.   (Bugaeva 1971, 107-108)

How illuminating it would have been to know the manner in which he changed the intonation "correspondingly." In most instances we must be left to guess on the basis of what we see on the page, however inadequate and incomplete an indication of intended intonation this may be.

The "Foreword" (dated June 2, 1930) to *Masks*, Bely's last novel, contains his only published remarks on layout in his prose:

When I write: "I—'bren-bren'—otzyvalis stakany" (And—"chink-chink"—responded the glasses) this means that the sound-imitation "bren-bren" is an arbitrary association in the author's language.

But when I write:

"I—

   —'bren-bren'—

            —otzyvalis stakany . . ."—

                        —then

that means that the sound imitation somehow specially affects the one who is thinking it; it means,—the author pronounces: "ii" (full of meaning, an attention-getting "i"), pause; and "bren-bren," as a sound falling into the consciousness.   (Bely 1932, 10)

He claims that *Masks* is an epic poem "written in a prose layout to save space and with the indication in the lines only of the main pauses and main intonational emphases'' (ibid., 11).

As a final instance of the documentation of Bely's view on visual effects, we have the recent publication (Teryan 1973) of three letters of 1931 by Bely to A. M. Miskaryan, the copyeditor of *Masks*. These letters are of value for being the only documentation of Bely's problems with typesetters because of his use of unorthodox layouts. Miskaryan was evidently doing her best to meet the author's requirements; but mistakes naturally crept in and evoked from Bely an explanation of his methods (already discussed earlier in this chapter). Particular typographic mistakes prompted him to explain why his layout is vital to a given passage, and one statement is of special interest because it advances the idea of layout as a means of economy:

> This layout takes account of: (1) the pause, (2) breathing, (3) intonation, (4) sometimes replaces explanation, (5) tempo, etc. Destroy the layout in some places—and the author will be forced to include a superfluous phrase to explain what was given without words by the simple layout of the phrases. (Ibid., 157)

COMMENTS

Bely's remarks make it clear that the purpose of his layouts is to convey, however imperfectly, the vocal realization, the intonation of the passage, that is, the *aural* expression of the text. In this sense the visual devices are comparable to a sheet of music with signs that guide the performer. Faced with having to employ a system of typography that functions well enough on the semantic or logical level, but very inadequately on the sonic-intonational level, an author interested in effects in the latter area can only feel envious of the composer. The difference between musical notation and literary typography is that the former has a generally accepted and clearly defined relation to sonic phenomena (it is a system set up precisely to indicate how a piece should *sound*) while the latter indicates mainly how a text should be understood syntactically, and has only an imprecise relation to how it should sound. Punctuation is something of a minimum system: it reproduces in print only those aspects of spoken language (primarily gross intonation types and pauses) that are absolutely necessary for a correct understanding of the text's semantic content and syntactic relations. In his experiments Bely obviously stretches the usual system of punctuation and typography. But an essential factor is missing from his attempts to invent a system with the precision of musical notation, and this factor is a clear set of statements about what his various practices are intended to *mean* in sonic terms. The reader can only guess this meaning on the basis of what he knows about the punctuation marks and typography as they are ordinarily used.

Although Bely seems to have intended his typographical practices to be interpreted sonically, from the reader's point of view the result is both more and less than what was intended. It is less because of Bely's failure to make explicit the relation of his system to sound and articulation. It is more in that his practices have a decidedly effective *visual* import that certainly adds a new dimension to his novel writing, a dimension not available in standard prose. It is less unique in regard to verse. Although Bely considered this visual aspect of his text a means of dramatizing its sonic qualities, he seems never consciously to have appreciated that these visual effects are also an *addition* to the sonic effects—an element independent of sonic effects, though one that closely combines with the sonic to provide a total audiovisual structure.

The visual import of some typographical practices is underlined by the fact that in some cases the punctuation or typography seems to indicate a reading that would be difficult or awkward to reproduce physically, but whose intellectual apprehension causes no problems. These are usually awkward pauses, such as:

> I znaya, chto,—
> —Ezheshekhin-
> sky vpal v trubu, tam zapolzal . . . (Bely 1922c, 67)

> And knowing that—
> —Ezheshekhin-
> sky had fallen into the pipe, was crawling around there . . . (Bely 1971b, 47)

Here, if the double dash is given a distinct pause value, the meaning of *chto* would be distorted. Or there are effects that would be too subtle to have a perceptible vocal realization, such as in fig. 31 above. Then there are effects that are purely visual, such as when *komnaty* are first grouped together typographically, then strung out in a line, as in fig. 33a, b; or in fig. 28, where the row of dots indicates the *absence* of a song; or,

> —"Etogo 'Lva' pomnyu ya . . ."
> —"?"
> —"Pomnyu zholtuyu mordu . . . ne lva a—sobaki . . ."
> —"??" (1922c, 45-46)[14]

> —"I remember this 'Lion' . . ."
> —"?"
> —"I remember the yellow snout . . . not of a lion but of a dog . . ."
> —"??" (Bely 1971b, 31)

No technique of careful or trained recitation could possibly create an aural effect equivalent to the visual effect of such passages, except perhaps with the aid of gesture or mimicry.

---

[14] Similar examples of the use of the silent question mark can be found in *Petersburg*.

Bely was, in fact, interested in gesture and wrote about it in various places,[15] but he does not seem to have realized the purely visual nature of gesture as a sign that may or may not be accompanied by vocal sounds. Indeed, it would be quite appropriate to consider Bely's visual effects as typographical gestures. Bely considered them as such, but only as sonic gestures, which may be a contradiction.

The tie between the visual and the aural is something Bely maintained as a principle ("Physiology knows that hearing and sight are organically linked in us" [Bugaeva 1971, 107]) and its operation is clearly evident in his works, though perhaps not in the way he understood this link. Whether hearing and sight are "organically" linked or not, they are combined by Bely in texts that create effects having both a visual and an aural side to them. Both sides are operative because the text is meant to be looked at (i.e., not recited) as well as heard (i.e., with the internal ear). In this way, Bely's works are in keeping with the avant-garde trend of some Modernist writers to whom the visual impact of the text is often as important as the aural impact. Although by comparison Bely was rather conservative in his experimentation (typeface and size are uniform, the lines are all set horizontally, standard rules for capitalization are followed), he was one of the few writers to use visual effects in large-scale works. Philosophically Bely remained a Symbolist while using some of the same devices as the Futurists. His involvement with the visual dimension of written language produced many fascinating and effective literary moments, including the masterpiece *Kotik Letaev*, which brilliantly illustrates the possibilities open to writers to create visual impact.

[15] Chiefly in *Glossaloliya*, but also in *Maski*, 10; "Budem iskat melodii (Predislovie k sborniku 'Posle razluki')" (1966); also in Bely (1971a), and Bugaeva (1971). Bely's studies of verse rhythm similarly assume a sonic content to gesture. His large unpublished study, "O ritmicheskom zheste," appears to fall in line with this understanding as well. (See Bugaeva and Petrovsky 1937, 624, for a description of this work.)

3. Kruchonykh

and the Manuscript

Book

THE FIRST MANUSCRIPT BOOKS

In mid-1912, Aleksey Kruchonykh (1886-1968) published his first literary works,[1] thereby initiating a series of manuscript books that was to continue into the 1920s and that constitutes his major contribution to the look of Futurist literature. Despite his reputation as the "wild man of Russian literature" (Tretyakov et al. 1923), Kruchonykh was a systematic archivist and bibliographer. He numbered his books, or "productions" as he often called them, and appended a handy bibliography of his works through 1924 to his *Transrational Language in Seyfullina* (1925, 60-62). Since this bibliography has proved to be rather thorough and accurate, though some of the listed titles have not yet surfaced anywhere, I will use it as the main reference for putting Kruchonykh's works in order (fig. 44a, b.c).

The first books by Kruchonykh, six lithographed pamphlets, are extreme rarities, as are most of the later ones. They are not readily available in the United States, or even in Soviet libraries, although recently some have come up for sale at Sotheby auctions and elsewhere and may eventually turn up in the collections of museums and wealthy libraries. They are also available now on microfiche from Chadwych-Healey Ltd. and Interdocumentation Corp. A good selection of Kruchonykh's works in photocopied book form was edited and published by V. Markov (Kruchonykh 1973). Three of the first six are included in the Markov book, as are ten later booklets and additional material; this anthology is thus the handiest source for an overview of Kruchonykh's works. Lacking more specific or contradictory information, I will assume that the bibliography, which is subdivided by years, lists the works in chronological order.

[1] Prior to this, Kruchonykh had published *Ves Kherson v karikaturakh, sharzhakh i portretakh*, two lithographed albums, in Moscow, 1910 (Compton 1978, 30).

Before we study the individual works by Kruchonykh and his collaborators, it is worthwhile to pause a moment to consider the technical conditions and limitations under which the books were produced. Donald Karshan (1975) in his print catalogue of Malevich, discusses these matters primarily in relation to the painter, but his analysis applies to many of the other works in which Malevich was not directly involved. Regarding the paper used for many of the books, Karshan notes that it was

... usually the cheapest and thus the most perishable variety; thin, brittle and made of wood pulp. The reasons for such a selection were twofold: In some instances it was simply a matter of the publisher, usually the writers themselves, not having the funds for better paper (there was a great scarcity of paper in Russia during those years); in other instances, common paper was deliberately chosen, as an anti-establishment gesture and extension of their ideological stance. At this time, Paris-illustrated books, such as those by Kahnweiler and illustrated by Picasso, were printed on luxurious hand-made papers. (Karshan 1975, 29)

On size limitations, Karshan explains:

The Malevich lithographs were nearly all very small, as compared to most prints of the same epoch published in France and Germany. This was probably due to the fact that only small limestone slabs for the making of the lithographic images were available to Malevich and his collaborators. And then, the format of the booklets themselves [was] quite small, particularly in the case of the Futurist pamphlets and books—a scale chosen as an anti-book gesture or anti-elitist symbol, but perhaps also influenced by budgetary limitations. Parisian publications of the same epoch were generally much larger in format, with generous margins around the images; were issued in special editions on different papers, often pencil-numbered and signed by the artist. (Ibid., 31)

Fig. 44. A. Kruchonykh, personal bibliography from *Transrational Language in Seyfullina*, 1925, pages 60-62.

Библиография А. Крученых.

1912 г.

Старинная любовь.
Игра в аду. Поэма Хлебникова и Крученых. Рис. Н. Гончаровой.

1913.

Мирсконца. Кр-х, Хлебников. Рис. М. Ларионова, Н. Гончаровой и др.
Пощечина общественному вкусу. К-х, Маяковский, Хлебников, Д. Бурлюк и др.
Помада. Полуживой. Пустынники.
Куп-аса в журн. „Летучая мышь".
Союз молодежи. Сборн. III. Кр-х и др.
Садок судей. Сборн. Кр-х и др.
Декларация слова, как такового. Листок. Возрощеон.
Взорваль. Кр-х и др. Бух Лесиный. Кр-х и Хлебникова. Поросята. Кр-х и Зина В.
Чорт и речетворцы. Исследование. Слово, как таковое. Исследование. Победа над солнцем. Опера Крученых, Малевича, Матюшина.
Дохлая луна. Сборник Кр-х и др.
Стихи Маяковского. Выпит Кр-х. Трое. Сборник Кр-х и др. Молоко кобылиц Сборник Кр-х и др.
Рыкающий Парнасс. Сборник Кр-х и др.

1914.

Утиное гнездышко дурных слов. А. Крученых, рис. О. Розановой.
2 е дополненное издание.
Взорваль. Поросята. Бух лесиный и Старинная любовь. Игра в аду.
Те-ли-лэ Кр-х и В. Хлебников. Предисловие А. Крученых к „Новому учению о войне В. Хлебникова.
Стрелец. Сборник I. Кр-х и др.

1915.

Тайные пороки академиков. Статьи Кр-х и др.
Заумная Гнига.
Война. Кр-х, цвети. резьба О. Розановой.

1916.

Вселенская война.

1917.

1918. Кр-х и В. Каменский.
Учитесь худоги, рис. К. Зданевича.

АВТОГРАФИЧЕСКИЕ НИГИ (Гектограф):

Голубые яйца. Нособойна. Балос. Новкази. Тун-шал. Город в осаде, Нестрочье.

1918

Илез. Ма-е. Фо-лы-фа. Ра-ва-ха. Бегущее. Разбожу рылу. Цоц. Восемь восторгов. Из всех книг. Наступление. Зьют. Ф-нагт. Начилдаз. Шбыц.

1919 г.

Речелом Тушанчик. Зугдиди (зудачества). Замауль. Двухкамерная ерунда. Милорд. Сабара. Железный франт. Саламак. Нсар-Сами. Избылец. Пролинский перископ. Консовый зинр. Апендицит. Лакированное трико.
Фениис №№ 1—2. Сборник С. Г. Мельниковой. Ожирение Роз. Малохолия в капоте (1—2 издание). Фантастический кабачек. Милиорк.
Куранты №№ 1—3.
Замауль 1, 2, 3 и Юбилейная.
Цветистые торцы.

1920 г.

Мир и Остальное К-х, Т. Вечорка. В. Хлебников.
Мятеж I—X.
О женской красоте. Доклад.
Алая нефть. К-х и др.
Статьи в газ. „Коммунист". „Бакинский рабочий" и др.

1921 г.

Зэудо. Цоца. Заумь.
Искусство журнал №№ 1—2—3. К-х и др.
Бизль. К-х и Хлебников.

1922 — 23 г.

„Голодняк". — „Зудесник".
„Заумники"—сборник Крученых, Хлебников, Петников, Родченко.
„Фактура слова".
„Сдвигология русского стиха".
„Апокалипсис в русской литературе".
„Фонетика театра" с предисловием Б. Кушнера.
„Собственные рассказы детей". Собрал А. Крученых.

1924 г.

„500 новых острот и каламбуров Пушкина". Собрал А. Крученых.
„Лоф агитки Маяковского Асеева Третьякова". Собрал и слабил примеч. А. Крученых.
„Заумный язык у Сейфуллиной, Вс. Иванова, Леонова, Бабеля. Ар. Веселого".

And finally, on the printing process itself:

Typography by letterpress is a *relief process*, as are photoengraved plates. That which is *raised* on the plate, such as a line, is printed (the reverse exists for traditional engraving, etching). Woodcut is also a relief process: that which is cut away, does not print; only the raised portions do. Consequently, the less costly process, say for the preparations of *Victory over the Sun*, was to employ the photoengraved plate for the Malevich image, and the David Burliuk woodcut which is printed on the back cover. The plate, the type, and the woodcut all printed on one press cycle. This is why the lithographs which appear with typeset in futurist books are always *handmounted* on the covers or *hand-inserted* within. A lithographic image cannot be pulled on the same press cycle as the type, which is printed by letterpress. This also explains the all-lithographed books such as *A Game in Hell*: one process all the way through the printing procedure. Many deluxe illustrated books in the west juxtapose lithographic or etched images, for example, with typeset, necessitating the costly use of two or more separate printing processes. (Ibid., 63)

To this, Susan Compton adds:

The degree of participation by the artist who originated the image or the handwriting would vary. The printing was done by the professional, rather than the artist himself, from a lithographic stone, or sometimes, a zinc plate. The artist rarely worked on the stone, but provided the drawing and writing on paper. Special transfer papers were available, ready prepared for an artist to draw on, either with a lithographic crayon or pen, though cartridge paper could also be used. (Compton 1978, 70-71)

There were several advantages to the process: transfer papers allowed the artist to draw or write forward, rather than in mirror image, as was done when working directly on stone; the artist did not need to work at the lithographers, but could prepare his drawings wherever and whenever he wanted; and the handwritten text and the illustrations did not have to be done together, but could be done separately and combined later. "The finished result," as Compton remarks, "is not inferior to work drawn directly on the stone" (ibid., 75). Many of the drawings led a life separate from the texts, either in exhibits or as illustrations in other books; for example, some of Larionov's illustrations for Kruchonykh's books also appeared in *Donkey's Tail and Target* (ibid., 75-76). Such practices sometimes led to disunity or dissatisfaction among the contributing parties (see the discussion below on *A Game in Hell*).

All six of the books by Kruchonykh surveyed in this section are, except when otherwise indicated, lithographed throughout; they are printed on only one side of the page, and are octavo or smaller in size. We must remember that book design and production were based not only on aesthetic principles but also on the available financial resources. Thus, if a book was to be lithographed throughout, it was simpler and more economical to have the text handwritten on the stone or on transfer paper, whereas typesetting would incur considerable additional expense. Of course, one might say that all art exists within technical constraints, and it is what is achieved within those constraints that matters—not the constraints themselves.

Kruchonykh's first monographic publication, *Old-Fashioned Love* (Kruchonykh 1973, 13-18; Compton 1978, 10), appeared around August 1912, the date of *A Game in Hell*, co-authored by Kruchonykh and Khlebnikov (Khlebnikov 1968-71, 4:440). It is listed as the first item in Kruchonykh's bibliography and perhaps it came out slightly before *Game*.[2] Immediately striking is the design of the book, which is really more the size of a pamphlet (14 pages plus cover). It is lithographed from a handwritten text of eleven pages; two full-page rayist drawings, and the front and back cover designs, headpiece, and tailpiece were all done by M. Larionov. The text itself was also calligraphed by Larionov (see "The Letter as Such," below). As Markov comments, "It was obviously meant to be a complete break with the tradition of symbolist deluxe editions. The illustrations were either primitivist in the manner of folk art, or imitative of children's drawings, but some of them could be termed nonobjective" (1968, 41).

Besides being shocked to find in his hands a published work by a modern author that was handwritten and illustrated with primitive drawings, the reader of *Old-Fashioned Love* was probably struck by the poor quality of the book: cheap paper, poor binding, and unevenly trimmed pages—a rather makeshift and naive product compared to the prevailing norms. This, of course, was precisely the point, as Markov notes. Yet once the shock subsided, the reader was surely impressed by the visual unity of the whole work,[3] which imparts the sensation of having been written and drawn by the same hand. In contrast to the usual design of an illustrated book of the time, in which text pages differed markedly from illustration pages in the production process (letterpress versus lithography, color gravure, photoengraving, etc.), kind of paper, and craftsmanship, the drawings and text of Kruchonykh's first publication were both lithographed on the same paper.

The fact that only one process is used throughout *Old-Fashioned Love* not only allows for a unity of impression between text and illustration, but also permits the easy interpenetration of the two components. Thus rayist doodles or decorations can appear on a page of text (fig. 45), and the page number can become incorporated into a drawing (fig. 46). On page 1 (fig. 47), little cubist flowers fall from the headpiece drawing of a nude and a vase of flowers into the lines of text

[2] Markov (1968, 42). Khardzhiev (1968a, 316) says they came out simultaneously.

[3] Compton points out that this sort of unity fulfills the hopes of Maurice Denis "who had called for a revival of the medieval approach to book design, for the consideration of a page as a totality" (1978, 11). She further points out that Denis's theories were republished in France in 1912 and that the end page of *Old-Fashioned Love* bears the designation: "sochinenie A. Kruchonykh, ukrasheniya M. Larionov," where *ukrasheniya*, an odd word to be used in this context, corresponds to Denis's term *decoration*.

below. Although drawing and text remain distinguishable in this instance, they unexpectedly share the same space, and it is probably not immediately obvious that the little geometric figures belong to the illustration. They almost look like accents over the vowels below them. The boundary between text and illustration is thus subtly obliterated. The text itself consists of seven poems that sometimes parody nineteenth-century love lyrics by juxtaposing romantic clichés with "stylistic dissonances or nonaesthetic details (e.g., pus, vomit)" (Markov 1968, 42). The poems per se are less innovative than the visual aspects of the book and do not establish Kruchonykh as a first-rate poet.

Larionov's illustrations reflect the mood of "romantic clichés" in the repeated images of a nude and a vase of flowers. The drawings themselves tell a mute story:

Front cover: Close-up vase of flowers (fig. 48).

p. 1: small reclining female nude with vase of flowers nearby, petals falling (fig. 47).

Fig. 46. A. Kruchonykh, *Old-Fashioned Love*, 1912, p. 3; drawing by M. Larionov.

g. 45. A. Kruchonykh, *Old-Fashioned ove*, 1912, page 2.

Fig. 47. A. Kruchonykh, *Old-Fashioned Love*, 1912, p. 1; drawing by M. Larionov.

Fig. 48. A. Kruchonykh, *Old-Fashioned Love*; front cover by M. Larionov.

p. 3: abstract rayist composition (fig. 46).[4]

p. 7: foreground, lady with umbrella; man in background walking on perpendicular path, street light shining (rayist style) (fig. 49).

p. 14: female nude, rear view (fig. 50).

Back cover: large overturned vase of flowers; small-scaled nude overlapping composition; birds or butterflies (Compton 1978, 71) flying off in opposite directions (fig. 51).

The scene on page 7 takes some effort to "read" (Compton 1978, 89) and does not have a precise connection with any moment in the text; but it can be seen as a composite of various lines of text. About the woman it is said, "Dearest of all are you in an old hat, rumpled sides," while she says, "I arrive at a sacred tremor, walking under your umbrella." The man "loves to stroll," but next to her so that she can't "tyrannize" him with a head-on glance or "boldly insult" him directly to his face. Nighttime episodes are included in an on-again, off-again love affair of pseudo-tragic triteness, which is well captured in this sketch and the others:

Then, triumphing amid the world,
You [the woman] groaned thus in the quiet of nights!
Despising you and jealous all the same
I chose the path of devils! . . .   (p. 11)

The fact that page 7 is ultimately "readable" inclines one to try reading the

[4] This and the illustration on page 7 are, incidentally, the first applications by Larionov of his theory of Rayism (Khardzhiev 1976, 60).

Fig. 49, A. Kruchonykh, *Old-Fashioned Love*, p. 7; drawing by M. Larionov.

Fig. 50. A. Kruchonykh, *Old-Fashioned Love*, p. 14; drawing by M. Larionov.

Fig. 51. A. Kruchonykh, *Old-Fashioned Love*; back cover by M. Larionov.

rayist sketch on page 3 for some objective content. The page must be turned so the page number is in the lower left corner, and in that position one can barely make out a nude figure sitting on the end of a bed (?) in a room, with a window in the upper left corner. Such a "reading" is possible only in the context of the other illustrations, and with the text as a guide.

Another item of interest is the orthography of the text. Although in many respects it moves away from the old orthography, it is inconsistent, no doubt intentionally so. For instance, on page 1, line 1, we have хочеш (for хочешь [you want]) and несчасным (for несчастнымъ [unhappy]); but in line 2 we have слѣдъ прекрасным (for прекрасным [fine]). Despite inconsistencies, mainly on page 1, there is a system of sorts that leans toward the new orthography by rejecting the use of ъ after final consonants; otherwise the text usually follows Grot's rules. The departures from these rules are done for phonetic accuracy. Standard punctuation is sometimes omitted. This revised orthography is very likely Kruchonykh's responsibility rather than Larionov's, since it follows Kruchonykh's own personal spelling (Janecek 1980c) as seen in most of the books he edited and/or wrote; in contrast, Larionov's *Rayism* (1913) used the standard Grot orthography.

A Game in Hell (1912a) is Kruchonykh's first collaboration with Khlebnikov. The poem, which describes a card game between devils and sinners in hell, was conceived by Kruchonykh as "a parody of the archaic idea of the devil done in the manner of a *lubok*" (Kruchonykh 1928, 24; Khardzhiev 1968a, 311). The collaboration arose spontaneously, as Kruchonykh reports:

David Burliuk acquainted me with Khlebnikov at the beginning of 1912 in Moscow at some debate or exhibition. . . . In one of the subsequent meetings in Khlebnikov's untidy

Fig. 52. A. Kruchonykh and V. Khlebnikov, *A Game in Hell*, first edition, 1912, with drawings by N. Goncharova. The complete book is shown.

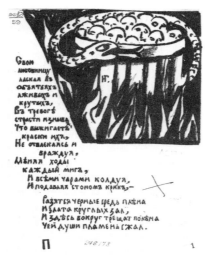

and student-like bare room, I pulled from my notebook two sheets of a draft of 40-50 lines of my poem *A Game in Hell*. I showed it to him humbly. Suddenly, to my surprise, Velimir sat down and began to add his own lines above, below and around mine. This was a characteristic trait of Khlebnikov's: he caught fire creatively from the slightest spark. He showed me the pages covered with his minute handwriting. We read it together, argued, corrected it again. Thus unexpectedly and unwittingly we became co-authors. (Khlebnikov 1968-71, 4:438)

So began a relationship that produced a number of joint books and manifestoes. The artist for the book this time was Larionov's lifelong companion Nataliya Goncharova (fig. 52a-o). The calligraphic style of pages 1 to 7 and 14 is archaic,

Fig. 52 (*continued*)

often resembling medieval Church Slavic *poluustav* lettering or later chancellery script (fig. 53). Old orthography is consistently observed. (Oddly, pages 8, 10, and 11 switch to the cursive style of *Old-Fashioned Love* and drop the ъ and old letter forms as if these pages were done by a different hand.) It is heavily illustrated in Goncharova's finest primitive manner, and every page of text except the last (p. 14) has an illustration, three of them (pp. 9, 11, and 13) full-page. Contrary to Larionov's practice, the illustrations are sharply separated from the text by a strong black-white contrast line. But the positioning of the drawings is striking, with the artist taking advantage of the margins to depict full-length vertical figures of devils. This shape resembles that of deisis icons and was used by

Goncharova elsewhere as well, most notably in her paintings of the four evan-
gelists (1910-11). Two pages contain a quadrilateral illustration, with one non-
rectilinear side consuming the upper right corner and squeezing the text diag-
onally to the left margin; two other pages devote the entire upper part to an
illustration. The alternation of these illustration shapes gives the book a complex
rhythm.[5] In contrast to the somewhat haphazard look of *Old-Fashioned Love*, *A
Game* gives the impression of genuine antiquity and primitiveness, and of well-
thought-out high art. The book has structure and rhythm, and the illustrations
are well suited to the style of the text, which has gained much by the participation
of Khlebnikov's poetic genius. Khardzhiev has called the book "one of the classic
examples of the unbroken unity of illustrations and text" (1968a, 311). This is
despite the recorded dissatisfaction of the artist in a letter to Kruchonykh:

5

A   B   C   BB   D   E (text only)

Page: 1 2 3 4 5 6 7 8 9 10 11 12 13 14
      A B C B B B B A BB C BB B   D E

The presence of the BB pages may indicate that Goncharova provided more illustrations than necessary
for the length of the text.

Fig. 53. Eighteenth-century *poluustav* manuscript of the
"Tale of Bova."

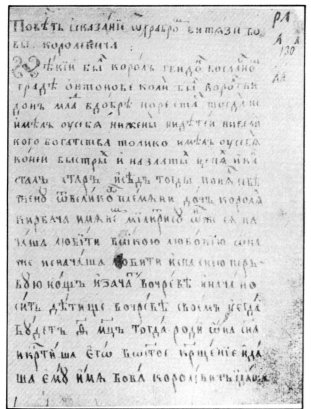

Fig. 54. A. Kruchonykh et al., *Worldbackwards*, 1912-13,
page with rubber-stamped text.

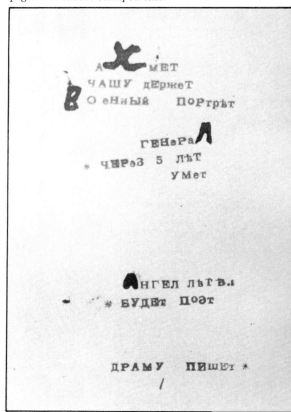

I received the proofs. They are printed very well, but positioned very badly. The drawing is placed on the stapled binding side [i.e., left]—this is very ugly; it would have been much better to place it on the outer edge of the page [i.e., right], which was what the whole composition of the drawings was predicated on and which gives more decorative unity and mass to the whole book. On those pages where the drawing is at the top, it would have been better to write the text right up or closer to the outer edge of the book. In any case, now it would be better to staple the page either at the bottom or the top, or so that the written side [the book was printed in recto] ends up not on the right side of the opened book, but on the left, i.e., facing the back cover as in old Hebrew and Arabic books. (Khardzhiev 1968a, 311)

This was not done, but the book hardly suffered as a result. Goncharova's remark about the positioning of the text indicates that although she did the drawings, she was not responsible for the calligraphy. Nevertheless, it is beautifully done by whoever did it, and Khlebnikov himself was pleased with the book, indicating "It has a sharp-witted appearance and cover" (1968-71, 3:297). It does not have the uneven, "sloppy" character of *Old-Fashioned Love*.

With *Worldbackwards* (1912b)[6] we move into something that is "much more experimental" (Markov 1968, 42) and away from what is merely a text with pictures, albeit a text handwritten by the artist himself. The title makes clear the author's intention to turn the usual norms upside down, and so he does. Although a section is devoted to Khlebnikov, it seems certain that Kruchonykh was entirely in control of this production.

The experimental nature of this work can be summarized as an obvious attempt to emphasize disorder or to avoid the unity that characterized the first two books. Everything is done to upset traditional notions of aesthetic organization: materials, and therefore colors, are mixed; two kinds and weights of paper are used in uneven alternation throughout, one whiter and thinner for the "stamped" pages, another heavier and thicker mainly for the lithographed pages; and a paper polyfoil leaf is pasted to the cover.[7] The artists, and therefore the style of illus-

[6] Although Kruchonykh lists the book as the first item under 1913 (fig. 44a), Markov, Khardzhiev (1968a, 311), Compton (1978, 125) and Chadwyck-Healey Ltd. place it in 1912. It is listed in the December 10-17, 1912, issue of *Knizhnaya letopis*.

[7] Compton indicates that the text is "enclosed in an ambitious paper cover on to which was glued an original collage by Goncharova. . . . Each copy has a variation in the shape of the cutout leaf design: some are cut in green or black shiny paper, others in gold-embossed paper, so that each type is individually distinguished from the others" (1978, 72). Indeed, the shape of the green leaf on the cover of the Chadwyck copy and of the copy from Herbert Marshall's collection illustrated in the *Bulletin of the Center for Soviet and East European Studies*, S. Illinois University (1978) 22:1, differs greatly. In the former it is mounted above the pasted-on author-title heading, while in the latter it is below it. The cover shown in Kovtun (1974, 59) shows an entirely differently shaped leaf made of patterned (evidently foil) paper. The title is below. Compton, in color illustration 2, shows a black upright leaf with title once again below. This is evidently the same copy as the one used by Chadwyck, i.e., from the British Library. Another cover is shown in *Ex Libris* 6, item 137. Yet another is held by the Lenin Library.

trations, are multiple: not only did Larionov and Goncharova make major contributions, but Rogovin and Tatlin also added a few drawings. The style of the latter two artists contrasts noticeably with the former two. And for the first time, the printing process is varied: the illustrations, with the exception of the leaf on the cover, are all lithographed as before, as is most of the text, but also included are thirteen pages of text done by a process that produces a colored copy instead of the black of the lithographed pages. The text in these instances is not handwritten, but rather it is rubber-stamped in typescript letters of varying sizes, mixing upper and lower case haphazardly (fig. 54). Added to some of these pages are much larger, handwritten letters in contrasting black, or in the case of the *n* in "Stikhi V. Khlebnikova" (verses by V. Khlebnikov) in red, which appear to have been done by hand on each copy.[8] One such page (p. 22) is mounted with the text running vertically, so that one must turn the book 90° to read the passage.

Only Goncharova's drawings are honored by a reference on the preceding page, and in one instance a drawing is heralded on the *two* preceding pages (pp. 23-24); the first of these also contains the title of Kruchonykh's travelogue, which begins on the page following Goncharova's drawing (p. 25). In another instance, such a reference is followed not by a Goncharova drawing, but by a piece of text with a drawing by Larionov (p. 48).

Also somewhat chaotic and unpredictable is the interpolation of blank pages made of white paper. These blanks precede illustrations (including some illustrations with texts), which can be seen through the transparent paper and thus act as veils, but they also resemble the slips used to overlay illustrations in elegant editions. At one point (pp. 39-40), two such blank pages follow one another, after the announcement of "Verses by V. Khlebnikov"; they are followed by a Rogovin drawing in which the artist has added doodles to his own rather wild handwritten copy of several verses (fig. 55). The page looks more like a piece of graffiti than a dignified presentation of a poem or illustration, which one would normally expect. In any case, the double blank page seems to be a mistake that playfully calls attention to the very existence and function (or lack thereof) of the blank pages themselves—a "baring of the device." The Lenin Library copy, however, lacks these thin and blank pages.

The texts vary, ranging from stanzas in traditional meters to unpunctuated automatic prose writing (Markov 1968, 42-43). The fact that some of it is lithographed handwriting and some is rubber-stamped typeset adds to the feeling of disparity. The lettering is usually chaotic in form, particularly in the prose travelogue, and the diverse handwritings on the pages containing both illustration and text suggest that the artist also did the calligraphy. This is most obvious in

---

[8] Compton (1978), in the note to color illustration 3, indicates these larger letters were "added by stencil or potato-cut." See also her p. 72. The descriptive details in my analysis of this work are based on the microfiche edition issued by Chadwyck.

the cases of Larionov (pp. 2, 48 [fig. 56], and 54; compare with *Old-Fashioned Love*) and Rogovin (p. 42 [fig. 55]), but is probably true of the Goncharova pages as well.

One particularly interesting new feature of this book—in view of its intentionally blurred organization—is a decided blurring of the boundary between text and illustration. There is a variety of instances in which letters themselves become part of the composition of an illustration, as in Picasso and Braque Cubist collages beginning in 1911. Goncharova, Shevchenko, Larionov, and others began to do this in 1912. Thus, in addition to illustrations such as those found in the earlier books, we have fig. 57 with the syllables *AX* and *ME* to left of the head echoing the word "axmet" on the following page of text (Compton 1978, 12, 95) and with the artist's name broken up in an attention-getting manner below. Or, in fig. 58, we see *MEE* (or ⴱ) and *ME*ъ(Λ) combined with musical notes and lines suggesting musical instruments. Even more fascinating is fig. 59, in which the creature in the drawing appears to be shouting "OZZ"; yet, since his ear is drawn in a stroke like the letters, the ear seems to be a letter *C*.

Rogovin's two drawings on pages 19 and 20 look like primitive cave writings, with stick figures prancing around in various positions. It takes one a moment

Fig. 55. *Worldbackwards*, 1912-13, page by I. Rogovin, poem by V. Khlebnikov.

Fig. 56. *Worldbackwards*, 1912-13, page by M. Larionov, text by V. Khlebnikov.

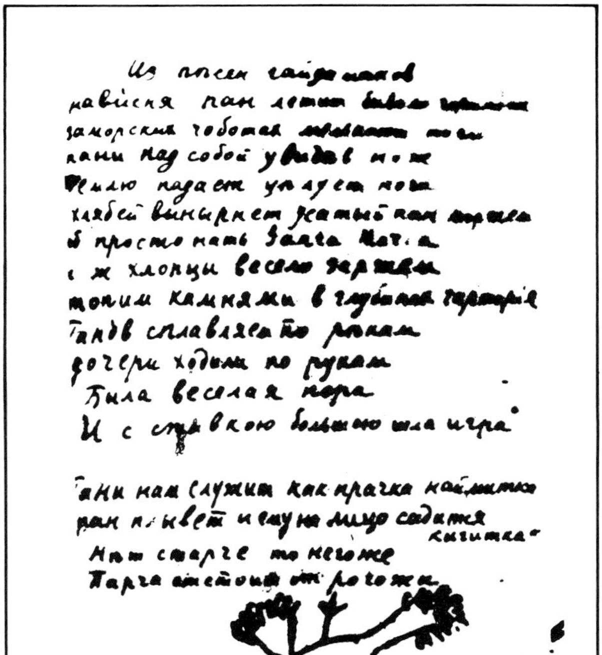

to realize that in the second sketch (fig. 60) the parade of "figures" up the right margin is the artist's signature, so much do the first two letters with their extra appendages (H, P) look like figures. In the Rogovin example shown in fig. 55 the script is so rambling and disconnected that it is hard to distinguish the text from the doodles. For instance, in the middle is it По Пушкиноты or is the П part of the doodle? The curves of the з at the bottom are rhythmically echoed around to the left, and the syllable -нимъ seems to run into the hair of the reclining figure right below it. This text is one of the most difficult pages to read in the book, so I will reproduce it here:

<table>
<tr><td>О Достоевский-мо бегущей тучи!</td><td>O Dostoevsky-mo of a running cloud!</td></tr>
<tr><td>О Пушкиноты млеющего полдня!</td><td>O Pushkinotes of sizzling midday!</td></tr>
<tr><td>Ночь смотрится, как Тютчев,</td><td>Night stares at you like Tyutchev,</td></tr>
<tr><td>Замерное безмерным полня.</td><td>Filling the beyond measure with the</td></tr>
<tr><td>(Khlebnikov 1968-71, 2:89)</td><td>measureless.</td></tr>
</table>

I leave the interpretation to the reader.

This page is followed by two pages of drawings by Larionov that are stylistically close to Rogovin's. The first of these has a caption written mostly in mirror-image letters (fig. 61). The text, deciphered, is:

Наш кочень очень озабочен	Our cabbage head is very very worried
Нож отточен точен очень	The knife is very very sharp

The second drawing has a caption also, but it is written in normal letters. Interesting here are the stick cave figures that seem to imitate Rogovin's signature in fig. 60 but do not spell anything (fig. 62). The natural gravity of the figures and

Fig. 57. *Worldbackwards*, 1912-13, page by M. Larionov.

Fig. 58. *Worldbackwards*, 1912-13, page by M. Larionov.

Fig. 59. *Worldbackwards*, 1912-13, page by M. Larionov.

the whole composition dictate that the page should be rotated 90° clockwise, but the caption would then be in the wrong position (first read, then rotate) (Compton 1978, 92).

   Kruchonykh's next three booklets, published in rapid succession in early 1913, add little in the way of new visual devices. *Pomade* (1913a; 1973, 53-71), illustrated by Larionov, is quite short (18 pages). Its cover is handcut from shiny, cinnabar-red paper and most of the full-page illustrations are mounted on gold leaf papers rather than stapled in as in earlier books. The lithographs are water-colored in twenty-five of the copies (Kovtun 1974, 62). *Pomade* gained particular notoriety for having introduced to the world three poems written in what was later called *zaum* (transrational language). Fig. 63 reproduces the famous *zaum* poem "dyr bul shchyl." The poems written after the three *zaum* poems are more traditional in form but have "shifted" syntax. Note also the continual alternation of cursive and printed letter forms and the complete absence of ъ (fig. 64).
Half-Alive (1913b), with marvelously expressive drawings by Larionov, is a single narrative poem, similar to *A Game in Hell* in its emphasis on the hellish. Compton (1978, 94) notes the echo of violence in the progressive disintegration of the nude figures. Finally, *Desert Dwellers* (1913c; 1973, 29-52), illustrated by Goncharova, is unique in separating the text completely from the illustrations. The drawings take up the full page, and there are no drawings as part of the text pages. Furthermore, the text, written in double columns, is bound in at the top of the page, that is, at right angles to the illustrations. This calls for a constant 90° rotation of the book back and forth, between text pages and illustration pages (fig. 65). The illustration and comment by Compton (1978, 33) indicate that this

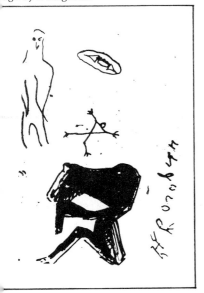

Fig. 60. *Worldbackwards*, 1912-13, page by I. Rogovin.

Fig. 61. *Worldbackwards*, 1912-13, page by M. Larionov.

Fig. 62. *Worldbackwards*, 1912-13, page by M. Larionov.

right-angle arrangement may have transpired by mistake. Inexplicably, the illustrations are twice as large as the text pages. To bind the two together necessitated the turning of the text pages on their sides to create the same size page as the illustrations. Compton's illustration 21 (ibid., 33) shows one of the text pages already cut to the smaller size, with two leaves placed one above the other to form a large page; however, the other pages are uncut. The text consists of two narrative poems, "Desert Dwellers" and "Woman Desert Dweller," the first of which is written in the nearly consistent chancellery script of *Game* while the second is in the mixed script of the other booklets. Moreover, the text and illustrations share the same mixture of "Byzantine severity and popular humor" (Chamot 1972, 84) and thus are harmonious complements.

The importance of these six booklets in the history of the Russian Avant Garde cannot be overestimated. In Markov's words, "In his first publishing ventures, Kruchonykh added his own note to Russian primitivism; created, mainly with the artists Goncharova and Larionov, the classic form of a Futurist publication; and inaugurated the most extreme of all Futurist achievements, *zaum*" (1968, 44). In terms of visual effects, *Worldbackwards* is the most avant-garde

Fig. 63. A. Kruchonykh, *Pomade*, 1913, showing the famous transrational poem "Dyr bul shchyl"; drawing by M. Larionov.

Fig. 64. A. Kruchonykh, *Pomade*, 1912, page of text.

Часы музыкѣ предавая
Иль смотришь снѣга чистый
свѣт
В небесном взором утопая
Мечтой ужчавшись в глуби лѣт

Или как тихая русалка
Глядишь глаза цвѣты тоски
Средь ночи бродишь в теми
парка
Иль вдруг разбудишь сткло
рѣки

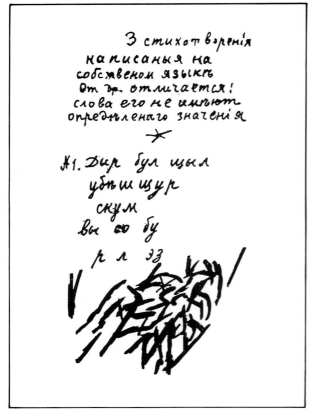

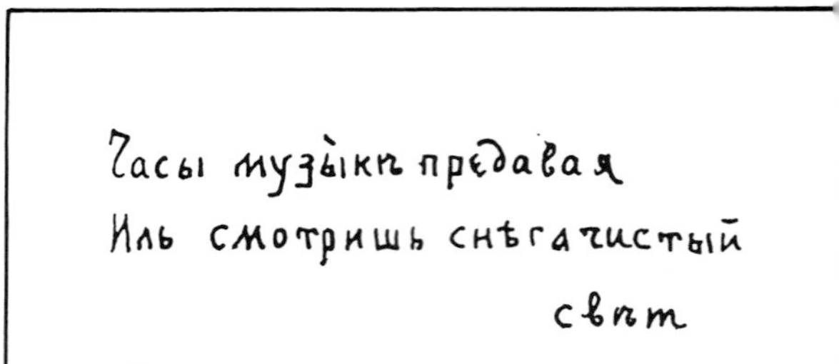

Fig. 65. A. Kruchonykh, *Desert Dwellers*, 1913; drawing by N. Goncharova.

of the avant-garde books in the set because of its anti-aesthetic disunity and emphasis on the Futurist collective, which stands "on the solid block of the word 'we' amid the sea of boos and indignation" (Markov 1968, 46).

After the publication of these booklets the collaboration of Goncharova and Larionov in the work of Kruchonykh tapers off; it is thus appropriate to pause and consider their role. Khardzhiev, in his necrological survey of their achievements, understandably emphasizes the importance of the two painters in these projects:[9] "Larionov and Goncharova created a new type of poetic book—entirely lithographed with a text written by the author or artist (*samopismo*)" (1968a, 310). He points out that this format permitted the close relationship of illustration to text and also provided a programmatic answer to the elegant graphics of the World of Art group. Furthermore, "The aim of Larionov's and Goncharova's illustrations was the illumination of the poetic work not by literary but by painterly means. Precisely this explains the adoption by the artists of the lithographic technique—its specific peculiarities did not limit the freedom of purely painterly solutions" (ibid., 310).[10] These statements appear to credit the artists with the lithographic innovations, but Khardzhiev had immediately before this noted that it was Kruchonykh, a trained graphic artist (Kruchonykh 1928, 59), who had first led the two away from the easel and to book illustration by suggesting they lithograph some of their paintings for postcards, which he then had published in mid-1912 (Khardzhiev 1968, 310). Kruchonykh later explained his own move away from painting toward literature in the following way:

In these years (1910-11), having a foreboding of the rapid death of painting and its substitution by something different, which subsequently took shape in photo montage, I broke my brushes ahead of time, abandoned my palette and washed my hands in order, with a pure soul, to take up the pen and work for the glory and destruction of Futurism—that farewell literary school which was only then beginning to burn with its final (and brightest) worldwide fire. (Kruchonykh 1928, 59)

Although Kruchonykh seems to have been the main editor and producer of the booklets, the venture was obviously a cooperative one. When the involvement of the two artists in this sort of work ended (the remaining books by other authors

[9] As does A. Nakov: "The artistic personality of Mikhail Larionov determined the style of the first phase in the history of the lithographed publications of the Russian Futurists. Throughout 1912 and up to the summer of 1913, Larionov (stimulated by Kruchenykh) produced several books that are not only entirely lithographed but were conceived and realized as works of art" (1976, 4).

[10] Also Khardzhiev (1976, 60). In an interesting technical remark, Khardzhiev notes: "In contrast to illustrations by Goncharova, who preferred to work with a lithographic pencil, the whole illustration series by Larionov in 1912-13, except for the first book [*Old-Fashioned Love*], was done with lithographic ink. This was an avoidance of three-dimensional spatial constructions and a move to schematic planar solutions. With the help of this new principle Larionov attained the full unity of book architechtonics" (1968a, 316). The difference between thick-lined planar ink technique and the more modeled, granular pencil technique is evident in many of the above examples.

in which Larionov and Goncharova participated will be mentioned at the end of this chapter), Kruchonykh continued to publish similar and varied works for some time after with the help of other artists. Moreover, Kruchonykh, with Khlebnikov, is responsible for the supportive theories that emerged soon after these first publications and which we will now consider.

THE EARLY MANIFESTOES

Kruchonykh was an avid manifesto writer. From the end of 1912, when *A Slap in the Face of Public Taste* appeared, through 1913 (the big year for manifestoes) and later, his name was attached to nearly all the major Cubo-Futurist (Hylaea) pronouncements. Since some of these were collective efforts, it is not possible, with one exception, to distinguish Kruchonykh's contribution from that of others; but given his radical temperament, it is likely that he supported or authored a few of the most extreme passages about which other signers, such as Livshits, might not have been so enthusiastic.

The untitled group manifesto in the Futurist miscellany *Trap for Judges* (February 1913) contains the first major statements about the visual level in literature. Among the "new principles of creativity" are: "1. We have stopped considering word formation and word pronunciation according to grammatical rules, having come to see in letters only *what guides speech*" (Markov 1967, 52). This formulation, by the testimony of Livshits (1933, 136-39; 1977, 126-28), was contributed by Khlebnikov. The second principle also sounds like Khlebnikov's: "2. We have come to ascribe content to words according to their graphic and *phonetic characteristics*" (Markov 1967, 52). It is noteworthy that the graphic composition of a word is advanced as a principle for the new art: the look can determine content. Phonetic characteristics can also determine content, and the two, although parallel, are nevertheless distinguished here. Khlebnikov, in his poetry and theories, indeed considers both phonetic and visual components. What is meant in the first principle by letters being "only what guides speech" is less certain. Livshits, who subscribed to this manifesto, nevertheless considered the statements to have "a certain indistinctness of thought and weakness of terminology" (Livshits 1977, 127).

The manifesto made other pronouncements. Nouns could be modified (or "characterized") not only by adjectives, but also by other parts of speech including "letters and numbers." Also, "assuming in handwriting a component of the poetic impulse . . . , in Moscow therefore we have put out books (autographs) of 'self-write' [samo-pisma]." This was the first time a theoretical connection was made to the expressive role of the handwritten text. Furthermore, punctuation marks were abolished in order to emphasize the "verbal mass." And, in the words of

N. Burliuk (ibid., 128)—not unlike Bely's in "The Magic of Words"—"We understand vowels as time and space (the character of aspiration), consonants are color, sound, aroma. . . . We consider the word the creator of myth, the word, dying, gives birth to myth and vice versa" (Markov 1967, 52).

The precise chronology of the remaining 1913 manifestoes is still unclear. Some were not published at that time, and others published in 1913 may have been written earlier. This was probably the case with "Declaration of the Word as Such," which was released as a flyer in the summer of 1913; it was included in the booklet *The Word as Such* (September or October 1913), and was republished frequently thereafter. Kruchonykh claimed to have written it in 1912, but this early date may have been a polemical exaggeration (Markov 1967, 64). The "Declaration" is important mainly for "giving the first theoretical foundation for *zaum* language" (ibid.). However, it contains several remarks with implications for visual effects. One involves Kruchonykh's renaming of the lily (*liliya*) with the neologism *euy* (еуы), which is appropriate in part because the shape of the letter "Y" resembles the shape of the flower. Khlebnikov also felt the new name was appropriate, adding, in a letter to Kruchonykh dated August 31, 1913, "The quick sequence of sounds conveys the taut petals (of the curved flower)" (Khlebnikov 1968-71, 4:367). This attitude is a reaffirmation of the pictographic principle claiming that the symbol should look like the object it represents. It also illustrates in practice the previous manifesto's principle of giving "content to words according to their graphic and phonetic characteristics," only it does this in reverse: the object and its shape are the given, and letters and sounds are selected to correspond to it, as presumably was done at the dawn of civilization.

Kruchonykh goes on to illustrate the universal language of vowels as shown in a poem composed exclusively of the vowel letters in the Russian "Our Father."[11] The formulation of this example was attacked by Baudouin de Courtenay for its terminological imprecision. His objection centers around the careless tendency to use the words "letter" and "sound," "vowel," or "consonant" without acknowledgment of the difference between written and spoken language (Janecek 1981a).

In a view that is generally accepted today, Kruchonykh maintains in his "Declaration" that poetry is untranslatable. He suggests that it would be better to translate by choosing words close to the original in sound rather than in meaning, that the sound patterns are more essential than the meaning. By extension of this principle, sounds are converted into sequences of letters, whose visual patterns are also essential. The only real alternative would be to transliterate a Russian poem into roman letters and to give a "pony." Thus the value of a poem is in its unique combination of letters, sounds, and meaning. Its meaning,

---

[11] Markov must be given credit for the discovery of the relationship between Kruchonykh's vowel poems and Russian Orthodox prayers.

traditionally the depository of the most value, is given the least importance, and is virtually ignored as a significant factor—a feature of Kruchonykh's program that establishes its avant-garde nature but limits its general applicability and acceptance.

Kruchonykh's most extensive statement in this period, and a solo effort, is the essay "New Paths of the Word," which appeared in the miscellany *Three* (September[?] 1913). The essay is subtitled "Language of the Future Death to Symbolism" and is in part an attack on that movement. It proclaims that "the word is broader than meaning," that it is not limited to thought but is "beyond the mind" (*zaumnoe*) as a result of its sonic and graphic components. In this context he declares that "Each letter, each sound is important!" (Markov 1967, 66). He also refers to "strange, 'meaningless' combinations of words and letters" (ibid., 68) produced by a new psychology. He illustrates these "incorrect" combinations in contemporary writings, including a reference to an article by S. Khudakov (see chapter 5) that Kruchonykh claims is imitative of "our speech," and cites examples of "all vowels, all consonants, and of scattered letters and words." Kruchonykh concludes his survey by summarizing: "These types do not exhaust all the possible incorrectnesses and unexpectednesses: (it is not by chance they are incorrectnesses) one can e.g. name unusualness of meter, rhyme, script, color and position of words, etc." (ibid., 70). He does not go into further details at this point.

Written shortly after "New Paths,"[12] the manifesto "On Artistic Works" in *The Word as Such* continues in the same spirit with additional examples of the new writing. It begins with the declaration: "May it be written and seen in the twinkling of an eye!" (Markov 1967, 53). One example is of interest for its analysis of the repetition of the "letter" *r* as the determining factor in the "artistic sentence" (and not the grammatical), that is, once the structure of letters is complete, "a period is placed and not sooner" (ibid., 55). This and other uses of "letter" where "sound" would usually be found (a lack of precision in distinguishing sound and sight) brought down the wrath of Baudouin de Courtenay. Beyond that, the authors state: "Futurist painters love to use parts of the body, sections, and Futurist poets love subdivided words, half-words and their whimsical clever combinations (transrational language) . . ." (ibid., 57).

Included in this booklet are a reprint of "Declaration of the Word as Such" and an untitled manifesto of sorts by Nikolay Kulbin that echoes some of the ideas of the other two manifestoes. For example: "The path of the word is *symbol, sound, script*. The life of consonants and vowels (see the declaration by Kruchonykh). The uniqueness of the letters!" (*The Word as Such*, 1913, n.p.).

The preceding statements show that visual effects were considered, by the

---

[12] By internal evidence; i.e., Kruchonykh refers the reader to "New Paths of the Word" (Markov 1967, 57), therefore probably October 1913.

by, as part of the whole avant-garde program, and were discussed along with those on *zaum* and other novelties. But, in the end, specifically visual matters were made the subject of a manifesto of their own.

The declaration, "The Letter as Such," one of the few direct programmatic statements on the visual aspects of literature, was written by Kruchonykh and Khlebnikov in 1913 but not published until 1930 (Markov 1967, 60-61; Khlebnikov 1930, and 1968-71, 3:248-49, 353). Trying to keep one step ahead even of their own avant-garde statements, the authors announce therein that the concept of the "word as such" is already generally accepted (which was not exactly true) and they have gone on to a more basic level, the letter. In logical genesis, this places "The Letter as Such" after "Declaration of the Word as Such."

To convey the full flavor of the manifesto, I present it here complete in translation:

The Letter as Such

There are no longer any disputes; about the word as such there is even agreement. But what is this agreement worth? It is necessary to remind oneself that those speaking (in hindsight) about the word say nothing about the letter!

Blind-born!

The word is still not a value, the word is still merely bearable. Otherwise why do they dress it in a gray prisoner's suit? You have seen the letters of their words—stretched out in a row, insulted, cropped and all equally colorless and gray—not letters but brands!

But ask any worder and he will say that a word written in one handwriting or set in one typeface is not at all similar to the same word in another written form.

After all, you would not dress all your beautiful women in the same government-issued caftans.

Of course not! They would spit in your eyes, but the word—it will be silent.

For it is dead (like Boris and Gleb).

It is stillborn in your hands.

Ah, cursed Svyatopolks!

There are two principles:

(1) that mood influences handwriting during writing;

(2) that the handwriting, idiosyncratically influenced by mood, conveys this mood to the reader independently of the words. Similarly one must ask the question about signs written, visible or simply perceptible, as by the hand of a blind man. Understandably, it is not obligatory that the worder be also the scribe of a self-runic book; perhaps it is better if he assigns this to an artist. But there were no such books yet. They have been provided for the first time by the futurists, namely: "Old-Fashioned Love" was transcribed for publication by M. Larionov, "Explodity" by N. Kulbin and others, "Duck nest" by O. Rozanova. Now is when one can finally say: "Each letter is—just kiss your fingers."

It is strange that neither Balmont, nor Blok—quite contemporary people it would seem—figured out that they should entrust their progeny not to a typesetter but to an artist. . . .

A text, transcribed by someone else or by its creator himself, but by one who is not reliving the original experience while transcribing, loses all the charms which its script furnished it with at the moment of "the terrible blizzard of inspiration."

V. Khlebnikov
A. Kruchonykh

One might wonder whether the interposition of an artist between the author and the reader does not vitiate the spontaneity of communication of mood that seems to be the main feature of Kruchonykh and Khlebnikov's first principle. What evidently is more important than the authenticity of the script source is the capacity of the script to convey the intended mood. Somewhat later (1915-16) Khlebnikov repeats this idea in "Proposals": "Handwriting, by its very calligraphic quivering, controls the reader. The mute voice of handwriting" (1968-71, 3:160). The author's own handwriting may not do this as effectively as that of a sympathetic artist, to whom it may be "subcontracted." Thus, the writers felt that the visual qualities of the text ought to be made expressive and can have an expressiveness "independent of the words." Even though they referred to handwriting, this principle may be applied to typeset texts as well, since typographic art and calligraphic art have similar aims, if different methods.[13]

It is necessary to point out here that Velimir Khlebnikov figures in this study in a subordinate role not because his contributions were minor, but merely because they were often published without his help and against his wishes (Khlebnikov 1968-71, 3:257). His works came to light through the efforts of other Futurists (D. Burliuk, B. Livshits, and, of course, Kruchonykh) and it is not certain if they appeared as Khlebnikov would have wanted; for example, many items were simply fragments. Though a brilliant poet, he was an irresponsible and capricious custodian of his own masterpieces. Leading the life of a scholarly hobo, he would leave manuscripts wherever he went as he wandered throughout Russia. It is possible that little of this treasure would have survived if his works had been left exclusively in his care. Luckily, his friends took charge of whatever came their way, but this also created a problem: his works were published without his validation. As Markov remarks, "Sometimes he clearly did not care what his publishers did." From another perspective, this neglect may have been fortunate. As his friend Dmitri Petrovsky reported, "Khlebnikov did not know how to read proofs. He never corrected; he simply rewrote everything in a new way." Knowing this, "His friends succeeded in keeping printers' galleys away from him, and he never supervised the publication of any of his works" (Markov 1962, 32-33). Thus it is impossible to involve him more deeply in our study, even though he was also the most obvious descendant of the hermetic tradition among the Futurists. His eastern orientation, cabalistic investigation of numbers, linguistic archeol-

[13] For a more detailed analysis of this manifesto, see Janecek (1980c).

ogy, and belief in the power of the word[14] inclined him very solidly in that direction, and he seems to have been a more likely ally of Bely than of Kruchonykh. He also made contributions in theoretic areas, as discussed earlier, and among his other tangentially applicable theoretic works we can include "Artists of the World" (1919) and "Our Foundation" (1920a).

THE LATER WORKS

The number of Kruchonykh's publications by 1930 runs to over 150. Many of them fall into the category of "more of the same": some are new editions of old works in whole or in part; others fall into groups characterized by a certain method of production or visual style. Still other works have never come to light. Nevertheless, there was still a variety of interesting new developments, on which I will focus here. The chief artists during this time were Olga Rozanova, Kruchonykh's wife, and, to a lesser extent, Malevich and others.

Let Us Grumble (1913d; Kruchonykh 1973) is a landmark only because it was the first solo book by Kruchonykh to be typeset. It has tipped-in illustrations (two by Malevich and two by Rozanova), and, as Compton remarks, these illustrations "clash with the format" (1978, 77). The content is alogical and the margins are unjustified, but otherwise this is a throwback to the traditional illustrated book. Prior to this, the only typeset works by Kruchonykh had been individual poems[15] and manifestoes contributed to Futurist anthologies. The first poem in *Union of Youth 3* (1913 , 68) is noteworthy for its mixture of upper- and lower-case letters, in one case in the same word (зАжАТый).

Following the print and illustration format of *Let Us Grumble*, a series of booklets appeared in 1913-15 that limited the illustrations to covers: *Piglets* (1913e, and second expanded edition, 1914a); *The Devil and the Speechmakers* (1913f); *Victory over the Sun* (1913g); *V. Mayakovsky's Poems* (1913h); and *Secret Vices of Academics* (1915a; on cover, 1916). (All except *Victory* are in Kruchonykh 1973.) Generally, these works demonstrate a transference to print of the haphazard orthographic and punctuation practices of the earlier lithographed books; but because of the limitations inherent in combining letterpress with illustrations, little or no concern was given to the coordination of text and drawing. In fact, illustrations are minimal in number and appear to be studiously unlinked with the text.

---

[14] Markov points out Korney Chukovsky's deprecating remark (written in 1914) on Khlebnikov's epic poems that the word is "merely a modest vehicle for expressing thoughts and emotions, subordinated to the very Logos, so ardently rejected by the futurists" (1962, 30).

[15] *A Slap in the Face of Public Taste*, 1913, 87-88; *Union of Youth*, 1913, 3:68-72; *Trap for Judges*, 1913, 2:63-66; *Croaked Moon*, 1913, 1:17; *Three*, 1913, 6-21; *Roaring Parnassus*, 1914, 71-72; Belenson 1915, 109.

Chronologically parallel with these printed booklets was a continuing series of lithographed, handwritten booklets similar to the earlier set of six. The main collaborator for these was Rozanova. They basically followed the previous format but do contain some new effects.

The first group, a set of three numbered by Kruchonykh as 7, 8, and 9, consists of, respectively, *Duck's Nest of Bad Words* (1913i), *Forest Boom* (1913j), and *Explodity* (1913k, of which there is a second edition, 1914b). Inexplicably, the first in the group apparently appeared last, at the end of 1913 or the beginning of 1914. To this group can be added the second edition of *A Game in Hell* (1913). The switch of artist-collaborator from Larionov and Goncharova to Kruchonykh's wife, Rozanova, avoided the misunderstandings and cross-purposes that occasionally cropped up as a result of the collaboration-from-afar in the earlier booklets. One can assume that the Kruchonykh-Rozanova collaboration was much more intimate and thorough.[16]

Forest Boom is in reality a new edition of *Old-Fashioned Love*, with some additions to the text and a four-stanza introductory page by Khlebnikov. A portrait of Kruchonykh by Kulbin is included, but the remainder of the artwork is by Rozanova. The influence of the first edition is particularly obvious in the decorations on the text pages, though Rozanova does not use the straight-line rayist technique, and she uses a pen or crayon instead of a pencil.

It is informative to compare the handwriting in equivalent places in the text (figs. 47 and 66). The first edition, according to Kruchonykh in *The Letter as*

[16] "Kruchonykh apparently moved to the capital (in March 1913) because of Olga Rozanova, who played an increasingly important role as collaborator in his books; by 1915 and 1916 these were made by their exclusive partnership, almost entirely by hand" (Compton 1978, 3).

Fig. 66. A. Kruchonykh, *Forest Boom,* 1913, page of text; drawing by O. Rozanova.

Fig. 67. A. Kruchonykh, *Old-Fashioned Love,* 1912, p. 8; drawing by M. Larionov.

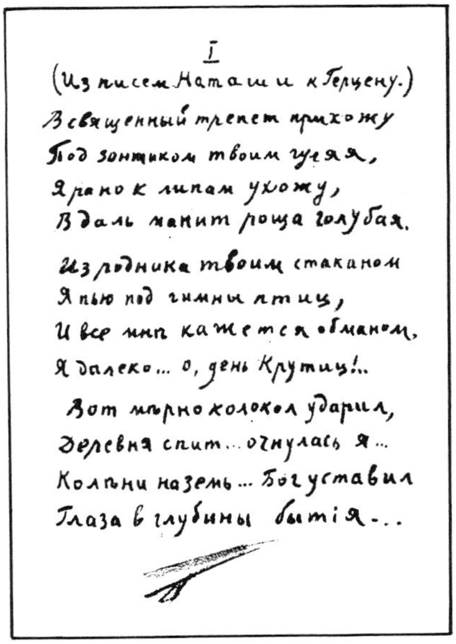

Fig. 68. A Kruchonykh, *Forest Boom,* 1913, page of text comparable to fig. 67.

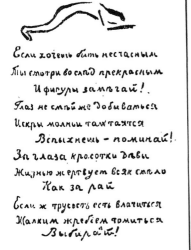

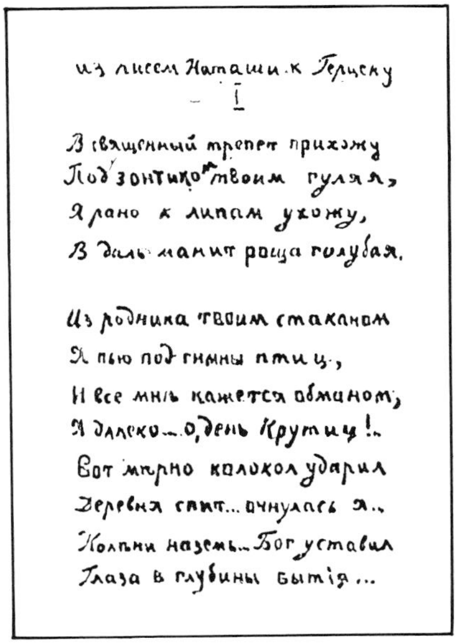

Such, was ostensibly calligraphed by Larionov, yet the second edition is remarkably similar. Some changes were made in orthography (regularization) and letter forms, yet the two seem to have been done by the same hand, leading one to wonder if Kruchonykh did not do both. Indeed, the handwriting in all of the script texts is similar enough to suggest that Kruchonykh wrote everything himself, without an artist-collaborator. In *Old-Fashioned Love*, it appears most likely that Kruchonykh wrote the text first and then Larionov added his decorations afterward, since the decorations are fitted to the text shape rather than the reverse. In *A Game* (first edition), as already indicated, the illustrations were prepared separately from the text and Kruchonykh combined the two; whether the text had been prepared before he received the illustrations is not clear. Rozanova and Kruchonykh probably collaborated fully in this new version, perhaps page by page. It is also possible, however, that Rozanova closely imitated Larionov's handwriting.

The changes raise a question about the principle promulgated in *The Letter* regarding the close association of mood and handwriting—that is, do the changes, however slight, wrought by a new edition produce a different mood as a result of new handwriting, letter shapes, illustrations, and so forth? For example, the new edition includes instances that are very similar to the first edition in handwriting style, as well as places where more angular letter forms have been substituted (м/Т, н/П, ᵭ/Б, etc.) (compare figs. 67 and 68). Can we perceive a different mood as a result of the shift to these angular letter forms? I think yes: the flowing, rounded script of *Old-Fashioned Love* (fig. 67) is lyrical, while the right-angled script that emerges in many places in *Forest Boom* (fig. 68) is lapidary. *Old-Fashioned Love* is in fact unique in consistently using rounded forms. Kruchonykh's other books use a constantly changing and unpredictable mixture of angular and rounded forms.

Fig. 68 also shows a characteristic baring of the device in the obvious correction of a "misspelling" (зонтико^м). It seems unlikely that such an error could be made in the first place, and it could well be an intentional effect to show that normal decorum (that is, redoing the page) is abandoned for reasons of spontaneity and/or informality, just as only the most persnickety letter writer would rewrite a page on which a mistake had been made.

Explodity resembles *Worldbackwards* in its heterogeneity: lithographed drawings by various artists (Rozanova, Malevich, Kulbin, Goncharova, Altman), lithographed text, and unevenly stamped text.[17] A new feature in several of the lithographs is the balance struck between text and illustration. Recall that *Worldbackwards* contained several drawings by Larionov that incorporated letters or syllables (figs. 57, 58, 59). In *Explodity* verbal and nonverbal elements in these

---

[17] Compton (1978, 76) characterizes *Explodity* as "more heterogeneous" than *Worldbackwards*.

cases are combined in equal proportions. Thus on leaf three (fig. 69) we have a *zaum* word (*belyamatokiyay*) and some miscellaneous letters combined with decorations (clumps of grass?) in a unified visual composition. The V-shape of the decorations is echoed in the letters ЛМКЙ. Some figures could be either verbal or nonverbal (♭ 7), or rather, they are poised delicately between the verbal and nonverbal. The grass motif is repeated in another drawing (fig. 70) and then in the text (fig. 71).

Regarding the obverse use of verbal material in Cubist painting, Robert Rosenblum comments: "Confronted with these various alphabetical, numerical, and musical symbols, one realizes that the arcs and planes that surround them are also to be read as symbols, and that they are no more to be considered the visual counterpart of reality than a word is to be considered identical with the thing to which it refers" (1966, 66). In Kruchonykh's work, the juxtaposition of letters and drawing indeed makes us appreciate the graphic-pictorial nature of writing.

In other instances in *Explodity*, instead of the drawing being contoured around the text, the words are shaped into the drawing to make a unified composition (figs. 72-74). In fig. 74 the letters give the appearance of being ejected from a source at the bottom (explosion? flower?). And finally, in one of the more famous hoaxes in Futurist history, Kruchonykh claims to have "at one moment mastered all languages to perfection." To illustrate this he uses *zaum* words that are supposed to be foreign (Spanish, Hebrew, Japanese) and illustrates them with lines of the "grass" motif that also look like Japanese calligraphy (fig. 75). The book concludes with the famous *shish* (fig) fashioned to look like Hebrew letters (fig. 76).[18]

[18] My colleague Boris Sorokin comments: "A 'shish' by the way, is more than a fig, although the

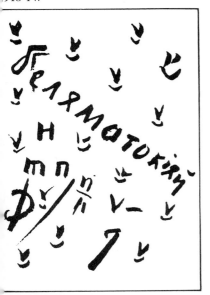

Fig. 69. A. Kruchonykh, *Explodity*, 1913-14.

Fig. 70. A. Kruchonykh, *Explodity*, 1913-14.

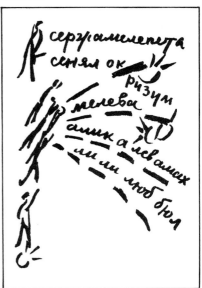

Fig. 71. A. Kruchonykh, *Explodity*, 1913-14.

The second, so-called "expanded" edition of *Explodity* that appeared in 1914 is in reality no more extensive than the first, but it does differ in a few respects: it has a new cover drawing by Rozanova; four of the stamped pages are converted to lithographed pages, such as those in figs. 69-76, with drawings around the margins; four stamped pages have been added, but four others have been deleted; one lithographed page of text has received a new rendition, but is still very similar to the first; and the caption page to Kulbin's portrait of Khlebnikov has been removed. Nineteen of the pages are identical, including those in figs. 69-76.[19]

The revised and expanded version of *A Game in Hell* was published at the end of 1913 (Khlebnikov 1968-71, 4:439-40). The artwork was redesigned, with the front and back covers done by Malevich and the remaining drawings done by Rozanova. The script style is modernized but, rather than being presented in the pure cursive of *Old-Fashioned Love*, it is in block lettering with a haphazard alternation of some cursive letter forms. The letter ъ was completely avoided,

---

word 'figa' is used as a synonym. But it is actually a euphemism. The gesture 'shish' (thumb between index and middle finger in a fist) is an ancient rude gesture, denoting vaguely the looks of a backside in the process of defecation and apparently means 'you'll get nothing from me but worthless shit.' The gesture is so old that no one even knows any more what it originally meant, but still retains its intended meaning of 'you'll get nothing from me.' Making it appear as if written in Hebrew letters is apparently a reference to the Yiddish 'kiss mein toches' [kiss my arse]—a similar gesture/phrase of contempt." Such playfulness, ambiguity and multi-level associativeness has been noted in the work of Picasso and other Cubists (Rosenblum 1973, 49-75).

[19] These results were arrived at by comparing the first edition at Pushkinsky dom and the British Library copy of the second edition on microfiche from Chadwyck Ltd., plus Compton 1978, 77, and *Ex Libris* 6, items 129 and 130. It is possible that other copies may differ from these.

Fig. 72. A. Kruchonykh, *Explodity*, 1913-14.

Fig. 73. A. Kruchonykh, *Explodity*, 1913-14.

Fig. 74. A. Kruchonykh, *Explodity*, 1913-14.

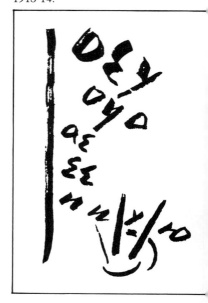

and there are a few other sporadic modernizations of orthography. The influence of the earlier version can be seen in the emphasis on vertical full-length figures,[20] but they are usually not set off from the text by a contrast line; rather, they tend to share the same white background as the text and the text is often shaped around the drawing (fig. 77). There is no punctuation. Perhaps because of the participation of two artists (Rozanova's contributions seem to me more effective than Malevich's) and because of the mixed script style, the result is to me less unified and aesthetically pleasing than the first edition, though I am no doubt applying traditional norms to a work that was trying to overturn such norms.

Malevich's contributions here and elsewhere are decidedly those of an outsider—one who is going his own independent way, yet one whose work is respected by fellow Avant Gardists. His lithographs, whatever their intrinsic merit (and I am personally not inclined to rate them as highly as other writers), seem extraneous to the works in which they appear, as if they were created with another purpose in mind and included only out of respect. Their style seems inappropriate and they do not fit the context of the book.[21]

Duck's Nest contains nothing new and, like *Old-Fashioned Love* or *Half-Alive*, gives a unified impression. Although it did not appear until after numbers 7 and 8, it may well have been prepared first, as the numbering suggests.

On some copies the lithographs have been colored. Kovtun comments:

[20] On the influence of Goncharova on Malevich's and Rozanova's work, see Bowlt (1980, 7, 10, 14).
[21] For a similar view, see Compton (1978, 76) and Nakov (1976, 4); for a somewhat different (more positive) view, see Karshan (1975, 35-36).

Fig. 75. A. Kruchonykh, *Explodity*, 1913-14.

Fig. 76. A. Kruchonykh, *Explodity*, 1913-14.

Not only the illustrations but also the pages with text are covered with paint. The artist made something like a score of colour out of the poems with stress laid on illustrations covering a whole page, where the colour gains primary importance. At the same time the reaction of the living word and the colour transforms the poems into a characteristic "colour poetry," analogous to "colour music." (Kovtun 1970, 46)

Kovtun makes the point that such hand coloring is reminiscent of folk art, and it is used more in Kruchonykh's second group of later works than in the first.

The second group (1914-17) consists of four works, each of which is unique and fascinating in its own way.[22] There is a marked move away from narrative text (however disjointed or fragmentary it may have been) toward pure pictoriality with a minimum of verbal material.

The only multicolored hectographed book by Kruchonykh, *Te li le* (1914c), is magical for its lyrical use of color hectography.[23] The colors are clear bright

[22] Not included in Kruchonykh's bibliography is another work of 1914: *Sobstvennye razskazy i risunki detey*, 16 pp., printed in recto with lithographed drawings on orange paper, probably a "forgery" by Kruchonykh.
[23] See Compton (1978, 32), for a brief discussion of this work in connection with Marinetti.

Fig. 77. A. Kruchonykh and V. Khlebnikov, *A Game in Hell*, second edition, 1913; drawing by O. Rozanova.

Fig. 78. *War*, 1915, leaf 8; linocut by O. Rozanova.

reds, blues, violets, and browns, with an upbeat yet delicate gelatinous or liquid quality.[24] The color reproductions in Compton (1978, nos. 1f, 12, 13) do reasonable justice to the book, which is truly lovely, though that would perhaps not be the term of approval sought by artists. The verbal contents by Kruchonykh and Khlebnikov, mostly already familiar material (Kruchonykh's poems from *Pomade*, Khlebnikov's poems from *A Slap* and *Worldbackwards*), are eclipsed by the striking artwork of Rozanova (and one drawing by Kulbin).

Zaumnaya gniga (Transrational Boog, 1915b) takes the reduction of text vis-à-vis graphics a step further. In a book of twenty-one pages, eight pages consist of Rozanova's full-page colored linoleum cuts of kings, queens, jacks, and aces of playing cards captioned in the border as part of the composition. Although they are Cubist in style, their manner of combining subject and title is strongly reminiscent of the *lubok*, since the linoleum-cut technique is modeled on *lubok* woodcuts. The "text" consists of red-stamped pages that are interlarded between Rozanova's pages. Each such page has a few words of syntactic and/or phonetic *zaum* (on the average a half dozen; in one case only one *otdykh* [rest]). The impressions are sometimes quite faint, which is in contrast to the strong, gruff impression of the linoleum cuts. The text appears fragmentary and unsatisfying in comparison to the fullness of the survey of face cards, though not all suits and ranks are covered. Cohen has aptly characterized the presentation as "a unique combination of the throwaway and the hieratic" (1976, 2). The book ends with a *zaum* poem by Alyagrov (better known as Roman Jakobson), which will be discussed in chapter 5.

One step further away from text and toward pure graphics is the volume *War* (1915c). Its most immediately striking feature is its quarto size, which makes it the first oversized book in the Kruchonykh canon. The work it most resembles is Goncharova's folio of lithographs of the same name, *Voyna: misticheskie obrazy voyny* (*War: Mystical Images of War*, 1914), after which Rozanova's work was probably modeled. The Kruchonykh-Rozanova book consists of a table of contents plus fifteen leaves, nine of which are full-page linocuts, of which two include fragments of newspaper reports in the composition (figs. 78, 79). This feature and the scale of the pictures make this book the most *lubok*-like of any Futurist work. One page is a collage, with three smaller linocuts included (fig. 80). The remaining five pages are short poems by Kruchonykh (2 to 4 lines each) done in a large block-lettered linocut. The table of contents is in reality part of the text: it includes not only the titles of the linocuts, but also *zaum* captions

---

[24] "Fifty copies were made by hectography, which is a gelatine duplicating process, like the old jellygraphs used by amateurs for reproducing a small number of copies. The advantage of the process is that colour can be used and *Te li le* was printed in numbered copies using pink, yellow, blue, mauve, and gold . . . all the colours sink into the paper to give unsurpassed unity to the pages. Kruchonykh reprinted his *zaum* poem which here begins *dyr bul shchyl* in splendid coloured writing: the ornament round it balancing the *zaum* words" (Compton 1978, 82).

for some of them. These were written by Kruchonykh and appear only in the table of contents. The uniformity of process—linocut throughout with the exception of the table of contents, which is done by letterpress—makes for a beautiful unity of style and mood. In contrast, the gruff technique, the primitive lapidary block lettering, and the dynamic graphics are intriguing yet stark. It is an impressive production. Rozanova herself called it her highest achievement in graphic work (Khardzhiev 1976, 61).

The use of block lettering is an interesting phenomenon. Its association with ancient script and the *lubok* is immediate even when the orthography is somewhat modernized. However, in the *lubok*, block lettering is determined by the medium itself: in a woodcut the path of least resistance is the straight line rather than the curved line, since it is harder to carve a curved line into wood. The later *lubki* that were engraved on copper show a more cursive script. In the lithograph and the linocut, the media used by Kruchonykh and his collaborators, block lettering is no more practical than cursive script. Its apparent purpose is to create an artificial association with the woodcut technique of the *lubok*.

Universal War: ъ,[25] the only work Kruchonykh places in 1916, is similar to

[25] The fact that Kruchonykh placed a huge letter ъ in the middle of the title page can be taken as

Fig. 79. *War*, 1915, leaf 9; linocut by O. Rozanova.

Fig. 80. *War*, 1915; collage with linocuts by O. Rozanova.

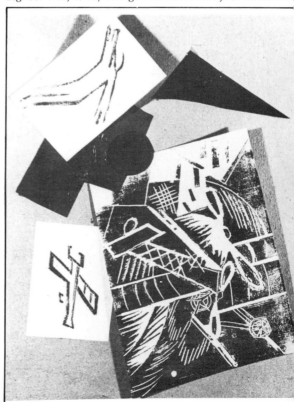

the preceding book in that its small amount of text comes at the beginning, like the table of contents of *War*, and consists of captions for each of the "leaves" of the book that follow. The captions consist of either a title alone, such as "Leaf 6 - Destruction of the Gardens," or a title plus a *zaum* poem. The book is unique in this series for being, it seems, a solo effort by Kruchonykh, as well as for the fact that the illustrations to which the captions refer are perfectly abstract, geometrical, brightly colored, pasted-paper collages with no apparent link to the text. This complete divorce of text from illustration puts it at one extreme of our study. The collages are so abstract that they are difficult to "read" even with the help of the captions, and each caption could have been matched to any one of the collages (illus. Rudenstine 1981, 458-60). Nevertheless, the text and illustrations are intended to be semantic, or rather methodological, equivalents, as the author's preface indicates:

> These collages are born of the same impulse as transrational language—of the freeing of creation from unnecessary comforts (rabid objectlessness). Transrational painting is becoming predominant. Earlier O. Rozanova gave examples of it, now a few other artists are developing it, including K. Malevich, Puni and others, having given it the unsuggestive name: suprematism.
> But I rejoice in the victory of painting as such, to the pique of hacks and the newspaperitis of the Italians.
> Transrational language (the first representative of which I happen to be) extends its hand to transrational painting.
>
> A. Kruchonykh

Be that as it may, the text and illustrations are so completely independent of each other that they form two separate entities that coexist between the same covers nearly without contact.

Compton (1978, 43) and Markov (1968, 335) claim that the collages were done by Rozanova, but there is no evidence to support this. (Indeed, the book *1918* (1917a) includes similar collages done exclusively by Kruchonykh.) It was also uncharacteristic of Kruchonykh to omit credit for a collaborator—in this case, his wife—and thus Khardzhiev attributes the collages to Kruchonykh: "The colored paste-ons (collage) of Rozanova served as a model for analogous works by A. Kruchonykh, who published the album *Universal War* in January 1916: 12 collages with *zaum* texts" (1976, 61). For proof of this attribution, we can turn to a letter to Kruchonykh from A. Shemshurin, dated July 4, 1916, and quoted by Khardzhiev:

Beyond the forms, the album is interesting also for being a very practical development of

---

an expression of his negative feeling toward war. This soon-to-be-nearly-eliminated letter with no sound value had already been eliminated by Kruchonykh in his personal orthography and might well seem the perfect symbol for the irrationality and anachronism of warfare in the modern world.

futurist publications. . . . In relation to publications you are taking a step forward. With Goncharova the futurist depends entirely on typography. . . . With Rozanova—typography is already eliminated, but there still is the mechanical element, since the color is imposed on one and the same plate. With you—the only mechanical thing remaining is scissors. (Ibid.)[26]

Kirill Zdanevich later gave high marks to Kruchonykh's ability to "position layers of paper, compose colors, and vary texture by the unexpected juxtaposition of materials" (ibid.; see K. Zdanevich 1919, 13).

Whatever Rozanova's role may have been in this last work, it cannot be denied that her influence on the works in which she collaborated was very great. The most notable new feature is the frequent presence of vibrant, at times lyrical, color. This vivifying force casts into shadow the more nihilistic, "adolescent," primitivizing foundation of Kruchonykh's art. One can both agree and disagree with A. Efros's characterization of Rozanova as the "intimate futurist" (1930, 231): "intimate" may be taken to mean delicate and refined, which is true of her work in many instances, but at the same time it fails to express her forcefulness and aggressive ideological affirmation.[27] Her death in 1918 issued in the most nihilistic period in Kruchonykh's career.

The first work produced by Kruchonykh in Tiflis and with the collaboration of Kirill Zdanevich instead of Rozanova, *1918* (1917a), is similar to the preceding work in two ways: it is in large format (approximately 22 by 33 cm); and it opens with text which is followed by a series of Suprematist collages, this time certainly by Kruchonykh himself. Included in the copy at Pushkinsky dom (Leningrad) is a signed collage by Malevich, much smaller than the rest, of a simple fish composed of patterned light-green wallpaper on a raspberry backing.[28] The entire book is made of brown construction paper with black and white lithographs pasted into the text portions. The work begins with two full-spread ferroconcrete poems by Kamensky (which will be discussed in the next chapter). They are followed by four pages that are divided down the middle, with the left side displaying text (the first a poem by Kamensky, the next three poems by Kruchonykh) and the right side displaying abstract lithographs by K. Zdanevich. These are followed by the Malevich collage, and then by Kruchonykh's collages. Judging from the handwriting, which is different from that in Kruchonykh's previous books, the cal-

---

[26] Nakov dismisses Khardzhiev's claim that Kruchonykh is the author of the collages with the bold statement: "A stylistic analysis of the work makes this hypothesis untenable" (*Tatlin's Dream*, 74). More recently, Hubertus Gassner claims that some of the collages "were executed by Rozanova, some by Kruchonykh himself" (Rubinger 1979, 235); but this claim is also made without evidence given to support it, as are similar statements in Rudenstine (1981, 458), and Rowell and Rudenstine (1981, 140).

[27] See Rubinger (1979, 68-70, 216-56), for the most extensive discussion of Rozanova to date.

[28] *Tatlin's Dream*, 48, shows a similar collage that, despite a legible signature by Malevich, is attributed to Rozanova in the caption.

ligraphy appears to be the work of Kirill Zdanevich. Zdanevich added decorations even to Kruchonykh's three texts, and the script of his initials on the drawings on pages 4 and 6 is the same as the text script. The same script is used in succeeding works, such as *Tsvetistye tortsy* (*Flowering Paving Planks* [?], 1919a), which were also done with Zdanevich's collaboration. The relatively thin pen lines of the script move away from the lapidary weight of the earlier books and toward the lightness and elegance of normal handwriting. The emphatic diagonal sweep of some of the letter lines is a new feature (figs. 81-83). Thus the influence of a new collaboration is reflected in its visual style, if not in the content of the poems, which is *zaum*. (Incidentally, page 5 [fig. 82] includes a printed note that the work was passed by the Tiflis police on January 2, 1917.)

The last of the group of unique publications is another collaboration with Kirill Zdanevich, *Uchites Khudogi* (*Learn Artists* [1917b]), which returns to the purely lithographed format of the early works. Once again there are more pages of graphics than text: of the twenty-five pages inside the booklet, six pages are pure text (handwritten in block lettering, five by Kruchonykh, one by Ziga Vladishevsky); three more by Kruchonykh are mainly text, but with force lines and

Fig. 81. A. Kruchonykh, poem from *1918*, 1917; drawing by K. Zdanevich.

other decorations added; the remaining fourteen are drawings by Zdanevich in a variety of Cubist, Expressionist, and near-abstract styles. Two pages, one by Kruchonykh and one by Zdanevich, are particularly noteworthy. The page by Kruchonykh (fig. 84) is a new development in his work, presaging things to come in its composition of disconnected letters and other geometric shapes of a Suprematist origin. With the possible exception of the column of three letters on the left (b a sh) they are not grouped into words or even syllables—*zaum* or otherwise—but remain purely graphic shapes of only protoverbal significance. In one instance it is not clear whether a shape is a letter or an abstract shape (see upper right corner: ⁄1); or rather, the shape is poised between being an abstract figure and a letter. Letters are treated merely as graphic elements on a par with other shapes. One might compare this with Cubist collage paintings of 1912 that incorporate letters or words, though here the synthesis is approached from the literary side. The difference is that in a painting the lettering functioned in part to emphasize or reestablish the planar surface of the painting to which the other elements of the composition could be contrasted,[29] while in Kruchonykh's com-

[29] For further discussion of this feature of Cubism, see Rosenblum (1973).

Fig. 82. A. Kruchonykh, poem from *1918*, 1917; drawing by K. Zdanevich.

position, no such tension emerges. Everything is comfortably and, one might add, uninterestingly situated on the same plane. No depth or levels are evident.

The page by K. Zdanevich of interest is a nude entitled "Masha" (fig. 85). The title of the drawing is incorporated into the composition, as is done with a number of his other drawings in the book. While in other instances the title forms a border or caption ("Man in the Sun" [fig. 86]), in this case the title and Zdanevich's signature are intimately incorporated into the curved and swirling lines of the drawing. The *M* continues the curves of the falling hair and the ш echoes the rhythmic strokes along the thigh. Even the з is to some extent echoed in the breasts. More intriguing yet is the distribution of the signature: it is scattered in several places and not all the necessary letters are there. The abbreviation of the given name to *Kir* (lower right) is no problem; but the surname, split into *Z d a n e* and *ich* (middle and upper right), is missing the letter *V* (*В*) and includes an unaccountably miswritten letter *n*, possibly the roman letter form. Since the principle of literally reading the inscriptions included in the drawings is well established throughout, the inclination to read the artist's name is obviously encouraged and then, in this case, frustrated by the splitting and the

Fig. 83. A. Kruchonykh, poem from *1918*, 1917; drawing by K. Zdanevich.

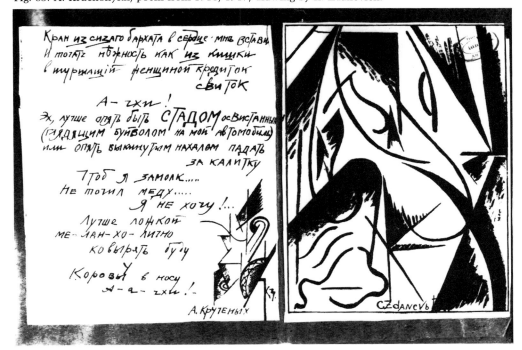

missing letter. It is bad enough that the last syllable should be placed above and slightly to the fore of the first two syllables, thus running counter to normal reading habits, but the absence of a letter is provocative. The natural response is to search for the letter elsewhere in the composition. Since the 3 imitates the shape of the breasts, is the *B* to be found there as well? If so, is it only a dirty mind that sees as a motivation for the miswritten *n* an anagram that spells *pezda*, a misspelling (pronounced the same) of *pizda* (cunt)? Such vulgarity is clearly not beyond the scope of the book, as Kruchonykh's poem preceding the illustration amply demonstrates (fig. 87):

A Belch

As a gander
    gorged himself on grain
I'll snooze
    next to the goose
Masha
    with a red puss
Whispers about love.

Fig. 84. A. Kruchonykh, graphic composition from *Learn Artists*, 1917.

Fig. 85. K. Zdanevich, "Masha," from *Learn Artists*, 1917.

The poem and the illustration both have the same less-than-respectful attitude toward the lusty Masha, and provide one of the best, if not most edifying, conjunctions of text and illustration to be found in these works.

The next major grouping, gathered and indented by Kruchonykh in his bibliography under the heading "autographic books (hectograph)," is indeed a set that is of a piece for a number of reasons, the chief being the method of production. They number thirty-six items, but only about half have come to light.[30]

The main feature distinguishing this group from those preceding and following it is the informality of their production, that is, the absence of formal publishing processes and machinery. However haphazard and offhand the earlier publications were made to seem, they nevertheless involved traditional means of production (printing press, lithographic materials, special papers, artistic collaborators) and required the services of a lithographic publishing house (most often "Svet"). The present set, on the other hand, was most assuredly produced by Kruchonykh himself with the help at most of a hectographic machine, which he probably operated himself. Use was made of whatever materials were available, including ordinary paper, stationery, lined notebook paper, graph paper, and so forth. In a number of instances, the booklets include pages done in pencil that are obviously the "original." Other pages are simply carbon copies of such originals. Clearly the number of copies of such a work must be quite small, limited as it is to the number of carbons that can be made from one impression (about ten). I will discuss later what other principle might have been at work to change this picture somewhat.

[30] A major group of them is located at Pushkinsky dom in the "fond russkikh pisateley v Gruzii." The Lenin Library also contains some items.

g. 86. K. Zdanevich, "Man in e Sun," from *Learn Artists*, 1917.

Fig. 87. A. Kruchonykh, "A Belch," from *Learn Artists*, 1917.

Отрынка.

Как гусак
объѣлся каши
Дрыхну
гуска рядом
Маша
с рожей красной
шепчет про любовь

а. Кручёных.

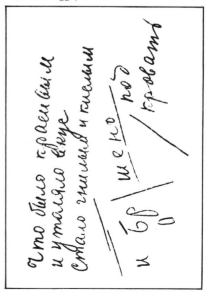

Fig. 88. A. Kruchonykh, page from *Sky-blue Eggs*, 1917.

All of the group that I have seen are quite similar in appearance. They are smaller in size than most previous publications (approximately 17 by 11.5 cm); consist of 10 to 16 pages, though most are 12 or 14 pages long; do not have a specially made cover; are limited in color to hectographic and carbon-paper colors (black, blue, purple); are written in thin lines, most likely by pencil, but on occasion include some stamped pages; are mostly in *zaum* and are textually fragmentary, each page being an isolated unit or composition; are devoid of elaborate illustrations and nearly devoid of independent ones, but often have simple lines as part of a composition of letters; and are often a combination of pages with horizontal and vertical text layouts. Most have *zaum* titles. Included among them as perhaps the most straightforward, if not eloquent, example of the correspondence of text layout to the text itself is the following example from *Sky-blue Eggs* (1917c) (fig. 88). The first three lines, which read, in translation, "What was beautiful/and satisfied taste/Became rotten and sour," are written in the standard manner, while the last line, "and thrown under the bed" is broken up and scattered across the page together with lines that, to me, suggest pick-up sticks.

Fig. 89. A. Kruchonykh, *F/nagt*, 1918, complete book.

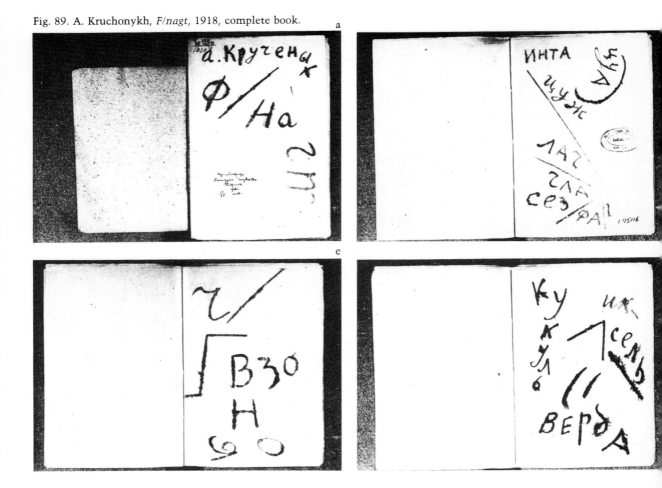

Given the "cottage industry" nature of these publications, their similarity, and the nihilistic decline in verbal content, one can conjecture that they were produced as follows. Kruchonykh, whenever the mood or the opportunity arose (or, perhaps more importantly, under conditions of scarcity, whenever materials became available), would write, compose, or hectograph a number of individual pages on whatever paper came to hand. Depending on supplies or on method of production, each page would be produced in a varying number of copies. With a selection of such pages ready, Kruchonykh would put them together into a booklet and provide it with a title. It is likely that some pages appear in several publications. A later booklet outside the series, *Zaum* (1921), confirms this suspicion to some extent. It consists of a new printed cover designed by Rodchenko that has been fitted over the earlier hectographed booklet, *From All Books* (1918b), which is an eloquent title in itself. The printed flyleaf of the "Declaration of the Transrational Word" was inserted in the middle, folded in half. *From All Books*, in turn, consists of pages from other books in the autographic series. Included in its entirety is *F/nagt* (1918a; title is meaningless), with a variant of one of its pages, as well as two pages that differ from each other only slightly. There are

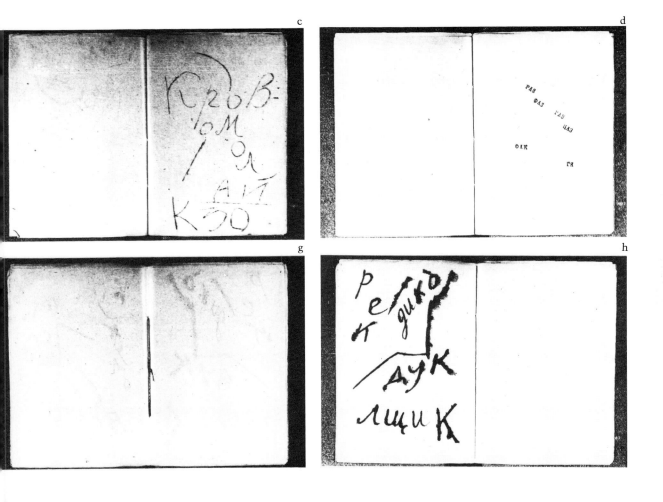

seven more pages before and after the *F/nagt* section; they may well make up another book in the series, but I could not verify this. Some of the pages of *F/ nagt* that appear in *Zaum* are darker and clearer than they were in the earlier book. They probably came sooner in the hectographic run than those in the first version. When seeing these booklets, one wonders if all copies of works with the same title—assuming there is more than one copy—have the same contents.

Whether this conjecture turns out ultimately to be true is not particularly important, however, since the booklets are repetitious and uniform enough to have entirely interchangeable pages. This is in striking contrast to Kruchonykh's earlier books, where an overall design and architecture were present. With this fourth group, Kruchonykh could be said to have passed from Futurism to a stance close to the empty game of life played by some of the Dadaists.

The best way to convey the flavor of a typical example of the group is to present one in its entirety. Commentary is not needed. You don't have to know Russian to follow along. If you know the alphabet, you can pronounce the sounds, but they do not mean much more to a Russian. In this case and others, a pure

Fig. 89 (*continued*)

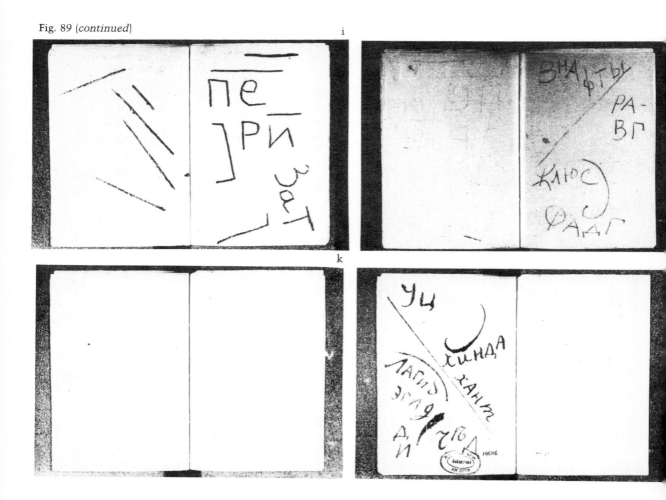

extreme is reached: the complete absence of what would genuinely be called a text. The example, *F/nagt* (fig. 89a-1) consists mainly of compositions of lines and miscellaneous letters that cannot be read except in the way one "reads" a painting. It is at this point that literature and painting intersect. All that is left of "the book" are its pages; all that is left of "literature" are its letters. This is a return to basics in its purest sense, a return to minimal requirements, the limit beyond which one cannot go and still use the terms "book" and "literature."

The last of the series, *Lacquered Tights* (1919b), exists in two versions, one the same as the rest of the series, and a second longer version elaborately typeset and designed, probably by Ilya Zdanevich, Kirill's brother. Under one title are joined antipodes of the publishing art: the minimal—a modest, hand-produced, almost childishly simple booklet; and the maximal—a tour de force of the type-setter's craftsmanship. This new flowering was produced by the involvement in Kruchonykh's works of Ilya Zdanevich, and took them in a direction that was influenced more by Zdanevich than by Kruchonykh. This will be discussed fur-ther in the chapter devoted to Zdanevich.

Of the remaining works by Kruchonykh to 1930 and beyond that were pro-duced without Zdanevich's help, little need be said. Most of them are typeset, but even those that are not show nothing new in the way of visual techniques or ideas. In appearance they are either similar to or more conservative than previous works. Some of these works, particularly those from 1919 to 1921, include hand processes, but by 1922 nearly all are printed in a more or less traditional manner.

Among the few handwritten books of the later years, I should mention *Iron-iada* (1930a) and *Rubiniada* (1930b), both of which were produced by a process called *steklopechat*,[31] which gives the text a slightly different grainy texture than pencil lithography. Notable is the variety of handwriting styles thrown together in the course of the text, sometimes several on the same page. The handwritings are so dissimilar at times that one doubts that they were all done by Kruchonykh (fig. 90a,b).

After 1930, Kruchonykh turned into a compiler and collector, devoting a major part of his energies to the creation of "albums," that is, scrapbooks of materials related to his major avant-garde friends and associates, such as Ma-yakovsky, Aseev, Pasternak, and Kirsanov (Korolyova 1978). These have consid-erable historical interest as sources for little-known materials; they have a kind of artistic coherence of their own, but do not add anything to the present dis-cussion. Kruchonykh became a bibliographer and archivist of the period of his glory and of later times, living modestly and quietly in Moscow until his death in 1968. He served as a valuable consultant to official archives and eventually

---

[31] The process of *steklopechat (steklografiya)* is similar to lithography, but uses a glass plate or cylinder. Maximum number of copies is approximately one hundred.

donated most of his materials to them (Korolyova 1978, 304).[32] The total number of "productions" for which Kruchonykh was chiefly responsible runs into the two hundreds, and probably well beyond three hundred.

AN EVALUATION

Kruchonykh's manuscript books took a leap back through history to what in Europe would be pre-Renaissance times. For a Russian, this leap was not as great as it would have been for a Western European because the time span was not nearly as long. The cultural effect of the Renaissance began to be felt in Russia only at the end of the seventeenth century and led immediately to a period of neo-Classicism that can be said to have continued until the twentieth century. This leap was easy also because much of Russian art was imitative and modeled on imported styles. The leap, then, was back to the older native traditions of the icon, the *lubok*, and the manuscript satire that in fact had never died out, but had continued their unrespected, unofficial existence even into the present century. For a European, such a leap would have meant a rejection of five centuries of organic development, but for a Russian it amounted to less than two centuries of relatively inorganic development.

In this connection another trend should be noted. The general European mood of *fin-de-siècle* exhaustion and a sense that the old culture was dying meant, as we can see in retrospect, that the post-Renaissance period was coming to an end. If, as Douglas Cooper states, "Renaissance artists opted out of recording that fuller truth about reality which is known to the human mind in favor of recording only what the eye sees of things, incomplete and deceptive though this may be"

[32] For a personal view of Kruchonykh in his last years, see McVey 1975.

Fig. 90. A. Kruchonykh, two pages from *Rubiniada*, 1930.

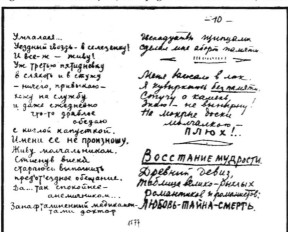
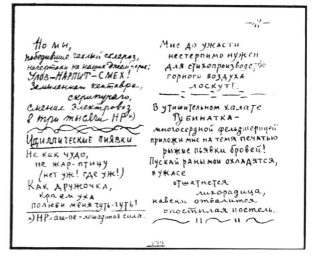

(1971, 11), the Symbolists had already paved the way for new developments by their "denial of the world of appearances" (Bowlt and Long 1980, 10). This new trend was to be a reestablishment of the pre-Renaissance attitude.

> Now Cubism involved a return to the earlier conceptual principle, insofar as the artist assumed the right to fill gaps in our seeing, and to make pictures whose reality would be independent of, but no less valid than, our visual impressions of reality, and was thus stylistically the antithesis of Renaissance art. (Cooper 1971, 11)

Kruchonykh was, as we have seen, closely associated with the early Russian devotees of Cubism and shared their aims.

In book culture this shift was reflected in Kruchonykh's rejection of the "straitjacket" of the mechanical post-Gutenberg book, with its neat rows of letters, in favor of the free treatment of the page space permitted by the more modern techniques of lithography and hectography, which return to the licenses of pre-Renaissance manuscript culture. Kruchonykh's way of freeing the text from its straitjacket is amply demonstrated above.

What is less amply demonstrated is his and Khlebnikov's contention that script conveys the writer's mood directly to the reader. More precisely, it is accepted as a truism by handwriting analysts that handwriting reflects the character and probably also the temporary mood of the writer, and they have devised elaborate systems for reading character and mood from the script. Although it is elusive, the scientific basis for handwriting analysis, or graphology, seems generally to be recognized, though more so in Europe than America. Handwriting is one of many human gestures that reveal personality and can be used as a descriptive tool clinically if properly handled. However, "it is never the form of single letters alone, nor any particular characteristic, but the combination and interaction of all parts of the writing pattern that reveal the personality of the writer." The trained graphologist can look beyond the writer's "intended communication" to discern "how emotive and unconscious factors have also shaped this hand. In other words, he reads the accompanying 'unintended communication,' a language without words, simultaneously with the intended" (Roman 1968, 441). On the other hand, a recent study (Jansen 1973) concludes that while handwriting analysis has a somewhat better than random correlation with personality evaluations established by a full battery of tests, trained graphologists are no more reliable than untrained university students at relating handwriting samples to a personality trait.

If the validity of the connection between handwriting and personality is questionable from a scientific viewpoint, the visual expressiveness of handwriting is considerably less so. In fact, this very expressiveness may have led graphology to its assumptions (whether true or false) because the expressiveness is so obvious. If one doubts that i-dots and t-bars placed high indicate for certain that the writer himself is idealistic and optimistic (Marcuse 1962, 44), his handwriting never-theless conveys that mood; if a jagged, irregular, and unharmonious handwriting cannot allow us to incarcerate the writer for criminal tendencies or mental in-stability, we are still likely to feel nervous reading his writing. The handwriting of true criminals may, on the other hand, be quite pleasing to the eye.

Once the focus is on the handwriting itself and not on the personality behind it, Kruchonykh's and Khlebnikov's provision for subcontracting the task to a skilled artist makes sense. The artist can control the expressiveness of the writing without necessarily breaking the author's intended mood by the intrusion of the artist's own personality.

The situation is similar to the effect of colors and sounds. In general terms, there is agreement (Jakobson and Waugh 1979, 189-94; O'Grady 1979, 157; Scha-piro 1973, 47-49). No one would claim that bright yellow is calming or scarlet is cold and distant, nor that a high note is heavy or a low note is bright. Similarly, a script with broad, heavy strokes would not be considered reflective of timidity or introversion. Whether such a script is the product of the author himself or a surrogate artist would not be vital to the impression. But whether one can proceed beyond a level of broad generality when the phenomenon is not narrow and homogeneous but complex and heterogeneous is another issue. Thus a flute melody may be sad if the high notes are in a minor key and the tempo is adagio, or it may reflect by turns a spectrum of moods depending on many factors, not the least of which is context or accompaniment. Listeners tend to disagree when the matter becomes both more complex and more specific. With handwriting, the same would be true. If block letters reflect rigidity and strength (they may also reflect an orientation to the archaic), and flowing, rounded script reflects a lyrical, flexible mood, what does a mixture of the two, as is often the case in Kruchonykh's early works, convey to the reader? Opinions would likely vary, as with the flute melody, and the effect could not be pinpointed precisely. This fact does not invalidate the method at all but, to the contrary, as in the case of the flute melody, it validates the method. Something is unequivocally expressed even if it is beyond verbal formulation. Just as a good painting defies verbal translation (and thereby asserts its artistic independence and proves its significance), so script is a visual phenomenon like painting and, somewhat paradoxically, asserts its independent value by defying verbal translation. If nothing else, a manuscript book reflects its author's rejection of domination by print culture and presents itself as a handwritten letter to the reader.

Compton makes a point in connection with the formation of the Hylaea group of Futurists with which Kruchonykh was most closely associated (Hylaea was the land of the Scythians, assumed to be early Slavs):

By emphasizing these primitive roots, the group of artists and writers wished to trace their heritage back to a pre-Classical settlement and link the present to the ancient past, by-passing the western European Classical inheritance by joining up with their own pre-Classical primitivism. In this way they both challenged the Russian symbolists with their themes of Apollo and Dionysus and found their own answer to the contemporary French avant-garde interest in non-Western and primitive art forms. (1978, 13)

Thus it was natural that the classical norms for art (harmony, balance, clarity, order) should be rejected in favor of their opposites.

Kruchonykh, generally recognized by his peers as the most radical and uncompromising adherent of this program, must therefore be considered as the group's leader, or at any rate its most characteristic product. It is safe to say that to the end of his days he never abandoned faith in the program, never threw up his hands and said it was all a mistake or that the time for Futurism had passed. He spent many later years continuing to argue in favor of its tenets.

The movement certainly had its greats (Khlebnikov, Mayakovsky), but what did Kruchonykh himself achieve? On the matter of whether the theories set out in "The Letter as Such" find adequate realization in Kruchonykh's art, one can confidently answer in the affirmative. Certainly there is no body of works that better illustrates the variety of possibilities available to the artist-bookmaker. The expressive high points of each major example have already been set forth above.

Kruchonykh did more than any other writer to integrate visual features thoroughly into his works. As we have seen, in a number of instances in the period 1914-20 he came close to striking a balance, or perhaps a variety of balances, between graphics and literature, while remaining basically a writer. But what of his writing? Personal opinions may vary, of course, but my own is that Kruchonykh's books are more interesting to look at than to read. However, a careful, thorough reading of his works, which is made more difficult and challenging by the format, remains to be done and will involve important considerations of *zaum* in theory and practice. For Kruchonykh, the word remains of utmost importance. To this effect, we can quote from his memoirs of 1933, wherein he reflects on his youth. It is a statement that puts him surprisingly close to Bely:

I was more "broad" a nature than was necessary for an artist. To only *see* the world was not enough for me. I had acute hearing. A silent picture, the tongue-tied medium of the artist deprived me of half the world, made it one-sided. My world had to sound; great mutes had to begin to speak. Of course, music alone would also not be able to satisfy me: it deprived the world of color, like painting deprived it of sound. . . . There is, however, no more natural, perfect and multifaceted means of expressing yourself in art than the word. One can live without painting and music, but without the word—there is no person! From painting I turned to poetry as the final, integral lever for moving the earth. (Ziegler 1978, 286)

We have surveyed the books in which Kruchonykh was involved, noted their astonishing variety, richness, and interest, and noted the ever-changing collaborations; there is no corpus like it in size and, one might say, in grandeur, in Russian or, as far as I know, any other literature. And the role Kruchonykh played in this incredible production was of the utmost importance for the final results. Compton is entirely fair when she gives chief credit for the design of the books to Kruchonykh:

> The originality of his approach can be measured by comparing the appearance of those which he initiated, right up to the 1920s with those to which he was only a contributor, or which were published independently. Those under his supervision surpass in design those of nearly all his contemporaries, his only rival being the poet Vasily Kamensky. (1978, 70)

Under the sign of the times of a "return to basics," Kruchonykh provided the best or, at any rate, most extreme examples of a return to the basic book. His approach to the practice of bookmaking was a classical case of "defamiliarization," such as Natasha's visit to the opera in *War and Peace*. It is as if Kruchonykh, intentionally playing the role of the primitive observer, was handed his first book on some occasion and, not knowing what it was for or anything about the millennial tradition of the book, set out to make some more of his own. By approaching the issue with fresh, naive eyes, and without cultural preconceptions that had developed over the centuries, he ignored all the existing norms of the bookmaker's and bookwriter's art and consequently exposed the true physical nature of the book. He deprived it of all but its minimal essence; in one notable instance he even deprived a book of its accurate name by misspelling it *gniga* instead of *kniga*, imparting to it some unkind associations (*gnida* "nit," *gnila* "rotted"). But the true basic nature of the book was always maintained: a series of pages of text fastened together at the margin.

In Kruchonykh's more radical examples, the book is little more than an assemblage of miscellaneous pages, each self-sufficient. The sequence is not important; the contents are varied in the extreme and bear no evident relationship to other parts of the book, being dispensable, interchangeable, not important; illustrations may or may not be present, linked to the text, or incorporated into the text; stock papers may be uniform or haphazardly miscellaneous; pages may be of nonuniform size; the text may be printed, stamped, typed, or handwritten; the text itself may be minimal, with barely any words—only letters, lines, or even blank pages.

Given the artistic talents of Kruchonykh and his collaborators, it is not surprising that a number of these books are in fact beautiful to look at. We must keep in mind, however, that for the Avant Garde—and in particular for Kruchonykh—beauty in any traditional sense was not a goal. The beauties we find in Kruchonykh's works are chiefly not his own doing but those of his collaborators, though he provided the framework for them and in many cases the stimulus for their actualization. Kruchonykh himself comes across as an artistic nihilist.

By reducing the text to a minimum (syllables, letters, lines), Kruchonykh indeed achieved one goal, that of simultaneity.[33] Such a page of "text" need not be read sequentially in linear time, but can be taken in at a glance and absorbed by the same process of free visual exploration used in studying a painting. Even on those pages with thorough *zaum*, a kind of simultaneity can occur, perhaps unintended, when the reader, having read a few such pages carefully, syllable by syllable, tires of it and "reads" a whole page at a glance with the mental comment: "More of the same." Whether such an experience produces a sense of "higher intuition" in the Uspenskian sense[34] is questionable, though a full answer to this question must hinge on a thorough study of the *zaum* itself.

This is perhaps the place to introduce several comments by Kruchonykh's erstwhile collaborator, Kazimir Malevich, who was himself an occasional *zaumnik*. In a letter to Matyushin (June 1916), Malevich wrote some trenchant criticisms of Kruchonykh's efforts. He characterized Kruchonykh as one of the

new poets who have waged a war against thought which has enslaved the free letter and who have attempted to bring the letter close to the idea of sound (not music). Hence the mindless and transrational [*zaumnaya*] poetry "dyr bul" or "vzdryvul." The poet has justified himself by references to the flagellant Shishkov, to the nervous system, religious ecstasy and thereby wanted to prove the rightness of the existence of "dyr bul." But these references led the poet into a dead end, bringing him to the same marrow, to the same point as before. The poet does not succeed in explaining the reasons for the liberation of the letter. . . . The word "as such" must be reincarnated "into something," but this remains *vague*. (Kovtun 1976, 190)

Malevich goes on to describe the letter as a kind of sound note, which is "more subtle, clearer and more expressive than musical notes," out of which "compositions of sound mass (former words)" can be constructed (ibid., 191). For Malevich even *zaum* words are still words, and therefore not liberated. A new, third path is needed:

In this way we tear the letter from the line, from its one direction, and give it the possibility of free movement. (Lines are necessary to the world of bureaucrats and domestic correspondence.) Consequently we come to the third position, i.e. to the distribution of sound masses in space similar to painterly suprematism. These masses will hang in space and

[33] In connection with simultaneity, the "simultané" of Robert Delaunay should be mentioned. It was publicized in *Apollon*, no. 1/2 (1914): 134, as a result of a lecture by A. A. Smirnov entitled "Simultané" at the Brodyachaya Sobaka cabaret. However, since Delaunay meant the following, it could play no significant role in graphics, where line is vital: "Line is limitation. Color gives depth—not perspectival, not successive, but simultaneous depth—as well as form and movement" (Cooper 1971, 84). For Delaunay, spots of solid colors give a sense of depth of varying intensities. In the Russian context it was Georgy Yakulov who best exemplified this trend. See also Bravsky 1913.

[34] P. D. Uspensky is quoted by Kruchonykh in "Novye puti slova," *Three*, September 1913 (Markov 1967, 66), and by M. Matyushin in *Union of Youth* 3 (1913): 26, from Uspensky, *Tertium Organum*, 1911; reprint Berlin, 1931, 65.

give our consciousness the possibility of reaching farther and farther away from the earth. (Ibid., 191-92)

Kruchonykh's works subsequent to this statement may well have satisfied Malevich, although this is not known. In any case, Kruchonykh was not inclined, as was Malevich, to journeys into outer space. Yet both artists share the tendency to negate. With Malevich this was in order to affirm and create something better or higher; with Kruchonykh the absence of mysticism places him dangerously close to not affirming or creating anything.

A unique enterprise that in some respects upstages Kruchonykh is Varvara Stepanova's handmade "anti-book," *Gaust chaba* (1919). It is made of newsprint bound into book format and contains pages on which either *zaum* words are scrawled or snippits of other newsprint are collaged (fig. 91). Newsprint, the ultimate manifestation of print culture, is thereby dethroned into being merely a material or background for the artist's (nihilistic) self-expression (Kovtun 1974, 57-63; Rubinger 1979, 270-84; Rudenstine 1981, 469).[35]

[35] Mention should be made here of several other Stepanova efforts along these lines. In the catalogue for "Tenth State Exhibition (Non-Objective Art and Suprematism)," 1919, she states: "The new type of Non-Objective poetry, consisting of sound and typography, is combined in my works with painterly sensation, which fills the dead monotonous sounds of the verse with a new, live visual experience. With the aid of pictorial graphic art I shatter the closely arrayed printed lines, progressing in this way towards a new art. On the other hand, while I am thus recreating the Non-Objective poetry contained in two books, *Zigra ar* and *Rtni khomle*, I introduce sound as a new quality into pictorial graphics, increasing thereby their quantitative potential" (Karginov 1979, 57). Pages from these two books are illustrated in *From Painting to Design*, 166, 167, 177 (color), and 179. Other items of interest in this catalogue are Stepanova's cover for a "series of graphic poetry" (p. 164) and her illustrations (pp. 211-13, 245) for a book by Kruchonykh, *Gly-gly* (1918), which is not listed by him in his bibliography and therefore may never have been published. The illustrations come from the Rodchenko

Fig. 91. Varvara Stepanova, page from *Gaust chaba*, 1919.

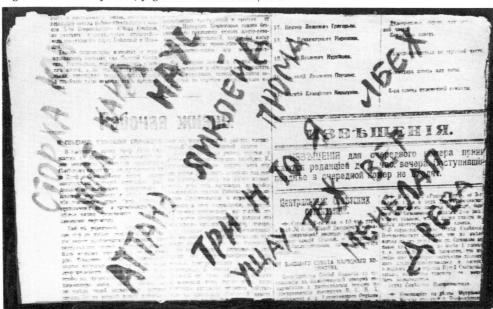

One can look at Kruchonykh's book publications as experiments in defining the limits of the book as an idea. In a number of instances he can be said to have reached those limits in one respect or another, but, in contrast to Stepanova, one does not get the impression of a destructive violence at work. Kruchonykh did not seem to want to do violence to the book, but rather, in a childlike, almost playful spirit, he wanted to establish its essence.

Without going into questions of direct influence or trying to be exhaustive, one can point to similar manuscript lithographed books of the period which, if not imitations of Kruchonykh, are at least products of the same impulse. Mayakovsky's *Ya!* (*I!* [1913]), with graphics by Chekrygin and L. Sh. (Zhegin), which is closest in visual style to *Pomade*, was published by the same G. Kuzmin and S. Dolinsky, and lithographed by the same Mukharsky. Goncharova and Larionov produced Bolshakov's book of poetry *Le Futur* (1913), with rayist illustrations, but a meticulously calligraphed text was done by Ivan Firsov (Chamot 1973, 498). In 1920 Goncharova herself illustrated Rubakin's volume of poems *The City* (1920), with text handwritten and lithographed by the author (ibid., 499-500). N. Aseev also published a manuscript-lithographed book of *zaum* poems *Zor* (1914), which was issued in Moscow but printed in Kharkov (Ciszkewycz 1980, 241). Two of Malevich's books are lithographed with manuscript texts: *On New Systems in Art* (1919) and *Suprematism: 34 Drawings* (1920). Khlebnikov's *Selected Poems* (1914) includes a lithographed section in the back called "Wooden Idols," with interesting calligraphy and graphics by Pavel Filonov. The great poet's *Ladomir* (1920b) is a manuscript book, as are others in the series *Unpublished Khlebnikov* (1928-33). In addition, I should mention the collection *Autographs* (1921), in which the contributing poets (including Bely, Bryusov, Tsvetaeva, Lunacharsky [!], and others) are featured with poems done in their own hand; another book of the same title, undated, has different contributors, mainly Imaginists. Bozhidar's *Tambourine* (1914) is without illustrations, handwritten in its own peculiar mixture of Cyrillic and Latin alphabets. Finally, there are some handwritten "productions" that are true manuscripts, that is, they seem to exist in only one copy meticulously done by the author. Such is the edition by Bely of his poem *To Christian Morgenstern* (1918), with anthroposophic illustrations by the author in watercolor.[36] A similar work, *Poem*, is reproduced in Malmstad (1968) at the beginning of volume 2. Even more remarkable is Kirsanov's meticulously calligraphed copy of *Rativor: A Bylina* (1921),[37] which is done in medieval script with red initials. Mayakovsky produced a similar book (see chapter 7).

---

archive, Moscow. See also Lavrentiev. These examples somewhat resemble *Te li le* in their colorfulness, but are more energetic. The texts are in *zaum*.

[36] IMLI, f. 11, op. 1, ed. 40.

[37] Ibid., f. 110, op. 1, ed. 1.

Important for the variety of visual effects he used was Aleksey Remizov. The battery of his devices ranges from double dashes and indentations, akin to Bely's, in many of his prose works (for example, *Olya* [1927]; *Along the Eaves* [1929]); to combinations of verse and prose; to beautifully and elaborately hand-calligraphed monkeys' *gramoty* (charters) in chancellery script that he gave to friends; to minutely written fragments with doodles (Belenson 1915, 84-85); to poems with idiosyncratic punctuation and fanciful layouts. The only thing he does not seem to have done is to use elaborate layouts of various typefaces, as done by Zdanevich. Remizov does not receive more attention in this study because he did not break new ground of a kind that would interest us in this context. With the exception of his prose layouts, in which he is preceded by Bely, the rest is, for all its personal expressiveness, backward-looking and conservative, or at the very least unprogrammatic, unsystematic, and without a perceptible goal, except, in the spirit of Fyodorov, to preserve the culture of writing in an age of print. Nevertheless, Remizov's efforts should not be belittled, for they provide us with numerous striking examples of visual literature of a high level.

Mention should also be made of the manuscript work in the modern Soviet context. So far as I know, no officially produced manuscript book has emerged from the Soviet Union recently except for the photocopy edition of K. Chukovsky's album *Chukokkala* (Moscow: Iskusstvo, 1979). Needless to say, freelance lithographed, mimeographed, or xeroxed works are officially frowned upon. *Samizdat* authors prefer to type their works for the obvious reason that authorship is less easy to trace that way. Nevertheless, the manuscript medium is still used on occasion among the more adventurous avant-garde writers.

In conclusion, I will cite a note of tribute to Kruchonykh by a colleague, Sergey Tretyakov:

> Besides his emotional sensitivity of ear, he has an undoubted visual sensitivity. Look at his lithographed or handwritten booklets.
>
> Letters and syllables at random of various sizes and scripts; less often these letters are printed, more often handwritten and then crookedly, so that not being a graphologist, one immediately senses a blocky, tight, bone-creaking psyche behind these letters. Besides, these letters are quite restless, —the boogeyman [Kruchonykh] says:
>
> lines are necessary for bureaucrats and Balmonts
> they are fatal!
> *Our words take flight!* . . . (*Nestroche*, 1917)

And indeed they do take flight, turn somersaults, play leapfrog, crawl and hop over the whole page. People are aghast: This is poetry? No, this isn't poetry. These are drawings; in them graphics dominate, but letter graphics which carry as an accompaniment the feeling of sounding and accretions of associations attended by speech-sounds.

Kruchonykh's graphic *zaum* went parallel to sonic *zaum* and has its place even now. This phenomenon is explained in my opinion by the fact that until now a boundary between visible language (letters) and audible (sound) has not been drawn. Not by accident in his time one of the futurists, finding in a poem a line about the sea tide with three b's

[§] found that the tails of the letter "b" above the line conveyed the splash of the waves.

And, of course Kruchonykh, the laboratorian, was right when he took into his laboratory on various bases both the visible and the audible, all the more since the visual effect of typefaces and handwritings was used by the Italian Futurists also (and even earlier by posters, signs, newspaper headlines, etc.). (Tretyakov et al. 1923, 5-7)

Kruchonykh's role was to reduce the book and the page to a minimum; yet no new principle of integration emerged out of this. It was Vasili Kamensky, working beside Kruchonykh, to whom a new principle of page organization can be attributed.

4. Kamensky

and the Ferroconcrete

Poem

If one takes seriously the idea that the page is a visual space like the surface of a canvas and that words distributed on the page exist in real space, then another path of activity must be explored: the structuring of the text according to the spatial relationships that result from positioning letters and words on the page. It is in following this path that Vasili Kamensky (1884-1961) made a significant contribution with his "concrete" (*zhelezobetonny*), more literally "ferroconcrete" or "reinforced concrete," poems. The striking similarity between the translation "concrete" here and the much more modern Concrete Poetry movement that began in the late 1950s is an accident of English homonymy. The latter movement defines "concrete" as "tactile, material" (as opposed to "spiritual, abstract"), while Kamensky thinks of "concrete" as something made of hardened cement, as in a building, sidewalk, or other such structure.[1]

Among the Futurists, the word *zhelezobetonny* was apparently used first by Kruchonykh in *Piglets*[2] (1913e, 8):

zhelezobetonnye giri-doma	concrete weights-houses
tashchut brosayut menya nichkom	drag, throw me flat on my face

Here it is not used metaphorically, but applied to buildings made of reinforced concrete.

Kamensky appears to have been the first to use the term metaphorically to characterize a certain type of poetry and, to my knowledge, he is the only one

---

[1] By way of a brief history of the development of reinforced concrete use we may note that its introduction was attributed to Joseph Monier in about 1868 and that its architectural use "coincided with the appearance of the modern style of architecture" at the beginning of the twentieth century (*Encyclopaedia Britannica*, Vol. 6 [1959], 209b).

[2] I am grateful to Vladimir Markov for pointing this out.

to have used it this way. He is also the only Russian poet of the time to have written such a "ferroconcrete" poem. He applies the term *zhelezobetonny* (for convenience we will hereafter use the translation "ferroconcrete") to a series of poems that share the following properties: (1) each is one page long; (2) they use the entire page as free space for distributing text; (3) they are essentially nominal, that is, they are lists of nouns, though parts of words and non-nominal words are sometimes included; (4) they generally lack overt syntactic structures; (5) the text is organized by word association, which is made by semantic, contextual, and visual links between words; (6) the structure is free in that the reader is free to read the elements of the poem in any order he chooses, letting his eye wander over the page at will as he would in examining a painting. Each of the ferroconcrete poems has a thematic focus and is built around the author's personal associations connected with the theme. Sometimes these associations can be idiosyncratic enough to be obscure to the modern reader, as they probably also were to Kamensky's contemporaries.

In contrast to the huge corpus of Kruchonykh's visual experiments, the number of Kamensky's ferroconcrete poems is quite small—nine, to be exact. These are the published poems; evidently more exist or have existed, judging by the catalogue of the Exhibition No. 4 (Moscow, 1914) in which eleven ferroconcrete works are listed. Only one of these, "Constantinople," can be linked with certainty to a known poem. Another, "Circus Cry," may correspond to our "Circus."[3] The following is a complete list of the nine published ferroconcrete poems and the volumes in which they appeared (repeated titles indicate another publication of the same work):

"Constantinople" (cloth flyer)

A Naked Man among Clothed (February 1914):
    "Cabaret"
    "The Mansion S. I. Shchukin"

Futurists: First Journal of the Russian Futurists (before March 1914):
    "Skating Rink"

Tango with Cows (March and April 1914):
    "Constantinople"
    "Cabaret"
    "The Mansion S. I. Shchukin"
    "The Nikitin Circus"
    "Skating Rink"
    "Bathhouse"

[3] 76 Ma + 4
77 Rue de Carrousel
78 Bacchanale
79 Constantinople
80 Journal
81 Journal 1276 3914 numéros
82 Voyage du moteur
83 Tombe d'un aéroplane
84 Radio-télégraphe
85 Cri du cirque
86 Les grands magasins Mir-Mériliz (Moscou) (Marcadé 1971, 335-36)

The Archer. I (1915):
    "Constantinople"
1918 (1917):
    "Tiflis"
    "The Sun (*Lubok*)"
    "K (Blade)"
Since the group is so small, it is possible to reproduce each example and discuss it in detail.

At the head of the discussion must be "Constantinople" (fig. 92). It apparently was the first work of the series, published three times, and the only one to receive an analysis by a contemporary. Since the major group of ferroconcrete poems (excluding those in *1918*) was clearly the product of the same impulse and time, temporal priority is not particularly important. Kamensky does honor the poem with the subtitle "first book of poetry to the world," which is meant to apply to its initial manifestation as a flyer printed on yellow sateen.[4] This is exactly the same as the version printed in *Tango with Cows* and, as a caption indicates, is intended to be placed on "walls and fences." Its third publication (Belenson 1915, 165) occurred as part of an analysis by A. Shemshurin. It differs slightly from the original in layout and typefaces, probably to make it compatible with the anthology in which it appeared; it also omits the marginalia of the original.

[4] An example of it in this form is to be found at IMLI, fond 205, op. 1, no. 1 (M.1914).

Fig. 92. V. Kamensky, "Constantinople," from *Tango with Cows*, 1914.

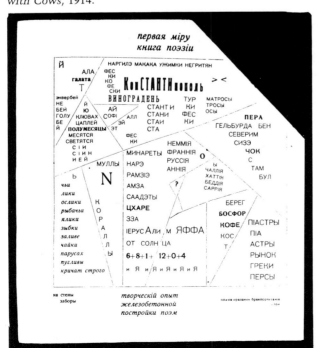

Shemshurin's commentary, based on conversations with the author and the only such analysis extant, is therefore extremely valuable, and it is tempting to proceed by quoting or summarizing his remarks. But since Markov already did this (1968, 197-98), we might profitably confront the poem "cold," going as far as we can on our way before consulting Shemshurin when our ingenuity and knowledge are exhausted.

The first visit by the poet to this famous city took place in 1904 and is described in his memoirs as follows:

The captain of a trade vessel—to whose son I had been giving lessons—offered me a cruise to Turkey along the shores to Trebizond and Constantinople.

The poet's heart began to throb—I dropped my lessons.

The ship with its cargo took his sadness [because of an unhappy love affair] to Bosphorus shores.

Trebizond met the traveller with a terrible storm, desperate tossing, the howl of sirens, after which the Constantinople bay calmed him with heavenly peace, the fantastic beauty of the welcoming confluence of two seas.

Constantinople with its seven hundred mosques and its grand harbor of the Golden Horn, its shipyards and the wonder of Byzantine art—Hagia Sophia, with its bright motley of eastern peoples, the mosque of Soliman, Pera, Dolma-Bahçe; Kadıköy, Galata, its huge silk-carpet bazaar, its coffeehouses—made a magical impression on the Poet.

The intoxicated Poet dizzied in the streets, entered the crowds of the bazaar, moved like a nomad from one coffeehouse to another, observing the people.

He forgot himself in distraction.

He didn't want to leave Constantinople, but it was necessary: the ship was leaving for Russia. (1918a, 81)

Kamensky's trip to Constantinople was an exciting chance opportunity that served as an escape from a discomforting love affair. The poet took advantage of it, obviously impulsively and without particular preparation. The city presented itself to his naive eyes as a series of impressions undifferentiated by cultural experience. Kamensky understood little or no Turkish or Greek and may not even have been able to distinguish the two languages. The complex cultural life of the city sent its sounds and sights in his direction and he recorded them, filtered through the prism of Russian associations and native wit, unimproved by much depth of background knowledge. Lunacharsky has noted a carefree intuitive attitude in Kamensky even when it came to the Russian language:

Kamensky is characterized by a high degree of freedom in dealing with the word. He doesn't look in any dictionaries so as not to make etymological or syntactic mistakes. He believes not only that in his Ural, Kama core there always lies . . . an inexhaustible fund of genuine words coming right from the soil, but generally is not afraid to manipulate words. He takes a word, stretches it out or cuts off some part of it. He combines it with another, twists it into a pretzel, turns it into a ball, throws and catches and bounces it on the ground, making it jump. (1963-67, 2:540)

This unscholarly attitude extends to foreign words as well, as we shall see.

It is immediately obvious that one cannot read this poem linearly, from left to right. The first item encountered on the upper left is an "Й"—not even a whole syllable—and there is space to the right. There are precious few series of words horizontally arranged, the most prevalent verbal structure being a column of individual words arranged in a straight vertical or at a slant. Thus syntax in its usually understood meaning is absent. As a result, lacking any linear-syntactic path to follow, the eye is freed to wander at will over the page, encouraged by certain patterns to follow various paths.

Within the frame of the poem, that is, by leaving aside the marginal titles, captions, and epigraphs (which do have syntax), the eye is drawn to the most prominent word centered in the upper polygon, which serves as the associational focal point and title: *Konstantinopol*. After reaching this focal point, the eye proceeds at will without rigid progression; thus the order of discussion of the remaining features will be rather arbitrary. As with a painting, there is a tendency to explore a pattern in one direction until it is exhausted or is intersected by another interesting pattern. The eye may return to one point several times and depart in a different direction until all the elements are encompassed. The order of each reading, even by the same reader, is likely to differ.

The polygon containing the title is the most complex in content. It is generally the beginning point of exploration because it contains the most boldly printed word. The most striking additional feature of this word is the capitalization of the second and third syllables. The piece STANTI is repeated below in a column of words that shrink by one letter as the list goes down the page. "Stanti" is, according to Shemshurin, the name of the city as heard by the poet (Belenson 1915, 166). If so, he heard it among the Greeks, not the Turks. The next word, *stani*, means nothing in Russian, but is close to a number of words (stan [noun], stany, stan! [imperative]). *Stai* might be the plural of *staya* (flocks) and would therefore be linked to the pigeons and herons to the left. *Sta* could be an inflected form of *sto* (one hundred).[5]

A more comprehensible shrinking column is found to the far right: *matrosy* (sailors), *trosy* (hawsers, ropes), and *osy* (wasps). The first two are obvious fixtures

[5] A comparable example of the shrinking poem by Kamensky occurs in *Roaring Parnassus* (1914, 46):

    YA
Izluchistaya
Luchistaya
Chistaya
Istaya
Staya
Taya
Aya
Ya

in a busy port city and the third could be an image of striped- or dark-uniformed men swarming over the "hive" of a ship.

The overwhelming image of this area is of the Turkish coffeehouse. The words across the top begin to paint this picture. A *narghile* is the renowned Turkish hookah or waterpipe. *Makaka*, a macaque, is possibly a trained monkey on view in the vicinity. And the *uzhimki negrityan* (negroes' grimaces) may be those either of servers at work or their customers. *Feski* (fezes) appear in four places in the area, each time divided into syllables. Twice the word occurs in the upper left below *narghile*, where another syllable *ko* is inserted in the middle so that the second *fe* is read also as the second syllable of *ko-fe* (coffee). The placement of the *ko* to the left forces you to read *ko-fe*, then go on to *ski*, at which point you must backtrack to reuse the *fe*. The division of *feski* in a different place (*fe-ski*) permits this double use. *Ko* also echoes the first two letters of the city's name, near which it is placed.

Feski occurs again at the bottom of the area by itself and then to the right below *tur-ki* (Turks), paralleling its letter structure. This last column is in the same typeface and size as the *stanti* column to the left and there are sonic resonances with it (*i, t, s*) and to the right as well (*tr, s, i*).

Vinograden, prominently displayed, is a neologistic form obviously conveying the presence of grapevines shading the coffeehouse garden (Belenson 1915, 166).[6]

The cryptic *v*'s on their sides are incomprehensible on their own. Shemshurin explains: "The signs 'more than,' 'less than' mark the impression of the arrival [by boat?] of the public and its departure into the city" (ibid., 166). Remaining are three short syllables, *et, ey,* and *all*. These are Turkish words. *All* is the short form of "to take." *Et* is "meat" as in Et Meiden, the famous "Meat Square" where the Janissaries were crushed in 1826. *Ey* is an interjection (also in Russian).

The triangle in the upper left corner begins with the nonsyllabic Й. The significance of this can be elucidated only with the help of Shemshurin:

One of the first impressions upon stepping onto the shore were some strange sounds. One could take them only for the cries of gulls, since at first it was not clear exactly where they were coming from. They were similar to the sound of the letter Й [y] if one shouted it forcefully and loudly. It turned out that it was boys shouting, begging for and thanking for alms. (Ibid., 166)

[6] This is the image of the Turkish cafe as popularized by Pierre Loti's novel-memoirs of Constantinople, *Aziyade* (1876) and *Fantôme d'Orient* (1892); English translation together as *Constantinople* (London, 1927), from which comes the following brief description: "That mean ancient quarter, where I recall vaguely having been once or twice to sit in the sunlight with Achmet, under the aged vine arbor, in the sad little garden of a Turkish cafe . . ." (p. 193). Loti's more favored place was in the suburb of Eyüp where the cafe in question has become a tourist attraction because of its romantic associations and excellent view of the city.

The next item *alá* (Allah) does not need explanation and leads to an association with *galáta*, the district on the European side of the Golden Horn where ships commonly docked. The name is applied also to a tower, the bridge that goes from the district to Istanbul proper, and a main street.[7] Oddly, it is only the latter that Kamensky had in mind, judging by Shemshurin's remarks, and the *T* is explained by Kamensky's having seen several buildings on that street with signs bearing that letter.

Enverbey, Enwer Bey or Enver Pasha (1881-1922), was a Young Turk who came to prominence in 1908-1909. In 1904, the time of Kamensky's first visit, Enwer had only graduated from military school, but by 1914 he had become Minister of War. Shemshurin's explanation is therefore anomalous: "The poet unites the impression of pigeons with the impression of Turkish military personnel who are sometimes called enverbeys." It is probable that in the interim between the experience and the composition of the poem, the poet's recollections were led astray by more recent events.[8] The honorific "bey" (lord, master) is a homophone with the Russian imperative "beat!" and with the final syllable in *golubey* (pigeons, genitive-accusative case), thus producing a trio of otherwise tenuous associations.[9] The "stanza," as Shemshurin points out, both begins and ends with Й.

If the eye follows the diagonal created by Й→T—*galata*—which continues as a genuine line, it lights on another section or "stanza" that also begins "Й," followed by ю and a series of words associated, it seems, partly by sound and partly by meaning. The association of Й and ю is unclear except for a certain similarity of letter shape. The ю is repeated in the middle of *klyuvakh* (beaks), which is for some reason in the prepositional case without its preposition. This is followed by *tsapley* (heron), a bird whose beak is a prominent feature, in the instrumental case, perhaps only because this is the one inflected form of that word that contains an Й. Also, the instrumental can be used for the comparison "like a heron." The next word *polumesyatsy* (half-moons), in boldface, has no obvious connection with the preceding word, except that it is an emblem of Turkey and Islam and generates a near-rhyme verb form *mesyatsya* (they are mixed, kneaded). Although there is no etymological link between *mesyatsy* and *mesyatsya*, they are so close in sound as to force a link into being. There is, of

---

[7] Historically the most plausible explanation of the origin of the name "Galata" is from the Genoese *calata*, "staircase," for the staired streets running from the harbor in that city. Galata has such a famous staired street. See Mitler (1979, 71).

[8] Enver-Bey is also mentioned in Marinetti's manifesto, "The Variety Theatre" (September 29, 1913) (Apollonio 1973, 127).

[9] Among the designations for various military or quasi-military types that might have been the original source the poet garbled are: *Zeibeck* (free soldier), *eshkenji* (regular troops), and *beckjii* (night watchman).

course, a syntactic link as well with the next word: *svetyatsya* (they shine) is syntactically parallel to *mesyatsya*; they are similar in sound and semantically logical (the half-moons shine). The "stanza" ends with a series of "Turkish" words that "are supposed to indicate the varying intensity of light" (ibid., 167). A number of actual Turkish words are not too far away from these "words" (*şahne* = sun; *şahane* = royal, tremendous; *sahin* = inflamed; *sahn-sîm* = moon's disc), but the closest approximations have nothing to do with light (*iyi* = good; *sí* = thirty; *siyy* = fellow; *sin* = fifteenth letter of the alphabet). Once again, the series begins and ends on an Й.

The organizing principle of this area is completely extrinsic and would certainly elude the uninformed reader. It is: "Impressions of mosques and the illumination of the sky. The spires of mosques [presumably minarets] are inscribed on the background of a sky which is somehow surprising for the poet. The spires recall the beaks of herons . . ." (ibid., 166-67). One might add the multiple crescent moons of the mosque domes and arches. By a small stretch of the imagination, the typical configuration of a mosque, such as the Nuru Osmaniye, with minarets on each side and a large central dome, resembles a letter ю or Й [ⓜ]. The half circle of the letter Й is a crescent moon of sorts.

A similar structure is the great cathedral Hagia Sophia, which cannot be omitted from an impression of the city and is given its own triangle to the right of the preceding area. The Russian as given is missing its endings (*Ay Sofi*), which leads one to search for them elsewhere, thereby noting letter links in all directions for all the letters given or needed. The missing *ya* is at the very bottom in the series of *i ya*'s.

The areas discussed above are divided from the ones below them by the only diagonal line that crosses the entire page.

Beginning at the far left of the lower area we find a list of italicized Russian words in various inflected forms, mostly plural, headed by a "soft sign" that enters into the word below it (чьи) and one other word (рыбачьи). All the words have to do with impressions of the port area: faces, donkeys, fishing yawls, ripples, gulls, sails, the bay, and frightening, stern shouting. Syntactic connections are weak, but possible if a few prepositions are supplied. Shemshurin adds that this area "contains something like a translation of a song heard by the poet near the bay. He didn't understand the words but supposed that the Turkish composers couldn't speak in song about anything but women under veils (*chi liki*), about gulls, etc." (ibid., 167). The next section to the right, beginning with *mullahs*, is best described by Shemshurin:

The figure with the French letter is somewhat more complicated than the rest and is explained thus: The poet encountered a multitude of mullahs on the streets and they all seemed to have one and the same face, so that sometimes it occurred to him: wasn't it one and the same mullah seeking an encounter? The poet is superstitious. The profession which brought him to Constantinople is dangerous. There are such occupations (submarine service, bacteriology, aviation, etc.) the indefiniteness of which, the novelty of the activity, the complexity of conditions for maintaining safety, in a word, the *unknown* frightens workers of culture. As always in such circumstances, some people begin to see signs everywhere either favorable for the project underway or unfavorable. The encounter with mullahs seemed to the poet to be this kind of evil omen from fate, the unknown. And so the poet indicated his recollection of the earlier fear of the unknown with the letter N. Below—corals in letters and dots: these are the talisman of a poet who believes in such means and uses them to combat fate. (Ibid., 167)

Thus are explained the series of numbers to the right and the question mark in its own triangle, that is, lucky numbers at dice (or dominos, since 0 and 1 are not numbers that would occur in dice games)[10] and the feeling of uncertainty. "The poet, too, wants luck, therefore he writes '*i ya*' [I, too]" (ibid., 168). The question-mark triangle has its mirror image below it; it is mysteriously blank.

The most puzzling area is the polygon to the left of the question mark. It begins with "minarets," but then continues with a list of words that seem to be names but could be identified only with the help of Kamensky's memoirs: "And I liked the names of Turkish women: Ramzie, Chiriban, Saadet" (1931, 50). The others are probably of similar origin.[11] A unique feature of this area is the fact that the text of the lower portion beginning with "Jerusalum and Joffa"[12] is intersected by a diagonal line and is thus divided into two areas, the only such occurrence in Kamensky's ferroconcrete poems. As a rule, an area is self-con-

---

[10] My thanks to Vladimir Bubrin for this insight. Bubrin's dissertation (1982) contains a chapter on the ferroconcrete poems as well as those discussed in my next chapter, in some cases analyzing them more extensively than I do. He also discusses a poem, "Kinematograf," which is not in my microfilm copy of *Tango with Cows*.

[11] *Ramzi*, a common man's name, is made feminine by the Arabic ending -e; similarly *saadet* (happiness) is made into a feminine name, *Saadete* (not *Saadety*); *Nare* may be from *Noor* (brilliance), also a common name; Hamza is a common man's name, after the uncle of the Prophet, and the *h* is often silent (*amca* has come therefore to mean "uncle"); *tskhare* may be *şaire* (poetess) which begins with a long *sh* sound; -*za* with a long *z* sound can be the verbal root "to give birth to." Turkish vowels are unstable and vary widely from dialect to dialect, which could explain certain discrepancies between standard forms and what Kamensky might have heard. I would like to thank my colleague, the specialist on Turkish history, Dr. Robert W. Olsen, for his helpful suggestions on these and all the other questions of Turkish language and culture connected with this poem.

That these are intended to be women's names is also supported by one of Kamensky's poems, "Persidskaya" (1918b), which paints a picture of the sultan entering his harem and contains these lines (p. 72): "Cham—chally-ay / Otday— / Vozmi. / Saadet— / Cheriban— / Ramzie— / Vsyo ravno. . . ." The first line quoted evidently relates to *challiya* in the next section of "Konstantinopol," discussed in this chapter.

[12] Markov explains that these two cities, then belonging to the Ottoman Empire, were mentioned to "probably [indicate] the poet's wish to continue his travels" (1968, 198). They are also linked to Constantinople by the itinerary of the Fourth Crusade (1202-1204), which never reached its presumed goal because of a diversion to the seat of the Eastern church.

tained. The phrase *ot solntsa* (from the sun) has various possible interpretations, none of them particularly satisfying. The interpretation of the upper portion to the right of "minarets" once again requires the assistance of Shemshurin. Noting that the question mark relates in part to the words *challiya, khattiya, beddiya*, he explains: "The poet was interested in what they meant and found out that this was Germany (*nemmiya*),[13] England (*anniya*),[14] etc." (ibid., 168), and apparently France (*franniya*) and Russia (*russiya*). The letter *o* has a completely hermetic explanation: "Zero with a little cross is a notation of a temperature which, it would seem, is very strange in Constantinople: when the poet arrived in the daytime it was 37°C, in the evening—zero" (ibid., 168).

The remaining areas are relatively straightforward. Below *challiya* and so forth we have: shore (*bereg*), Bosphorus (*Bosfor*), and, once again, coffee. *Kos* in Russian could be the genitive plural of *kosa*, the most likely contextual meaning of which would be "spit," that is, a point of land. The "T" echoes the "T" to the upper left.

At the bottom right corner, the poet plays around with the word for the Turkish coin *piastry*, finding in it *pia* (Latin: sacred, godly, motherly), probably referring to the city, and *astry* (asters),[15] perhaps seen in the market (*rynok*) where Greeks (*greki*) and Persians (*persy*) abound. This also echoes *turki* in the title area.

The simplest area to interpret is that to the far right in the middle. *Pera*, in bold face, is the modern European quarter of the city above Galata. *Gel burda ben severim size chok Stambul* is Turkish for: "Come here I love you alot Istanbul." The wording is peculiar in some respects. *Burda* is the locative form, not the directional form (*bura[ya]*) as it should be (Russian: *gde* vs. *kuda*);[16] the inclusion of *ben* emphasizes "I"; and *size* is the polite form of the pronoun. Additional emphasis is given to *chok* by its slightly bolder typeface.

A general evaluation of the whole poem might lead one to be less than fully satisfied with the final result. Some of the impressions are distorted by apparent ignorance (*enverbey, gel burda*). Others are so cryptically or elliptically presented that it is impossible to gain the desired meaning without authorial explanation (for example, the zero and the > <). Others are only suggestive and not clear. And some are quite clear and easily comprehended. One can certainly argue that the cryptic places are simply solecisms; yet the total effect is reasonably successful and even the cryptic parts can be defended as expressing the sense of

[13] The Turkish name for Germany-Austria happens to be derived from the Slavonic (cf. J. W. Redhouse, *A Lexicon: Turkish and English* [London 1980]), thus the similarity to the Russian *nemetsky*.
[14] Kamensky uses this as the name of a girl in the poem "Morskaya" (1916, 19): "Est strana Dalnyaya / Est strana Daniya / Est imya Anniya / Est imya—Ya." But it is not the Turkish name for England.
[15] If the word was misheard, Kamensky might have been thinking of *aspry*, another Turkish coin.
[16] In the poem "Persiya" from *Stenka Razin* (1916, 78), the correct form *bura* is given: "Ay khyal bura ben / Siverim chok."

mystery and confusion that a complex alien city is likely to produce in a new visitor. Unaided, the reader may not get the precisely intended impression in all instances, but the life and cultural richness of the city does come across in great measure, particularly when one considers the rather small space occupied by the poem.

Visually, the work is more successful. One explores the page, gathering verbal data, both random and ordered, in much the same way one would explore the city itself. What emerges is a complex web of associations where the visual parameters play no small role. If as a text the poem gives a disconnected impression, as a picture it is rather tightly constructed. Links between areas and items are evident everywhere on a variety of levels, from the intersecting diagonals in which the page shape itself participates by its cut-off corner to the scattered individual letters and combinations (КО, IЯ-ИЯ), to the rhythms of word columns and repeated letter shapes, to repeated words (*kofe, feski*), to topographical links (Galata, Pera, Hagia Sophia, Bosphorus, minarets, Jerusalem, Joffa). What is missing are syntactic links—that is, sentence structure, the logical organization that puts everything in its "proper" place. There is a little syntax (*ne bey golubey, gel burda ben severim size chok*) and some potential syntax (*chayki parusakh puglivy krichat strogo*); but most of the text consists of nominative lists, of syntactically independent units linked by other means. This construction frees the reader from linearity. These are Marinetti's "parole in libertà," and the reader may follow any of the available paths or his own whim in exploring the page, just as a visitor may wander through a city by himself without a guide confining him to a specific itinerary.

With Kamensky's remaining ferroconcrete poems we cannot depend on the exegetical assistance of the author or his surrogate. Fortunately, they are generally less difficult to decipher, and we should be able to do this on our own.

The main group of poems, of which "Constantinople" is one, is clearly the product of the same impulse; the poems were probably produced in close succession, perhaps in a matter of days. The order of production is not known and seems irrelevant, so for the sake of convenience we will consider them in order of publication, as far as this can be established. All were published in the first half of 1914.

The next publication, after "Constantinople," was the small booklet *A Naked Man among Clothed* (February 1914a), which includes two ferroconcrete poems, "Cabaret" and "The Mansion S. I. Shchukin."

"Cabaret" (fig. 93) contains associations centered around that subject that are clearly drawn from impressions of various such establishments in diverse places. The general layout is strikingly symmetrical and simple. The clipped-off upper right corner is balanced by a triangle in the lower right and there is a horizontal central dividing line that runs across the page. Another feature calling attention to the clipped corner is its use as a typesetting line for the name "Maksim," one of only two instances of a diagonally laid-out piece of text in the printed ferroconcrete poems (see also fig. 95); everywhere else the type is set horizontally. The central areas above and below the dividing line are both fairly similar in content, involving a jumble of food, drink, music, laughter, and money in a variety of manifestations. In the first category we have: fruits, champagne, Aï, and roasted almonds; in the second: singing, chansonettes, tango, and a gong. The laughter comes, of course, from the crowds of people—apaches, negroes, gypsies, Italians, madames, girls. In connection with the latter, the repetition of "Melle" in juxtaposition to rather large sums of money (10 rubles, 25 rubles) suggests a bit of the skin trade. Scattered about are also names of various cabaretlike places: the bar "Yar,"[17] the cabaret "Zone," Maxim's, a *taverna*, the chansonettes of a *café chantant*, and in the lower right corner a Turkish cafe (memories of Istanbul!).

This "Turkish cafe" area is interesting for its play on *my* and *chal*. *My* (we) by itself provides an echo to the prominent *my* in the center of the page that fits into the phrase "champagne we drink." The *my* on the right generates *chalmy* (turbans). The syllables reversed become *mychal* (he mooed). A bit of humor is interjected, as well: the entrance charge appears to be 1 ruble (*vykhod 1 r*), while the exit charge is 1000 rubles (*vykhod 1000 ru*). *Vykhod* could also be a perform-

---

[17] Probably at the Restaurant "Yar" in Moscow's Petrovsky Park on Tverskaya Street, famous for its gypsy singers.

Fig. 93. V. Kamensky, "Cabaret," from *Tango with Cows*, 1914. Uniform with the version in *A Naked Man among Clothed.*

Fig. 94. V. Kamensky, "The Mansion S. I. Shchukin," from *Tango with Cows*, 1914. Uniform with the version in *A Naked Man among Clothed.*

Fig. 95. V. Kamensky, "Skating Rink," from *First Journal of the Russian Futurists*, 1914.

ance fee or a financial yield. The bottom line expresses this wish: "To go away sunshine lie shore Bosphorus."

The puzzling "NTS" next to *mychal* piques one's curiosity. The answer is found in combination with the "TA" above and to its left, which forms "TANZ" (German, dance) and is close to its Russian offspring *tanets*. Kamensky seems to use word fragments as a technique for getting the reader to search the poem for the missing pieces. Thus *avtomob* (-*il*) (automobile) and *shof* (-*yor*) (chauffeur), below what may be a license plate number (the 6's, the letter B, and the number 3 echo each other's shape), lead us in search of the last syllables; but the closest we come to finding the needed syllables is in *vi-i-li-i-yu-iiii* and so forth, which might indicate a song or the screech of an automobile. I have not gone over every single word in this poem, but the only cryptic point left is the presence of sulphuric acid (H_2SO_4) below the name (?) Prid (or Pried) or maybe *pridat* (add).

"The Mansion S. I. Shchukin" (fig. 94) deals with the exhibition gallery-home of the famous Moscow art collector, Sergey Ivanovich Shchukin (1851-1936).[18] His residence housed an impressive collection of modern European (mainly French) masters and served as a chief source of inspiration for avant-garde Russian painters when they could not travel to Paris. The collection (now in the Hermitage, Leningrad,[19] and in the Pushkin Museum, Moscow) included Impressionists and moderns, in particular Picasso, whose paintings (over 50) "actually swamped Sergei's collection" (Ginsburg 1973, 482).[20] His house was always open to friends when he was in Moscow, and on Sundays it was open to the general public. Kamensky was obviously one of the many who took advantage of Shchukin's hospitality.

The layout of the poem resembles a map of the house, with its central entryway, main staircase (*lestnitsa*), and rooms in various locations displaying artistic focal points. Thus, to the left we have Cézanne and some of his subjects (Mont St.-Jean, a blue dress [*Dame en bleu*], ladies, fruits), with the comment "remained understandable." Above we have Monet with flowers (several paintings), gulls (*Les mouettes*, 1904), and the "fruits, of day, wine" of *Le déjeuner sur l'herbe*. To the upper right, we have Picasso and some of his subjects. Kamensky singles out *Espagnole de l'île Majorque*, *La flûte*, *Le violon*, *Tête de mort senile*, and *Baignade* for mention. To the lower right is a modern French "room": Gauguin (*Vainaoumati téi oa*), Van Gogh (*Arene d'Arles*), Pissarro, le Fauconnier, Maurice Denis, Derain, Constantin Meunier, and, again, Picasso. Below is a Matisse room, probably the actual grand salon that contained twenty paintings by the master, including *Le jardin de Luxembourg*, *Le bois de Boulogne*, *Les ca-*

---

[18] See Ginsburg (1973), 482-85. For a detailed description of the contents of S. I. Shchukin's collection, see Tugenkhold (1914). A list of holdings is found also in Marcadé (1971), 274-77.
[19] See Desargues (1961) for reproductions of many of the paintings referred to in the poem.
[20] See *Paris-Moscou* (1979, 26, for figures; p. 31 for photos); and Barr (1951, 24-25, for photos).

pucines à la danse (*Tanets vokrug nasturtsiy*), and *Café arabe*. Picasso is represented here also. Note that the stairway "leads" to Matisse. Shchukin had commissioned and, after much indecision, ultimately hung Matisse's two huge panels, *The Dance* and *Music*, on the grand staircase of the house (Ginsburg 1973, 483). The display of painters and subjects naturally includes some verbal and visual play by Kamensky, such as, in the Cézanne "room," the repetition of the second syllable of *damy* and *frukty* to highlight the personal pronouns *my* (we) and *ty* (you, informal); and in the Monet "room" the sequential sound linkage of *Mone net ten drapri pri mne* (Monet no shadow draperies by me), the last link containing all but one of the components of the first.

Finally one should note that, in contrast to the other ferroconcrete poems, most of the areas here are open toward the central area, suggesting open doors and the freedom to wander as in a museum. There are, however, three enclosed areas that relate either to the house (upper left triangle) and its piano; or to artistic and/or atmospheric vocabulary: air, color, smell, words, light (lower left quadrilateral); or to objects and fragmentary reactions: Moroccan woman (Matisse: *La Marocaine*), vase of flowers (I love the spring girl, beginning . . . of beliefs . . . of arrival flight), and the play on "Pikassomnoy" where the central syllable has a dual function—*Pikasso* and *so mnoy* (with me).

The *First Journal of the Russian Futurists* (before March 1914) contains one ferroconcrete poem, "Sketing Rin" (fig. 95), that uses a Russian borrowing of the English "skating rink," though Kamensky omits the final consonant. *Roliki* and the lines of *o*'s make it additionally clear that this is a roller rink (as opposed to a *katok* for ice skating), an uncommon institution for which there was no native word. Here words with *o*'s and similar round shapes predominate; music, motion, and legs are the prominent themes. The waltz is even beaten out: *t-ta-ta*. We have both diminishing columns of words (*podskoki, skoki, koki, ko*) and augmenting ones (*my, umy, dumy*), plus a long linkage of sequential associations running diagonally across the top.

Kamensky's key work *Tango with Cows* (March-April 1914b) contains all of the poems discussed thus far ("Skating Rink" has a different layout, however; see fig. 96) plus two additional poems, "The Nikitin Circus" (fig. 97) and "Bathhouse" (fig. 98). The former is basically a list of attractions (names of performers, types of acts, and so forth), plus the sights and sounds of a circus performance. One can, of course, glean from this the impression of a typical circus; but it has not been enlivened imaginatively to any great extent, nor have the names been made meaningful to the reader.

On the other hand, "Bathhouse" is the most accessible of the ferroconcrete poems in that its images merely require a nodding acquaintance with that institution. Closer to home, a gymnasium locker room with showers and a sauna supplies most of the needed associations. At the same time, progression through the poem corresponds more closely to reading a page from the upper left corner to the lower right than has been the case with the other poems. We enter the bath by paying 20 kopecks to the cashier, and we exit with a glance in the mirror and 30 kopecks for a cabby to take us home. In between we are confronted with the rich panorama of bathhouse life.

Having paid the all-important (thus boldly indicated) 20-kopeck entrance fee, we are confronted by abbreviated signs indicating the way to the men's sector (MUZH) and the women's sector (ZHEN). The diagonal to the right creates a sense of expanding space as we go from the cramped cashier entrance to the dressing rooms. The hot and cold faucets are clearly marked; in the dressing room we are surrounded by sagging bare bellies and underwear that the author delicately deemphasizes (VISYAT, ZHIVOTY, *belyo*), and, of course, the sensation of steaminess. A slight grunt (*kryak*) may be ascribed to the effort of undressing among the more elderly clientele.

Once undressed, we may proceed at will to any of the usual activities. Each has its own compartment or area. In the lower left a limp, aching back may be soaped, as described in a contracting column of words. Next door is the steam room with its slippery, slimy boards and tub. A shot of steam merges with a pleasurable "mm" of contentment. The bath attendant keeps the steam coming, producing a "steamy thought." A bast sponge is applied (*vekhotka*). The "soft sign" is the keynote to this area, possibly turning *gul* and *par* into imperatives and, below this, prolonging the slipping and sliding.

In the triangle at top center are the showers, the homonymy of the repeated DUSH suggesting the meaning "shower of souls." The water splashes and sparkles as a figurative elephant is hosed down, ears and all, thus picking up a fragment of the word for shower in USH (of ears).

. 96. V. Kamensky, "Skating
nk," from *Tango with Cows*, 1914.

Fig. 97. V. Kamensky, "The Nikitin Circus," from *Tango with Cows*, 1914.

Fig. 98. V. Kamensky, "Bathhouse," from *Tango with Cows*, 1914.

Below and to the right is an area that is a symphony of sights, sounds, and smells: the coldness of feet on tiles, the smell of birch branches, drops of moisture weeping from the ceiling; there are shoulders (rhyme: *tech-plech*), washrags, throat clearings, grunts of pleasure and effort, as well as a moment of sympathy for an old man having a rough time or simply looking pitiable. On the way out one can weigh one's body (*Te/lo*) for 5 kopecks; result: 5 poods 9 pounds. The *-lo* of *Te/lo* echoes the bottom fragment of the back-washing area.

In the small triangle at the mid-right are the palindromes *nos* and *son*, suggesting that a good bathing clears the "nose" or makes it tingle and makes one "sleepy."

The image of crackling cartilage in the last area of the poem is doubtless that of the salt fish that, with beer, ends the perfect bathing experience. The quadruply repeated *shch* onomatopoetically underlines the sound of the anticipated gustatory delight. There is also a sheet with which to dry off and in which to wrap oneself; it can be rented for 10 kopecks. The sound of the word *prostynya* (sheet) seems to generate the association with piglet (porosyonok)—and thus with the elephant above—and with the animal contentment and corpulence of the typical client. The earthy satisfactions found in the classical Russian bathhouse have been presented in refreshing, concentrated fullness.

All of the poems published in 1914 use the new orthography fairly consistently, except for the constant presence of *i*. The occasional "lapses" may be printer's errors, or they may reflect the actual spelling Kamensky encountered (chiefly in "The Mansion S. I. Shchukin").

The term "ferroconcrete" applies reasonably well to the visual impression of fixed blocks of material linked or reinforced by the iron rods of diagonals.[21] In addition to the generally similar layout of this major set of ferroconcrete poems and the features outlined earlier, another common feature emerges only after careful analysis: all poems deal with enclosed spaces of definable dimensions. There are three house-sized buildings (cabaret, Shchukin's house, bathhouse), two public places (skating rink and circus), and the largest "space," the city of Constantinople. It is possible but unlikely that some of these buildings were actually made of reinforced concrete, since its architectural use began only in the early twentieth century. In the most successful poems, "Bathhouse," "The Mansion S. I. Shchukin," and "Constantinople" (in roughly that order), the physical shape of the page corresponds to the locus rather closely, almost as if it were

---

[21] Compton (1978, 83) elaborates the reinforced concrete image: "If the five-sided page is seen as the mould, the lines dividing it up can be interpreted as rods giving the poem strength. Since the Russian Futurists had been criticizing Marinetti for the onomatopoetic character of his poetry, it is fitting that in his new writing Kamensky began to explore words in a new kind of framework. He appears to have chosen the term 'ferroconcrete' to describe the arrangement of words on the page in direct contrast to the Italian Futurists' 'words in freedom.'"

a map of the place. In the least successful poems, "Skating Rink" and "Circus," the layout does not correspond well to the subject and it does not contribute to one's feeling of being there.

I agree with Markov that "in spite of their bizarre appearance [these poems] are essentially impressionistic" (1968, 198). But I would add that they are impressionistic on a variety of levels—linguistic, topographic, imaginal, sonic, visual—and that these impressions in the best of the poems create a rich fabric of vicarious associative experiences for the reader and do so in a small space, succinctly. It is only the most inferior poem, "Circus," that comes across as little more than a list of facts on one level of experience.

If pure impressionism is bad, it is because the reader is obliged to put the miscellaneous pieces together. One may criticize the poet for requiring the reader to be familiar with the subject of the poem in order to get the poet's meaning ("Constantinople" in particular requires authorial glosses for much of its content). But the other poems are generally as accessible as any other kind of sophisticated poetry, although one must be ready to approach them simultaneously as literature and as a visual experience.

Kamensky's remaining three ferroconcrete poems, those in Kruchonykh's collection *1918* (Tiflis, 1917), produced in collaboration with Kruchonykh and Kirill Zdanevich, are very different from those of 1914. The most immediately obvious difference is in the means of production: handwritten lithography rather than the letterpress of the earlier poems. The next obvious difference is the presence of drawings as part of the first two poems, both of which are in double-page format. Beyond this it is best to consider the poems separately.

"Tiflis" (fig. 99), the first item in the collection, is really just a map of the city, with features most significant to the poet pointed out. Thus we have the river Kura with its two bridges, Vorontsov and Veriis; Mt. David and its funicular to the upper left; and Mt. Kazbek to the mid-right. Oddly, the map is upside down (north on the bottom and south on the top); at each end of the river the direction to the major coastal cities of the Caucasus is mentioned, but Baku is actually to the east of Tiflis and Batum is to the west. Also marked are three important buildings: to the right, *Z. zhivut Kir., V. i Il Zdanevich* (Here live Kirill, Valentina Kirillovna [mother], and Ilya Zdanevich); in the middle, *kipan* (Kipianovskaya Street) *No. 8* (also Kamensky 1916, 133-34), with the letter я coming out of the chimney in smoke, indicating the residence of the poet; to the left *Dukhan* (restaurant) *No. 2 Saero* (a Georgian wine). The post office is indicated above the large black circle, and Golovinsky Avenue, where the Caucasian Printing Association was located (see chapter 5), is marked along the upper bank of the river.

Below the display title of the city is the phrase "the circus where I" and a figure falling from a horse. The box office is also sketched in. This incident is explained in a poem from *Barefoot Girls* (1916, 134-35) called "Ya—v tsirke" (I am in the Circus), where the poet describes his performance tour at the Esikovsky Brothers Circus in Tiflis beginning on October 19, 1916, in which for seven shows he recited poetry on horseback dressed in a brocade kaftan.[22] Why the figure in the drawing is a female and why she is falling remains a mystery.

Toward the bottom of the map are several rather cryptic items. Below the black circle (a reference to Malevich?) is the word *tolpa* (crowd), with a triple "a" in a column, which may be intended to refer the reader to the list of ethnic groups within the city (Georgians, Armenians, Persians, Russians). Each of these nationalities is represented by an expression in its native tongue written in Cyrillic. The Russian "Saryn na kichku" means roughly "Forward, gang!" (a Volga pirates' cry) and is one of Kamensky's favorite expressions, also featured in *Stenka Razin* and a number of other works.[23] The diagram of Saturn with the inscription *Saturnoch* (a compound of Saturn and *noch* [night]) seems to belong to the next poem. Finally, the poet provides an elaborate signature in the lower right corner.

The second poem, "Sun" (fig. 100), is given the subtitle *lubok*, but it more resembles Bely's anthroposophical-astrological diagrams than it does a typical *lubok*. The central image can be formulated as "The bright sun[24] is the face of a

[22] For more on Kamensky in Tiflis, see 1931, 237-42.
[23] See the poem "Tiflis" (1914) in Kamensky (1916, 75-76), as well as an excerpt from *Stenka Razin* (p. 126). The phrase later served as the title of an entire collection of poems (1932).
[24] The neologistic expression "Solntsen-yartsen" is developed in a poem of the same name (1916, 30):

Fig. 99. V. Kamensky, "Tiflis," from *1918*, 1917.

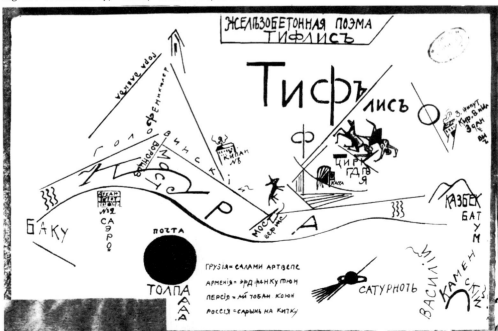

genius," or, in other words, genius is like the sun. Shooting off from the sun and its "divine eye" are rays leading to four vowel letters. Why И is omitted is not clear. Positioned around the circle and on the various rays are words—some neologisms, others not—which relate to the central image. The north-south-east-west rays each contain a formation based on *solntse*: north, "solstice"; south, an echo of the word itself; east, sun confluence; west, becoming the sun.[25] At an angle from each main ray is a subsidiary one: north, meadow of days; south, a play on *keliya* (monk's cell), which translates as "a cell—fir trees—I";[26] east, oranges; west, youth. In some measure, the rays extending in each direction reflect the vowel they lead to. Thus, for north, both words have a stressed A; for south, the main ray works to eliminate everything but the last letter, E, and the side ray has words with stressed e; east, oranges reflect the roundness of the O; west, the ю of *Yunost* (youth) is repeated after the word. Of course both O and ю echo the central circle figure in their shapes.

Around the central circle are words that seem to apply to the "seasons" of

"Solntsen v solntsen. / Yartsen v yartsen. / Razduvayte parusa. / Golubeyte molodye / Udalye golosa. / Slavte zhizn / Privolno-volnuyu / Golubinnuyu privol. / Poyte zdravitsu / Zastolnuyu / Bezshabashnuyu razdol." Translated, we have: "Sunshine into sunshine / Brightness into brightness / Fill the sails. / Turn sky blue, young / Valiant voices / Glorify life / Free-as-can-be / Blue freedom. / Sing to health / At banquet tables / Reckless liberty."

[25] Comparable passages in the poetry are: "Solntsesiyanie / Solntsestoyanie / Solntsesliyanie / V nashikh zvenyashchikh serdtsakh / Ell—le-le" (1916, 29); and also "I—solntse—siyanie / I—solntse—sliyanie / I—solntse—stoyanie / I—solntse—potok" (1918b, 81).

[26] Hermitlike isolation is described in Kamensky's first book *Zemlyanka* (1910).

Fig. 100. V. Kamensky, "Sun," from *1918*, 1917.

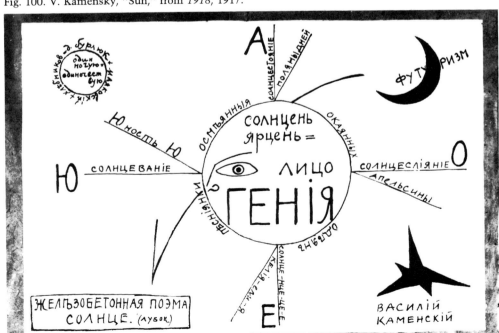

genius: "derided," "cursed," "garbed," and a neologism *pesneyanki* ("songsters," f.).[27] Supplementary heavenly bodies complete the picture: the crescent moon of Futurism, the star of Vasili Kamensky, and another round body circled by Futurists (D. Burliuk, Mayakovsky, and Khlebnikov) containing the short verse *odin nochuyu odinochestvuyu* (I sleep alone. I am lonely).[28]

The third poem in *1918* should perhaps not be considered a ferroconcrete poem at all since its layout is that of a regular poem. However, the title "*K (Klinok)*" (K [Blade]) (fig. 101) suggests the focus of the poem in the letter shape of K. It contains words that prominently display this letter and are more or less related to the shape (pickax, anvil, forging stick, sharply, pierce, cries of the cuckoo and the jackdaw).

Despite the obviously great potential for visual poetry afforded by Kamensky's ferroconcrete poems, the poems of *1918* are already less interesting and

[27] Although it would be difficult to perceive from the present work, these words refer indirectly to the seasons, as the following poem (1916, 5) clearly indicates: "Leto: / Osmeyanka / Osmeyannaya / Osmeyannykh / Osmeyan. // Osen: Okayanka / Okayannaya / Okayannykh / Okayan // Zima: / Odeyanka / Odeyannaya / Odeyannykh / Odeyan."

The version of this poem as it appears in *Moloko kobylits* (Kherson, 1914) omits the season designations but adds the following first stanza: "Odeyanie / Pesniyanka / Pesniyannaya / Pesniyannykh / Pesniyan."

The word *pesniyanka* appears also in another poem (*Croaked Moon*, 2d ed. [1914], 47): "Na stupenyakh pesnepyanstvuyut / Pesniyanki bosikom / Rastsvetaniem tsvetanstvuyut / Taya nezhno snezhny kom."

[28] Also included as a one-line poem in Kamensky (1918b, 6).

Fig. 101. V. Kamensky, "K (Blade)," from *1918*, 1917; drawing by K. Zdanevich.

inventive than those of 1914. These bold and unique experiments lack further development in Kamensky's *oeuvre* mainly because he was less a poet-painter than a poet-orator-musician. He was, in Boris Slutsky's words, one of those poets who

construct their poetry aimed at not so much a reader as a listener, what is more—a mass listener. Kamensky was one of the powerful precursors of the contemporary poetry of the Polytechnical Museum. Hence his verboseness, his repetitions, his love of slogans, of poetic aphorisms, his sonic drive. The heard word needs repetition, and explanation to a much greater extent than the read word. (1977, 22)

One of Kamensky's earlier fans, A. V. Lunacharsky, described him as "a poet from the line of meistersingers, in the style of recent French chansoniers. Here is a semi-dramatic, semi-musical performer of his own 'songs' " (1963-67, 539). A survey of the rest of Kamensky's poetry provides convincing evidence of these remarks, particularly in his frequent onomatopoetic passages. The ferroconcrete poems are uncharacteristic of Kamensky and are a flash in the pan, however striking they may be.

The last of the ferroconcrete poems "K (Blade)," though not a true ferroconcrete poem, is more typical of Kamensky's poetry in the larger sense and is not unique among his works. Other poems of his are devoted to an intense play on one sound, for example, "ю" (1916, 17), which leads us to a consideration of his theoretical pronouncements.

Kamensky, unlike Bely and Kruchonykh, was not given to theorizing. His statements on visual effects consist of one major three-page statement (actually a chapter) (1918a) and a few other brief remarks. The major statement is given here in full:

ю.
What is the Letter.
Vasili Kamensky teaches.
The letter is the ideal-concrete symbol of the impregnation of the world (the word)—the shattered flash of lightning, summoning up thunder (the word)—the beginning of a well-spring rushing out of a foothill in order, in headlong confluence with other springs, to form a stream or rivulet (the word) which flows into the glorious movement of a river (thought) down to the ocean of word creation.
The Letter is an explosion, the Word—a flock of explosions.
Each Letter has its own Fate, its own Song, its life, its color, its personality, its path, its odor, its heart, its purpose.
A Letter—this is a completely separate planet of the universe (words are concepts).
A Letter has its own sketch, sound, flight, spirit, its solidity, its rotation.
The born Word is a divine wedding of several pairs or threes of Letters.
The vowel is the wife.
The consonant—the husband.
Consonants are roots of Letters, fathers.

Vowels are movements, growth, motherhood.

The drawn bow of a hunter is a consonant, and the released arrow—a vowel.

Each Letter is a strictly individual world, a symbolic concentration which gives us an exact definition of internal and external essence.

An example is—

YU	YU
YUnochka	Young girl
YUnaya	Young (fem.)
YUno	Youngly
YUnitsya	Juvenates itself
YUnami yunost	By youngs youth
V iyune yunya.	Juvenating in June
YU—kryloveynaya leynaya	—wing-wafted flowing
YU—rozoutraya raya	—rosy-morninged of heaven
YU—nevesta Sta Pesen	—bride of the Hundred Songs
YU—zhena Dnya	—wife of Day
YU i YA. (1916, 18)	

If one encounters YU in thousands of words and in any lanaguage—YU always brings a word femininity, sonorality, rosy-morningedness, flexibility, arousal.

The letter *K* gives a word hard-cold-sharp materiality: *koren, klinok, kamen, kirka, kost, suk, kovka, kol, kisten.*

The letter *M* is the call of animals: the mmu of a cow, the mme of a sheep, the meow of a cat, ma-ma the call of a baby, *moya, my, molitva, milaya, primanka*—the feeling of life's warmth.

The letter *O* is a wheel of space [*koleso prostora*], *vozdukh, nebo, vysoko.*

The letter *N* is mysticality: *nekto, nevedomy, noch, nachalo, kanun*—negation: *net, ne, nikogda, nemoy.*

The word OKNO [window] = O + K + N + O = means: space and matter (glass and wood + boundary of night + air = OKNO).

Fig. 102. V. Kamensky, "K Stone," from *Soundry of Springstresses*, 1918.

The letter *B*—is a divine-[*bozhestvenno-*] elemental beginning: *bog, bytie, bibliya, byk* (sacred), *budushchee, burya, bedstvie.*
    E—den, tsvet, selene derevo, eley.
    A—arka, raduga, mat, au.
    R—krov, trud, grom, raskal, ugar.
    [И] *I*—is a link,[29] addition, water: *pit, lit, nitka, vino.*
    The word *nebo* [sky] = n + e + b + o = means: unknown + light + divinity + air = *nebo.* (From Kamensky's lecture on word creation [1918a, 123-25])

Kamensky openly illustrates his system in one particular poem "K (Kamen)" (K [Stone]) (1918b, 9; fig. 102), which is not unlike the previously discussed "K (Blade)" from *1918*. It includes an explanation-epigraph straight from the system just described:

    (Derivation of the word *Kamen.*
    + K—sharp—cold—hard
    + A—conjunction—liquid—beginning
    + M—world creation
    + En—sound of falling.)

Such a system is well within the hermetic tradition carried on by Bely (*Glossolalia*), Khlebnikov (in essays of 1919-20) (1968-71, 207-43), and others. Its mystical, theurgic orientation fits better into the Symbolist orientation than the Futurist orientation, if we take Kruchonykh as a typical representative. Or rather, it shows again that the Futurists were often not as far removed from the Symbolists as they insisted.

    It is important to note that while Kamensky uses the term "letter," he does not concern himself much with the letter as a visual, graphic entity. His only remarks—and weak ones at that—that concern the visual aspects of a letter are: "The letter has its own sketch [*risunok*]"; "The letter O is a wheel of space," suggesting a correspondence between round shape and meaning; and "A is an arch, rainbow," also suggesting a shape-meaning correspondence. But these relationships are based on sound almost as much as on shape. Later, Kamensky remarked in retrospect:

This whole "graphic" typographical technique of broken lines of verse and the constructionism of the "ferroconcrete" poems (in the *Journal* and in the book *Tango with Cows,* 1914), all this word structure was developed by me to emphasize the rhythmic beat of the verse material. (1931, 193)

This puts him squarely in line with Bely and, as we shall see, with Mayakovsky. Yet, as with Bely (but to an even greater extent), he was wrong about what he did. There is a decided visual dimension to the ferroconcrete poems that cannot

---

[29] *I* means "and" in Russian.

be subsumed under the rubric of "rhythmic beat" or any other sonic phenomenon. There is space, there is shape, and there is visual linkage that is important and meaningful to the reader.

A significant role was probably also played by the influence of Marinetti, by the Italian Futurist manifestoes, and by the typography of *Lacerba*. If so, Kamensky's response was instantaneous. Marinetti arrived in Moscow on January 26, 1914, and left from Petersburg in early February. *Naked Man* and *Tango* were listed in *Book Chronicle* for publications appearing February 19-26 and March 13-20, respectively. Marinetti's relevant manifesto, "Destruction of Syntax—Imagination without Strings—Words in Freedom," had been published in *Lacerba* in June 1913, and the even more relevant "Technical Manifesto of Futurist Literature" appeared in May 1913, but neither was published in Russian translation until February 1914. No doubt Kamensky became aware of these works as a result of Marinetti's visit.

The following passage from "Destruction of Syntax . . ." seems directly relevant to the ferroconcrete poems:

> Now suppose that a friend of yours gifted with his faculty [of changing the muddy water of life into wine] finds himself in a zone of intense life (revolution, war, shipwreck, earthquake, and so on) and starts right away to tell you his impressions. Do you know what this lyric-excited friend of yours will instinctively do?
>
> He will begin by brutally destroying the syntax of his speech. He wastes no time in building sentences. Punctuation and the right adjectives will mean nothing to him. He will despise subtleties and nuances of language. Breathlessly he will assault your nerves with visual, auditory, olfactory sensations, just as they come to him. The rush of steam-emotion will burst the sentence's steampipe, the valves of punctuation and the adjectival clamp. Fistfuls of essential words in no conventional order. Sole preoccupation of the narrator, to render every vibration of his being. (Apollonio 1973, 98)

If Kamensky fulfilled the requirements for synaesthesia and destruction of syntax advanced here and in the "Technical Manifesto," his emotional dynamism was less than intense. The ferroconcrete poems, as their name suggests, are more static than a steam engine. But what they lose in dynamism and thereby in temporal thrust, they gain in structure and thereby in focused simultaneity.

Yet whether Marinetti's visit provided the impetus for Kamensky's experiments or not (Kamensky claimed independence from Marinetti [Markov 1968, 151-52]), the "ferroconcrete poems" are generally the closest thing to "words in freedom" to be found among the Russians. We should also note that Marinetti's onomatopoetic orientation, which repelled many of the Russians, was in consonance with Kamensky's own inclinations. Thus Kamensky's imitations of real places in the space on a printed page parallel his onomatopoetic imitations of the sounds of nature in his other poems.

Another way of looking at the ferroconcrete poems is to see them as the endpoint of a transition in art forms from oral poetry, which, like music, is sequential but has reference points to anticipated or remembered segments (in music: tones or series of tones; in poetry: rhymes and parallel constructions of all kinds); through written poetry, which retains the sequential features of oral poetry but whose visual form allows immediate reference between lines outside a temporal sequence (you can look ahead or back whenever you choose); finally, to what we have in Kamensky, which, like painting, allows for what Jakobson calls a "reciprocal referral of the factors in question" (1980, 25). That is, the sequential feature of syntax is reduced to a minimum and any piece of text can be linked to any other in whatever temporal order the viewer chooses within certain implied guidelines.

In written language the syntactic-contiguity feature is visible on the page in the string words on a line, while the paradigmatic-comparison feature, though implicit, is invisible. When syntax is destroyed or only implied, as in the ferro-concrete poems, a new balance is struck between the two features. Visually linked words can be treated either syntactically or paradigmatically, or rather syntax and paradigm are *equally* implied.

Certainly this temporary preoccupation with visual expressiveness was a detour from Kamensky's basic orientation. He had begun as a poet, then turned to painting for a while, coming under the influence of his Futurist friends, and later sidelined the painting. For various reasons, he might be inclined to downplay this detour post facto. But it is there.

I have not yet discussed his other typographically oriented poems of 1914 because they are fundamentally different from the ferroconcrete poems and closer to a style brought to a peak by Ilya Zdanevich. These experiments, referred to by Kamensky above as "broken lines of verse," are indeed closer to his mainstream and to the techniques of a number of the other Futurists. They will be considered in the next chapter.

Nevertheless, it is with his ferroconcrete poems that Kamensky made a unique and personal contribution to visual literature, and in this he stands alone and unimitated.

5. Typography

Zdanevich and Others

The key figure in the flowering of typography was Ilya Zdanevich (1894-1975), and its center was Tiflis from 1917 to 1921. Comparable phenomena preceded him, however, and we will look at these before discussing Zdanevich himself.

Despite the rather dramatic effects produced immediately by Kruchonykh with his lithographed books, little experimentation was undertaken by anyone in the area of typography until Kamensky's *A Naked Man among Clothed* and *Tango with Cows*. The only minor exception prior to this was David Burliuk's occasional use of boldface or italics to emphasize words in some of his poems.[1] Nearly all the early Futurists' works were typeset according to convention and were even in the old orthography,[2] which Kruchonykh had upset early on. At best, typographical variety was limited to the use of several different fonts in the course of a collection, with some poems set from one font and others from another (for example, *The Bung*, 1913, *Mares' Milk*, 1914, and *Croaked Moon*, 1914).

As Markov has pointed out (1968, 415), the Futurists were actually not even the first Russians to use capitalization for idiosyncratic effect. In the eighteenth century V. K. Trediakovsky wrote an epigram in which his opponents were purposely insulted by his use of lower-case letters to refer to them while the rest of the text was written in upper case (*Russian Epigram*, 33, 271).

To be sure, posters advertising Futurist events, because of the very nature of display typesetting practices, tended to be more adventurous. In fact, the experiments undertaken with books may well have been inspired by the uncon-

[1] For example, his contributions to *The Bung, Croaked Moon* and *Roaring Parnassus*.
[2] The only exceptions are *Trap for Judges* (1910) and Khlebnikov's *Roar!* (1913), which use a modernized orthography.

strained layouts of posters and their visual effectiveness in drawing the attention of the passer-by (fig. 103).

KHUDAKOV, LOTOV, THE RAYIST POETS, AND D. BURLIUK

It is worth mentioning here an article by one S. Khudakov that appeared in *Donkey's Tail and Target* (July 1913). Markov indicates that Khudakov is probably a pseudonym (1968, 184), and internal evidence leads me to believe that it belongs to Zdanevich. The following discussion is thus based on this assumption.

Khudakov's thorough knowledge of avant-garde painting and literature, his closeness to Larionov and Goncharova in regard to the former[3] and his ultraradical stance in regard to the latter; his evident respect for Italian Futurism;[4] his fondness for pseudonyms; and his general goading extremism fit Zdanevich's character perfectly. In his ultraradical literary position he characterizes Khlebnikov as an epigone of the Symbolists on a par with Sergey Gorodetsky. Even Kruchonykh

[3] Under the pseudonym of Eli Eganbyuri, Zdanevich had written the first monograph-catalogue about these two artists in 1913. He also had coauthored with Larionov the manifesto "Why we paint ourselves," *Argus* (December 1913), 114-18.
[4] Zdanevich's knowledge of Marinetti's activities and his own activities as a purveyor of Marinetti to Russia are discussed in *Iliazd*, 9, 12, 44.

Fig. 103. Poster for Futurists' lecture in Kazan, February 20, 1914.

is not adequately avant-garde; for example, Khudakov felt that *Pomade*, Kruchonykh's only book that was praised faintly for being one of the few "where the word begins to be free," was written in "a delicately sentimental spirit characteristic of that author, with an indefiniteness in its tendency to make the word self-valuable" (Khudakov 1913, 143).

A book singled out for higher praise by Khudakov is Anton Lotov's *Record* (1913; forty copies; illustrated by Larionov). While Markov has even doubted the existence of the book (1968, 403), Khardzhiev believes the author is Bolshakov (1976, 47).[5] Judging by the three substantial excerpts Khudakov quotes from the Lotov book, it is interesting less for its visual effects than for its use of *zaum*. Such is also the case for Khudakov's quotations from Konstantin Bolshakov's manuscript and from the Italian Futurist Palazzeschi [misspelled Palachesci]. The article describes the Italian principles for freeing syntax: verbs only in the infinitive form, only verbally related adjectives, no conjunctions, no adverbs of place or time, no punctuation, more interjections. In contrast to Kamensky's practice, "numerals are not used—the great object of futurist poetry is in endlessness and the number is boundary" (Khudakov 1913, 139). All of this is designed to make language more dynamic. Khudakov attributes these principles to Palazzeschi (also Compton 1978, 83-84) and connects them to the quoted poem, supposedly of 1907. However, these points also closely parallel those made in Marinetti's "Technical Manifesto of Futurist Literature" (May 11, 1912). And Zdanevich himself, in his lecture of September 21, 1921, in Paris entitled "The New Russian Poetry," describes Lotov and Sergeev as "writing rayist poems; creating extraordinary typographic compositions in Moscow" at the end of 1912 (*Iliazd*, 12).

What is most valuable for us, however, is Khudakov's citation of a number of so-called "rayist" poems by the otherwise unknown and evidently unpublished "young" poets N. Bleklov, A. Semyonov, and Reyshper. The examples are reproduced in full with connective comments from pages 144-47 in fig. 104a-d.

Their similarity to the free layouts of Italian Futurist "parole in libertà" of *Lacerba* is not surprising. But the use of vertical and diagonal lettering and geometric figures in Semyonov's poem is unique in the Russian context, though it is only slightly more advanced than parts of Kamensky's ferroconcrete poems

---

[5] Earlier Khardzhiev had thought Lotov was Zdanevich (1968a, 311), which Zdanevich has denied to Markov (1968, 403; *Iliazd*, 12). Zdanevich, as a one-time Dadaist, might not be above a false denial. The title of Terentev's brochure on Zdanevich, *Rekord nezhnosti* (1919a), seems to echo Lotov's title.

In a note Khardzhiev says: "The collection by A. Lotov *Rekord* dedicated to N. Goncharova and illustrated with pneumo-rayist drawings by Larionov, was 'published' in a quantity of forty copies. Not one of them has to this day been uncovered. The initial unraveling of the pseudonym (Lotov—Ilya Zdanevich) was based on the erroneous oral communications of A. Kruchonykh and V. Kamensky. The title of A. Lotov's play 'Pyl-ulitsy pyl' was soon replaced by another ('Plyaska ulits') and the author named K. Bolshakov (cf. sketches by N. Goncharova and the production design by M. Larionov in the journal *Teatr v karikaturakh*, M. 1913, No. 4, and the note 'Futuristicheskaya drama' in the newspaper *Stolichnaya molva* M. 1913, Oct. 7)" (1976, 47).

and Kruchonykh's works. Kruchonykh, in fact, accused these poets of plagiarism (Markov 1967, 69; 1968, 184).

Comparable examples can be found in the work of Ignatev:

Opus 45 Ivana Ignateva	Opus 45 by Ivan Ignatev
N.	N.
Velichayshaya	The greatest
Ѣ	Ѣ
Re.	Re.
umom As	by mind Aboutone
e	s
Б	e
ѣ	l
	f

This is followed by the note: "Opus 45 is written exclusively for visual perception, to hear and recite it is impossible." In *Crushed Skulls* (1913, 12), opus 45 is followed by another note: "In view of technical impotence—I. V. Ignatev's opus 'Azure Logarithm' cannot be reproduced by typolithographic means." One can

Fig. 104. S. Khudakov, pages from *Donkey's Tail and Target*, 1913, showing rayist poems by N. Bleklov, A. Semyonov, and Reyshper.

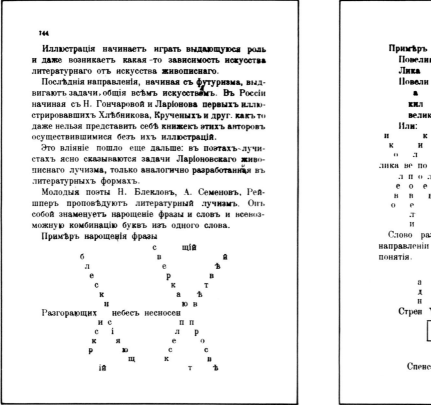

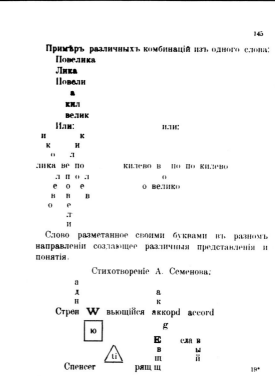

only wonder at the complexities that defied the printing resources of the time, given the possibilities available.

Other members of the Russian Avant Garde experimented with other forms of unorthodox verse typography. For instance, Vadim Shershenevich printed his books of poems *Crematorium* (1919) and *Horse like a Horse* (1920) so that the verses were justified at the right margin instead of the left. He borrowed this device from the Novy Satirikon poet Pyotr Potyomkin, author of *Ludicrous Love* (1908). And in Vasilisk Gnedov's contributions to the collection *Skydiggers* (1913), the first five pages consist of poems with one long "word" per line—that is, there are no spaces between words.

Unless the rayist poems are Khudakov's fabrication, there appears to have been a group of young radicals around Larionov (another possible Khudakov) who produced such poetry for a short time (Markov 1968, 403). That nearly all of it appears to have remained unpublished might be due to the difficulties of setting it in type, as well as to contemporary economic obstacles.

Khudakov's article is interesting also for its comments on the avant-garde illustrated books:

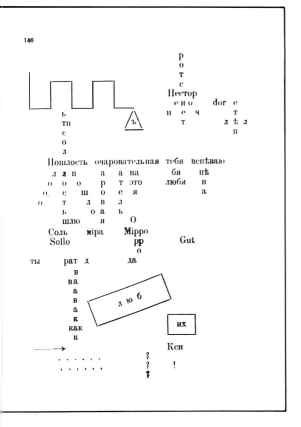

[Lotov's] book is illustrated with the pneumo-rayist drawings of Larionov. It has now become fashionable among contemporary poets to decorate their collections with the drawings of Goncharova and Larionov. But evidently the artists themselves pay little attention to what book they are illustrating, since they have done a lot of illustrations for the poetic works of terribly different poets. On one hand, this is good; but on the other, the illustration loses its meaning for the given book itself and lives an independent life. (Ibid., 142)

Such a comment is true enough for many of those artists' efforts (see chapter 3 on Kruchonykh) and also seems to discount the idea that Khudakov is Larionov himself, who would probably not be so self-critical.

In discussing the rayist poets and the merely mentioned orphist poets, Khudakov adds:

The last two movements appeared as a result of the influence of painting theories bearing the same names.

Now painterly art is beginning to impinge on literary art more.

Illustration begins to play a major role and there even arises a sort of dependence of literary art on painterly art. (Ibid., 43-44)

The rayist poems quoted are presented, of course, as an illustration of rayist painterly principles applied to literature, an oversimplification to which Kruchonykh rightly objected.

The *First Journal of the Russian Futurists* (1914), edited mainly by Shershenevich because Burliuk, Kamensky, and Mayakovsky were on their famous tour of the provinces, contains, in addition to the first efforts in this area by Kamensky, the most daring of David Burliuk's typographical practices. His repertory of effects went beyond emphasizing key words with italics or by capitalization to include: mathematical symbols ($=$, $+$) that have no sonic value (that is, one cannot verbalize the sign without disrupting the obvious meter or, in one instance, the rhyme scheme);[6] *razryadka* (a Russian practice of spacing between letters for emphasis, equivalent to italics); parentheses in odd, unnecessary places; and the use of a bolder, different style font for certain key letters in some poems. An example of the last device is the poem "Railroad Whistlings" (ibid., 38-39) with its special letter form for *r*. This device is motivated by sonic requirements. As Burliuk notes in the parenthetical statement that follows the poem: "(On the sound *r* is concentrated a feeling of harsh severity): *d* and *t*—a feeling of firmness, stability" (ibid., 39). *D* and *T* are, however, not distinguished by a special letter form. The explanation of the function of special typographical devices as expressive (recitational) clues makes this one of the rare instances of such straight-

---

[6] For example (p. 39): "Paravozik kak ptichka / Svisnul i net / *Luna = kovychka +* / Vozvyshenny predmet."

forwardness that we will encounter in the decade 1910-20. Another occurs later for the letter *L* (ibid., 44).

Ordinarily, the reader is left to his own devices to make sense of what he sees on the page. For example, the next poem, "Steam Engine and Tender" (fig. 105a-c), uses special letter forms for other consonants (*v, k, b, r, n,*) for no apparent reason. In "Railroad Whistlings," however, one can easily discern that the fonts are used to call attention to the triple (in the case of *r,* quadruple) repetitions of the sound (see also ibid., 46). Below this is a rare instance of a baroque-style double-columned poem (paramoeon) where the two sides can be read separately or together. (Another example of this is Sergey Tretyakov's poem "Veer" [Fan, 1913] in his *Iron Pause* 1919, 16.) The rhyme scheme of each half emphasizes its independence, while the one solid line across "Pastukh korosty i ovets" (Shepherd of scab and sheep) creates a pressure to read the two together. This line is clever in including an internal semirhyme—*rost*—to rhyme with *rot* (mouth) in the first column, and *ovets* to rhyme with *mertvets* (corpse) in the second column. There is also a baroquelike macaronic rhyme *arendator* (renter)—*Vat r.* The whole poem is a tour de force of eclectic period visual verse effects. Another of the poems, "Zimni poezd" (Winter Train, ibid., 42), is shaped roughly like an inverted pyramid and ends on a single letter, similar to sections of Kamensky's ferroconcrete poems. Included in the series are also slanted or zigzag layouts and fragments of words, with the remainder filled in with dots, no doubt to titillate the prurient imagination.

Generally this series presents an interesting battery of visual effects with good possibilities for development. Some are too obvious (for example, emphasizing sound repetition), but others are intriguing and worthy of further attention.

Fig. 105. D. Burliuk, "Steam Engine and Tender," from *First Journal of the Russian Futurists*, 1914.

Unfortunately, Burliuk did not develop them in his own poetry but remained instead within conservative limits, though he played a role in the radical design of Mayakovsky's *Tragedy* (see chapter 6).

KAMENSKY AND TYPOGRAPHY

This brings us back to Kamensky.

The second, revised edition of *Croaked Moon* (1914) included among its new items two poems by Kamensky, the first of which "From Hieroglyphs to A" (fig. 106) involved some mild typographical nuances in the style of Burliuk, such as capitalized words, an equal sign, numbers (+3, 15), and a long dash at the end. The poem is striking for its use of urban imagery, which is rare in Kamensky (Markov 1968, 179).

In addition to his ferroconcrete "Skating Rink," *The First Journal* included five more poems ("Tango with Cows," "Summons," "Gypsy Woman," "Wanderer Vasili," and "BA-KU-KU"), all of which are typographically expansive. By this I mean that they outshine previous experiments by Burliuk, including those in

Fig. 106. V. Kamensky, "From Hieroglyphs to A," from *Croaked Moon*, second edition, 1914.

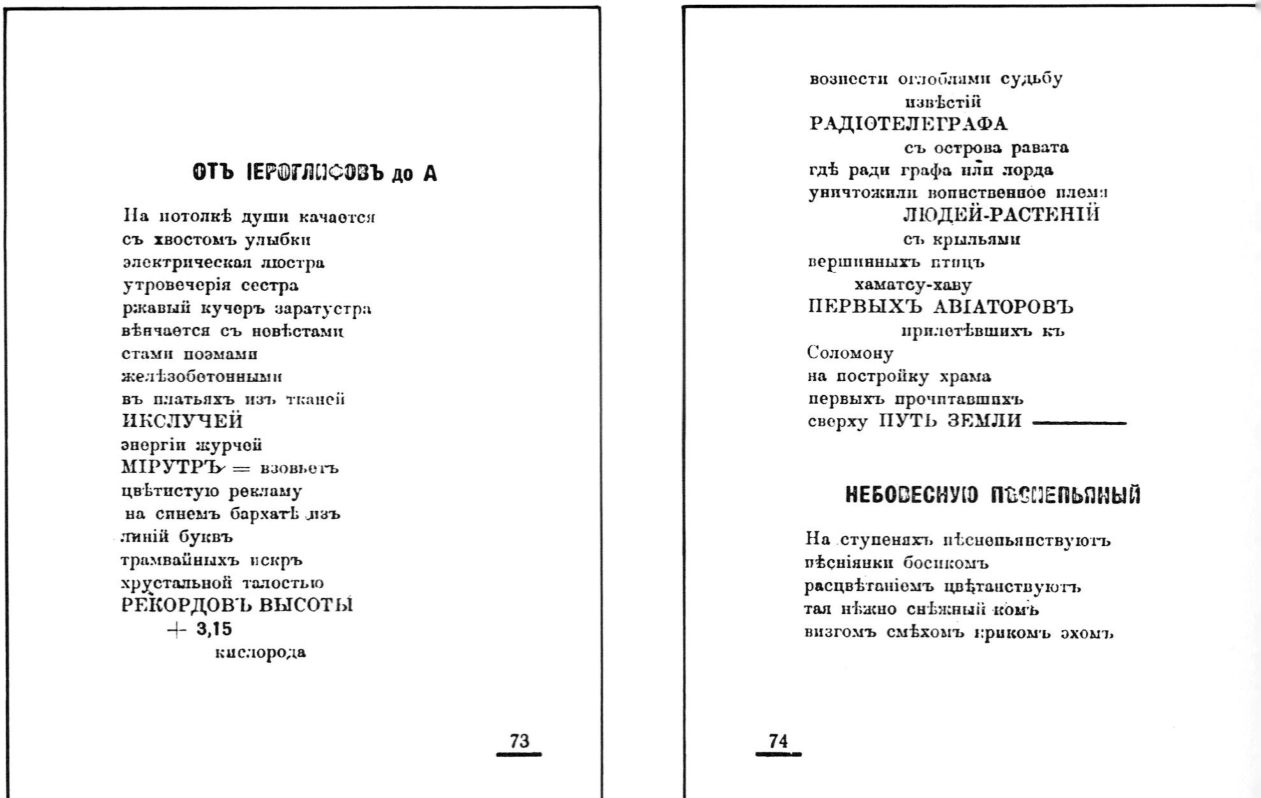

ОТЪ ІЕРОГЛИФОВЪ до A

На потолкѣ души качается
съ хвостомъ улыбки
электрическая люстра
утровечерія сестра
ржавый кучеръ заратустра
вѣнчается съ невѣстами
стами поэмами
желѣзобетонными
въ платьяхъ изъ тканеи
ИКСЛУЧЕЙ
энергіи журчеи
МІРУТРЪ = взовьетъ
цвѣтистую рекламу
на синемъ бархатѣ изъ
линій буквъ
трамвайныхъ искръ
хрустальной талостью
РЕКОРДОВЪ ВЫСОТЫ
+ 3,15
кислорода

вознести оглоблями судьбу
извѣстій
РАДІОТЕЛЕГРАФА
съ острова равата
гдѣ ради графа или лорда
уничтожили воинственное племя
ЛЮДЕЙ-РАСТЕНІЙ
съ крыльями
вершинныхъ птицъ
хаматсу-хаву
ПЕРВЫХЪ АВІАТОРОВЪ
прилетѣвшихъ къ
Соломону
на постройку храма
первыхъ прочитавшихъ
сверху ПУТЬ ЗЕМЛИ ————

НЕБОСВЕСНУЮ ПѢСНЕПЬЯНЫЙ

На ступеняхъ пѣснепьянствуютъ
пѣсняики босикомъ
расцвѣтаніемъ цвѣтанствуютъ
тая нѣжно снѣжный комъ
визгомъ смѣхомъ крикомъ эхомъ

73

74

The First Journal, just discussed. Kamensky immediately moves beyond Burliuk's practice of having a basic typeface, with occasional "decorations," to a broad variety of faces in which it is often difficult to distinguish a "basic" or predominant one.

Of the five poems, "Tango with Cows" (fig. 107) is the most radical in its use of the typesetter's resources. It includes not only unpredictably mixed upper- and lower-case letters, but also boldface in several sizes, italic upper case, and several display letter forms. It even positions two letters (*A* and *O*) on their sides in the word *gramofon* (gramophone). The letters in the word *mosty* (bridges) are distributed in a zigzag, and a long line preceding *revnosti* (jealousy) produces a visual pause and dislocation that separates the noun from its adjective immediately above. All of this is effusive and fun to look at but relatively unexpressive, except that it corresponds to the generally alogical collagelike tenor of the poem itself, as suggested by the title.

The remaining poems are progressively more conservative, but each has its own visual personality or typographical "key." For "Summons" (fig. 108) it is *razryadka* (spacing between letters), which gives the poem a feeling of spacious horizontal linearity. The poem focuses on Kamensky as the pioneer aviator, even giving his credentials in a footnote. "Gypsy Woman" (fig. 109) is dominated by upper-case lettering, perhaps to reflect the larger-than-life romantic profile of the gypsy. "Wanderer Vasili" (fig. 110), with only a few exceptions, does not mix letter styles within words and is predominantly in normal lower-case type, with selected words or lines emphasized in upper case or italics. "BA-KU-KU" (fig. 111) is notable for the visual rhythms created by repeated letters such as *tEl-EgRaFnYe S, PRoVoLoKA, v gOlOve* (telegraph with, wire, in the head), and of

Fig. 107. V. Kamensky, "Tango with Cows," from *First Journal of the Russian Futurists*, 1914.

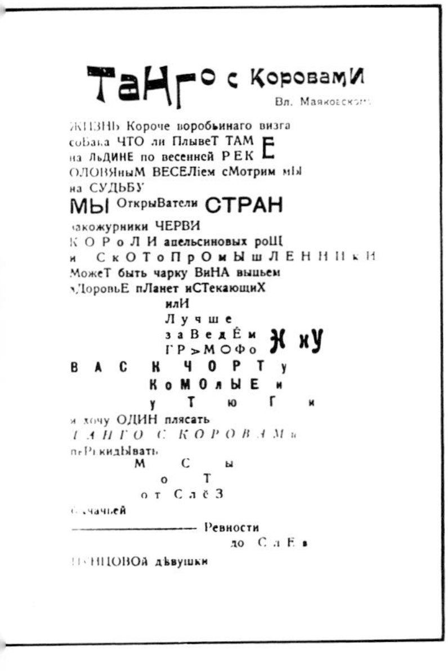

Fig. 108. V. Kamensky, "Summons," from *First Journal of the Russian Futurists*, 1914.

Fig. 109. V. Kamensky, "Gypsy Woman," from *First Journal of the Russian Futurists*, 1914.

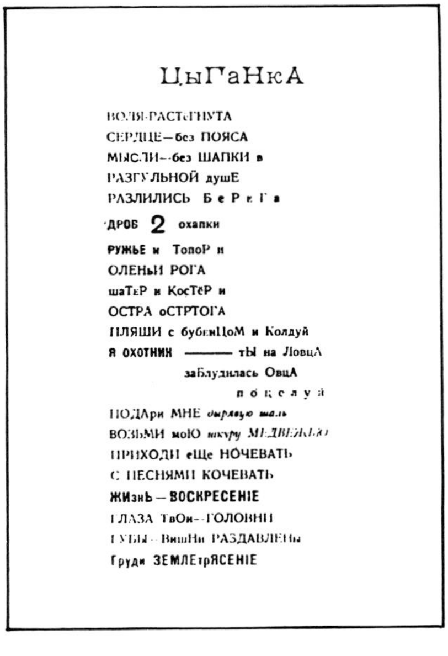

course the key unit KU, *kU-kU-shka kU* (cuckoo koo). In fact, this last poem, though more conservative than the first, comes closer to making sensible expressive use of the devices employed. In the other poems, expressiveness would be posited at the risk of seeing something that is not there.

The first book of the period to use striking typography was *A Naked Man among Clothed* (1914), which included, in addition to the two ferroconcrete poems "Cabaret" and "Mansion S. I. Shchukin" (discussed in the last chapter), a one-page poem that begins with *kokofoniyu dush* (cacophony of souls) and uses a whole spectrum of type fonts. (This poem is another version of "Summons" and also appears in *Tango with Cows* in a slightly expanded version, so I will consider it as part of that work.) The first part of *A Naked Man* also includes some additional verse by Andrey Kravtsov, and makes use of various fonts in addition to its basic italic style. Since this verse was a flash in the pan and it is not clear that Kravtsov did the typography himself, I will not consider him any further.[7]

This brings us back again to a discussion of *Tango*, this time for its innovations in typography. The ferroconcrete poems comprise the second half of the book. The first half consists of a series of "typographic" poems, as Kamensky has called them (Litvinenko 1970, 201), in which typography is used in an unconventional manner. They follow more traditional poetic styles than the ferroconcrete poems; no lines define spatial areas of the page and the type is set horizontally. What is unusual is the mixture of typefaces on the lines and often within individual words.

The first poem, "Vasya Kamensky's Airplane Flight in Warsaw" (fig. 112),

[7] For more on Kravtsov, see Markov (1968, 199-200). Kamensky himself is reported to have considered Kravtsov "not interesting" (Spassky 1940, 23).

Fig. 110. V. Kamensky, "Wanderer Vasily," from *First Journal of the Russian Futurists*, 1914.

Fig. 111. V. Kamensky, "BA-KU-KU," from *First Journal of the Russian Futurists*, 1914.

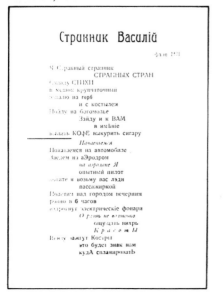

looks like a figure poem of a triangle, but it is accompanied at the bottom by the instruction to "read from the bottom up." It is not, however, a figure poem in the traditional sense, since the shape reflects not some object but rather the process of rising to the heights. The poem is a brilliant visual and sonic evocation of an airplane takeoff. Below a ground line the title is scattered in large letters. As we rise, the letters become less and less massive as they pass from boldface caps to thin italics and end in the dot of an *i*. Each line is an independent unit and in several cases breaks off in midword. Three vertical corridors, determined by the spacing in the bottom line, are forced into the upper lines without regard to word boundary, resulting in some spaces at midword and a lack of space between some words (for example, in the third line up). The poem follows the fragmentary impressions of the pilot as he prepares to take off: "Aerodrome Crowd Mechanic hustles / Contact Propeller Started Up." This is followed by sensations of flight and sky panoramas. The rising tension is reflected in shorter and shorter fragments of thought that end on the high-pitched *i* as the plane disappears from sight. At the end of the poem a sudden shift of perspective occurs: up to that moment we are with the pilot sharing his impressions, but then he slips away from us as if we are still on the ground.

The next poem, "Telephone" (fig. 113), is Kamensky's most elaborate exercise in typography and compares favorably with Zdanevich's *lidantYU azabEEkan*. No line is left untouched by typographic extravagance, and dozens of typefaces, display and normal, are brought into play. The poem conveys one side of a telephone conversation, beginning with the dialing of the number. The second line evokes a phone ring; the third contains a preliminary verbal exchange identifying

Fig. 112. V. Kamensky, "Vasya Kamensky's Airplane Flight in Warsaw," from *Tango with Cows*, 1914.

Fig. 113. V. Kamensky, "Telephone," from *Tango with Cows*, 1914.

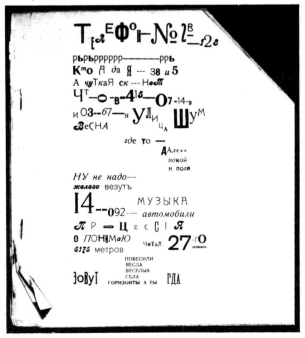

the speakers to one another and ends with what appears to be a body temperature in centigrade indicating a high fever. The next line refers to a "sensitive ch[eekbone?]" (from a toothache?). The remainder of the poem consists of one side of the conversation interlarded with the speaker's mental impressions of his surroundings (such as street, noise, hauling of iron, music, automobiles, and a [funeral] procession). Generally the conversation is on the left side of the page and the external impressions are on the right. A particularly expressive moment occurs midway when a large blank area on the left seems to convey a long monologue by the person on the other end of the line, while, at the mention of "spring" (*vesna*), the poet thinks to himself, "somewhere—far away peace and fields." What emerges is the perception that the poet seems to be physically sick, is tired of the urban bustle, and longs for escape to the country. The typography reflects this emotional disarray, especially when the various numbers are mentioned. Only when the poem speaks of rural matters—"peace and fields," "they stowed the oars, merry villages," "horizons but you"—does the typography gain order and regularity. The column of four words at the bottom is noteworthy as a poetic sound invention; otherwise the poem has no verselike structure. The poem ends elusively on the word fragment "GDA," which by itself could be interpreted as the last syllable of one of the adverbs *kogda* (where), *togda* (then), or *inogda* (sometimes). Yet since the poem has only one other fragment, there is an inclination to interpret it in another way as well. The last line could read: "The horizons call but you are where?" if instead of GDA one reads GDE, which

Fig. 114. V. Kamensky, "Tango with Cows," from *Tango with Cows*, 1914.

would complete the syntactic structure and transform the fragment into a complete word.

The remaining four poems—a neater version of "Tango with Cows" (fig. 114a,b), another variant of "Summons" (fig. 115), "Cinema" (not shown), and a poem written when the poet was eleven years old, which was given a new typographical treatment (fig. 116; see also Kamensky 1918, 38-39)—are relatively tame. The dominant style is italics, but certain words are emphasized in large boldface. The book ends with an ad for *The First Journal of the Russian Futurists* and Kamensky's *Mudhut* (1910) (fig. 117), which is as elaborate as anything else in the book, except perhaps for the front cover (fig. 118). Regarding the latter, Markov says, "The letters of the title and subtitle . . . are placed on the cover in such an involved way that they are scarcely legible" (1968, 199). (On all these poems, see also Bubrin 1982, 126-45.)

Kamensky's own comments on *Tango* are illuminating, despite a certain post facto ring:

> Together with the journal I published a colored pentagonal booklet of ferroconcrete poems *Tango with Cows*—these were poems of constructivism, where for the first time (as also in the journal) I employed ruptures, dislocations, and a stair of stressed lines of versification.
>
> For example (from *First Journal of the Russian Futurists*):

Perekidyvat	To build
mosty	bridges
ot slyoz	from tears
bychachey	of bulls
revnosti	jealousy
do slyoz	to tears
puntsovoy devushki	of a crimson girl

> All these "graphic" typographic techniques of broken verse lines and the constructivism of "ferroconcrete poems" . . . all this word construction was begun by me to emphasize the rhythmic stress of the verse material. If earlier I wrote (*Trap for Judges*):

Byt khochesh mudrym?	You want to be wise?
Letnim utrom	In the summer morning
Vstan rano-rano,	Get up very early,
Khot raz da vstan,	If only once but get up,
I, ne umyvshis,	And, without washing,
Idi umytsya na rostan.	Go wash in the melted snow.

> Now, in 1914 ("Telephone" from *Tango with Cows*):

Vesna	Spring
Gde-to	Somewhere
daleko	far away
pokoy	peace
i polya.	and fields.

> Here the obvious rhythmic stress looks like stairsteps—the word lives at full value and is pronounced abruptly, with separation.

Fig. 115. V. Kamensky, "Summons," from *Tango with Cows*, 1914, showing verso page of wallpaper on which the book was printed.

Fig. 116. V. Kamensky, "barefoot through nettles," from *Tango with Cows*, 1914.

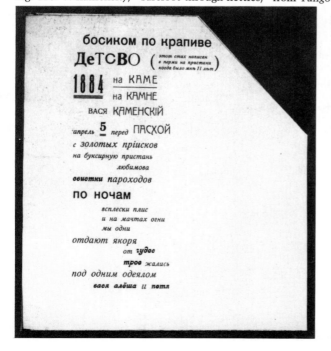
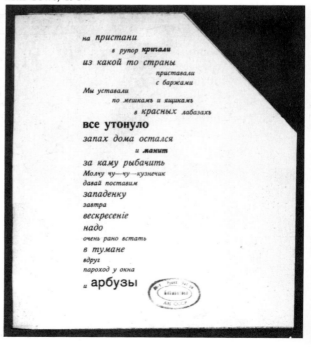

I intentionally took as an example "ordinary" words in order to show how individual, broken-off lines give this "gde-to," "daleko" an aura of special significance.

In this rhythmic method there is no ordinary "cluster of words" and "carillon of sounds," but a sense of precision, a strike of the hammer on the anvil of the word construction, letter construction, number construction.

The emphasis of separated words, letters, the introduction into verse (in boldface) of numbers of various mathematical signs and lines—make the thing dynamic for perception, more easily rememberable (you read, as if musical notes, with the expressiveness of the indicated stress).

I am not now speaking about the possibility of giving by letters alone a graphic picture of the word. For example, in the same poem "Telephone" I depict a funeral procession in letters this way: ProTSeSsIya (procession). Each letter of a different typeface, in addition a narrow *o* placed horizontally, which indicates—the coffin. The very word "protsessiya" is stretched out to look like a procession covering one long line. In this way the *word*, designed for conveying the most precise concept in the given and all other cases, gives the highest precision.

This especially concerns verses where the verbal conception is raised to a cult, where the concrete form exalts content.   (1931, 192-95)

These comments, published in 1931, owe a bit of hindsight to developments by Mayakovsky after 1914. Note that the layout in the quoted poems differs from that in the original in the direction of Mayakovsky's later stepladder line. And the use of the term "constructivism" is an anachronism; the term did not come into use until 1920 (Bann 1974, xxvii). Nevertheless, much of the explanation, in particular the analysis of "protsessiya," no doubt accurately reflects Kamensky

Fig. 117. Advertisement page from *Tango with Cows*, 1914.

Fig. 118. Front cover of *Tango with Cows*, 1914.

at the time. However, the use of typography to convey emphasis is not developed into a clear system that is of value to the reader; rather, it seems to have a decorative function.

ZDANEVICH'S *ASLAABLICHE* AND THE TRANSCRIPTION OF *ZAUM* IN DRAMA

Though no writing system ever corresponds perfectly, grapheme to phoneme, with the oral language it represents, the relationship between written and oral language is conventionally established. Literate people automatically make the necessary adjustments, substitutions, additions, and subtractions with no great difficulty, and the process is virtually subconscious. However, in the context of *zaum*, where the conventional relationship cannot be relied upon, the process breaks down. A given series of letters is not the conventional representation of a recognizable oral word, and the conversion is not automatic.[8] Imprecision in the correspondence between written and oral language would be highlighted were it not for the absence of an a priori oral correspondent, making the issue of imprecision immaterial. The *zaum* word is a precise visual representation of itself. A reader looking at a *zaum* text may wish to verbalize it, and is probably expected to do so,[9] but he does so at his own risk, since the conventional relationship is lacking. But "risk" is perhaps too strong a word, since a mispronounced *zaum* word is not likely to be the cause of a misunderstanding.

More specifically, in Russian the reader is uncertain about where to place the stress in multisyllabic words, as he is with attendant questions of vowel reduction on nonstressed syllables in such words. Should final consonants be devoiced? And so forth. In much of the *zaum* literature, the question of pronunciation need not be answered definitively; indeed, the ambiguities and variety of possibilities may be part of the game, one of its major charms. But in works for the theater, such variety is not practical, since an actor must decide on one pronunciation, at least for a given performance.

---

[8] Actually, even with normal reading material, the process is not quite this simple all the time, and a distinction has to be made between familiar words and new words. As expressed by de Saussure, "We read in two ways: a new or unknown word is spelled out letter by letter; but a common, ordinary word is embraced by a single glance, independently of its letters, so that the image of the whole word acquires an ideographic value" (1959, 34). Whether a word new to the reader can be converted by him into a correctly pronounced oral word depends on a variety of factors involving the writing system, the skill of the reader, and the given word itself. A *zaum* word is therefore not necessarily more difficult to pronounce "correctly" than a word that is new to a certain reader but actually exists in the language.

[9] Shklovsky, in fact, makes the point that the kinetic sensations from articulation are a major source, perhaps the prime source, of pleasure in the "transrational word" (1919, 24).

Among the *zaumniki*, Ilya Zdanevich[10] was one of the few to recognize the need for precision in the written representation of *zaum* and to address the problem seriously. In connection with this we will look at his series of five one-act plays, called collectively *dUnkeeness (aslaablIche): Yanko king of albania* (1918), *Dunkee for Rent* (1919a), *Eester ailend* (1919b), *azthO zgA* (1920), and *lidantYU azabEEkan* (1923).[11] The texts of these plays were typeset under the direct supervision of Zdanevich, initially with his personal participation in the typesetting process itself.[12]

I received the following information from a conversation with V. A. Katanyan in May 1979. The first encounter between Zdanevich and Katanyan occurred in 1917 in Tiflis, when Zdanevich invited Katanyan to meet him at a printing house. According to another source, Zdanevich had become an apprentice at the Caucasian Printing Association (Kavkazskoe tovarishchestvo pechati at 26 Golovinsky Street) in the autumn, and later he himself printed *Yanko*.[13] Katanyan reports that when he entered, he found Zdanevich in the process of setting the type for *Yanko*. Soon after, discouraged by the slowness of work at the first printing house, Zdanevich moved over to the Printing House of the Union of Georgian Cities (Tipografiya Soyuza Gorodov Respubliki Gruzii). According to Katanyan, Zdanevich had developed a sizable income as a result of some secret business dealings with the English, and he could afford to hire a craftsman, Andrey Chernov, who, comments Zdanevich, "executed according to our directions the

---

[10] For Zdanevich's activities relating to Futurism, the prime source is Markov (1968); see also Spassky (1940, 15-21). For a more recent study, with emphasis on Zdanevich's Parisian period (after 1921), see *Hommage à Iliazd* ("Iliazd" is Zdanevich's pseudonym), which is an entire issue of *Bulletin du bibliophile* (1974, no. 2) devoted to Zdanevich; and in particular, see *Iliazd*, the catalogue of the exhibition of his works at the Centre Georges Pompidou, May 10-June 25, 1978. The latter includes a critical article by Olga Djordjadze, "Ilia Zdanevitch et le futurisme russe" (pp. 9-22), a detailed biographical calendar, a complete annotated bibliography of Zdanevich's publications, and a photocopy of *lidantYU fAram*.

[11] The plays are presented here in final order as five acts of the whole cycle; the dates given are publication dates found in the printed editions. The dates provided by the author himself in a bibliography found in *lidantYU* (p. 4) are somewhat different: 1917, 1918, 1919, 1920, and 1922, respectively; but they also do not correspond with the years in which the plays were written. The editions of the second, third, and fourth plays mention a benefit performance for the actress S. G. Melnikova, at which presumably the plays were performed; the respective benefit dates were May 3, 1918; July 19, 1918; and November 22, 1918. This shows that at least the initial versions of the plays were written in 1918 or earlier; *Yanko*, printed in May 1918 according to its colophon, was first performed on December 3, 1916 (*Iliazd*, 50). Although *lidantYU* was published three years after *zgA*, it appears to have been written close to the other plays, since it is listed among other works by the author as *pechataetsa* (in press) in *Eester ailend*, 1919, 2.

[12] To date, only *lidantYU* is available in reprint (in *Iliazd* and on microfiche from Interdocumentation, Switzerland). The original editions are all extreme rarities. Of the five plays, only *azthO zgA* is known to be available in a library (Widener Library at Harvard) in the United States.

[13] The printing of *Yanko* occurred in late 1917 or early 1918, not a year later as stated in *Iliazd*, 14, since the finished book appeared in May 1918.

composition of all the 41° editions during 1919-1920, the date when I left Tiflis for Paris, via Constantinople" (*Iliazd*, 14). Thus for some time at least, Zdanevich stopped getting ink on his fingers, though he obviously supervised the composition and printing very closely.[14] According to Katanyan, two hundred or fewer copies of each book were printed, immediately distributed, and sold, though the cost of printing such a limited edition was not recovered by the sales. Later in Paris, however, the price of the editions, which were also limited, and collector demand were high enough to enable Zdanevich to live on the income from one or two publications a year. We can therefore be confident that the finished products reflect his wishes at that time. Whether the five plays represent a unified whole is a question that will not be addressed here; however, the span of five years between the composition of the first and last plays produced some differences at least in the use of typography to communicate the desired effects. This aspect is what will be discussed here.

Zdanevich retains Cyrillic and its conventions (such as "hard" and "soft" vowel letters) rather than using a more exact phonetic transcription. As a starting point for analysis, we must therefore draw up a list of discrepancies between standard orthography and pronunciation of modern literary Russian. They fall into several large categories that can be subdivided:

I. General sound-letter discrepancies
    1. reduction of unstressed vowels *o, ya, e*
    2. devoicing of final voiced consonants
    3. consonantal assimilation in clusters
    4. lack of a special convention to represent the phonetic hardness of *zh, sh, ts* as opposed to the phonetic softness of *shch, ch*.

II. Particular sound-letter discrepancies
    1. adjectival ending -ogo pronounced -ovo
    2. reflexive suffix -sya pronounced -sa
    3. *yo* not distinguished from *e*, i.e., dieresis not given
    4. initial letter *i* pronounced de-jotized
    5. *ch* pronounced *sh* in certain contexts (chto, konechno)

III. Prosodic features not usually reflected in orthography
    1. stress
    2. intonation, except as indicated by punctuation
    3. pauses, except as indicated by punctuation

IV. Features of orthography not reflected in pronunciation
    1. spacing for proclitics and enclitics (e.g., prepositions and particles)
    2. capitalization
    3. consonant clusters simplified: rus(s)ki, so(l)ntse, poz(d)no, luch(sh)e, grazh(d)ane, ko(g)da, etc.

---

[14] For details of Zdanevich's printing principles and practices, see *Iliazd*, 36-37, 52.

Since all of the plays contain some non-*zaum* Russian, usually at the beginning in the mouth of the *khazyain* (host), we can see that from the outset Zdanevich is consciously trying to bring his spelling close to the pronunciation within the confines of the Cyrillic alphabet and with more or less conventional usage. Thus on page 1 of *Yanko* we have: хазяин, гражани, знаменитава, изыка, бис (без), схожыи, рускими, ых, чюжова, князь, биржофки (fig. 119). Stress is indicated here by setting the stressed vowel and preceding consonant in boldface type. If there is more than one consonant preceding, only the last one is in boldface. Of the standard discrepancies listed above, only a few are not addressed, namely: *ë* is still written as *e*; there is no punctuation at all (with a few exceptions) and no capitalization; and proclitics and enclitics are spaced. In fact, Zdanevich rarely used punctuation in *dUnkeeness* and in general does not concern himself with trying to transcribe intonation precisely.

However, Zdanevich's efforts to be precise in other ways are characterized by a certain inconsistency or sloppiness. Thus in the opening speech of the *khazyain*, side by side with ых (their) and изыка (language), we find и таму (and such) and ляшковай (Lyashkova), that is, reversions to standard orthography. Also the name *Yanko* is spelled everywhere with a final unstressed *o*, except in inflected forms, where it is given the feminine endings that presuppose the reduction of the *o* to an *a*, thus associating the noun with feminine rather than neuter gender.[15] Other peculiarities are the predilection for the Moscow-dialect pronunciation of the adjectival ending -ый as reflected in the transcription -ай (круль албанскай), and the anomalous unjotized spelling ыво жы for его же (his). Zdanevich's phonetic system gives a strange appearance to the text, making it seem

[15] Grot considers the declension of masculine names ending in *o* as if they were feminine nouns to be a colloquial variant "not contrary to the spirit of the language" (1885, 26).

g. 119. Ilya Zdanevich, *Yanko king albania*, 1918, page 1.

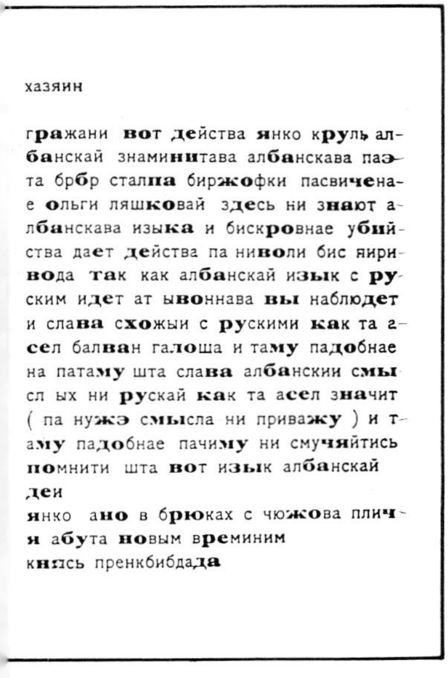

Fig. 120. Ilya Zdanevich, *Yanko king of albania*, 1918, pages 2-3.

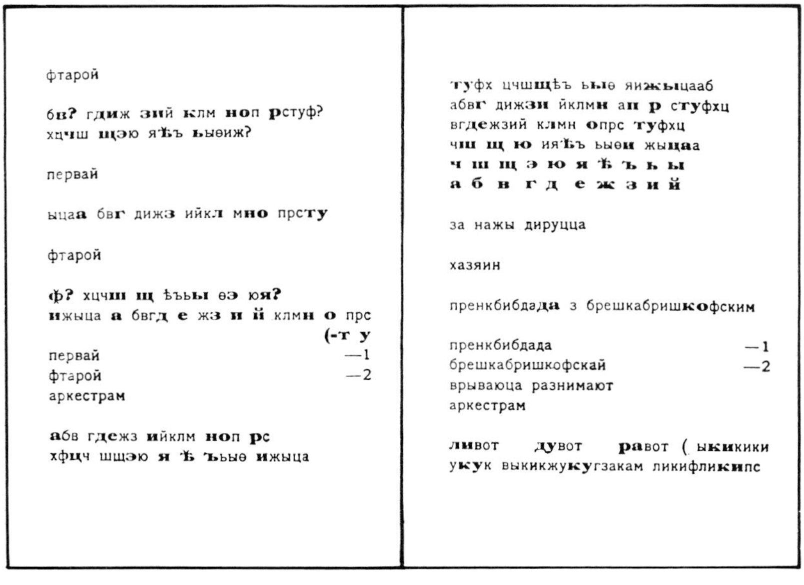

хазяин

гражани вот действа янко круль албанскай знаминитава албанскава пазта брбр сталпа биржофки пасвиченае ольги ляшковай здесь ни знают албанскава изыка и бискровнае убийства дает действа па ниноли бис яиринвода так как албанскаи изык с руским идет ат ывоннава вы наблюдет и слава схожыи с рускими как та асел балван галоша и таму падобнае на патаму шта слава албански смы сл ых ни рускай как та асел значит (па нужэ смысла ни приважу) и таму падобнае пачиму ни смучяйтись помнити шта вот изык албанскай деи
янко ано в брюках с чюжова плич я абута новым времиним
князь пренкбибдада

фтарой

6и? гдиж зий клм ноп рстуф?
хччш щэю я ъ ььеиж?

первай

ыцаа бвг дижз ийкл мно прсту

фтарой

ф? хцчш щ ъььы эо юя?
ижыца а бвгд е жз и ий клмн о прс
(-т у
первай —1
фтарой —2
аркестрам

абв гдежз ийклм ноп рс
хфцч шщэю я ъ ььые ижыца

туфх цчшщъ ьые яижыцааб абвг дижзи йклмн ап р стуфхц вгдежзий клмн опрс туфхц чш щ ю ияъ ыеи жыцаа ч ш щ э ю я ъ ь ы а бв гд е жз и й

за нажы дируцца

хазяин

пренкбибдада з брешкабришкофским

пренкбибдада —1
брешкабришкофскай —2
врываюца разнимают
аркестрам

ливот дувот равот (ыкикики укук выкикжукугзакам ликифликипс

nearly *zaum* even though most of the words in the opening speech of *Yanko* are genuine Russian. Thus the boundary between Russian and *zaum* is blurred.

Nevertheless, not all of the problems with reading the ensuing *zaum* speeches are alleviated by this phonetic system. For instance, there are many "words" with no vowels, only consonants. These derive from a straight listing of the alphabet itself (fig. 120). Thus we have words where the stress evidently falls on a consonant! Or should they be read with the standard vowels added, as done on the preceding page (for example, аб бевегбевиг ге де е)? Then there are ъ? and ь? Also, there are letters from the old orthography such as *i*, ѣ, Ѳ, and *v* whose pronunciation is in doubt: are ѣ and *e*, Ѳ and ф, *v*, and и to be distinguished? Moreover, in addition to other forms of imprecision, there are dozens of unstressed *ya*'s, *e*'s, and *o*'s to be found in the *zaum*.

We find, in general, a competition between visual effects and phonetic precision, here chiefly between the visual string of letters in alphabetic order broken up into words, and the sounds an actor would be called upon to produce when reciting the text on stage. But elsewhere there are lapses without this visual motivation—for example, a whole series of two-syllable *zaum* words such as ли̱вот ду̱вот ра̱вот where the second syllable contains an unstressed *o* written as such. Should one apply *okane* (nonreduction) or *akane* (reduction to *a*)? If the former, then we are dealing with dialectal *zaum*; if the latter, then we have imprecision in spelling. The actor, in short, has some tricky problems left to solve.

The suggestion of dialectal *zaum* might be somewhat facetious, but it does raise the question of an author's ideolect or dialect as a factor in phonetic transcription. Even a superficial knowledge of Russian dialects allows one, with reasonable certainty, to discount the possibility that the evident inconsistencies of transcription are attributable to dialect. Although Zdanevich, a native of Tiflis and son of a Russian professor of French, may or may not have been influenced by southern dialects in his own speech, he clearly focuses on standard literary Russian. Katanyan said that although Zdanevich lisped (*kartavil*), he had no observable accent in Russian. He also said that Zdanevich was a brilliant reader of his *dras* (as Zdanevich called his plays), reading them with a full voice that made a strong impression on the audience.

However, Igor Terentev suggests that ideolect played a role here:

Ilya Zdanevich's voice is well enough audible in *Yanko*, and he focuses visibly on the letter "ы," which allows for easy adoption of the upper "й":
"албанска̱й изык с руским идет от ы̱воннава."
[T.'s spelling corrected to match Zd.'s original.] "ы̱вонный язык" opens up all the pure Russian possibilities, which in *Yanko* however are not used: there is no woman, not one "ьо"—not a drop of moisture.[16]

[16] Terentev's brochure has a huge letter ю on the cover superimposed over the title. On the connection between ю and moisture (*vlaga, vlazhnost*) in Lermontov, see Levinton (1981).

The unusual dryness of the verbal texture, the stiff paper and the dried-yellow-bile-colored cover—forced many to take Ilya Zdanevich as an academician and bureaucrat. (1919a, 10)

This last comment about Zdanevich being "academic" is incredible and obviously said in jest. Nevertheless, as Terentev has it, Zdanevich set out to relieve this "dryness" in his later *dras* by the introduction of anal eroticism, expressed in tenderly inflected *zaum*, and by the introduction of female characters. Be that as it may, the most likely explanation for inconsistencies is imprecision in applying the system of transcription. On the other hand, the case of ливот need not be automatically characterized as a mistake, since the author is free to call for any combination of sounds, and an unstressed *o* pronounced as such is perfectly within the articulatory capacities of a southern Russian. The problem is merely in the uncertainty about whether the author wants vowel reduction here or not. Perfect consistency one way or the other would remove the doubt.

Perhaps the most interesting technical question is the one concerning simultaneous recitation, that hallmark of Dadaism of which Zdanevich's plays contain numerous examples. The first simultaneous poem evidently is dated February 26, 1916, as reported by Tristan Tzara in "Zurich Chronicle" (Motherwell 1951, 235). It was recited in three languages. On the other hand, the Motherwell anthology provides a photocopy of the text of "L'amiral cherche une maison à louer: Poème simultan par R. Huelsenbeck, M. Janko, Tr. Tzara," in which the "Note pour les bourgeois" written by the same Tzara states: "La lecture parallèle que nous avons fait le mars 31, 1916, Huelsenbeck, Janko et moi, était la première réalization scénique de cette esthétique moderne" (ibid., 241). Although it seems unlikely that Zdanevich attended either of these events, if indeed there were two of them (*Iliazd*, 49-50), a copy of the text of "L'amiral" may well have reached him. Zdanevich's first play premiered on December 3, 1916, and the fact that the title character was given a name corresponding *mutatis mutandis* to one of the participants in the Dada event seems more than a coincidence. Dare we claim incidentally that the final vowel in the Russian name was intentionally left as Yank*o* to approximate the French pronunciation? In any case, the Dada event was preceded by theatrical syntheses among the Italian Futurists that included a brief simultaneous recitational of four actors in a playlet by Balla (Tisdall and Bozzolla 1978, 107).

Zdanevich's plays use basically two types of ensembles: the first consists of two or more actors who recite the same text in unison (in *Yanko* the term for this is *khoram* "in chorus"), and the second consists of several actors who recite different texts simultaneously (in *Yanko* the term is *arkestram*, "in orchestra"). The first type presents no technical problems once the text is clearly established: the author merely writes the text for a single reader and indicates which actors compose the chorus. The actors must of course practice in order to produce a good ensemble. The second type is obviously more complex, particularly if the author is interested, as Zdanevich appeared to be, in having the various texts correspond temporally, as in a piece of chamber music. Such an effect is, I think, without precedent in literary history and is rightly claimed by the Dadaists as one of their most unique contributions to world literature. There are no past conventions on the stage or on the printed page for handling this situation. Zdanevich opts in *Yanko* for a rather confusing set of guidelines. The first instance of the direction *arkestram* occurs on the fourth page. While the actors are identified and even assigned numbers in the right-hand margin, the text itself is presented for a single actor. One is forced to conclude that the odd lines are for the first actor and the even lines for the second. This is made more obvious in later instances where the style of the two parts is more clearly differentiated. It would have been much clearer if the numbers at the right had been repeated in the margins of the text as well. It is also not clear whether the parts are supposed to correspond at points other than at the beginnings of the lines (perhaps not even there), since Zdanevich made no attempt to align the parts in any consistent manner.

Later (p. 13; see fig. 121) we come to the first instance where parts of the simultaneous recitation are clearly meant to come together in a unison of several syllables and then go their separate ways again. The ensemble is for three parts, the third part apparently being for the two robbers in unison. (I have added the marginal numbers in fig. 121 to help distinguish the parts.) The principle used here is that the larger the letters in the text, the more parts are included. But one must also distinguish larger letters that indicate stress position. Thus *bmimas*

Fig. 121. Ilya Zdanevich, *Yanko king of albania*, 1918, page 13; numbers in the lower right margin by G. J.

мачтаел азьювапдош
гор а гор а горе гори горо гогор
(—угол
стаят
аркестрам

шэк тук моб —1
бличик мутикикавута бликутжутара—2
аб вг де жз ий кл мн апр ст уф —3
вып глам геп 1
мизивизидицол авжык каючахавиркуя 2
хацэ чишэ щэ ѣъ ь ыю ия өнжыца 3
руж тоц хафхур 1
чичкавихат хавидихой вуишнач ивадат 2
абвг деж зийкл мноп с туфхц 3
боз 1
бмиМАс бмиМАс видидагуей 2
чшщ ѣъьы июя о ижыцаа бвгд 3
вап лыс гун — 1
лидигуивирол самбо — иЗЕж 2
(—ча виона — 3

Fig. 122. Ilya Zdanevich, *Dunkee for Rent*, from the miscellany, *S. G. Melnikovoy*, 1919.

52

зохна
падант абнимант
жыних 6
аркестрам

сФЛЮ. ЮФЯ: ФАЮ. ЫФПЛЮЯЮ
ХАЛАЛИТА. КУРУЯ ФЛЬ-П
юБЯ. ФА ФАЛЬФАЮ: КУМАЧЕН
ПЯЛЬЮСЬ. ПХАХЛИ: МСУСЛИ: ЕН СЬ
мЯСНИ: СОН. ЯМСИ. ЮПХИ: ХОН СЬ
ИЖЫЦА. ИЖЫЦА АКАЯ. АЖАКА

53

ЮШУЮ: ЛИЖЫЦА ИСЯФЫ. ВЕИТИ
БУЯК. УИТ. Н. МУХА. ХОН
ЛАЯПА: ТОЮФКА. БРЮХА. Ф.—АА. ГОН
ФЯФСАЮ. ХЛЯРЦА. ЯЯ. ХЛЮЮЮ. ЯРЦА УЛЮЮ
ХЛЮЮ: УЮ: НУЖЫ. СТАРЦА ПУЗЫРЯ
ФРЯ
ПИРИГОНИЧЬ. ЮХАРЯ
УМИСЬ. Я. ФИЖ. ЛЬ. ЛЬ.

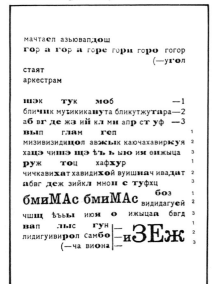

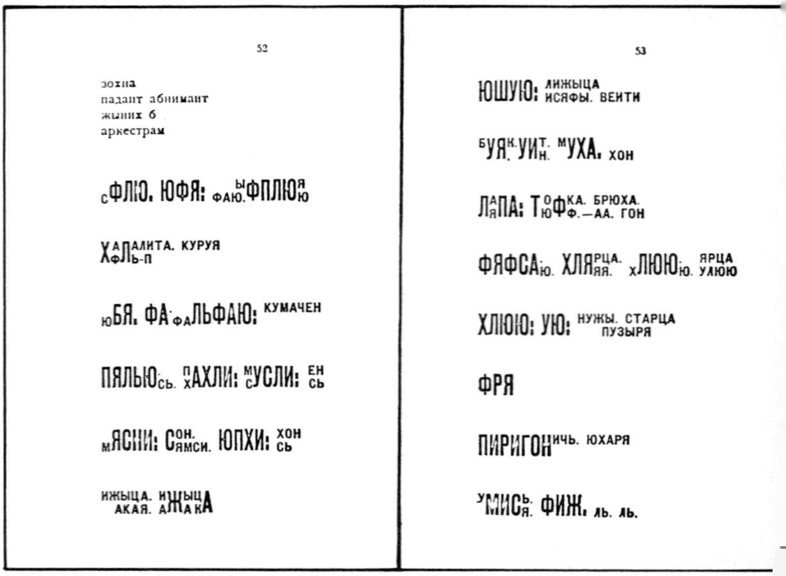

bmimas is for parts 1 and 2 with stress on *ma*, while *zezh* at the bottom of the page is for all three parts with stress on *ze*, the preceding *i* evidently being for parts 2 and 3 only. The open parenthesis indicates a continuation of part 2.[17] The parts themselves are differentiated in content: part 1 is mainly monosyllabic, part 2 contains long words, and part 3 is the alphabet. The main difficulty for actors in such a play would be in the proper timing of the unisons.

Typographical use remains much the same for the next play in the series, *Dunkee for Rent*, except that stressed syllables are indicated by capitalization of the vowel only—certainly an improvement in economy and precision. Although there are no unison choruses, the polyphonic ensemble, a minor feature in the preceding play, here becomes a major element. Obviously Zdanevich knew a good thing when he saw it and wanted to develop it further. Thus we have a duet (fig. 122). Problems of ensemble are minimal in such cases because so much of the text is shared. It seems that the periods indicate a full pause, and what looks like a large colon is evidently a full pause for both unison parts. Missing, however, is any indication of stress position, although of course unison vowels would sound

[17] An illustration of this basic principle of operation can be found in Terentev (1919a, 18). The example there is taken from *Eester ailend*.

Fig. 123. Ilya Zdanevich, *Dunkee for Rent*, from *S. G. Melnikovoy*, 1919.

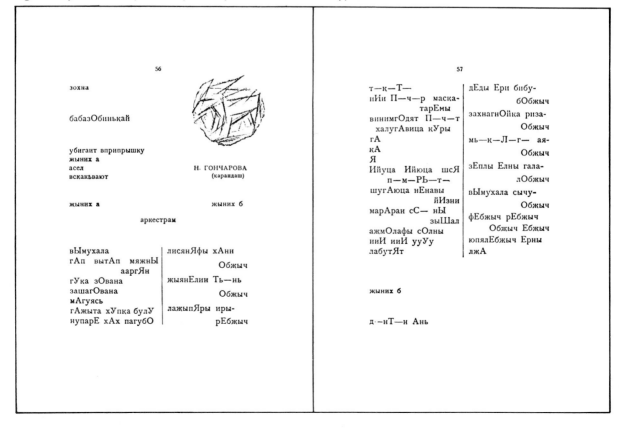

more emphatic than solo vowels. In this play Zdanevich introduces, on a one-time basis only, another type of ensemble format (fig. 123), which consists of a duet written in parallel columns. Having derived a means for producing precision in ensembles (the preceding example), Zdanevich may have chosen this style as a means to convey ensembles that have greater freedom. Here the texts contain no unisons and seem to correspond to ensembles such as the one on the fourth page of *Yanko*.

Dunkee for Rent and *Eester Ailend* were both published in 1919; but although the latter was most likely written after the former (assuming the order of writing corresponded to the order of the plays in the final arrangement of the series), it was printed before it.[18] Conclusive evidence for this can be found in the list of the other works by the author on page 2 of *Eester*, where the status of *Dunkee* is "in press" while *Eester* is obviously already in print. Typographical usage leads one to this conclusion, in any case. Stress is marked in *Eester* for both the vowel and preceding consonant; these are italicized, however, and are not as easy to distinguish as capitalization or boldface. *Arkestram* ensembles are marked in the same style as *Dunkee* for shared sounds, which is the first use of such a typographical technique. *Eester* even contains a four-part *arkestram* ensemble (fig. 124)—a further step in the direction of complexity and by no means easy to read in this format.

In terms of phonetic precision *Eester* makes no advances; indeed, it takes some steps backward, making this play less precise than either of the preceding ones. Thus in the Russian portion we have:

Eester		*Yanko*	
бедная	(poor)	пасвиченае	(dedicated)
аслабят	(they will weaken)		
паследява	(final)		
чужая	(alien)	чюжова	(alien)
вспухшый	(puffed up)	биржофки	(stock market?)
мудрости	(wisdom)		

In the *zaum* portion, matters are even worse, leading one to believe that unstressed vowels *o, e,* and *ya* should not be reduced and that soft and hard variants of all the sibilants are to be used (for example, жгорчыл, жежэ, свычачеблу, лугавща, щухапудра). Even ь makes a new appearance in unexpected places (for example, кишь, акалдышь, мусмишь), nearly all such forms ending in what looks like the second person singular verb desinence. That these are meant to be perceived as verb forms might well explain the retention of the final ь. Indeed, many of the other failures of phonetic precision might also be an attempt by the

[18] *Eester* was later performed in a danced version by Lisica Codreano in Paris on April 29, 1923 (*Iliazd,* 55).

author to retain recognizable morphological patterns, with such morphological recognizability taking precedence over phonetic precision. Or perhaps as *zaum* words approach standard patterns, the author's blindness to imprecision increases. The typographical error hardest to detect is one in which the mistake results in another correctly spelled word (for example, "of" for "on," or "sway" for "away"). Or, when a Slavist transliterates from the Cyrillic to the roman alphabet, he may not notice he has written "peka" instead of "reka."

In several areas *azthO zgA* shows advances over *Dunkee*, its immediate predecessor in publication. Capitalization of the stressed vowel continues, as it will for *lidantYU*, but stress is now reincorporated into the ensembles with shared sounds by making the stressed vowels slightly larger than unstressed vowels. Since there are only three ensembles—all duets—this effect is not complicated and is easily perceived (fig. 125). In the area of phonetic precision, the dieresis is finally introduced to mark the difference between *e* and *ë*. And proclitics are attached to the following word, for example, иадвакАт (andthelawyer; p. 9); фканЕц (intheend; p. 10); насцЗни (onstage; p. 11). On the negative side, while the reflexive particle -ся is written -ца when combined with a preceding *t*, for example, прасыпАица (awakes; p. 11), if it follows a vowel it remains ся, for

g. 124. Ilya Zdanevich, *Eester ailend*, 1919.

example, забрыкАфшавася (who began to kick; p. 9). Instances of unstressed я written as such continue to be found in other contexts as well.

Of interest also in *azthO zgA* is the unexplained, peculiar introduction of *izhitsa* (*v*), for example, зчзавинчЯниим (p. 9), evidently to represent "slAbyi padObiya y" (weak equivalent of *y*), as indicated ultimately in *lidantYU*. In the example, this serves as a semivowel between a preposition and the initial consonant of the following word when together they form a double consonant. In standard orthography this would be spelled: с завенчанием (on your wedding). Another example: лфтиЯтчр = ль в театр (whether to the theatre). Also, ъ is introduced in unexpected places, for example, актърИсу (actress; p. 9). The general effect is to mimic certain singing styles (Shalyapin, gypsy romances), where such semivowels are added for expressive purposes (see Selvinsky below). In addition, the letter *h* makes its first appearance in *zgA* (p. 13). In *lidantYU*, *h* is characterized as standing for "zvonkay kh" (sonant *kh*).

The culminating play of the series is *lidantYU azabEEkan*. It is the longest and most complex, if not the greatest, work of *zaum* in world literature.[19] In his notes of 1922, Zdanevich wrote of *lidantYU*:

The idea of the book, of the typographical characters of *zaum* have attained in this book their highest development and their perfection. This is not the extinction of the work, it

[19] On the painter M. Le-Dantyu and his role as a model for the hero of Zdanevich's play see Compton 1978, 64-65, and Zhadova (1975, 154, note 3, and 126).

Fig. 125. Ilya Zdanevich, *azthO zgA*, 1920.

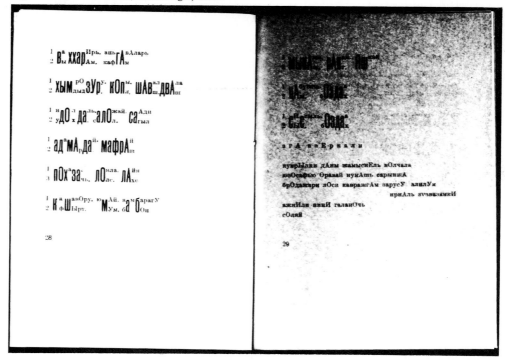

is its summit. This book is the synthesis and the overture, seen in regard to *zaum*, of everything that has happened during the last ten years in the radical Russian Avant Garde. (*Iliazd*, 22)

Introduced, finally, is a table (called "uslOviya chtEnya," conditions for reading) that explains the various symbols, terms, and practices employed in the text (fig. 126). A number of new symbols are used for newly introduced sounds, including a tongue click, and previously used practices explained. The terms for types of ensembles have changed: *khoram* is now called *saglAsna*, and *arkestram* is called *sabOram*. And the practice of using various depths of indentation to indicate "beginning of a speech," "beginning of an expression" is introduced, which is a helpful syntactic signal, given the general absence of punctuation. Finally, there is a list of features that are "omitted in this edition," but presumably should be a part of a proper performance; it even includes instructions for "the number of syllables per minute."

The system designed by Zdanevich for conveying these other features is contained in his archives (fig. 127a,b).[20] Pitch (*vysatá tóna*) is indicated by a vertical line above and below a median position; volume (*síla gólasa*) is indicated by a horizontal line of varying length; the two lines are marked as intersecting above the stressed vowel. A caesura is marked by a double vertical line, and pauses of various kinds by periods. A later refinement dated February 27, 1922 uses solid, open, or divided circles for further precision. Tempo is given in numbers for "syllables per minute." The entire system is illustrated in the first line

[20] I would like to express my thanks to Mme. Helène Zdanevitch-ILIAZD for graciously supplying this material.

Fig. 126. Ilya Zdanevich, *lidantYU azabEEkan*, 1923.

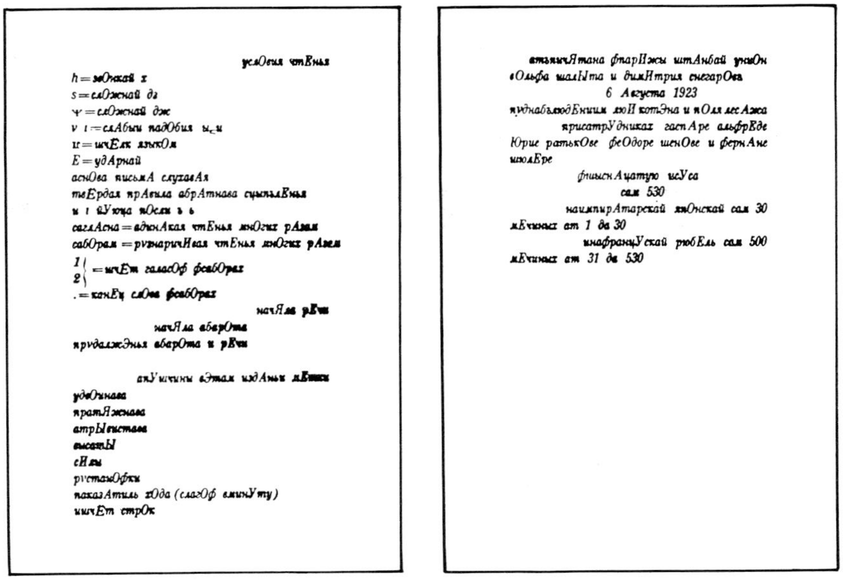
услОвия чтЕнья
h = мОжкай х
s = слОжнай дз
ѱ = слОжнай дж
ν ι = слАбыи падОбия ы и
ɯ = щЕлк языкОм
E = удАрнай
аснОва письмА слухавАя
тьвЕрдая прАвила абрАтнава сцыпльЕнья
ы ι йУюща пОслы ъ ь
саглАсна = адинАкая чтЕнья мнОгих рАлей
сабОрам = рузнаричНая чтЕнья мнОгих рАлей
1 | 2 | = щчЕт галасОф фсабОрах
. = канЕц слОва фсабОрах
начЯла рЕчи
начЯла абарОта
прудалжЭнья абарОта и рЕчи
апУщиныи вЭтам издАньи лЕпки
удвОинава
пратЯжнава
атрЫвистава
высатЫ
сИлы
рустанОфки
паказАтиль хОда (слагОф вминУту)
щичЕт стрОк

атпичЯтана фпарИжы штАнбай унюОн
вОльфа шалЫта и димИтрия снегарОва
6 Августа 1923
пуднабъюдЕнием люИ котЭна и пОля лесАжа
присатрУдниках гаспАре альфрЕде
Юрие ратькОве феОдоре шенОве и фернАне
шюлЕре
финыскАцатую исУса
сам 530
наимпирАтарскай япОнскай сам 30
мЕчиных ат 1 да 30
инафранцУскай рюбЕль сам 500
мЕчиных ат 31 да 530

of fig. 127a. The second page (fig. 127b) repeats information given in the published version, but adds details on the role of ь and ъ as separators, and clarifies the use of "soft" vowels with jotization.

A glance at the first page of the play's text makes it clear that something else has been introduced, namely, the use of a variety of typefaces, sizes, and line positions, purely for visual effect rather than for practical purposes (fig. 128). An actor might find this hodgepodge counterproductive because it makes the script much harder to read than conventional typesetting (stress position is less clear, for instance); however, it makes the text a visual feast with a graphic value all its own, which in its own right might be stimulating to an interpreter. We must remember, however, that Zdanevich was by then living permanently in Paris and felt in the end that he was publishing a monument to an era gone by. His desire for a live performance had waned, since a performance seemed out of the question in 1923 and in a French environment, and he saw no harm in enlivening the text visually at the expense of readability.[21] His new techniques for phonetic precision

[21] Relevant here are the following comments on *lidantYU* by Zdanevich, as quoted in *Iliazd*, 60-61: "Ce livre est mort car son temps est passé. Il n'y a pas longtemps encore, quand je l'écrivais, ce livre était la vie. Maintenant il n'est que le testament d'un temps irréversiblement disparu.

"Je me demande si vivra longtemps dans notre mémoire ce temps d'affirmation, d'espoirs naifs, de deraison, de jeunesse et de lutte. Je me demande si nous nous souviendrons encore longtemps de ces jeux de l'esprit, de cette audace indispensable."

Fig. 127. Ilya Zdanevich, "Verse Signs," manuscript (courtesy of Helène Zdanevitch-ILIAZD).

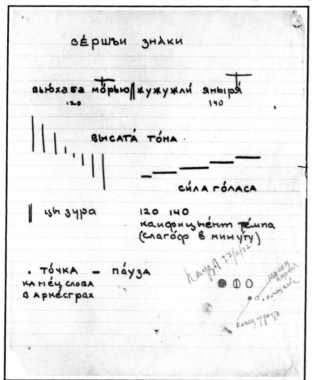
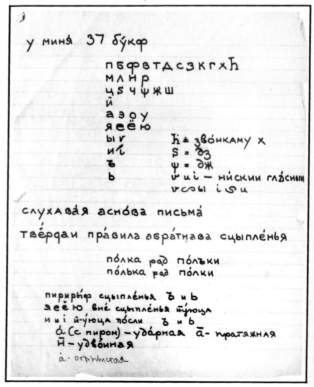

include an odd one in which consonants ending words that are not proclitic adhere to the following word, thus anachronistically and incorrectly restoring open syllables, for example, нииспытА фпатърЕта (nottryin gaportrit); гастИнцэ мзнАхарю (azapresen tuthasorserer); цАръстии мбОжым (heve nhelpm) (fig. 128).

In spite of these efforts at what seems to be overscrupulous phonetic precision, the old faults, though somewhat fewer, remain in evidence. Unstressed *ya*'s and *e*'s are still found in the Russian part of the text (in the *zaum* they abound), as are initial *i*'s. With the introduction of *ё* comes the possibility of unstressed *ё*, and examples of this also abound in the *zaum*. Sibilants are carefully used in the Russian, but there are a few lapses in the *zaum* (снЯчая, p. 12, and жю, p. 26; fig. 129), which may be intentional. The letter щ is not found in the text, but these are a few examples of what probably serve as substitutes: шчя (fig. 129), злышчь, and хишчь (p. 55).

Choruses attain a stunning level of development in this play. In particular,

"Je jette ce livre, adieu jeunesse, adieu zaoum, adieu long chemin de l'acrobatie, de l'équivoque, de la froide raison, de tout, tout et tout" (texte inédit, Paris, 1923).

Fig. 128. Ilya Zdanevich, *lidantYU azabEEkan*, 1923.

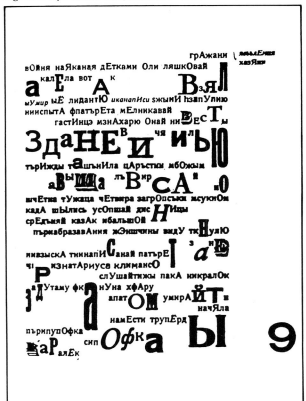

the polyphonic (*sabOram*) type achieves a remarkable elaborateness, reaching a final chorus with eleven voices! Given this complexity, Zdanevich wisely avoids the typographical effusions found on the solo pages. Instead, he uses a system of representation that supersedes in effectiveness that used for the preceding plays. A good example is found on pp. 26-27 (fig. 129). Here the words in the various parts are simply listed in a column. When the stressed vowels are meant to be simultaneous, they are lined up vertically; when in series, they are spread out at an angle whose slant indicates how close in time they should be. While the exact tempo is not given, the spacing gives a fairly good idea of the relative timing. The content of each part is immediately clear, and use of this text for performances would not be a problem, even with as many as six, seven, or eleven parts (fig. 130). Zdanevich had thus solved the problems inherent in simultaneous recitations, and the further possibilities for using the device are (or were) unlimited.

One can imagine even without the direct experience that the effect of eleven different words simultaneously spoken or shouted would be a striking one, comparable to a complex orchestral chord in which the instruments and notes (here the voices and phonetic components) could not be isolated, but would form a

Fig. 129. Ilya Zdanevich, *lidantYU azabEEkan*, 1923.

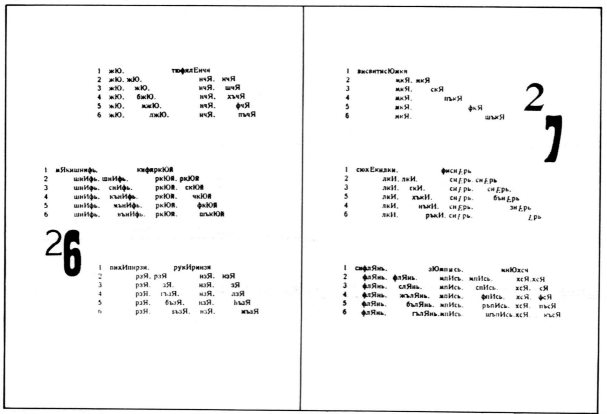

textural amalgam. Whether they were real words or *zaum* words would hardly matter. As Zdanevich remarked in a Paris lecture on November 27, 1921: "Dans la poésie orchestrale, le langage poétique quitte brusquement le cadre individuel et se libère définitivement" (*Iliazd*, 94).

Zdanevich was the first to devote extensive attention to typography as a device for greater precision in the transcription of language—more so than was the case with standard (old or new) orthography. But others had already been concerned with the matter. For instance, stresses were marked on Khlebnikov's poem "Bobeobi pelis guby" when it appeared in *A Slap in the Face of Public Taste* (1912, 7) and in *Te-li-le* (1914c); and the poem by Alyagrov (Roman Jakobson) at the end of *Transrational Boog* (1915b) had used italics to indicate stress position:

Алягров
мзглыбжвую йихъяньдрью чтлэщк хн фя съп скыполза
а Втаб-длкни тьянра какайзчди евреец чернильница

Разсѣяность.
удуша янки аркан

Fig. 130. Ilya Zdanevich, *lidantYU azabEEkan*, 1923.

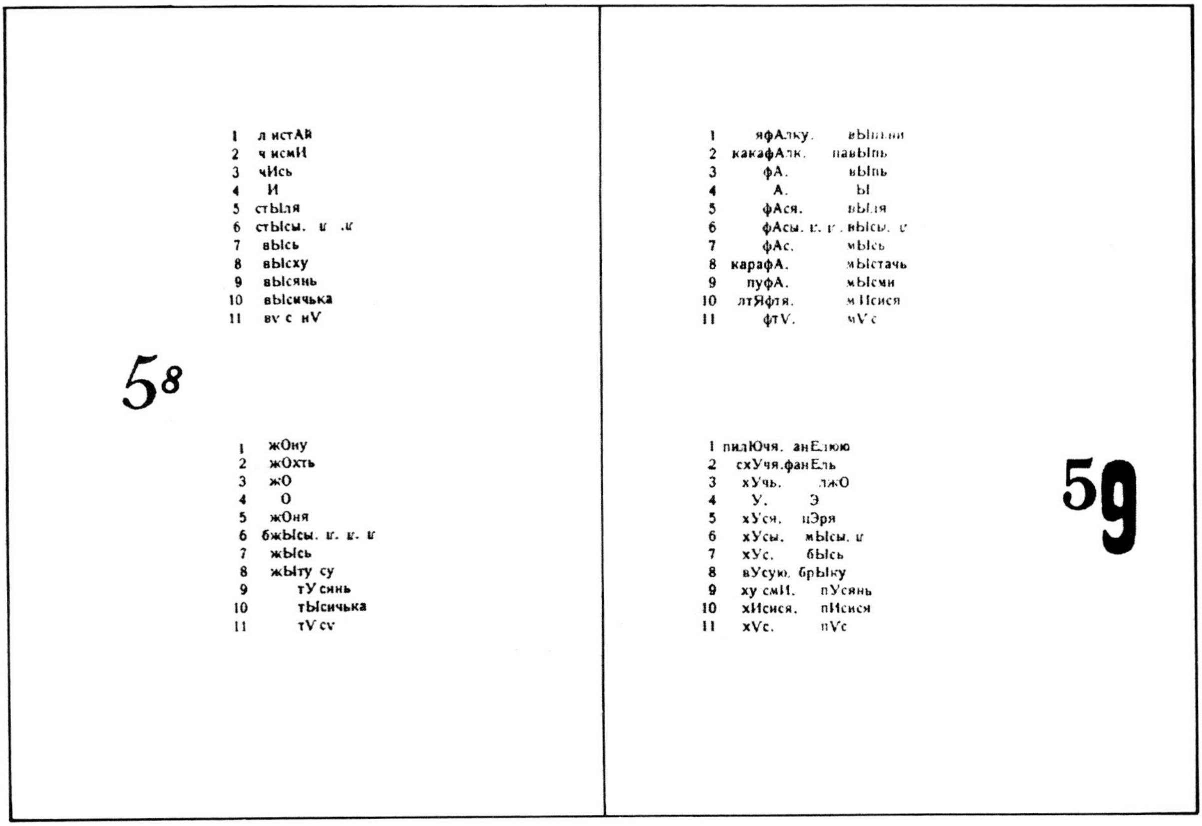

1 л истАй
2 ч исмИ
3 чИсь
4 И
5 стЫля
6 стЫсы. ľľ .ľľ
7 вЫсь
8 вЫсху
9 вЫсянь
10 вЫсичька
11 вv с нV

58

1 жОну
2 жОхть
3 жО
4 О
5 жОня
6 бжЫсы. ľľ. ľľ. ľľ
7 жЫсь
8 жЫту су
9 тУ синь
10 тЫсичька
11 тV сv

1 яфАлку. вЫлми
2 какафАлк. павЫпь
3 фА. вЫпь
4 А. Ы
5 фАся. вЫля
6 фАсы. ľľ. ľľ. вЫсы. ľľ
7 фАс. мЫсь
8 карафА. мЫстачь
9 пуфА. мЫсми
10 лтЯфтя. мИсися
11 фтV. мVс

1 пилЮчя. анЕлюю
2 схУчя.фанЕль
3 хУчь. лжО
4 У. Э
5 хУся. цЭря
6 хУсы. мЫсы. ľľ
7 хУс. бЫсь
8 вУсую. брЫку
9 ху смИ. пУсянь
10 хИсися. пИсися
11 хVс. пVс

59

канкан армянк
душаянки китаянки
кит ы так и никая
армяк
этикэтка тихая ткань тик
ткания кантик
а о оршат кянт и тюк
таки мяк
тмянты хняку шкям
анмя кыкь
атразиксіію намёк умён тамя
мянк—ушатя
не аваопостне передовица
передник гублицю стоп
тляк в ваго передавясь

But Zdanevich was the first to work out a fully developed system which included not only stress, but vowel reduction, consonantal elisions, and so forth, as well as (on paper if not in print) tempo, pitch, and volume, making each of his books a "véritable partition" (*Iliazd*, 8).

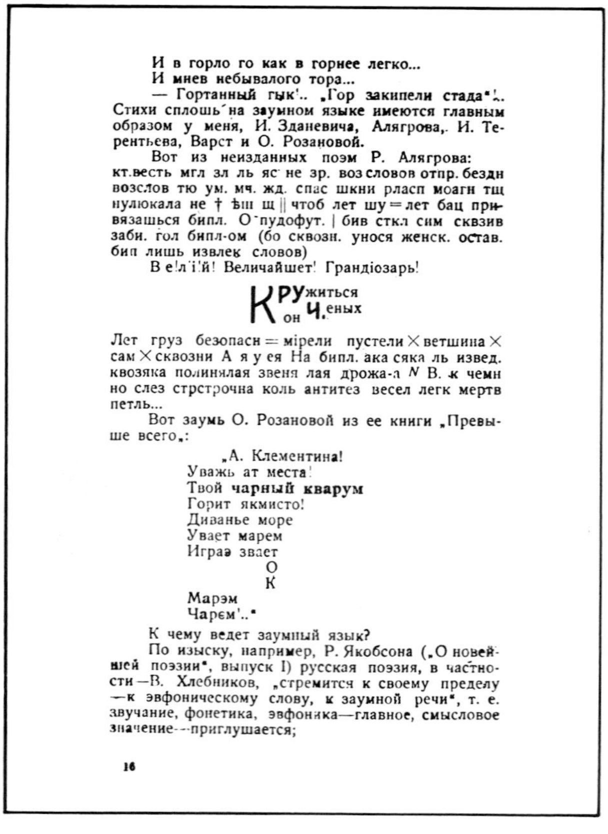

Fig. 131. A. Kruchonykh, G. Petnikov, and V. Khlebnikov, *Zaumniki*, 1922, showing (one-third down the page) a letter poem by R. Alyagrov (Jakobson).

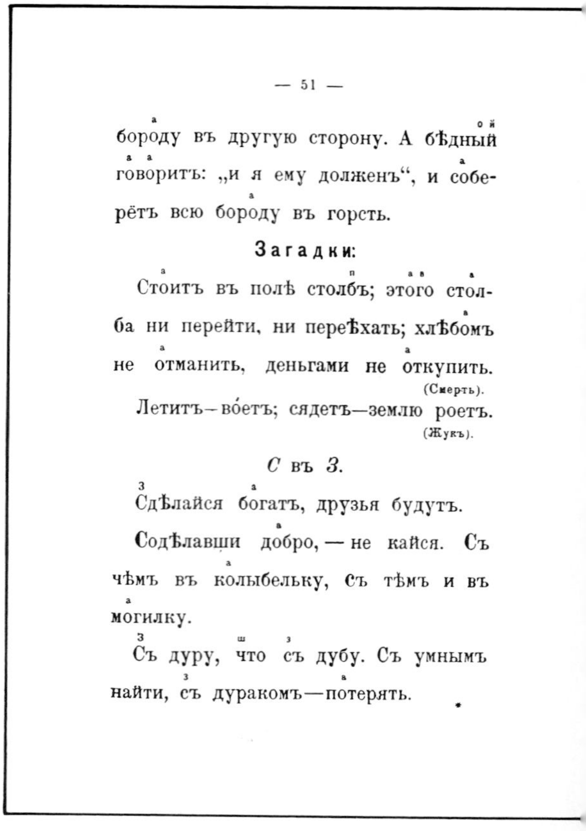

Fig. 132. L. N. Tolstoy, *Alphabet Book*, 1871-72.

Jakobson himself had also been experimenting with verse graphics and was interested in similar experiments by others, as a letter to Khlebnikov (February 1914) indicates:

Remember, Viktor Vladimirovich, you told me that our alphabet is too poor for poetry and how could one not reach a dead end with alphabet-letter verses. I am becoming more and more convinced that you are mistaken. These days I've come to a curious new idea, which is why I am writing to you. This novelty is the interweaving of letters, a kind of analogy to musical chords. Here one can achieve a simultaneity of two or more letters and, besides this, a variety of shape combinations which establishes various mutual relationships between letters. All this enriches verse and opens up new paths. . . . When I asked you what *you* have come to, the answer was—to numbers. You know, Viktor Vladimirovich, it seems to me one can create verse from numbers. The number is a double-edged sword, extremely concrete and extremely abstract, arbitrary and fatally exact, logical and meaningless, limited and infinite.[22] Pardon me for the rhetoric. You're well acquainted with numbers and therefore if you consider a poetry of numbers perhaps an unacceptable paradox but a witty one, please try to give me if only a small sample of such poetry.

Khardzhiev, the owner of the letter, says that it contains examples of Jakobson's letter-poems, but he does not share them with us. Jakobson also reportedly sent Kruchonykh some samples and asked for his opinion. (Later, in 1915, Kruchonykh himself wrote a "poem of numbers," but it does not survive [Khardzhiev 1976, 56-57].) In *Zaumniki* (1922), Kruchonykh quotes a short selection of Jakobson's *zaum*, which happens to include a piece that looks like a Zdanevich chorus (fig. 131). If we read it as a chorus, we get two independent words, *kruzhitsya* (turns) and *konchenykh* (should be *konchennykh*, finished); but if we read it zigzag fashion, following the large letters, we get Kruchonykh's name. This is clearly an example of the "interweaving of letters" that Jakobson had sent Kruchonykh in 1914, and means he preceded Zdanevich in using this device and even superseded him by allowing a third, zigzag reading in what would otherwise have been a two-part chorus.[23]

[22] Marinetti at exactly this time was also declaring a taste for numbers that led him to incorporate them and also other mathematical symbols in his writings. See "Geometric and Mechanical Splendour and the Numerical Sensibility" (March 18, 1914) in Apollonio (1973, 158-59).

[23] In response to my inquiry about this subject, Professor Jakobson sent the following reply (April 28, 1981): "The question of the interplay between speech sounds and letters and the possibility to utilize these interplays in verbal art, particularly on its supraconscious (*zaumnyj*) level, vividly preoccupied me in 1912-1914; and they were intensely discussed in my correspondence of 1914 with Krucenyx and Xlebnikov. The selection of those elements of phonetic transcription which could and should be utilized for the printing of various poetic experiments was touched upon next to the daring problems of poetic experimentation with diverse combinations of sounds and letters, and even numbers. I personally was particularly preoccupied with these problems and prepared in 1914 a number of theoretical notes and of poetic experiments. Most of them perished, while some others can be still found among Moscow collectors of literary archives. When I think about my reasonings and exercises of the mentioned cycle, I would characterize them now as centered around paronomasia as a fundamental and vital poetic device. The latter found its development in my later and even recent studies

One should not assume, however, that these were the first attempts to deal with the phonetic discrepancies between Russian pronunciation and script. L. N. Tolstoy was something of a pioneer in this regard when he designed his *Azbuka* (*Alphabet Book*, 1871-72) to teach peasant children the rudiments of language and reading. After presenting the letters and short words in the book, he introduces short texts to illustrate the standard differences between orthography and orthoepy. Whenever a difference occurs, the pronounced sound is given in small type above the word in the text (fig. 132). If the orthography were modernized and the small letters were substituted directly in the word, the result would be similar to Zdanevich's technique. The next pedagogical step presents texts in which the letters with different pronunciations are italicized, but the key is not given (fig. 133). This mixture of typefaces has a familiar look. Later the italics are removed. The book ends with two verse folk tales in which the stresses are marked by an accent. In the *Novaya azbuka* (*New Alphabet Book*, 1875), a new

---

on verbal art. As to the question of wider insertion of phonetic variations into poetry, one might quote particularly poems written and printed in the 1920's by the poet Sel'vinskij whose experiments were repeatedly cited and praised by Majakovskij during his public debates in Prague." For more on Jakobson's avant-garde activities, see Winner (1977).

Fig. 133. L. N. Tolstoy, *Alphabet Book*, 1871-72.

— 61 —

просила. Орёлъ взялъ её въ когти, поднялъ вверхъ и пустилъ: она упала на камни и разбилась.

Голова и хвостъ змѣи.

Змѣиный хвостъ заспорилъ съ змѣиной головой о томъ, кому ходить впереди? Голова сказала: „ты не можешь ходить передомъ, у тебя нѣтъ глазъ и ушей". Хвостъ сказалъ: „а за то во мнѣ сила, я тебя двигаю; если захочу, да обернусь вокругъ дерева, ты съ мѣста не тронешься. Голова сказала: „разойдёмся!"

И хвостъ оторвался отъ головы и поползъ впередъ. Но только что онъ отползъ отъ головы, попалъ въ трещину и провалился.

Хорёкъ.

Хорёкъ зашелъ къ мѣднику и сталъ лизать подпилокъ. Изъ языка пошла кровь, а хорёкъ радовался, лизалъ, — думалъ, что изъ желѣза кровь идётъ, и погубилъ весь языкъ.

Fig. 134. L. N. Tolstoy, *New Alphabet Book*, 1875.

79

Кто сидѣлъ на моемъ стулѣ и сломалъ его!

Медвѣди пришли въ другую горницу.

Кто ложился въ мою постель и смялъ ее!

Зеревѣлъ Михайло Иванычъ страшнымъ голосомъ.

Кто ложился въ мою постель и смялъ ее,

зарычала Настасья Петровна не такъ громко.

А Мишенька подставилъ скамеечку, полѣзъ въ свою кроватку и запищалъ тонкимъ голосомъ:

Кто ложился въ мою постель!

И вдругъ онъ увидалъ дѣвочку и завизжалъ такъ какъ будто его рѣжутъ:

Вотъ она! Держи, держи! Вотъ она. Вотъ она! Ай яяй! Держи!

Онъ хотѣлъ ее укусить. Дѣвочка открыла глаза, увидѣла медвѣдей и бросилась къ окну. Окно было открыто, она выскочила въ въ окно и убѣжала. И медвѣди не догнали её.

Какъ дядя Семенъ разсказывалъ про то, что съ нимъ въ лѣсу было. (Разсказъ.)

Поѣхалъ я разъ зимою въ лѣсъ за деревами, срубилъ три дерева, обрубилъ сучья, обтесалъ, смотрю ужъ поздно, надо домой ѣхать. А погода была дурная: снѣгъ шелъ и мело. Думаю, ночь захватитъ и дороги не найдешь. Погналъ я лошадь; ѣду, ѣду—все выѣзду нѣтъ. Все лѣсъ. Думаю, шуба на мнѣ плохая, замерзнешь. Ѣздилъ, ѣздилъ, нѣтъ дороги и темно. Хотѣлъ ужъ сани отпрягать, да подъ сани ложиться, слышу недалеко бубенцы погромыхиваютъ. Поѣхалъ я на бубенчики, вижу тройка коней саврасыхъ, гривы заплетены лентами, бубенцы свѣтятся и сидятъ двое молодцовъ.

Здорово братцы!—Здорово мужикъ!—Гдѣ братцы дорога?—Да вотъ мы на самой дорогѣ. Выѣхалъ я къ нимъ, смотрю, что за чудо—дорога гладкая и не заметеная.—Ступай, говорятъ, за нами и погнали коней. Моя кобылка плохая не поспѣваетъ. Сталъ я кричать: подождите братцы! Остановились, смѣются.—Садись, говорятъ, съ нами. Твоей лошади порожнемъ легче буdevice is used in the story of the three bears, whereby the size of the typeface conveys the volume of the voice, from Papa's down to baby's (fig. 134). This practice is also familiar to us. The latter book continued to be used until after the Revolution and by 1910 it had already gone through twenty-eight printings, for a total of nearly two million copies (Tolstoy 1978, 18). Of course, Tolstoy's readership differed greatly from that of Zdanevich, and his devices were designed for very different purposes, but the effects are still similar.

THE MELNIKOVA ANTHOLOGY

The typographic profusions of *lidantYU* represent a different, parallel side of Zdanevich's creativity that had been largely subordinated to the practical needs of transcription. Yet it was there all along.

The following memoir by Paustovsky makes one feel that only a portion of Zdanevich's Tiflis productions has come to light. Paustovsky was introduced to the Zdanevich family in Tiflis in 1923. Ilya had already left for Paris two years earlier for a visit that turned out to be permanent.

Throughout the whole apartment were scattered many books, mainly thin ones with vociferous titles and similarly loud covers. On them were drawn colored semi-circles, women's breasts and broken rays.

The most popular book of verse was considered the one entitled *"Tsveti, poeziya sukina doch"* (Bloom, poetry, you bitch's daughter!).[24] It was typeset in all the typefaces that could be found in Tiflis—from poster-size to petit and from italic to elizevir. Between individual words were inserted various lines, rows of dots, clefs, letters from the Armenian, Georgian and Arabic alphabets, musical notes, upside-down exclamation points, ducal crowns (these insignia survived in pre-revolutionary printing offices only for visiting cards), vignettes depicting cupids and rose garlands.

I studied this book with pleasure as a kind of collection of typefaces.

There were many books in *zaum*. One of them was entitled only with the letter ю (1966, 2:456-57)

From this description one could easily suspect that *lidantYU* was not necessarily Zdanevich's most typographically adventurous work. He had obviously been operating in this vein before his departure for Paris. Some day more of this work may surface. What little else there is from the Tiflis period comes down to the following: two covers for books by Kruchonykh—*Lakirovannoe triko* (Lacquered Tights) and *Milliork*—and the Melnikova anthology (Zdanevich et al. 1919).

Zdanevich had fallen in love with the beautiful actress Sofya Georgievna

[24] A passage very similar to this occurs in Terentev (1920, 7, fig. 151, and also in fig. 145). It seems possible that Paustovsky's memory confused the title of a book with this striking passage. The same may be true of the book titled *YU*, which may have been Terentev (1919a) and has a large letter *YU* on the cover.

Melnikova, who was associated with the Russian avant-garde group 41° in Tiflis and had participated in many of its activities and events.[25] It seems the feeling was not entirely mutual. Zdanevich decided to pay homage to her by dedicating to her a collection of works by 41° members. Katanyan recalls that Zdanevich went around to his friends trying to drum up enthusiasm and contributions. He finally succeeded, albeit with some difficulty, in putting together the desired anthology, which appeared under the 41° imprint in 1919. In addition to Zdanevich's *Dunkee for Rent*, it included contributions by Nina Vasileva, Tatyana Vechorka, Dmitri Gordeev, Katanyan, Kruchonykh, Terentev, Aleksandr Chachikov, Nikolay Chernyavsky, Grigori Shaikevich, and others (Markov 1968, 361-64; Nikolskaya 1980, 312-13). Terentev, Kruchonykh, and Zdanevich are listed as editors, though the role played by the first two, except in regard to their own contributions, is unclear. Of interest to us, besides Zdanevich's contribution (discussed above), are the contributions of the other two editors and of Chernyavsky. Since Terentev developed his own style and body of works, I will discuss him in a separate section later.

To his play Zdanevich added two remarkable one-page typographic compositions. They are tours de force of typesetting and compare favorably with Marinetti's most elaborate efforts of the same time. The verbal elements in both are *zaum* drawn from the play and neither is readable in the normal sense. They are, rather, visual experiences, with letters and syllables as shapes and rhythmic features. In the first, *zokhna* (fig. 135), the verbal elements are more prominent

[25] For a description of the literary life of Tiflis at the time, see Nikolskaya (1980).

Fig. 135. Ilya Zdanevich, ''zokhna,'' from *S. G. Melnikovoy*, 1919.

Fig. 136. Ilya Zdanevich, ''zokhna and her suitors,'' from *S. G. Melnikovoy*, 1919.

than the nonverbal; but in the second, a fold-out page, *zokhna i zhenikhi* (zokhna and her suitors) (fig. 136), the nontextual shapes overlie and dominate the textual elements to form a unique composition that is a blend of Cubist collage, Surrealism, and Futurism-Dadaism. Zdanevich occasionally became a purely graphic artist. The newspaper *41°* (only one issue, July 14-20, 1919) reportedly contained "2 vignettes and 1 woodblock print" by him (Ex Libris, no. 6, item 67).

Kruchonykh's contribution, a cycle of poems "Muzka" (Musey) (Zdanevich et al. 1919, 95-120; Kruchonykh 1973, 461-86), shows the influence of the *41°* typographic milieu by being more elaborate in its use of typefaces than is characteristic of him, though it is not more elaborate than Kamensky had already been.[26] There is a basic typeface, and other larger fonts are used for emphasis, most often at the end of a line or a page, when the same font is used for a whole word or phrase. Often such words are followed by an exclamation point, which gives the obvious impression that they are meant to be shouted (fig. 137). In the rare instances when a letter or letters are emboldened within a word, more often than not it is the stressed vowel or syllable that is emphasized. Thus the general impression is that the typography is closely tied to recitation, as in Zdanevich's first four *dras*, rather than being a more or less independent element, as in Kamensky. The typography goes beyond the merely practical, and in this Kruchonykh moves somewhat away from Zdanevich's principles and toward Kamensky; the text remains rectilinear, however, and does not impede reading. Since Kruchonykh's basic orientation had not been recitational, perhaps it is accurate to

---

[26] "Similar books had been published by Kruchonykh before, but he had never displayed so much imagination or variety in his use of print. Both were missing, however, when he later reprinted some of his Caucasian poetry in Moscow" (Markov 1968, 340).

Fig. 137. A. Kruchonykh, "Musey," from *S. G. Melnikovoy,* 1919.

Fig. 138. A. Kruchonykh, "Musey," from *S. G. Melnikovoy,* 1919.

Fig. 139. A. Kruchonykh, *Lacquered Tights,* 1919; cover design by Ilya Zdanevich.

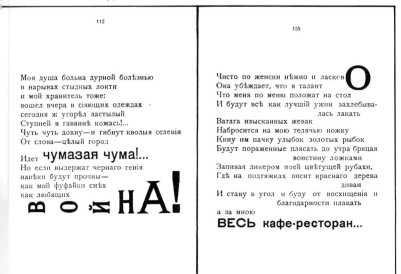

say that in 1919 he had fallen under the spell of Zdanevich. The title of the poem gives a clear indication of the tone of work. *Muzka* is the Muse with a derogatory suffix and, although this is Kruchonykh's tribute to his muse, she remains a vulgar sort (or at least his depiction of her is) and the typography often highlights the raunchy language and tone. The poet's relationship with his muse is tinged, or rather saturated, with eroticism; one instance of typography departs from the recitation-oriented toward the purely visual, where the poet writes, "In a purely feminine way, tenderly and caressingly, she convinces me that I am a talent," and the word "caressingly" (*láskovo*) ends in a huge unstressed vaginal "O" (fig. 138). Despite the late date (1919), Kruchonykh retains a number of features of the old orthography (ѣ , i, -ago), which is a surprising expression of conservatism, or perhaps a nod in the direction of the classicism of his theme.

The printed version of Kruchonykh's *Lacquered Tights* (1919c), with the cover designed by Zdanevich (fig. 139), appeared at roughly the same time as the Melnikova anthology and includes poems from "Muzka" plus a number of others. Typographically both books are similar, but *Lacquered Tights* is somewhat more conservative, as a comparison of corresponding pages shows (figs. 137 and 140). Not all of the typography is this bland (fig. 141), but since the book is longer than the selection from the Melnikova anthology, and the quantity of display typefaces is not greater, the proportion of normal text with capitalizations is higher. *Milliork* (1919d), with a similar cover by Zdanevich (fig. 142), is even more conservative. Note that both covers are created by printing the title layout twice but rotating it more than 90°.

Nikolay Chernyavsky's contribution to the Melnikova anthology consists of three choruses of the *arkestram* type, printed in exactly the same manner as the

Fig. 140. A. Kruchonykh, *Lacquered Tights*, 1919.

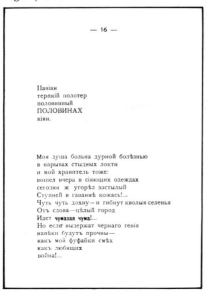

Fig. 141. A. Kruchonykh, *Lacquered Tights*, 1919.

choruses in *Dunkee for Rent*. Each is one page long; the first is for three voices, the second and third for two. Only the third has a title, "Brick Chimney" (figs. 143, 144). Obviously Chernyavsky picked up the technique from Zdanevich. The difference is that while Zdanevich's choruses were basically in *zaum* with only occasional recognizable words, Chernyavsky's are basically in Russian. It is no trick to make up nonsense choruses in this manner, but it is considerably more difficult to combine real words. It would be truly virtuosic if each of the voices had a poem in clear, normal Russian. However, the resulting poems, once separated out, yield an alogical text where the syntax is reasonably straightforward, but the meaning is "shifted." The first voice of the first poem can suffice as an illustration:

Dyuzhina bochek stav na
    utory povita
Remnem obruchey
Zapakhlo kraska pyzhas
    lyubo nyukhu
Chervatochiny shcheli uma-
    shche zhirnym mylom.

A dozen kegs pla on
    notches plaited
Like a belt of hoops
It smelled color puffed
    appealed to sniff
Worm-holes cracks tir
    ed (?) with fat soap.

Fig. 142. A. Kruchonykh, *Milliork*, 1919; cover design by Ilya Zdanevich.

Such poetry was written by a number of Futurists, including Khlebnikov, but three short examples (all that Chernyavsky is known to have published) are not enough to judge his talents.

Two additional features are worth noting. One is the occasional use of phonetic spelling (for example, "a" for unstressed "o"), where the shared sound requires it (see fig. 143, first line: Uzhin karoche, where the last word would ordinarily be spelled koroche, and Chervatochiny; and fig. 144, second line: vyles should be vylez). Phonetic spelling is also used in some instances without this necessity, but elsewhere standard spelling is maintained. Another feature seems to be the result of printing errors that caused the accidental omission of the periods that mark word boundary. If read as is, we get mistakes, or at least inconsistencies, such as: fig. 143, *imnet, vklube*; fig. 144, *zhmenya, v paru sv rukav, garzhi*, and *zdesyatykh, uleyzdes yaty*. There is even an actual spelling error, shown in fig. 144: *skhodnoa*, for *skhodnaya*. Such misprints are doubtless unintentional human errors resulting from the use of a new and complex printing technique. The technique, of interest in itself, might have produced something valuable if it would have been developed further.

Chernyavsky is the subject of a note in Kruchonykh's *Ozhirenie roz* (Obesity of Roses, 1918c), p. 13:

The *zaum* works of Nikolay Chernyavsky (well-known in literary circles as a collector of fairy tales) unfortunately cannot be reduced to typographic reproduction; at the present time they are being printed lithographically according to the drawings of the well-known futurist artist Kirill Zdanevich.

One hopes that such works will eventually turn up.[27]

[27] For more on Chernyavsky, see *Iliazd*, 12, 15, and Markov (1968, 362).

Fig. 143. N. Chernyavsky, poem from *S. G. Melnikovoy*, 1919.

Fig. 144. N. Chernyavsky, two poems from *S. G. Melnikovoy*, 1919.

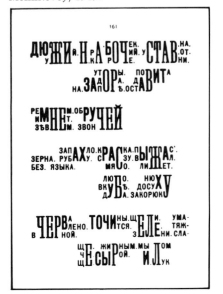

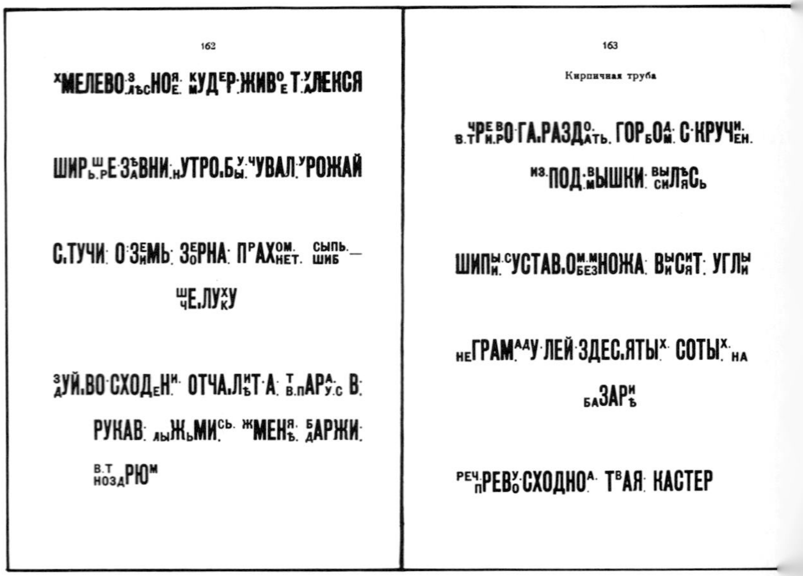

TERENTEV

If Kruchonykh was under Zdanevich's spell only temporarily, the third member of the Tiflis 41° triumvirate, Igor Terentev (Markov 1968, 358-62), can be said to have stood on Zdanevich's shoulders.[28] Terentev's contribution to the Melnikova anthology, "Gotovo" (Ready), contains the most radical typography of the collection, excluding Zdanevich's two "compositions." Terentev, more than anyone else, is fond of positioning letters at right angles to the normal position or turning them upside down. He likes to use shared letters—that is, large letters that are used simultaneously by two words, as in a Zdanevich chorus,—and he is fond of mixing typefaces and using oversized letters in unusual positions. All of these features are illustrated in fig. 145. In these innovations Terentev is not much more advanced than Kamensky had already been five years earlier. Unique to Terentev among the Russians is his occasional practice of positioning a whole mid-word syllable vertically (fig. 146), though this technique was used by the Italian Futurists already in 1913.

[28] Zdanevich describes Terentev as "benjamin remarquable du futurisme débuta par mes soins avec *Les 17 ontils du non-sens* où est exposée la première loi poétique de 41°" (*Iliazd*, 14, 52).

g. 145. I. Terentev, "Ready," from *S. G. Melnikovoy*, 19.

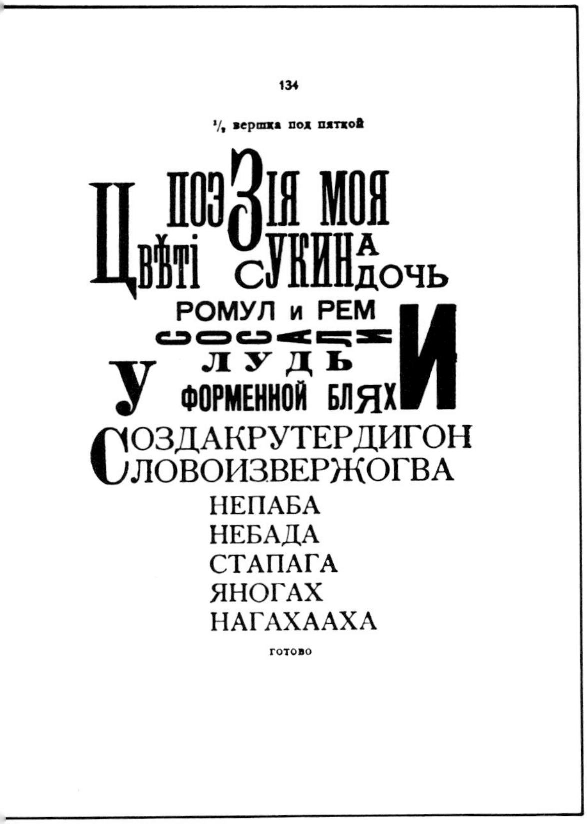

134

¹/₂ вершка под пяткой

Цвѣтi поэзiя моя сукина дочь

РОМУЛ и РЕМ

ЛУДЬ

У ФОРМЕННОЙ БЛЯХИ

СОЗДАКРУТЕРДИГОН

СЛОВОИЗВЕРЖОГВА

НЕПАБА

НЕБАДА

СТАПАГА

ЯНОГАХ

НАГАХААХА

готово

Fig. 146. I. Terentev, "Ready," from *S. G. Melnikovoy*, 1919.

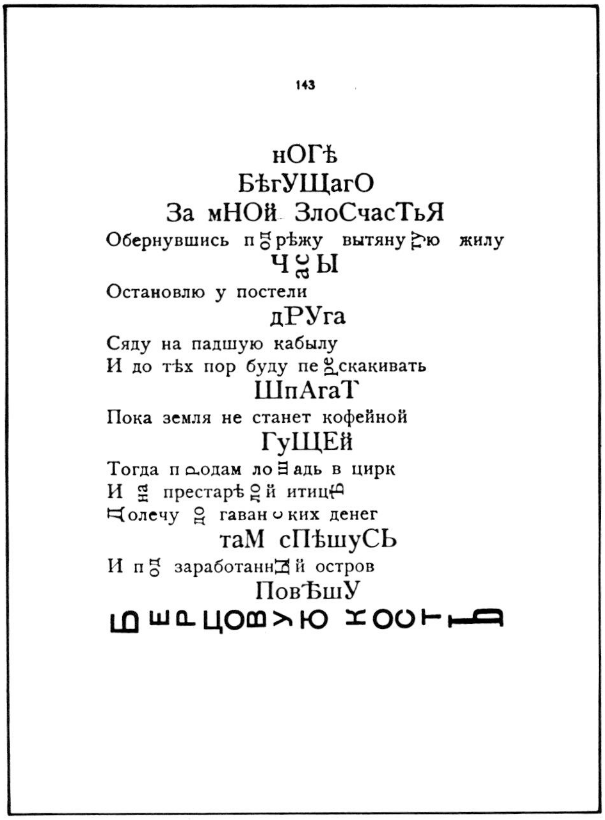

143

нОГѢ

БѢгУЩагО

За мНОЙ ЗлоСчасТьЯ

Обернувшись п рѣжу вытяну ю жилу

Ч Ы

Остановлю у постели

дРУга

Сяду на падшую кабылу

И до тѣх пор буду пе скакивать

ШпАгаТ

Пока земля не станет кофейной

ГуЩЕЙ

Тогда п одам ло адь в цирк

И престарѣ й итиц

олечу гаван ких денег

таМ сПѣшуСЬ

И п заработанн й остров

ПовѢшУ

цовую

In the course of the same year (1919) in Tiflis, Terentev managed to produce four of his own books—*Cherubs Whistle* (1919b), *Fact* (1919c), *17 Nonsensical Tools* (1919d), and *Tract on Thorough Obscenity* (1920?) (Markov 1968, 360)—plus a brief artistic biography of each of his colleagues—*Record of Tenderness* (1919a) on Zdanevich, and *Kruchonykh The Grandee* (1919e). The biographies are significant for being the only ones to appear in their subjects' lifetimes,[29] but they are typographically unexceptional. The other four books did not add much that is new to the already used battery of typographic devices. *Cherubs Whistle* limits itself, like Burliuk, to capitalization of selected letters and words. *17 Nonsensical Tools* contains some interesting pages (figs. 147-49), with each of the "tools" having its own characteristic typeface and layout. The last example is striking for its similarity to some of Lissitzky's designs for *For the Voice* (Mayakovsky 1923c).

A facetious aspect of *17 Nonsensical Tools* is found in the subtitle, which states "in the book there are no misprints." In fact there are. For example, there is an upside down *T* in the typographically normal introduction (Terentev 1919d, 3), and *teotiki stikha* and *kabyla Pegas* (both ibid., 8), but these are intentional misprints. This raises the quasi-issue of the misprint as a discrepancy between what you see and what you are expected to understand. Another famous example is, of course, *Zaumnaya gniga* (discussed earlier). This has some potential for developing into visual punning if the matter is taken more "seriously."

The *Tract* contains some elegant typefaces, including cursives and Church Slavic (fig. 150). One such fancy display typeface is used ironically to convey the sentiment "Bloom, you daughter of a bitch!" (fig. 151). There are also some

[29] With the exception of the special issue of *Bulletin du bibliophile*, 1974, no. 2, devoted to Zdanevich in the year before his death.

Fig. 147. I. Terentev, *17 Nonsensical Tools*, 1919.

Fig. 148. I. Terentev, *17 Nonsensical Tools*, 1919.

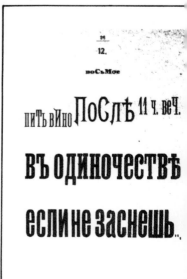

macaronic words and expressions that mix the roman and Cyrillic alphabets. Markov notes that "the letters х, ы, and ю are systematically singled out as typical for the true Russian idiom. Often, typographically emphasized parts reveal similarity to, or identity with, taboo words" (1968, 360) (fig. 150), for example, *MUDosti* (a possible misprint of *mudrosti* [wisdom], but *mud-* suggests "testicles"). There are, in addition, some zigzag and zoom effects, such as on the last page (fig. 152) where the words that say "I bless the universe with a fig sign" seem to zoom in and out of outer space. This is a device borrowed from the Italians.

Terentev was at the forefront of the typographical Avant Garde, but he cannot be credited with any unique achievements in that area. Although he did add a few personal nuances to the repertoire already in use, his orientation was mainly decorative. That is to say, with the exception of a few instances, some of which have been noted above, his use of typography was relatively arbitrary and without marked expressive or practical purpose. His use of capitalization, for example in *Cherubs Whistle*, was random rather than functional (to convey stress or emphasis), and his use of the various typefaces and layouts enlivened the look of the page without having any other apparent goal. They did not go so far, however, as to belabor the reading process greatly, as was the case with *lidantYU azabEEkan*.

A. N. CHICHERIN

Zdanevich may have been well on his way to working out a complete system for transcribing all the features of spoken language, but the prize for the most thoroughly realized system must go to the Constructivist Aleksey Nikolaevich

g. 148 *(continued)*.

Fig. 149. I. Terentev, *17 Nonsensical Tools*, 1919.

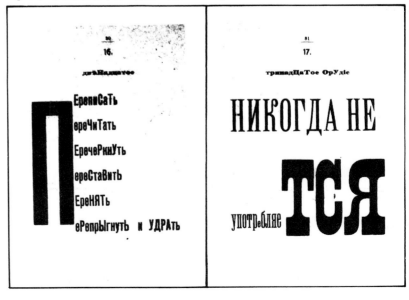

Chicherin (1889-1960). Chicherin remains a rather shadowy figure at the moment, despite his evidently prolific creativity (fig. 153).[30] *Mena vsekh* (*Change of All*, spoonerism for *Smena vekh*, "Passage of Ages," February 12, 1924), for which he acted as "constructor" and major contributor, is of particular significance. It was preceded by a small book of poems entitled *Plaf* (1920), which appears to have gone through three printings (fig. 153).[31] In addition to *Change of All*, I am familiar with his *Kan-Fun* (1926), which presents in detail the theory behind the practice in *Change of All*. Let us look at the earlier work first.

The system of signs in *Change of All* for relative stress, pauses, slurs, and so on takes two pages to present (fig. 154a,b). Even so, the author must admit at the end that "due to the lack of typographic signs, timbres and intonations cannot be printed in this book with the exactness of the original text." He emphasizes that Moscow dialect should be used for recitation of the poems, which date from 1921-23.

The result, as a glance at the first poem shows (fig. 155), is by no means easy to read. All of the signs are functional, like the musical notation from which

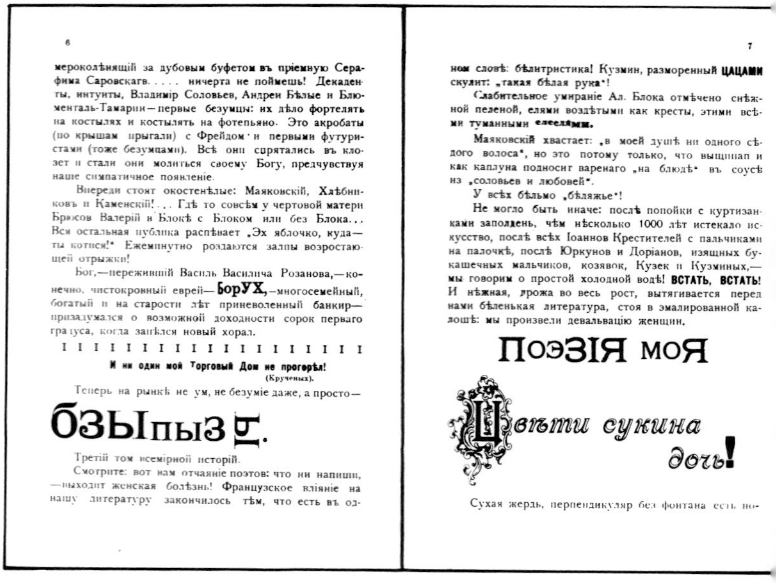

[30] According to Tarasenkov (400), *Zvonok k dvorniku. Poema*, listed in *Change of All* was published in Moscow in 1927. Not listed in fig. 153 but listed in Tarasenkov are: *Shlepnuvshiesya aeroplany* (Kharkov, 1914, 8 pp.); *Bolshak, Poema* in *Styk* (Moscow: V.S.P., 1925, 126-32); and *Krutoy podyom. Lirika* (Moscow 1927, 32 pp.). This last item is not the work of A. N. but of A. V. Chicherin. Chicherin is also mentioned as being one of the most talented, technically accomplished poetry reciters of the period. See Bernshteyn (1926, 43).

[31] I am grateful to Aleksandr Ocheretyansky for information on the existence and dating of a 1922 edition and a 1927 edition, both published in Moscow, the latter held by the Lenin Library.

Fig. 150. I. Terentev, *Tract on Thorough Obscenity*, 1919.

Стих 1. Вот к сожалѣнію дошли мы до черт знает какой **МУД**ости!
Начинается блаженство учеников и ни в чем неповинныя жертвы.
Мы въ кафэ сидим как три митрополита, три папы, три бабы, три зуба:
Крученых, Зданевич и Терентьев...

Стих 2. Вот нѣкоторыя слова: упразднить, испразднить, исправить, правило, порожній, прах, на всѣх парах..... отсюда вывод:
Мы ПРАВДУ матКУ рубим потные от счастья шТОПОРЫ ФУТУРИЗМА
(с тѣх пор, с той поры, топор).

Стих 3. Вопервых —
—самый крѣпкій и разнообразный: anglічане говорят только на провалившемся языкѣ (Тифлис=**Ш**ифилис), italiанцы — высуня (bona сѣра), поляки на зубах (цикаво пшез джви патшить), а французы — однѣми губами (Minion!) Русскій ничѣм не брезгает: **Х**аркает, **Ы**кота и высочайше **Ю**кает! Отсюда **ВСЕЛЕНСКОЕ ЗНАЧЕНІЕ** русской ругани: — верхній регистр! Елки палки! И нижайшее почтеніе на **Ы**: „упал на л**Ы**ки (Анчар).

Стих 4. Слово футуризм — означает поипоязычному свое нѣкоторое, а для нас фютюр=фитюлька! Правильнѣе говорить: фу ты, ну ты, ножки гнуты,

Fig. 151. I. Terentev, *Tract on Thorough Obscenity*, 1919.

6

мероколѣнящій за дубовым буфетом въ пріемную Серафима Саровскагв..... ничерта не поймешь! Декаденты, интуиты, Владимір Соловьев, Андреи Бѣлые и Блюменталь-Тамарин — первые безумцы: их дѣло фортелять на костылях и костылять на фотепьяно. Это акробаты (по крышам прыгали) с Фрейдом и первыми футуристами (тоже безумцами). Всѣ они спрятались въ клозет и стали они молиться своему Богу, предчувствуя наше симпатичное появленіе.

Впереди стоят окостенѣлые: Маяковскій, Хлѣбниковъ и Каменскій!... Гдѣ то совсѣм у чертовой матери Брюсов Валерій в Блокѣ с Блоком или без Блока... Вся остальная публика распѣвает „Эх яблочко, куда — ты котися!" Ежеминутно раздаются залпы возростающей отрыжки!

Бог, — переживший Василь Василича Розанова, — конечно, чистокровный еврей — **БорУХ**, — многосемейный, богатый и на старости лѣт приневоленный банкир — призадумался о возможной доходности сорок перваго градуса, когда запѣлся новый хорал.

I I I I I I I I I I I I I I I I I I I I

И ни один мой Торговый Дом не прогорѣл!
(Крученых).

Теперь на рынкѣ не ум, не безуміе даже, а просто —

бЗЫпыЗ.

Третій том всемірной исторій.

Смотрите: вот вам отчаяніе поэтов: что ни напиши, — выходит женская болѣзнь! Французское вліяніе на нашу литературу закончилось тѣм, что есть въ од-

7

ном словѣ: бѣлитристика! Кузмин, разморенный **ЦАЦАМИ** скулит: „такая бѣлая рука"!

Слабительное умираніе Ал. Блока отмѣчено снѣжной пеленой, елями воздѣтыми как кресты, этими всѣми туманными елеелями.

Маяковскій хвастает: „в моей душѣ ни одного сѣдого волоса", но это потому только, что выщипал и как каплуна подносит варенаго „на блюдѣ" въ соусѣ из „соловьев и любовей".

У всѣх бѣльмо „бѣляжье"!

Не могло быть иначе: послѣ попойки с куртизанками заполдень, чѣм нѣсколько 1000 лѣт истекало искусство, послѣ всѣх Іоаннов Крестителей с пальчиками на палочкѣ, послѣ Юркунов и Доріанов, изящных букашечных мальчиков, козявок, Кузек и Кузминых, — мы говорим о простой холодной водѣ! **ВСТАТЬ, ВСТАТЬ!** И нѣжная, дрожа во весь рост, вытягивается перед нами бѣленькая литература, стоя в эмалированной калошѣ: мы произвели девальвацію женщин.

ПоэЗІЯ моЯ

Цвѣти сукина дочь!

Сухая жердь, перпендикуляр без фонтана есть но-

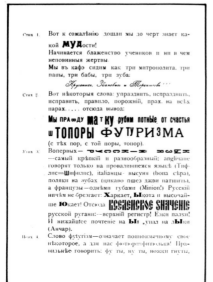

some of them have been borrowed, and not decorative; yet even in this first relatively simple case it is no small trick to remember them all. Once the signs are mastered, however, the text can be recited and its unusual requirements met. For example, the line:

Tudy-syudy—up // p'ridi!l'li,
    s suk' // kiny d' // deti . . .

requires a kind of stuttering (or drunken hiccuping)[32] repetition of the first consonants of *sukiny deti* (bitch's children) and mid-word pauses. The author has failed to explain the mid-word exclamation point, but one can guess that this conveys a rising, exclamatory intonation at the point indicated—a stressed vowel. As with Zdanevich's *dras*, Chicherin's poems are a combination of Russian and *zaum*. Phonetic spelling is used throughout, but Chicherin is much more precise and faultless in his transcription.

After a few pages of such texts, just as one is beginning to get used to the system, a surprising thing happens: the text begins to grow less prominent and

[32] Markov made this suggestion in a letter to me.

Fig. 152. I. Terentev, *Tract on Thorough Obscenity*, 1919.

Fig. 153. "Books of the Constructivist-Poets," *Change of All*, 1924.

КНИГИ КОНСТРУКТИВИСТОВ-ПОЭТОВ

А. Н. ЧИЧЕРИН и Э.-К. СЕЛЬВИНСКИЙ

„Знаем" (Издание 1-е) . . . . (разошлось)

Корнелий ЗЕЛИНСКИЙ

„Дематериализация" культуры (история технической
 логики). . . . . (готовится)
Та ovta (песни о сущем). . . . . (готовится)
Грузофикация поэзии (исследование) . . . . . . (печатается)
Логика квант (конструкции слова) исследование. . . (готовится)

Эллий-Карл СЕЛЬВИНСКИЙ

Творчество	„Рысь"	(печатается)
	„Хукк"	"
	„Бар-Кохба"	"
	„Особотдарм 2"	"
	„Бриг богородица морей".	"
	„Студия" книга корон сонетов . . .	(готовится)
	„Маленький восточек".	"
	„Гимназические стихи" (1915-1919 г.)	"
Теория	„Поэтика и политическая экономия". .	"
	„Технический кодекс конструктивизма" . .	"
	„Органическая теория искусства" . . .	"
	„Теория тональности стиха и иллюстрации к ней". .	"
	„Лермонтов под скальпелем конструктивиста" (исслед.)	"

Алексей Николаевич ЧИЧЕРИН

Творчество	„Плафь" изд. 1-е	(разошлось)
	„Плафь" изд. 2-е	"
	„Плафь" изд. 3-е	(шрифтуется)
	„Тырло"	"
	„Аллеббарда Белиберды	"
	„Роман в 2-х животах с результатом" изд. пряничное .	(печатается)
	„Авеки веков" (мрачная поэма) изд. пряничное . . .	"
	„Звонок дворнику" (поэма)	"
	„Мякгй памол" (поэма).	"
Теория	„Трактат конструктивиста"	(готовится)
	„Энантиосемия"	"
	„В знак"	"
	Русский ритм"	"
	„Такт, тембр, темп, и интонации слова" . . .	"
	„Строй конструэмы"	(печатается)
	„Анализ восклицательной интонации (нагрузка на вос-
клицательный знак)".	"
Исследование	„Каламбуры Достоевского"	(готовится)
	„Бредовой метод Достоевского"	"
	„Мастерство Достоевского"	"
	Случай Энантиосемии у Достоевского" (статья) .	(печатается)
	Анализ ритма „Трех ключей" Пушкина . . .	"
	„Портрет Матрены" (из романа А. Белого „Серебря-
ный голубь")	(готовится)

the sign system more prominent. On page 50 the first and last lines give extra space to signs (fig. 156). By page 54 (fig. 157) the page begins to look more like a modern musical score for chorus than a text for reading. On page 57 (fig. 158), the text amounts to one line and the sign system and its explanation take up the rest of the page. Page 58 (fig. 159) is an entire page of explanation of signs for page 59 (fig. 160), which has indeed turned into a musical score; however, the explanation helps not at all in decoding a nearly undecipherable "text." At this point the reader-reciter is bound to throw up his hands in frustration. The lines, curves, and dots take on a visual significance as a geometric composition but prevent oral interpretation. The next page (fig. 161) goes further: a title, two "chapters" and a geometric design for a text—no words, syllables, or even musical notes, except the word *kanets*, "the end." The next page (fig. 162), with curves and circles and a square root of 2, has a title, "a veki vekov" ("and ages upon ages"), but no chapters or "end." The next page (fig. 163) is a pure geometric composition with a few recognizable signs (+, . . .) but no text whatsoever. The last page (fig. 164) contains a portrait of Chicherin and the words, "Chapter of a poem," plus a long *zaum* word with a few signs above it.

This development is astounding. Having established an elaborate system for

g. 154. A. N. Chicherin, "Basic Devices," *Change of All*, 1924.

Fig. 155. A. N. Chicherin, poem from *Change of All*, 1924.

Fig. 156. A. N. Chicherin, poem from *Change of All*, 1924.

Fig. 157. A. N. Chicherin, poem from *Change of All*, 1924.

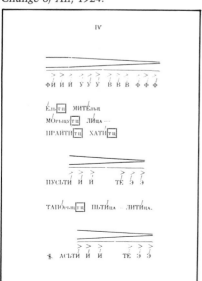

Fig. 158. A. N. Chicherin, poem from *Change of All*, 1924.

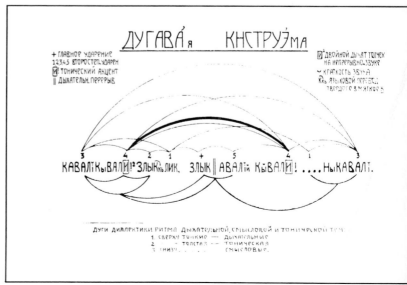

conveying the minutest feature of a text to be recited, Chicherin progresses to a point at which no text is present and the signs themselves become abstract elements in a geometric composition. One wonders if this is a parody of the original idea. But this is not so, as is indicated first of all by K. Zelinsky's theoretical article, "Constructivism and Poetry," which introduces *Change of All*. The central idea of the essay is that "culture dematerializes" and that technological progress produces an efficiency in which less matter creates more energy or does more work. He says:

Constructivism somehow battles against "weightiness," against the instinctual attraction toward the earth, against putting oneself in a motionless prone position in matter. . . . The technical logic of constructivism . . . removes anything personal. It knows only one law: the shortest distance between two points.   (Chicherin et al. 1924, 23)

Zelinsky describes this concentration of means with respect to verse in the following way:

The loading [*gruzofikatsiya*] of verse, i.e., the increase of the semantic-constructive effect, is a natural result of focusing the action of all artistic means as though on one point which serves as the central prop and is loaded with the "material" of the verse. (Ibid., 26)

Since the goal of such poetry is extreme concentration, the poet departs from normal conversational language, and, as Zelinsky notes, "The ear which has been serving our ordinary speech does not immediately accommodate itself to the condensation of speech" (ibid., 26). Such condensation results in distortion and

Fig. 159. A. N. Chicherin, "Signs used in 'Novel'," *Change of All*, 1924.

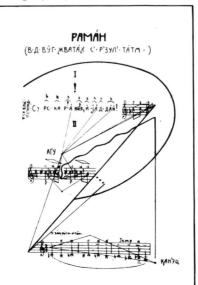

Fig. 160. A. N. Chicherin, "Novel," *Change of All*, 1924.

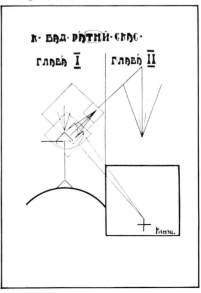

Fig. 161. A. N. Chicherin, poem from *Change of All*, 1924.

abstraction, a movement away from "earthbound" natural speech toward constructive concentration of energy—exactly the progression followed by Chicherin in his series of poems in *Change of All*.

Zelinsky continues:

Sometimes to the unprepared person it is incomprehensible, as an algebraic formula is incomprehensible to a layman.

This applies especially to A. N. Chicherin.

He is a representative of the tendency I earlier called formal constructivism. Chicherin has geometrized sound.

His constructions are extremely complex sonic patterns, phonetic lace. One must hear and read him many, many times in order to comprehend him.

His device of sonic dotted lines (upsetting the theme from its basic phonetic composite) is a bold attempt to work out an entire sonic fabric on the level of local semantics.

This is why, when listening to A. N. Chicherin's masterly reading, one must not lull oneself on the crests of sonic waves, but try to understand thoroughly the constructive nature of his lines.

In relation to "dematerialization" of poetic means, Chicherin has gone very far and before us are his experiments in an idiosyncratic geometric "stenography" which he rouses by a sonic ripple, supplied in addition with a musical pattern. (Ibid., 27)

Formal constructivism is characterized by Zelinsky as a drive toward a feeling of perfection by presenting geometrical plans that get at the bare essence of a thing, as, for example, the Cubists did earlier (ibid., 16).[33]

[33] For another description of the Constructivist program of Chicherin and Zelinsky, see Weber (1976). This includes the translation of two Constructivist manifestoes and several illustrations.

Fig. 162. A. N. Chicherin, poem from *Change of All*, 1924.

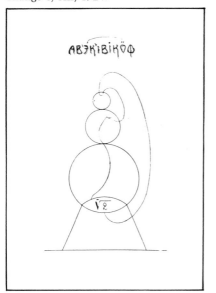

Fig. 163. A. N. Chicherin, poem from *Change of All*, 1924.

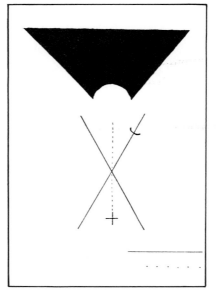

Fig. 164. A. N. Chicherin, poem from *Change of All*, 1924.

Ilya Selvinsky, the third contributor to *Change of All*, takes a path that is just as viable, but less abstract. Using some of the same punctuation devices, he conveys more accessible subjects, such as a gypsy song (fig. 165). Here the extra vowels in the traditional gypsy vocalization style are minutely transcribed. In other places he even indicates where a breath should be taken (ibid., 39; see also Khardzhiev and Trenin 1970, 281-82).

Chicherin's own treatise on this topic, *Kan-Fun* (1926), is the most fully developed programmatic statement made by any figure important to our study. The title is a contraction of Constructivism-Functionalism, and the work consists of excerpts from a larger (unpublished?) study called "Theses for a Treatise on Two Schools."[34] In its thoroughness it deals with other matters, such as social questions and a theory of rhythm, that are not germane to this study and therefore will not be discussed. In this pamphlet he writes, "The goal of the sign is the formation of a given state; the sign is a corrective of life's affairs" (Chicherin 1926, 25). The "sign of poetry" is organized according to the law of "maximal load of necessity on a unit of organized material, in a minimal space, with unbroken, concise, exhaustive viewability in a meaningful form" (ibid., 8), all of which can be taken to mean maximum meaningfulness with minimal material resources.

For the formation of poetic fullness in a sign only that material is suitable which is capable of existing in minimal space with the greatest leveling of parts in the interest of the whole, and, furthermore, is capable in this minimum of spatial compression, which complicates loading, of being combined with other material. (Ibid., 8)

[34] Chicherin also contributed remarks, dated June 14, 1924, to Kruchonykh (1924, 53-55).

Fig. 165. I. Selvinsky, "Gypsy Waltz on the Guitar," *Change of All*, 1924.

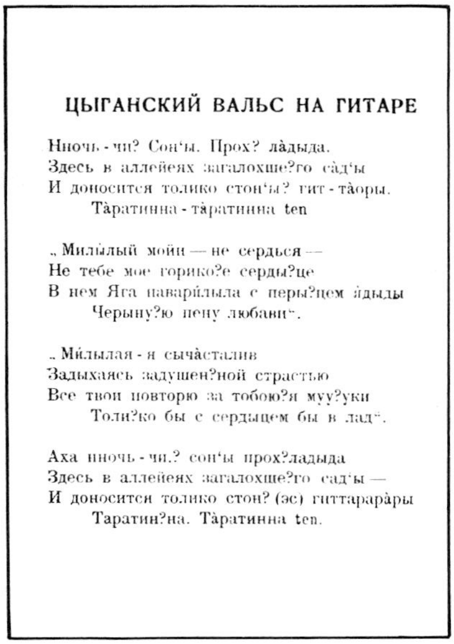

ЦЫГАНСКИЙ ВАЛЬС НА ГИТАРЕ

Нночь - чи? Сон‘ы. Прох? ла̀дыда.
Здесь в аллейеях загалохше?го са̀д‘ы
И доносится толико стон‘ы? гит - та̀оры.
Та̀ратинна - та̀ратинна ten

„Милылый мойн — не сердься —
Не тебе мое горико?е серды?це
В нем Яга наварйлыла с перы?цем йдыды
Черыну?ю пену любави“.

„Милылая - я сыча̀сталив
Задыхаясь задушен?ной страстью
Все твои повторю за тобою?я муу?уки
Толи?ко бы с сердыцем бы в лад“.

Аха нночь - чи.? сон‘ы прох?ладыда
Здесь в аллейеях загалохше?го сад‘ы —
И доносится толико стон? (эс) гиттарара̀ры
Таратин?на. Та̀ратинна ten.

Not only is crude, everyday language not adequate for this task, but even the most precise and subtle words say "much more than is wanted."

The material for a poetic sign must be different, wordless material which submits to the fundamental law of constructivism. . . . Poets have long ago "felt" and fearfully wanted to "express themselves without words." (Ibid., 8)

But if the word is inadequate as poetic material, what *is* adequate?

Chicherin turns with admiration to prealphabetic days when the "language of the cosmos" was given in figures and "relationships of lines," when words were expressed in whole forms, that is, in pictograms, and not broken up into the pieces of letters and sounds (ibid., 9). He disputes the view that literate culture progressed linearly from pictograms to ideograms to phonograms and the alphabet, each supplanting the prior state; rather, all these systems coexist and should be thought of as horizontal parallels. The system used depends on the goal and the means of perception. The alphabet

. . . is a system of phonograms—signs indicating particular sounds and therefore for perception by hearing. The law of constructive poetics predetermines perception of its signs by means of sight—through the eye.

The first place in a poetic "language" must be occupied by a sign of pictorial presentation, called a pictogram, and an image in an object; and an ideogrammatic construction of linear relationships—as a sign with an inclination to abstraction—can be in the second place. The path of development of Constructivism is toward picture and object constructions without names. (Ibid., 10)

Thus he has explained to us how poetry can turn into a geometric composition by way of a quite serious program. There is, of course, an obvious contradiction or misnomer in calling a wordless, soundless visual composition "poetry" except by analogy with another art, as sometimes Kandinsky's paintings are called "musical" and Bruckner's symphonies are called "architectural." As an immediate if incomplete solution to accomplishing this pictorialization or deverbalization of poetry, Chicherin recommends the use of all available resources of the printer's cabinet, such as punctuation, mathematical symbols, musical signs, borders, tailpieces, and emblems—anything with a pictographic or ideographic value (p. 12).

One sidelight on visual perception of a text is Chicherin's proposal that reading time be made more efficient by printing texts in lines to be read alternately from left to right and right to left (p. 19). In theory this would alleviate the wasted time and energy of having the eyes return to the left to begin each line. Chicherin quips that the unnecessary space covered in the course of reading a book would equal the distance of the Transsiberian Railroad. He may or may not have been the first to propose such a form of efficiency, but since then studies have shown that the mental energy required for adjusting to reading alternate lines in reverse direction is much greater than that required to skip over to the left margin for each line. The proposal is thus actually not physiologically practical or efficient.

Since Chicherin remains a shadowy figure, it is useful to add some autobiographical information contained in *Kan-Fun*. Chicherin mentions two editions of *Plaf* (written in 1919 and printed in 1920 and 1922) in which he first applied the Constructivist principles of poetry developed by him theoretically in 1918. Here he describes the "measure" (*takt*) as the new unit of rhythm rather than the verse foot. He worked on a treatise, "Measure, Timbre, Tempo and Intonation in the Word," and gave a course on phonetics sometime during 1924-26 at the Herzen House organized by the All-Russian Union of Poets (pp. 15-16). In addition to *Change of All*, he mentions another publication, *Styk* (1925), a number of periodical articles (unspecified), and a "construction" called *Aveki Vekov* (1924), which was made of gingerbread in fifteen copies and no doubt does not survive in that form (p. 5). The *Change of All* bibliography (fig. 153) lists this work as a "(gloomy poem) gingerbread publ. (in press)," along with "Novel in Two Stomachs with Result," also with the designation "gingerbread publication." It should be noted that two pages from *Change of All* (figs. 160 and 162) also bear these labels and one can only imagine what the work would look like constructed in gingerbread and inscribed with elaborate designs. The *pryanik* had actually reached the state of a high art in Russia and its use for such constructions is not unthinkable.

Even this incomplete glimpse at Chicherin's work confirms that he was a major theoretician and an important literary figure. S. Vysheslavtseva, a contributor to the Formalist journal *Poetika*, wrote an article, "On the Motor Impulses of Verse," which deals with the role of articulation in the reading (silently or aloud) of poetry. The first person she mentions is Chicherin. After noting that poetry was originally considered a declamatory art and had later become more visual than aural, she points out a recent return to the role of recitation for the fullness of poetic impact. "Concrete phrasal rhythms, concrete speech intonations enter into many poetic works as a fundamental element of construction, and the printed text, deprived of corresponding detailed signals, is sometimes simply incomprehensible and requires declamatory decoding by the author himself (A. Chicherin)" (Vysheslavtseva 1927, 45).[35] Indeed, when we are faced with the task of decoding a printed text that is burdened by Chicherin with signals for accurate recitation, we can only bemoan the fact that the author did not take advantage of the new technology of sound recording instead of the medium of print. As Gale Weber (1976, 296) has noted, "Chicherin's experiments were not regarded with esteem by his fellow Constructivists and, in any case, were far too abstract to play even a minor role in the development of literary Constructivism, let alone in Soviet literature as a whole." Boris Agapov tried his hand at a much

[35] For a report on Chicherin's reading of Mayakovsky's "Chelovek," see Rayt (1963, 237-38).

simpler system of declamational notation (figs. 166, 167) in *Economic Plan* for *Literature* (1925), the next Constructivist miscellany, but this, too, went nowhere.

LISSITZKY

Zdanevich and Chicherin, who began with an orientation toward phonetic transcription, ended up shifting out of it and into a greater emphasis on purely visual features. Once typographical means began to expand to meet the need to communicate vocal recitation, the means seem to have taken over and become an end in themselves. The poets were standing, so it seems, at a crossroads, at the intersection of text as the conveyor of oral language and the text as conveyor of graphic values—that is, at the intersection of literature for the ear and literature for the eye.

In this context, a consideration of El Lissitzky's theories is appropriate. Lissitzky was one of the most articulate Russian advocates of visual expressiveness in books. His pronouncements on the matter are clear, uncompromising, and radical enough to place him at the opposite pole to the more traditional linguists,

Fig. 166. Boris Agapov, "Ski Run," first page, *Economic Plan for Literature*, 1925.

Fig. 167. Boris Agapov, explanation of symbols in "Ski Run," *Economic Plan for Literature*, 1925.

such as Baudouin de Courtenay, who discount the visual aspects of literature. If Lissitzky had produced original literary works and not limited his activities to graphic design, painting, architecture, and theory, a whole chapter could have been devoted to him in this study. The one minor exception to his usual work is his "Pro 2 kvadrata" (About Two Squares, designed in 1920 in Vitebsk, published 1922 in Berlin), which has a text of thirty-three words for its six graphics (Lissitzky-Küppers 1968, Illus. 80-91). The book opens with the exhortation, "Don't read! Take paper, columns, wood: compose, color, build"—that is, don't be a passive observer, be a doer. The story is simple. There are two Suprematist squares, a black and a red, who come to earth from afar. They find everything a mess and attack it. A red structure is then built upon the black square. That takes care of Earth, and the two squares go on to new planets. The illustrations bear a clear relation to the text, but the narrative thread is explicit only in the text,[36] which is laid out in an expressive manner below the illustrations.

Also noteworthy is Lissitzky's striking Constructivist design for *For the Voice* (Berlin 1923), a collection of Mayakovsky's poems (Lissitzky-Küppers 1968, Illus. 95-108). Both this design and that for "About Two Squares" are characterized by a clarity and elegant simplicity that make their structure and message easily perceptible without making them trite. Lissitzky attempts to make parallel or common elements (letters, words, ideas) visually parallel or overlapping—for example:

$$\text{Б} \genfrac{}{}{0pt}{}{\text{е}}{\text{о}} \; \overset{\smile}{\text{И}} \qquad \text{and} \qquad \genfrac{}{}{0pt}{}{\text{Кра}}{\text{Я}} \; {>} \text{СНО}$$

beat   red
fight   clear

It is as a theoretician, however, that Lissitzky is particularly significant. His most succinct and categorical manifesto is the following:

1. Printed words are seen and not heard.
2. Concepts are communicated by conventional words and shaped in the letters of the alphabet.
3. Concepts should be expressed with the greatest economy—optically not phonetically.
4. The layout of the text on the page, governed by the laws of typographical mechanics, must reflect the rhythm of the content.
5. Plates must be used in the organization of the page according to the new visual theory: the supernaturalistic reality of the perfected eye.
6. The continuous sequence of pages—the cinematographic book.
7. The new book demands new writers; inkwell and quill have become obsolete.
8. The printed page is not conditioned by space and time. The printed page and the endless number of books must be overcome. THE ELECTROLIBRARY. (*Merz*, No. 4, July 1923, Leering-van Moorsel 1968, 329)

[36] In this respect, I differ from Compton, who states: "The words are hardly important, each page is dominated by suprematist forms" (1978, 114).

This manifesto proclaims the visual nature of the book; but it also challenges bookmakers to be economical and direct and to take maximum advantage of the given technical means, in this case typographical resources. In a letter to Malevich dated September 12, 1919, Lissitzky wrote: "I consider that thoughts which we imbibe from a book with our eyes must saturate all forms perceptible to the eyes. Letters, punctuation marks, which bring order to our thoughts, must be studied, but in addition the flow of lines comes down to certain condensed thoughts, and it is necessary to condense them for the eyes, too" (Khardzhiev 1962, 154).

As a major figure in the Constructivist movement, Lissitzky was a vigorous proponent of functional art and downplayed the element of personal expressiveness. In *Elementare Typographie* (1925), he wrote: "For modern advertising and for the modern exponent of form the individual element (the artist's own touch) is of absolutely no consequence" (Gould 1966, 49). So he would not be expected to endorse Bely's, Kamensky's, and, in particular, Kruchonykh's efforts in regard to visual expressiveness. In his opinion, the artist should serve a cause and not merely reflect his personality in his art. Lissitzky's emphasis was on modern technology and how it could be used to improve life for the people. Egocentricity, a trait prominent among all the Futurists, was absent in Lissitzky, which may have made him more genuinely future-oriented than they were, but it also resulted in a paucity of original literary efforts. Lissitzky also never made a significant shift away from the visual arts to the literary arts, as did many of the Futurists, and he always remained a designer-painter-architect. Nevertheless, he was partly indebted to the Futurist view, as was noted:

It is not difficult to find here a continuation of the concept of the visual values of writings developed by the creators of lithographic books, although Lissitzky had precluded any type of manual activity. He was of the opinion that a revolution in the traditional book could be achieved by industrial printing, but he did borrow from the Futurists their ideas on optimum visual stimuli. (Bojko 1972, 17)

According to Lissitzky, the time of the Russian Revolution seems to have been the historical moment at which the new possibilities in typography were appreciated. In a guidebook to the All-Union Polygraphic Exhibition in Moscow (1927), he wrote:

Until the revolution our artists neglected the composition of print. It was only after the revolution that artists, striving as they did in every discipline to find the appropriate artistic substance of that discipline, began creating a new type of book out of typographic material. These endeavors moved in two directions. The first aimed at achieving a book's "architecture," i.e., programming the whole as well as individual pages. Designing in line with this concept was based on the proportions and relationship of a page's individual elements, the relationship of the typographical composition to the paper area, the contrast and size of type, and most importantly the exclusive use of typographical material and specific printing processes, e.g., colour overlap. In the second tendency, which might be called artistic montage, most essential was the use of print composition as a building material for assembling a cover, individual pages, and posters. (Ibid., 17)

Such things went on before the Revolution in something of a free-style manner (Kamensky, Kruchonykh), but Lissitzky had in mind a more goal-oriented approach:

You should demand of the writer that he really presents what he writes; his ideas reach you through the eye and not through the ear. Therefore typographical form should do by means of optics what the voice and gesture of the writer does to convey his ideas. (Lissitzky-Küppers 1968, 356)

Yet Lissitzky did not envision the use of typography as a notational system for transcribing details of speech or gestures. This would result in a text that is neither readable nor an adequate conveyor of live speech. Rather, he thought of typography as a tool to present visual equivalents or analogies to aural expressiveness:

Language is more than just an acoustic wave motion, and the mere means of thought transference. In the same way typography is more than just an optical wave motion for the same purpose. From the passive, non-articulated lettering pattern one goes over to the active, articulated pattern. The gesture of the living language is taken into account. (Ibid., 355)

The page must become articulated and alive, but according to the principles inherent in the visual components as well as the aural components of the text: "Today we have two dimensions for the word. As a sound it is a function of time, and as a representation it is a function of space. The coming book must be both" (ibid., 357).

Even though we came across many interesting and impressive experiments throughout this chapter, we must still conclude that the proper balance of both factors sought by Lissitzky was not attained. Lissitzky's own productions are perhaps the best attempts, within their limits, to reach a synthesis of a text for the eye and the ear. Lissitzky saw that "letterpress belongs to the past. The future belongs to . . . all photomechanical processes" (ibid., 356). He saw in this new technology new and productive horizons:

You can see how it is that where new areas are opened up to thought- and speech-patterns, there you find new typographical patterns originating organically. These are: modern advertising and modern poetry. (Ibid., 357)

The connection between advertising and poetry is significant. Lissitzky predicted that "the next book-form will be plastic-representational" and would guide the shift (which he saw already taking place in America) to making "the word the illustration of the picture" (p. 357). However, historico-political exigencies prevented the organic development of this progression toward the achievement of a full-fledged school of "visual poetry" (p. 359) in Russia. But the flowering of typography in Tiflis in 1919 under Ilya Zdanevich came very close.

6. Mayakovsky

and the Stepladder

Line

In contrast to the other Futurists, about whom the literature is still relatively small but growing, the literature on Vladimir Mayakovsky (1893-1930) is huge. By virtue of Stalin's declaration that he was the "best, most talented poet of our Soviet epoch" and that "indifference to his memory and his works is a crime," Mayakovsky has become one of the most written-about poets in modern times.[1] What is amazing about this monumental attention, however, is a paucity of commentary on Mayakovsky's typographical arrangements, which are the most immediately striking feature of his poetry and one of the most widely imitated.

EARLY EXPERIMENTS

Direct contact and involvement in the activities of his Futurist colleagues naturally led Mayakovsky to dabble in similar visual effects. He, too, had begun his career as a painter and had turned out some credible paintings and drawings in his early days.[2] He continued to draw and paint even after he began transferring his main focus to poetry in 1912 under the influence of David Burliuk. When asked in 1924 in a *Komsomolskaya pravda* questionnaire to give his profession, he wrote "poet and painter" (Lapshin 1963, 43). And even with its relative conservatism,[3] his painting and drawing had the same "return to basics" theoretical foundation: "In poetry he maintained 'the self-valuable,' *samovitoe* word; in painting—'color, line, form as self-sufficient quantities' " (ibid., 46).[4] In Maya-

---

[1] See Brown (1973, 369-70), for a succinct report on this event.
[2] On Mayakovsky the artist, see Khardzhiev (1976, 8-84); Lapshin (1963); Katanyan (1963).
[3] Repin, upon seeing Mayakovsky's drawings, is reported to have called him an "inveterate realist" (Chukovsky 1967, 334).
[4] The quote inside the quote is from Mayakovsky (1955-61, 1:290). Hereafter references to this edition will be made in the text as PSS, followed by volume and page.

kovsky's own elaboration in the theses for a lecture of November 20, 1912, entitled "On the Latest Russian Poetry," we have the following:

Analogic paths, leading to the achievement of artistic truth, in painting and poetry. Color, line, surface—the independent goal of painting—painterly conception, the word, its shape [*nachertanie*], its phonetic side, myth, symbol—poetic conception. (PSS I, 365)

Yet there were exceptions to his generally Realist orientation in painting. At the exhibition "1915" he showed a top hat cut in half and a Cubist picture.[5] Two such Cubist paintings, dated 1915 and 1918,[6] are illustrated in color in Khardzhiev (1976), along with a 1913 drawing to illustrate the poem "To Signboards" (fig. 168). In the latter, which is as much at a midpoint between text and picture as some of Kruchonykh's poems of that time (cf. discussion of *Explodity*), verbal elements (the numbers 4, 7, letters p ѣ, and the artist's bold, then fading, signature at the top) freely mix with purely linear elements in the total composition. In the poem, however, it is not easy to see any connection between the two:[7]

[5] Khardzhiev (1976, 20): "Mayakovsky exhibited the futurist painting 'Ruletka' which was then acquired by Pavel Kuznetsov, and the épatage 'Self-portrait': half a top-hat and a black glove nailed or glued to the wall, painted over with black stripes."
[6] The 1918 painting "Zholtaya kofta" (Yellow blouse) is the one discussed as "Avtoportret v zholtoy kofte" (Self-portrait in a yellow blouse) in Khardzhiev (1968b, 38-39). It is one of three paintings exhibited at the "First Exhibition of the Professional Union of Artists-Painters in Moscow," May 26-July 12, 1918. Another, "Ulitsa" (Street), is illustrated in Khardzhiev (1968b, 39); and idem (1976), between pp. 128 and 129. While the first is Cubist, the second is closer to Impressionism in style.
[7] For a new study that goes very far toward revealing the links between the poem and the illustrations, see Stapanian (1982). Her dissertation (1980) explores in detail the analogies between Mayakovsky's early lyrics and painterly concepts of the time.

Fig. 168. V. Mayakovsky, drawing for "To Signboards," *Prayerbook of Three*, 1913.

To Signboards

Read sheet-metal books!
Beneath a gilded letter flute
Crawl salmons smoked
And gold-curled rutabagas.

And if with mongrel gaiety
The "Maggi" bouillon logo twirls—
The dead march bureau
Will file its caskets by.

When, glum, pathetic,
Lamppost signs are doused
Go fall in love beneath a tavern sky
With china teapot poppies!   (PSS I, 41)

Mayakovsky's literary efforts were immediately strong, avant-garde, and original. The encouragement of David Burliuk and the example of Khlebnikov led Mayakovsky to radical experiments with poetic language—not so radical as to reach *zaum*, but radical enough to provide some unique examples of layout-word relationship structures.

What has been termed Mayakovsky's "verse cubism" (Metchenko 1940, 32)[8] consists of chopping up words to emphasize a palindromic relationship, such as this often-quoted verse:

U-	S-
litsa	treet
litsa	face
U	S
Dogov	Of Great Danes
Godov	Of years
Rez	Shar
Che	Per
Che	Thro
Rez	Ugh
Zhelenznykh koney s okon begushchikh domov	Iron horses from the windows of speeding houses
Prygnuli pervye kuby	Jumped the first cubes.

This is the layout of its first publication in the flyer "A Slap in the Face of Public Taste" (1913; also *Prayerbook of Three*, 1913, 36). The layout of the earlier editions differs notably from the later ones, now canonized as "final," in the distribution of the words on lines, use of capitals, and punctuation. The canonic version is:

[8] Khardzhiev credits the initiation of this term to Malevich. In a private conversation with Khardzhiev, Malevich called the poem "Iz ulitsy v ulitsu" (From street to street) the most successful example of 'verse cubism' " (1976, 67).

U-
litsa.
Litsa
u
dogov
godov
rez-
che.
Che-
rez
zheleznykh koney
s okon begushchikh domov
prygnuli pervye kuby.   (PSS I, 38)

Notice the loss of symmetry with the change in capitalization. Also, the addition
of periods unnecessarily limits the syntax to one of several possible alternative
readings. This affects one place in the poem especially (*rez/che.*).

The original layout of later lines is:

Pyostr kak fo- rel sy N	Speckled like a tro ut so N
Bezuzornoy pashni	Of a designless ploughland
Fokusnik	A magician
Relsy	Draws
Tyanet iz pasti tramvaya skryt tsiferblatami bashni	Rails from the trolley maw hidden by the clock faces of a tower

Prayerbook of Three has a compromise version:

Pyostr kak fo-
Rel-sy-
N
Bezuzornoy pashni
Fokusnik
Relsy   (p. 38)

The later version has the following layout:

Pyostr, kak forel
syn
bezuzornoy pashni.
Fokusnik
relsy
tyanet iz pasti tramvaya,
skryt tsiferblatami bashni.   (PSS I, 38)

While the "difficult metaphoric structure" remains, the "cubism" of the earlier layout with its unexpected hyphenations and isolated letters has disappeared. The text may be easier to read now but the belabored, hard-won rhyme *(fo)rel sy(n) = rel sy* went underground and might not be noticed even by an attentive reader.

An earlier example of such a belabored rhyme,

I na	And against
Neyo, legko vstayushchikh zvyozd opyorlis	It, of the easily rising stars rested
Nogi.	The legs.
No gi-	But the des-
bel fonarey, (*A Slap*, 91)	truction of streetlights,

remains, however, close to its original configuration:

legko opyorlis nogi.
No gi-
bel fonarey,   (PSS I, 34)

These changes in layout fall in line with what Mayakovsky saw in the 1920s as his role as a poet of the masses: "It must be said that these things [experimental early poems] were most confusing, and they more than anything caused talk about their being incomprehensible. Therefore in all later things the question of comprehensibility stood before me, myself, and I tried to make things so that they could reach the greatest quantity of listeners" (Metchenko 1940, 30-31). Even though Mayakovsky strove to be more understood by the masses, his earlier layouts were still more suited to the nature of these poems, and they better revealed the formal properties that were the dominant features of the works and the raison d'être for their metaphoric complexities.

The most radically concentrated experiment of the *stolbik* variety was the short poem first entitled "Spring" (*Croaked Moon*, 1913, 21) and then immediately expanded to "Exhaustive Picture of Spring" (*Croaked Moon*, 1914, 59). The latter title in Russian (*Ischerpyvayushchaya kartina vesny*) has exactly the same number of syllables (12) as the entire poem:

Lis—	Leaf—
Tochki	lets
Posle	After
Tochki	period
Strochek	Lines
Lis	of foxes
—Tochki.	—periods

The later version, though more "readable," is much less visually arresting and symmetrical:

Listochki
Posle strochek lis—
tochki. (PSS I, 50)

A similar effect is completely submerged in the later layout,

Le   We
Zem   Crawl
Zem   ear-
Le   th
Vykolot belma pustyn (*Croaked Moon*,   to beat the whites of deserts
1913, 22)

which becomes:

Lezem zemle pod resnitsami vylezshikh   We crawl earth under eyelashes of nearly
    palm   leafless palms
vykolot belma pustyn (PSS I, 53)   To beat the whites of deserts.

The later line in the same poem (p. 23),

Doroga   Road
Pog   Horn
Ada   of Hell,

is likewise converted to a part of a single line. We should note, however, that later the process was reversed and some of the earlier long lines were arranged in columns.

Mayakovsky's early poems included an effect (such as the one mentioned in chapter 2 in connection with Tsvetaeva) of a hyphenated word with another line inserted between the halves of the word so as to suggest two concurrent expressions, one silently thought (narration), one spoken aloud (dialogue?), as in this poem (1913):

V avto   *In a car*

"Kakaya ocharovatelnaya noch!"   "What an enchanting night!"
"Eta,   "She
(ukazyvaet na devushku),   (points to a girl),
chto byla vchera,   The one from yesterday,
ta?"   that one?"
Vygovorili na trotuare   They said on the sidewalk
"poch-   "post-
perekinulos na shiny   was flung at the tires
ta." (PSS I, 58)   office."

This is motivated by "the illusion of a dynamic landscape" seen from a car (Khardzhiev and Trenin 1970, 110). Though such a device is perhaps more effective in print, it is possible to convey it in recitation by a careful modulation of intonation and loudness.

Taking his cue from Kruchonykh,[9] Mayakovsky published his first individual edition in lithographic form with handwritten text. This was the short collection of four poems *Ya!* (*I!*, May, 1913, 300 copies), with cover by the author and other illustrations by his classmates at the Moscow School of Art, Vasili Chekrygin (Khardzhiev 1968b, 37), and L. Zhegin (L. Shekhtel). The text was handwritten by Chekrygin (Khardzhiev 1976, 60).

If we compare the lithographed first edition of *I!* with the *Croaked Moon* letterpress versions (which are almost exactly the same in text) and the later "canonic" layout, we find that the two earlier versions are very similar in their freedom of word positioning. However, although the printed texts observe a uniform left margin, the lithographed text is freer: long lines go all the way to the left and shorter lines are positioned toward the center, but they do not adhere to any uniform vertical line (figs. 169, 170, 171). Note the presence in a number of places throughout the poems of an embryonic stepladder effect, more frequent in the lithographed version than in the printed one. But because of its simplified layout, the printed version gains in one respect: instead of having a center of gravity in the middle of the page, as in the lithographed version, its center is toward the left margin. As a result, any words or parts of words positioned in the middle stand out more. Thus the rhyme *Vyi/-vye* (Necks/[police]-men) is

[9] Khardzhiev prefers to credit Larionov (1968a, 316). He sees the cover as a variation on Larionov's cover for *Half-Alive* (1976, 60).

ig. 169. V. Mayakovsky, page 1 from *I*, 1913.

Fig. 170. V. Mayakovsky, page 2 from *I!*, 1913.

Fig. 171. V. Mayakovsky, "I," version from *Croaked Moon*, second edition, 1914.

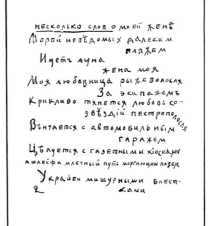

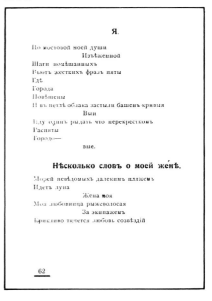

more highlighted in the layout of the printed version because the two words are lined up, for emphasis, one below the other in mid-page. A similar effect in the next section comes out just as clearly in both lithographed and printed text (Mayakovsky 1913, 3, and *Croaked Moon*, 1914, 63).

The writing of the lithographed text can be characterized as sloppily formal in the old orthography, with some elements of elegant manuscript style (long strokes for l, m, r, a), but with clumsy, heavy-handed parts and occasional instances that look like overwrites and corrections. The writing style corresponds reasonably well with the illustrations, but whether the illustrations correspond with the text is another question.

Zhegin reports on the creation of *I!*:

The cover for the booklet "I" was worked on for an endlessly long time. On it are laid out quite decoratively a sort of black spot and the inscription: V. Mayakovsky. "I!" [fig. 172] This spot, which could be taken simply as an inkblot which had spread, has as its foundation a real prototype: the "butterfly" necktie which Mayakovsky then wore. This necktie appears in the photographs which survive from this time. . . . [fig. 173]

The staff-publishing-house quarters were my room. Mayakovsky brought the lithographic paper and dictated to Chekrygin the verses which the latter transcribed in his precise handwriting with special lithographic ink.

Fig. 172. Cover to V. Mayakovsky, *I!*, 1913.

Fig. 173. Photo of Mayakovsky, 1918, showing his "butterfly necktie."

The four drawings done by Chekrygin by the same method (lithographic), in themselves remarkable, however are only extrinsically connected with Mayakovsky's text.

"Well, Vasya," muttered Mayakovsky, "you've drawn an angel again. You ought to have drawn a fly, maybe. You haven't drawn a fly for a long time."

Work on the design of the booklet took a week or week and a half....

In two to three weeks "I!" ... was printed in three hundred copies. Mayakovsky distributed them in the stores where they were rather quickly sold out. (Zhegin 1963, 100-102)

Because of Chekrygin's preoccupation with biblical themes in his own painting (Golgotha, a series on the Resurrection of the Dead), his illustrations for *I!* are "little connected with the text." Indeed, the illustrations by Chekrygin (Mayakovsky 1913, 9, 10, 11, 15) do appear to be religious. The first (fig. 174) shows a horse and rider confronted by a serpent (St. George and the dragon?); the second is a group of figures dressed in biblical garb (Christ and his disciples?); the third is a kneeling figure (Christ or a prophet praying in the wilderness or Gethsemane?); and the fourth (fig. 175) is a figure of a bearded man (similar to the main figure in the two preceding illustrations) who is raising an arm as if to bless a gazelle before him. Perhaps this corresponds to the line, "I am lonely like the last eye of a man going toward the blindmen" (ibid., 14). But none of these subjects can be clearly linked to the text, which is largely urban in imagery, except that a chiton is mentioned in one line (ibid., 13). All four have partly undecipherable captions written in mirror image, as in *Worldbackwards* (fig. 61). Yet the artist's signature immediately above is in correct image.

Fig. 174. V. Chekrygin, illustration for V. Mayakovsky, *I!*, 1913.

Fig. 175. V. Chekrygin, illustration for V. Mayakovsky, *I!*, 1913.

Three illustrations by Zhegin (ibid., 4, 5, 6) are also included in *I!* and are somewhat closer to the context. The first is of a seated woman beside a vase of flowers, which might correspond to the line, "Mama, if I start feeling sorry for the vase of your torments . . ." (ibid., 8). The second is of a nude woman (?) warming her hands at a campfire, and the third is of a standing nude couple about to embrace; but neither has a direct referent in the text. After all, even the section about "my wife" has in mind "the moon, my wife," and not a human mate.

The obvious models for Mayakovsky's work are Kruchonykh's early manuscript books. *I!* shows no particular inventiveness beyond the models.

The only other known manuscript edition by Mayakovsky is a one-copy, handmade edition of the poem "Backbone Flute," which was dated November 21, 1919. It was calligraphed by Lilya Brik, to whom it is dedicated, and has a cover and four watercolor illustrations by the author. Five pages from this edition are reproduced in Khardzhiev and Trenin (1970; between pp. 32 and 33; also see pp. 22, 71n. 37). The text is written in a beautifully flowing script and Mayakovsky's illustrations border on the Constructivist in their spare geometricity.

The text of *Vladimir Mayakovsky, A Tragedy* presented to the censors on November 9, 1913, was a typed copy (now in TsGALI, Moscow) without any indication of typographical effects. Since the work was a drama for which Mayakovsky envisioned an immediate stage presentation, a format for an eventual published version was probably not even part of the original conception. The publication of the text was doubtless considered only after the excitement of the stage presentation at Luna Park, Petersburg, on December 2 and 4, 1913. Mayakovsky, who played the leading role in his own work, was probably too busy setting up his production to think of it in other terms at that time. Zheverzheev points out, however, that when Mayakovsky revised his text with a view to publication, "he strove to give the stage directions a significantly more pictorial quality" (1940, 353) in order to make up for the absence of various visual features of the production (sets, props, blocking, and gestures) in the printed text. Mayakovsky was concerned with improving the reader's ability to visualize the stage action, but he does not appear to have been concerned with the look of the text per se. That was left to two of the Burliuk brothers.

As was noted in chapter 5, David Burliuk was fond of mixing typefaces in his own poems to emphasize important words and sounds. However, when Vladimir and David Burliuk designed *Tragedy* for publication (Moscow, March 1914), such purposive principles do not seem to have been applied. The use of a variety of typefaces in the book is largely decorative, without much expressive purpose or a practical goal.[10] Some words and letters are given visual emphasis through

---

[10] Oginskaya (1973, 32) holds a more positive position on the matter: "The phonetic texture of the word rests on the typographically torn-up script of the letters. The complicated semantics, the metaphoric and syntactical constructions find themselves in profound interaction with devices for

boldface, sans-serif, italics, or other faces; but there does not seem to be a rationale for many of the choices made. A popular technique was to make the last letter of a line triple-sized, so that it appears to be shared by two words, as in a Zdanevich chorus; in all instances (pp. 5, 6, 11, 28, 36, 37), however, the enlarged letter belongs only to the bottom word, and one has to read ahead to avoid the misleading initial impression that it also belongs to the top word. In one case (fig. 176) confusion results: is "vsem nam rodam" (to all us races) or "vsem narodam" (to all peoples) the desired reading? Such large individual letters also occur at the end of a line and at the beginning, and more rarely at the head of a word in midline (fig. 177).

The orthography is generally modernized, with a few exceptions, and the layout is well designed for easy reading. The semiabstract clean-line illustrations by the Burliuks go well with the text, providing it with stimulating visual associations in a "shifted," alogical style comparable to the images in the text. What hand Mayakovsky himself had in the preparation of the published version is not clear, however.

The remainder of Mayakovsky's early poetry shows nothing new in layout or design. The early layouts remained traditional, and later changes only broke up some lines into columns or introduced quatrain stanza breaks where there had been none. We will, however, consider "Poslushayte!" (Listen!) when we discuss Mayakovsky's reading of his own poems in a later section of this chapter.

---

laying out the printed text. The splintered texture aids a penetration into the unusual meaning of the poet's lyrical monologue. The graphic outlines of this type allow an examination of the verses together with the illustrations." But her presentation is devoid of specifics that support this evaluation.

Fig. 176. V. Mayakovsky, *Vladimir Mayakovsky, A Tragedy*, 1914.

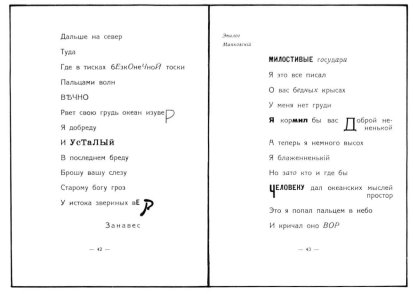

Fig. 177. V. Mayakovsky, *Vladimir Mayakovsky, A Tragedy*, 1914.

I also wish to mention two of Mayakovsky's other enterprises involving text with his own illustrations. One is the *Soviet Alphabet Book* (1919),[11] which included a propaganda couplet for each letter. The letter in question, which begins the couplet, is made of human figures who also create a tableau to illustrate the idea contained in the couplet (fig. 178). Letters formed of human figures belong to a tradition that in Russian culture dates back to at least 1694 and the publication of Karion Istomin's *Letterbook*, which contained similar illustrations by Leonti Bunin (fig. 179).[12] Here, however, the letter-figure stands alone and is only tenuously related to the text. Mayakovsky's contribution is to link letter-shape, text, and theme tightly together.

 The other notable enterprise is the famous series of ROSTA window posters (1919-22) for which Mayakovsky provided texts and often his own illustrations. These emerged from the satirical *lubok* tradition and other sources; but for all their probable propaganda effectiveness as political cartoons, they contain little

[11] Three to five thousand copies were illustrated, hand-colored, and produced by hand on abandoned lithographic equipment by the author. See Speech at Komsomol House, March 25, 1930 (PSS XII, 428-29), for Mayakovsky's recollections about the book.

[12] In connection with this, we should note a book by A. A. Shemshurin, an associate of the Futurists, on Istomin's alphabet books, *O gravirovannom i rukopisnykh litsevykh bukvaryakh Kariona Istomina* (Moscow, 1917), which deals with the dating of copies and other technical matters.

Fig. 178. V. Mayakovsky, *Soviet Alphabet Book*, 1919.

in the way of new visual devices.[13] These dynamic illustrations were at least as responsible as the text for having an impact on the subliterate population at which they were chiefly aimed (fig. 180). The storyline was supposed to be clear even without the text. Commenting on the change from Mayakovsky's earlier posters, one critic notes: "If the first posters were verses with drawings, then from this time on the 'Windows' presented themselves as drawings with verses" (Lapshin 1963, 48).

As in other political cartoons, there is frequently a complex interdependency between text and sketch. In many instances, the sketch completes the idea, answers the question, or intentionally contradicts the text, which would be an unfinished thought without it (Duvakin 1952, 397-98). This interrelationship is often more intimate than is the case with other works we have considered, but it is time-honored and traditional in its sphere.

STAGES OF LAYOUT DEVELOPMENT

Mayakovsky's layout practices went through three more or less distinct stages: (1) traditional (1912-16); (2) *stolbik* (column) (1916-22); and (3) *lesenka* (stepladder)

[13] For a brief survey of the techniques used, see Reeder (1980).

Fig. 179. Karion Istomin, *Letterbook*, 1694; illustration by Leonti Bunin.

Fig. 180. V. Mayakovsky, ROSTA window poster, 1920.

(1923-30). These phases correspond rather closely to the stages that Bely went through somewhat earlier, but in Mayakovsky the latter two stages are more precisely delineated chronologically. We must keep in mind, however, that many of the layouts presented in PSS do not reflect the original versions, but are the product of retroactive revision by later editors and perhaps the author himself. So the final versions present a blurred view of the chronological development of layout in Mayakovsky.

Traditional layouts (almost exclusively quatrains) coexist from the very beginning with *stolbik* layouts. But by 1916 the quatrain layout becomes rare and the *stolbik* is the layout of choice. Actually, Mayakovsky remains true to the quatrain structure, but divides it up into more than four lines. Thus the quatrain, rhyming A b A b,

Net. Eto nepravda, Net! I *ty?* No. It's not true, No! You, too?
Lyubimaya, za chto, za *chto zhe?!* Dearest, what for, what for?!
Khorosho—ya khodil, ya daril tsve*ty,* Fine—I went, I gave flowers,
Ya zh iz yashchika ne vykral I didn't steal silver spoons from the drawer!
    serebryanykh *lozhek!*

is actually layed out in a *stolbik* as follows (1916):

Net.
Eto nepravda
Net!
I *ty?*
Lyubimaya
za chto,
za *chto zhe?!*
Khorosho—
ya khodil,
ya daril tsve*ty,*
ya zh iz yashchika ne vykral
    serebryanykh *lozhek!*   (PSS I, 103)

Such a layout creates strong pauses and a halting pace which is clearly motivated by the short, emotion-laden phrases and which is much more appropriate than the flowing progress suggested by the layout of the quatrain (Eagle 1976, 2; 1978, 73). At the same time, the rhyme scheme becomes submerged (Zhovtis 1971, 63). In fact, it takes some effort to find it, even on the printed page.

This contrasts with Bely's earliest practice (1903) of having *all* the lines rhyme in a *stolbik*, even though the pattern might be irregular. The meter remains untouched and the layout could be shifted to a quatrain, but then the rhymes, which are foregrounded (semantically and/or sonically) in the *stolbik*, become submerged internally (Eagle 1976, 4-5). Bely's *stolbik* has a double purpose (pausing, richer rhyming), while Mayakovsky's introduces only additional line-break pauses while the quatrain rhyme scheme is untouched. For Bely, the increased rhyming was a way to "annul the significance of the end rhyme" (Eagle 1976, 5) by diluting its exclusive prominence in the sound structure of the stanza, while for Mayakovsky the "end" rhyme is a factor of utmost structural importance, one to be intensified, if anything, to give it maximum prominence. As Mayakovsky later stated (1926):

I always place the most characteristic word at the end of the line and find a rhyme for it no matter what. As a result, my rhymes are almost always unusual and in any case have not been used before me and are not in the rhyme dictionary.
    Rhyme binds the verse; therefore its material must be yet stronger than the material which has gone into the remaining lines. (PSS XII, 106)

Shtokmar's contention (1952, 303ff.)—although it has been attacked by Paperny (1957, 22) and Tomashevsky (1959, 481)—that rhyme is the prime organizing feature of Mayakovsky's verse is justified in one respect, in that rhyme is often the most obvious *fixed* feature that determines the subdivision into verses. There are exceptional cases where verses are unrhymed, but these are very rare.
    Moreover, in the *stolbik* layout, while it is often difficult enough to locate straightforward rhymes, Mayakovsky makes it at times even more difficult by positioning line breaks in places that go counter to expected pausing or normal syntagmatic divisions. One kind of conflict is the following:

kakoy raskryt za *soboy*	what is exposed behind
eshcho?	still?
Dymnym khvostom po vekam volochu	With a smoky tail through the ages I drag
operennoe pozharami *poboishche!*	a fire-plumed slaughter!
(PSS I, 232)	

The rhyme italicized here involves a midrhyme break (*soboy/eshcho*) if the line division is to mean anything at all, yet the recognition of rhyme depends on ignoring the line break. Comparable instances occur later with the *lesenka*.
    Another kind of conflict is the following:

skvoz dymy	through the smoke
svetlye *litsa ya*	I see bright
vizhu.	faces.
Vot,	Look,
priotkryv pomertvevshee oko,	having opened a stiffened eye,
pervaya	first
pripodymaetsya *Galitsiya.* (PSS I, 235)	arises Galicia.

Here the rhyme is entirely in a line-end position, but the close syntagmatic bond between *ya* (I) and *vizhu* (see) makes an enjambed reading virtually irresistible, thus diluting the impact of the rhyme.

Mayakovsky's "moment of innovation," to use Robert C. Williams's perhaps too monistic formulation (1977, 140),[14] can be said to have occurred with the invention of the *lesenka* (stepladder) in connection with the long poem *Pro eto* ("About This") in 1923. If we were to convert the above-quoted quatrain into a *lesenka* (though Mayakovsky did not himself do so with this poem), we would lay it out thus:

Net.
    Eto nepravda.
            Net!
               I ty?
Lyubimaya,
    za chto,
        za chto zhe?!
Khorosho—
    ya khodil,
        ya daril tsvety,
ya iz yashchika ne vykral serebryanykh lozhek!

When dealing with either the *stolbik* or the *lesenka*, it is useful to distinguish between the "line" and the "verse." Following a number of analysts of Maya-kovsky's poetry, we will call a "verse" that segment of text that ends with a rhyme even if it does not all fall on the same horizontal line. A "line" is that segment which is on the same horizontal typographical line. In the *stolbik* a "line" looks like a traditional verse, while in the *lesenka* it is synonymous with a "step" in the staircase.

The *lesenka* layout in *About This* (1923a) is actually somewhat different than the standard one that Mayakovsky developed soon after. The next step is not always begun below the space after the preceding word, but is often pushed farther to the left below the preceding step (fig. 181). Thus the eye must travel back rather than continuing on more smoothly.

M. L. Gasparov (1974) for the first time points to an external stimulus on Mayakovsky in the development of the *lesenka*:

At the end of 1922 around the very time of Mayakovsky's entering into work on *About This*, there came to light Andrey Bely's small booklet *After Parting* with a preface (marked June 1922) "Let us seek melody" in which a program was advanced: "to seek intonation in an idiosyncratic layout which conveys intonation to the viewer"—and as an example precisely a stepladder layout is proposed.

[14] It is an oversimplification to think that any creative career can be reduced to one such moment, but Williams happens to have chosen the one that concerns us most.

*The Dnepr is marvelous in still weather, when freely
and flowingly
      dash—
            —Through forests
                  and valleys—
                        —Its full waters.*

. . . Mayakovsky's interest in Bely's "formal innovation" is witnessed further by his autobiography *I myself*; the thematics of the collection *After Parting* were close to Mayakovsky at the end of 1922, and the preface to it must have drawn the attention of the poet if only because of the hidden barb directed scarcely elsewhere than against him: "not long ago in Moscow everyone wrote in the same slack meter with alliterated consonances instead of rhymes. . . ." Therefore Mayakovsky's acquaintance with such a new book of poems as Bely's *After Parting* could hardly be doubted, and the influence of Bely's experiments on Mayakovsky's *lesenka* reform is very probable.   (Gasparov 1974, 436-37)

I might add that Bely's poems in *After Parting* provide numerous examples of diagonal layouts akin to the *lesenka*, but with the use of double dashes.

The change in layout of *About This* actually occurred as something of an afterthought. The first and second drafts are done in *stolbik* layout, as is the first half of the third draft. Halfway through this third draft, steps begin to appear occasionally, beginning on page 17. Paperny gives detailed attention to the first instance of *lesenka* in this draft. In order to analyze a moment that was to have a profound effect on the future look of Russian poetry, Paperny is well worth quoting in full:

Fig. 181. V. Mayakovsky, a page from *About This*, 1923; photomontage by A. Rodchenko.

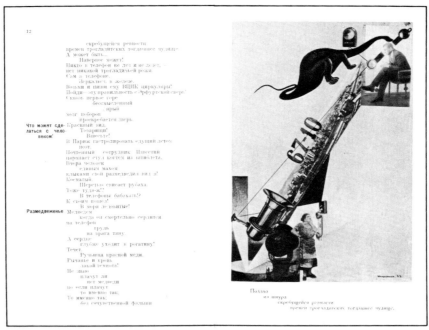

Already in the first draft, in the monologue of the Man on the bridge, there appeared the words addressed to the hero:

Ne dumay spastis	Don't think to save yourself
Eto ya tebya vyzval. (p. 11)	It is I who summoned you.

The same, but with a slight change, appears in the second draft (p. 14). Wanting to give the phrase great energy and dramatic expressivity, Mayakovsky in the third draft throws out the word *tebya* (you) and lays the words out thus:

Ne dumay bezhat!	Don't think to run
Eto ya	It is I
—vyzval. (p. 17)	—who summoned.

That is, he placed the word *vyzval* not under the preceding *eto ya*, but below to the right such that the one verse *eto ya—vyzval* was simultaneously both divided and at the same time isolated; it stretched stepwise from left to right; its beginning and end were clearly visible to us. Perhaps Mayakovsky didn't even pay attention to what he had written, but all the same—one can say without exaggeration—this was a discovery. The succeeding lines were again written in a *stolbik*, but on the following pages once again with increasing frequency, "steps" began to appear:

. . . Poka—	. . . Until—
po etoy	down this
po Nevskoy	Nevsky
po glubi	depth
spasitel lyubov	savior love
—ne pridyot ko mne . . . (pp. 17-18)	—comes to me . . .

The second part of the poem "Night before Christmas," having been begun in *stolbik* in the third draft, then is written in continuous *lesenka* with rarer and rarer exceptions. (Paperny 1958, 264)

In the printed version *lesenka* is used throughout. As Gasparov notes, because the poem was conceived in *stolbik* form and converted to *lesenka* only toward the end, its use of line divisions remains similar to Mayakovsky's earlier usages.

The real change of psychology occurs with Mayakovsky's next efforts:

The visual image of the verse changed at once: by writing in a *stolbik* the division into verses is lost in the division into lines; by writing in a *lesenka* both divisions present themselves to the reader with equal prominence. And not only to the reader, but also the writer; the new graphic showed Mayakovsky his own verse in a new light. Before this the fragmenting of the line evidently was used by the poet "by ear," only in individual lines— now he begins to use it consciously in each line. The poem *About This* was written still with the earlier attitude to the verse, and therefore, though it was printed in *lesenka*, the subdivision of the verse was in the previous style; but *Mayakovsky's Gallery* was written with a new enriched feeling for the verse and therefore the subdivision of the verse in it is entirely different. (Gasparov 1974, 435-36)

What is different, as Gasparov's study dramatically shows, is a new emphasis. For accentual and other types of verse in early Mayakovsky and late Mayakovsky, Gasparov has calculated the number of steps to the verse from undivided to four pieces. In the case of the *stolbik* the pieces are arranged, of course, in a column, so, following Shtokmar, a verse is defined by the rhyme scheme. Gasparov also calculates the tendency, when arranging the size of pieces (figured by the number of stresses in each piece), to have longer pieces at the end of the verse (growing), at the beginning (shrinking), or evenly divided (symmetrical). I have compressed his chart into the accompanying table by averaging his figures into "before" the change (including *About This*), and "after" the change (including *Mayakovsky's Gallery*). I have also singled out the results specifically for *About This* (finished February 1923) and *Mayakovsky's Gallery (MG)* (written April-May 1923) to show the clearness of the change and to locate it chronologically at March 1923.

In percentages (rounded to whole percent)

| | Number of pieces | | | | | Arrangement | | |
	1	2	3	4		Growing	Shrinking	Symmetrical
Before	39	42	17	2		28	7	65
After	(.2)	30	63	7		62	6	32
About This	32	44	21	3		27	10	63
MG	0	30	60	10		64	6	30

The "before" figures show that Mayakovsky preferred either to leave the verse undivided (39%), as are a number of entire poems in 1912-14 and occasionally thereafter, or to divide the verse into two lines (42%). He also heavily favored the symmetrical arrangement of lines (65%) (see also Gasparov, Table 12, 433), such as:

Eta tema pridyot,
               kaleku za lokti   (PSS IV, 137)
This theme will come
           a cripple by the elbow

After March 1923 there are virtually no undivided verses, and about two-thirds of the verses are divided into three lines, and one-third into only two. In arrangement there is a marked preference for the "growing" arrangement (62%), such as:

bylo
    skandalom,
               ne imeyushchim primera   (PSS V, 111)
There was
        a scandal
           without a parallel

Gasparov goes into other facets of this shift, but we can limit ourselves to the general observation that a change in layout practice seems to have *caused* a change in other areas of Mayakovsky's versification. The change in layout opened the door to new possibilities. It may be the case that some of these shifts, such as the regularization of syntax, of stress frequency toward the four-stress line,[15] and of stanza patterning,[16] would have occurred anyway,[17] but it is doubtful that many of them would have occurred so sharply and suddenly without the support of the *lesenka*.

One cannot leave *About This* without mentioning the dramatic photomontages by Rodchenko, which were in themselves a major event.[18] These photomontages are ideal illustrations for the poem, since they incorporate pictures of Mayakovsky and Lilya Brik, the main "characters" in the poem, as well as other photographic images of old-fashioned everyday life (*byt*), all arranged in a shifted, dislocated, half-humorous, half-grotesque, sometimes threatening way that corresponds to the mood of the work very well. According to one writer, Rodchenko "found the plastic equivalent of the poetic principle, since poetry is the drawing together of distant concepts. The collision of different critical masses presages an explosion. A catastrophe" (Uvarova 1968, 31).

Mayakovsky's Gallery (1923b) (PSS V, 101-48), the first work conceived from the beginning under the new *lesenka* system, is unfortunately dated in subject matter. It is a booklet that consists of a series of satiric verse portraits of prominent "anti-Soviet" figures, namely, Poincaré, Mussolini, Lord Curzon (English Conservative), Pilsudsky, Hugo Stynnes (German capitalist), Emile van der Velde (Belgian socialist), and Gompers. Each poem is fitted by the author with two illustrations, one a grotesque caricature portrait, the other showing the person in action; both of these give graphic shape to the images in the poems. A tight relationship exists here between the text and illustrations. Although the writing of the text largely preceded the drawings, as one scholar describes it, the drawings

[15] Gasparov's table 2 (1972, 411) shows a gradual, generally smooth increase of the four-stress line from 1913 (*A Tragedy*, 48%) to 1927 (79%), with a noted shift from the flexible early to the stricter late manner occurring between 1922 and 1923, i.e., before the change to the *lesenka* (p. 412).

[16] In Gasparov's words, "The early Mayakovsky preferred to emphasize the beginning of the stanza, the late Mayakovsky—the ends of stanzas. The first of these devices is more experimental, the second—more traditional (stanzas with a shortened last verse . . . are the most common type of stanza with varied line lengths in classical verse)" (ibid., 414). This is on the basis of the observation that "As in the early Mayakovsky, in the later the longest verse in the stanza is the first, the shortest— the last; but in the early Mayakovsky the lengthening of the first verse is more noticeable; in the later—the shortening of the last" (Kondratov 1962, 107-108).

[17] As Goncharov notes: "Mayakovsky's syntactic system underwent an evolution from palpable dislocations in the early works to a sharp decline of elements of 'telegraphic' syntax in the later works. It is characteristic that, if in the poem *War and The World* [1916], according to B. Arvatov's calculations, a third (33%) of the sentences are incomplete, in the poem 'At the Top of My Voice' [1929-30] not a single one is of this type" (1972, 96).

[18] Rodchenko did not invent the technique, however. Williams points out that Raoul Hausmann did his first photomontages in 1918: "Berlin Dada journals were full of photomontages and visual collages by 1922, and provided a novel influence on a number of Russian artists, among them the painter Rodchenko, El Lissitzky, and the film director Sergei Eisenstein" (1977, 143).

stimulated additional lines in the text (Pravdina 1965, 222). Nevertheless, there is nothing innovative here: it is simply an old-fashioned book of emblem poems. Mayakovsky's series of *Agitlubki* (propaganda broadsides), also of 1923, follow a similar format (PSS V, 167-250).

WHAT IS THE *LESENKA*?

With the discovery of the *lesenka*, Mayakovsky's poetry entered a new visual phase in which the remainder of his poetic *oeuvre* was to be written. Yet analysts have had problems discovering the principle Mayakovsky used in placing the *lesenka* steps. Compared to discussions of other aspects of Mayakovsky's creativity, little study has been devoted until recently to dealing with this most obvious feature of his later versification.

By way of an initial overview, we can refer to James Bailey's succinct outline of the various functions of the *lesenka*: "Increasing the number of phrasal groups in a line, indicating how a poem should be recited, setting off some words for special emphasis, delineating internal rhyme and other sound repetitions, and marking a caesura in long lines" (1979, 258). To this we can add an approach involving syntagmatic segmentation advanced by G. Pechorov. In this section I will discuss the nature of the *lesenka*, and leave for the next section the issue of recitation.

The most obvious place to begin is with the *lesenka* as a breaking device. Clearly, the step down automatically produces a break because of the slight dislocation of the next word from its expected position. Less distance is covered by the eye in this case than is required to return to the left margin, so, all other things being equal, the step down produces a break of lesser magnitude than a line end.

In a passage that sounds like Bely's complaints of a somewhat later date (see chapter 2), Mayakovsky himself writes in "How to Make Verses" (1926):

Having made a verse intended for print, one must take into account how the printed text will be perceived precisely as printed text. One must pay attention to the averageness of the reader, one must by every means bring the reader's perception to precisely that form which its maker wanted to give the poetic line. Our ordinary punctuation with periods, commas, question marks and exclamation points is extremely impoverished and unexpressive in comparison with the shades of emotion which the complicated person now puts into a poetic work.

Meter and rhythm are things more significant than punctuation and they subordinate punctuation to themselves when punctuation is used in the old standard way. (PSS XII, 113-14)

He gives several examples showing how this is true and how the average reader ignores the sense of the line, regardless of the punctuation, in favor of a mechanical, doggerel rhythm.

The lines:

Dovolno, stydno mne	Enough, I'm ashamed
Pred gordoyu polyachkoy unizhatsya . . .	To lower myself before a proud Polish woman . . .

are read like a provincial chat:

Dovolno stydno mne	(I'm rather ashamed)

In order for them to be read as Pushkin wanted, one must divide the line like I do:

Dovolno
        stydno mne . . .

With this division into half-lines neither semantic nor rhythmic confusion will result. The division of lines is often dictated also by the necessity of fixing the rhythm unmistakably, since our condensed, economical structure of verse often forces the excision of unessential words and syllables; and if one does not make a stop after these syllables, often one larger than that between lines, then the rhythm is broken. This is why I write:

Pustota . . .	Emptiness . . .
Letite,	Fly,
v zvyozdy vrezyvayas	Tearing toward the stars.

Pustota stands apart as a single word characterizing the skyscape. *Letite* stands apart so there would be an imperative construction: *Letite v zvyozdy*, etc. (PSS XII, 114)

Mayakovsky's insistence here that a midverse pause that results from excision of unessential words may be longer than a verse-end pause—a remark frequently quoted by scholars to show that such pauses are indeed vital to Mayakovsky's rhythm—is perhaps too forceful a statement. The line quoted can be quite adequately read with midverse pauses shorter than the verse-end pause. Only in the case of enjambed verses might there be a strong argument for shortening the verse-end pause, and enjambment is very rare in Mayakovsky (Timofeev 1941, 67). Thus the *lesenka* step serves to make sure that the naive reader puts the pauses in the right places and thus interprets the words correctly.

Gasparov sees in Mayakovsky's statement a twofold orientation: "(a) a pause is an element of syntax, a kind of additional punctuation mark which adds to the logical segmentation an emotional segmentation . . . (b) a pause is a specific element of rhythm which marks the dropping of a syllable" (1974, 439). Even in traditional layouts without steps it has been calculated that as a special "punctuation mark" in versification the line break more than doubles the frequency of punctuation marks in verse speech as compared to prose (Timofeev 1958, 70). In Mayakovsky, then, "the pause, which existed in classical versification as a possibility, here becomes an indispensable condition" (Zhovtis 1968b, 147). By employing the *lesenka*, Mayakovsky introduces a new means of creating such pauses, and thereby considerably increases their number in his verse. However, Gasparov notes that Mayakovsky's theory of the *lesenka* as a pausing device diverges from his practice. "If a pause is an element of syntax, then it must in no way contradict the natural, logical segmentation of the sentence." But Gasparov can list a series of examples where it does so (e.g., "A u/madamuazel-/ magazin bakaleyny" And the/mademoiselle has-/a delicatessen). He further notes that Mayakovsky's rich and complex syntax is regularly reduced to only a few favorite *lesenka* patterns. "The lesenka is laid over the logical segmentation of the text in a simplified schema which does not always correspond to the logical segmentation" (1974, 439).

On the other hand, consideration of a pause as a rhythmic element presupposes a clear metric scheme with precise syllable counts and predictable stress positions. To "drop a syllable" one must have a clear place where such a syllable is required by the meter; then the syllable can be replaced by a pause marked by a step down. Much of Mayakovsky's poetry uses syllabo-tonic meters, but, as Gasparov continues, in Mayakovsky's accentual verse such a scheme is weak or absent. In fact, the *lesenka* is used regardless of the metric structure chosen. Once again, the *lesenka* is laid over such a structure and is not a part of it, though it may reinforce it. Thus both aspects of the *lesenka* as a pausing device are not without problems when it comes to Mayakovsky's actual use of them.

Some scholars, in fact, have wanted to avoid the idea that line break automatically equals pause. Goncharov cautions: "*It would be incorrect* to absolutize the typographic layout of the verse and not see a flexibility and very non-unilinear interaction between verse structure and the graphic confirmation which gives the verse its second life" (1970, 59). Pauses can, of course, be produced by other factors, such as normal punctuation, natural segmentation, juxtaposition of stressed syllables, and difficult consonant clusters; and there are occasional instances in Mayakovsky's poetry where a pause indicated by a step is problematical, that is, it seems wrong or awkward, and one is inclined to disregard it; but by and large the *lesenka* divisions are the most reliable indicator of where to place pauses.

However, Goncharov's contention that a "system of pauses" emerges has been proved by Gasparov and Bailey to "have no scholarly justification" (Bailey 1979, 259). By applying statistical methods, Gasparov was able to detect only Mayakovsky's "tendency to use more steps in the opening line and fewer in the fourth line of each quatrain" (ibid., 258). Bailey successfully replicates Gasparov's results in an analysis of "Jubilee" (1924; PSS VI, 47-56). Bailey further notes: "Since Majakovskij employs a *lesenka* in all his meters, one can only conclude that it alone does not create a particular verse form" (Bailey 1979, 258).

Less convincing is Bailey's statement that "One also has doubts about how accurately the *lesenka* reflects intonational features because, for instance, V. Kachalov in his recording of several excerpts from Majakovskij's 'Jubilee' appears to ignore many pauses between the steps of the *lesenka* and add others where none are indicated" (ibid., 259). It is a mistake to assume that any one reading is authoritative. Even the author's own reading may not be the final or only word; and we do not, in most cases, have that on record. In addition, Mayakovsky has pointed out in print at least one of Kachalov's mistaken readings (see next section).

The evolution of Mayakovsky's rhythmics underlies the evolution of layout, but presents a more complicated developmental picture.[19] In the early period (1912-13), syllabo-tonic meters predominated. Khardzhiev and Trenin (1970, 72) have pointed to "But All the Same" (end of 1913) as a poem transitional to the freer rhythms of tonic or accentual verse that begin to take over in 1914-15. In this period there are also transitional "hybrid" forms (ibid., 204), such as "Anthem to a Judge" (1915) with irregularities in its unstressed syllable count, and "Man," which mixes sections of syllabo-tonic and accentual verse. Gasparov's succinct characterization of the period of accentual verse is this:

From the early works to the later, Mayakovsky's verse evolves: in 1919-1922 his rhythm weakens to minimal organizedness (especially in couplet stanzas), after 1923 it organized itself anew, but in a somewhat different manner. Namely: (a) the organization of the verse by number of stresses increases, by quantity of interstress intervals and anacrusis—it decreases, (b) the organization of the stanza (emphasis on its last verse) by length of the verse and rhyme increases, it decreases in the intonational *lesenka*. (1974, 467-68)

A major consideration in this rhythmic evolution is that verse, in order to retain its vitality and avoid falling into a monotonous doggerel, must maintain rhythmic tension. Tension is created by interplay of some regularized feature, such as a meter, and the language of its realization. Rhythm must be kept alive by the conjunction of opposing forces. In syllabo-tonic verse, the regularity of stress positioning is countered by the use of unstressed icti in a variety of configurations. The general principle seems to be that when one feature is regularized, then another must be deregularized to compensate for structural rigidity and to provide flexibility. The liberating feature of the *lesenka* was the introduction of breaks in a flexible and irregular way. With the resultant sharply increased number of breaks per verse, as Zhovtis notes, "The intonational symmetry of the verse in this way is destroyed from inside" and thus also its traditional "compactness" (1968b, 148; 1971, 62-63).

Another classical symmetry destroyed by Mayakovsky's layout, as noted by Zhovtis (1971, 64), is the lack of correspondence between the tirade and the stanza—that is, between the stanza as defined by layout and the stanza as defined by rhyme scheme.

The other functions of the *lesenka* listed by Bailey ("setting off some words for special emphasis, delineating internal rhyme and other sound repetitions, and

[19] Based on Zhirmunsky (1975, 559-68), who summarizes the results of others.

marking a caesura in longer lines") are obvious and easily understood. The last does not need our attention, but the other two are deserving of comment.

The "setting off" function for emphasis is perhaps the most straightforward aspect of the *lesenka* and the *stolbik*. As Roman Jakobson wrote already in 1923: "Mayakovsky's poetry is a poetry for the most part of isolated words" (1969, 107). The visual isolation given to individual words or small groups of words can serve to give them emphasis, as we have already seen in connection with Bely's prose and poetry. However, the matter has a somewhat different complexion in Mayakovsky once the *lesenka* becomes a universal. If *every* small segment of text is stepped down in the course of an often lengthy poem, the visual impact of the resulting fragmentation is much diminished. One step is no more prominent than another, in contrast to Bely's prose where a fragment isolated between double dashes is juxtaposed to blocks of prose that extend to the margins. Many later writers have therefore tended to use the *lesenka* more sparingly than its originator did in order to preserve its impact.

Mayakovsky himself, having sacrificed the emphasizing function to a large extent by overuse, needed then to resort to other means of emphasis, such as italics, boldface, and hyphenation between letters. Another favorite device of the time was to end a stanza on a one-word verse. Timofeev counts over a hundred such instances in the postrevolutionary period (1952, 170). Several examples:

```
Nam                                         We're
      ne strashno                                 not afraid
            usilie nichyo.                              of anyone's force.
Mchim                                       We rush
      vperyod                                     ahead
            parovozom truda,—                         a locomotive of labor,—
i vdrug stopudovaya vest—                   and suddenly a ten-ton piece of news—
            s Ilichom                                               Ilich has had
udar.  (PSS VI, 294)                        a stroke.
Vlast                                       Power
      k bogatym                                   will turn
            rylo                                        a snout
                  vorotit,—                                to the rich,—
                        chego                                    why
                        podchinyatsya                                succumb to
                              ey?!                                        it?!
Bey!!  (PSS VIII, 238)                      Hit!!
```

Also, the *lesenka* restores the genuine possibility of having internal rhymes, something the *stolbik* virtually eliminates by using end rhymes. Yet internal rhymes, even though they are an obvious path to take since the steps in the *lesenka* provide analogous visual positions between which a relationship can be created, remain a minor feature of Mayakovsky's versification. For the most part, he produces sonic echoes between lines—sometimes between a rhyme word and later verse-internal words, sometimes between miscellaneous verse-internal words. The layout can help the reader become conscious of such relationships more easily, but essentially they depend on the sound structure alone. A typical example of a sonic echo is the following:

Mne
    dazhe
        pidzhak ne zhal obodrat,
a grud i boka—
        tem bolee.
Otsyuda
    dash
        khoroshi udar— (PSS VI, 74)

I don't
    even
        care if my jacket gets torn
my chest and sides—
        the less.
From here
    you give
        a good punch—

Nevertheless, there are occasional true internal rhymes, such as:

Ot etogo *Tereka*
    v poetakh
        ist*erika*. (PSS VI, 74)

This Terek
    gives poets
        hysterics.

Here the *lesenka* provides a sense of verse unity while at the same time it has several line ends that can be rhymed. The above rhyme is a perfect rhyme and, since it occurs in the first verse of the poem "Tamara and the Demon," it creates a certain expectation that internal rhymes will occur elsewhere. Indeed there are others, not so perfect, but within the range of Mayakovsky's usual practice of inexact rhymes:

revet
    staratsya v golos vo *ves* (PSS VI, 75)
A *darom*
    nemnogo *darit gora*: (PSS VI, 76)

To roar
    to try at the top of the voice
and freely
    the mountain gives a little:

There is what might be called an eye rhyme (though this is largely alien to Mayakovsky's practice):

Ya znayu *davno vas*,
        mne
          mnogo *pro vas*
(PSS VI, 76)

I've known you long,
        to me
          much about you

Perhaps the most brilliant realization of the possibilities for internal rhyme effects is the following:

Vverkh—		Up—	
	flag!		the flag!
Rvan—		Rabble—	
	vstan!		arise!
Vrag—		Enemy—	
	lyag!		down!
Den—		The day—	
	dryan. (PSS VIII, 267)		is trash.

Here there are not only end rhymes, and internal rhymes within the verse (*Rvan— vstan, Vrag—lyag*), but also rhymes that run diagonally (*Vrag—flag, Rvan—dryan*). This kind of dynamic compression is also found in the later Tsvetaeva.

A more recent attempt to unravel Mayakovsky's rhythmics with the help of layout is made by G. Pechorov (1970, 1971) based on syntagmatic rhythms. Pechorov's analysis takes the concepts and terminology of syllabo-tonic versification and substitutes the syntagm for the syllable. He advances such terms as the "s-anacrusis" (syntagm-anacrusis), the "s-trimaker" (a three-syntagm, three-stress line), the "emphasistress rhyme," and the "s-ictus."

Pechorov notes that Mayakovsky's use of the term "stands apart" (quoted earlier in this chapter) shows an intuitive appreciation of the concept of the syntagm, which had not yet been defined or named by linguists (1970, 156). Syntagmatic segmentation is a feature bound up with the intonation and pausing of spoken language, as Herb Eagle notes:

The choice of precisely how to break up the utterance is not determined by rules of grammar and syntax. Choices are continually being made by the speaker, and the syntagmatic segmentation which is chosen is capable of reflecting subtle differences in meaning (often a speaker's segmentation, for reasons of special emphasis, can be quite idiosyncratic). (1976, 8)

Therefore, when Pechorov states that "at the rhythmic foundation of Mayakovsky's verse lay the syntagm" (1971, 161), we are not entirely relieved of insecurity, since the nature of the syntagm in relation to Mayakovsky certainly involves "special emphasis" and is often "quite idiosyncratic." To Pechorov's statement, I would like to add the qualification "at the rhythmic foundation of Mayakovsky's verse lies the syntagm *as it is reflected in the layout of the poem.*" Of course, the understanding is that layout is merely a means of allowing the reader of the printed page to recite the given poem in the way the author intended. In this regard, Mayakovsky's goals are similar to Bely's and Zdanevich's.

Pechorov himself underlines the importance of layout: "The position of a word, more so the place (position) of such a significant element as an emphasistress, has a colossal (definitional and functional) significance" (1971, 161). His analysis of "Left March" (1918; PSS II, 23-24) to a large extent demonstrates his appreciation in practice of the function of Mayakovsky's layout, yet it has enough anomalous points to make one doubt the usefulness of his elaborate critical apparatus. Nevertheless, Pechorov's approach is reasonably on target and is certainly an improvement over some earlier critics such as Ermilova (1964) and Kondratov (1962), who were content to dispense with the *stolbik* or *lesenka* as an unnecessary decoration; rather, they are essential to a correct reading and interpretation of Mayakovsky's poetry.

Artobolevsky reports that while Mayakovsky often left the punctuation of his works to the typist or editor, he "carefully did the intonational division of verses into stepped lines himself" (1940, 273-74). Artobolevsky adds that Mayakovsky was concerned about the layout and typeface of a work when it was published for the first time. Later publications of the work were evidently less well looked after, unfortunately. "As always, Mayakovsky's layout reflected the intonational wishes of the author and helped the reciter. The question of Mayakovsky's 'letter' is the question of Mayakovsky's thought. Behind his every 'letter' are the living sounds, intonation, thought" (1959, 265).

Arutcheva's study of Mayakovsky's notebooks shows that the indication of steps in the *lesenka* is the last step in the composition. With few exceptions, Mayakovsky lays a poem out in steps only for the final draft, at which point he also adds the routine punctuation. "When he writes poetry, Mayakovsky doesn't need either punctuation marks or steps at all. For him they are merely a means of conveying to the reader the rhythm of the poem, the intonation, and pauses necessary for reading" (1958, 355). This does not, of course, mean that they are an afterthought and not inherent to the original conception. Rather, they are very likely a part of it from the very beginning, but the poet knows how he wants the lines recited and does not need to note this down for himself, just as a composer might do the orchestration of a piece as a last step, knowing all along which instruments should play what; or a painter might know the color scheme of a painting while still perfecting the composition of the initial drawing. This, however, confirms the impression that for Mayakovsky the layout is only a guide for recitation and has no independent visual significance.

Furthermore, Gasparov calculates that Mayakovsky's early works contained a contrasting use of verse subdivisions because the odd verses in a stanza tended to be more subdivided than the even ones, thus: "for the beginning of the stanza (as for the beginning of the verse) a fragmented intonation was characteristic; for the end of a stanza (as for the end of the verse)—a flowing intonation." However, "In the late Mayakovsky this compositional use of contrasting divided and undivided lines disappears and all the verses receive a uniform 2- or 3-step layout"

(1974, 438). Mayakovsky's preferred schema in a three-step layout was to have one stress group in each of the first two steps and two stress groups in the third (1-1-2). The psychological effect of this, according to Gasparov, is to equate the three steps so that the longer third step is "lighter" (ibid., 441). Thus a "progressive lightening of the verse" predominates in the late Mayakovsky.

This would seem to contradict Gasparov's own contention that the *lesenka* is a liberating factor. He seems to be saying that it is a regularized feature and a formant of the rhythm lacking in the metric structure. He is talking about the last period and about the role of the *lesenka* in accentual verse, and this limits the scope of his comments. Yet a randomly chosen poem, "Perekop Enthusiasm" (1929; PSS X, 7-9), illustrates the typical situation as Gasparov describes it. The twenty-eight verses of the poem fall into seven quatrains with the rhyme scheme a b a b. This is the most regular feature of the poem. The meter is basically four-stress accentual verse with four verses having only three stresses. Twenty of the twenty-eight verses follow Gasparov's "progressive lightening" pattern of step-stress relationship (1-1-2), including two whole quatrains (the fourth and the seventh). The other eight verses in six other patterns are randomly scattered. If the accentual structure is slightly more regular (24 of 28 verses with four stresses), the rhythmic indefiniteness of accentual verse in general makes the regular *lesenka* structure a more palpable rhythmic feature, but not one so rigidly implemented as to be monotonous, even in the late verse.

All of this still serves to illustrate Bely's principle: "The freer the meter, the more it depends on typographic means."[20] In Zhovtis's words, "The exceptional significance of Mayakovsky's *lesenka* consists in that it introduced into poetry its own way of dividing the sentence without destroying in the process those specific verse links which existed in symmetrically constructed classical verse" (1968a, 128). The *stolbik* had introduced subdivisions of the verse, but it also weakened or destroyed its unity by making the subdivisions equal to a complete verse and not subordinate to it. It weakened the rhyme by removing it from a predictable, symmetrically placed location at the end of the line (Ermilova 1964, 237, 239). In a significant way it contradicted Mayakovsky's emphasis on the importance of rhyme by making rhyme-ended lines visually equal to nonrhyme-ended lines. Furthermore, Mayakovsky's sonorous but frequently inexact rhymes were harder for the eye (if not the ear) to pick out than were more traditional exact rhymes. The *lesenka* avoided both of these disruptive features, introducing subdivisions while preserving the unity of the verse and the importance of rhyme, thus restoring the harmony to Mayakovsky's system of versification. It was in this respect a more conservative measure than Bely's *stolbik* and double dashes.

Herbert Eagle describes the advantages:

[20] As quoted in Zhovtis (1968, 155). The quoted passage, however, is not in the location indicated by Zhovtis (Bely 1929, 11), and I have not been able to locate it elsewhere.

In Majakovskij's verse the reader (especially the unsophisticated reader toward whom Majakovskij now aimed his poetry) could easily lose the sense of the meter because it was often accentual (itself a departure from the usual), because there were a relatively large number of deviations from the dominant pattern in terms of number of stresses and also because Majakovskij often switched from syllabo-tonic meters without any marked transition (in his longer poems). The explicit step-ladder form at once solved all these problems by indicating clearly what the verses were, what the syntagmatic segments were, and what the rhymes were. (1976, 9)

However, as a consequence of restoring the harmony and clarity of the verse to something close to a traditional configuration, the potential rigidity had to be counteracted by subdividing the verse in a flexible, varied, and unpredictable way according to intonational needs.

It appears to make little sense to search for more definite patterns in the steps of the *lesenka*. Its role in rhythm and intonation seems much like that of soundplay: a free, unregulated, flexible means of expressively highlighting unique moments. What soundplay is to rhyme, the *lesenka* is to meter. Its value is precisely in its freedom and unpredictability.

HOW TO READ MAYAKOVSKY

If Mayakovsky's layout is meant to be a guide on how to read him, then we should now consider this in more detail. Clearly, the first instruction is: read aloud! All who heard Mayakovsky and report on it agree that his rich, booming bass voice was an ideal vehicle for the oratorical, projective style of most of his poetry.

The principal difference between Mayakovsky's verse and the verse of all preceding Russian poets is that Mayakovsky's verse is designed for the voice, for loud recitation for a mass auditorium. Furthermore—Mayakovsky's poetry found its fullest embodiment specifically in *his* voice, in the author's recitation. (Khardzhiev and Trenin 1970, 165)

Another way of saying the same thing is Spassky's statement that in reciting his poetry Mayakovsky expressed himself most fully (1940, 31). It is therefore best to begin by understanding how Mayakovsky himself read his poetry before we tackle the subject of how we should do so.

As with Bely, there is recorded evidence of Mayakovsky's voice, which we will consider shortly. There are also a number of written descriptions of his performances, most of which are too general to be of use to us, or else they provide only isolated details. Let me provide a few glimpses from less well-known sources.

Gruzinov writes:

When he read "150,000,000" Mayakovsky mainly emphasized its complicated rhythm.

Trying to make it easier for his listeners to follow one or another rhythmic passages of the poem, Mayakovsky lightly tapped his foot in beat with the words being pronounced and made measured movements of his body to the left and right, accompanying the body movement with hand gestures. More than anything I remember Mayakovsky's flowing hand motions when he was reading. Reading a poem, he moved his hands like a conductor before an orchestra seen only by him. (1978, 190)

A. N. Chicherin provides specific details on Mayakovsky's hand gestures during recitation. At the performance on February 2, 1918, at the Polytechnical Museum, Mayakovsky read "Man." Chicherin describes his elaborate motions:

As I still remember, when, in reading the lines from "Man":
How
can I not sing of myself
if all of me—
is a complete wonder,
if my every movement—
is huge,
an inexplicable marvel . . . ,
at the word "movement," Mayakovsky, who had up to then been standing motionless, suddenly flung out his arms straight to the sides at shoulder height. With this gigantic crucifixion he stood there ten or fifteen seconds, looking questioningly at the public, and— continued:
Go around the two sides.
At each
you'll marvel at the five rays.
It's called "Hands,"
A pair of magnificent hands!
He paused, and—
Notice:
I can move from right to left . . .
And he slowly bent the right arm at the elbow, having lifted his palm up like they do when voting: he moved his hand to the left, lowered it and propped it on his side; then he put his left hand in voting position and swept it to the right:
and from left to right:
Notice:
and having slowly raised both arms, with the words:
I can choose
the best neck
I will wring . . .
he delightedly tightened his fists and with controlled power he lowered his hands to his sides.
He picturesquely read the lines about the voice:
I can "O - ho - ho"
it'll flow high, high . . .
Mayakovsky sang, raising his voice with each sound higher and higher, and—suddenly:

> I can "O - HO - HO"
> and the hunt of the poet falcon—
> the voice
> will softly descend to the depths
> he rumbled through a hoarse "octave" and—was silent.   (1939, 14-15)

Katanyan, on the other hand, paints the picture of a more reserved performer of a later period (1927-30):

> He, the poet, believes in the convincing force of the precisely chosen word obtained "from artesian human depths" and it must be because of this that his gesticulation was so economical. In no measure illustrative or theatrical. One could not call it oratorical either. Perhaps most correctly—it was rhythmical.
> This was mainly one gesture of the right arm, broader or more collected from down to up, and simultaneously from right to left, from open hand to tightened fist, with a fluid taking and compressing motion. Sometimes it turns into something else: the fist loosens and the open palm (back of the hand up) flies straight out from him and higher than the shoulder.   (1958, 315)

Mayakovsky's was a performance that encompassed not only the voice, but the whole body. He was consummate not just as an orator, but as a complete performing artist. The gestures that were part of the effect must, however, be ignored insofar as they are a feature that is not to be found in the text, except by implication. A reciter is free to add them as he sees fit, but a reader will not find reason to do so.

Also not usually reflected in text is the author's ideolect, his personal way of pronouncing certain sounds, though some commentators have noted details (ibid., 315; Chukovsky 1963, 128, and 1967, 329; Chicherin 1939, 17).

Let us next see what we can learn from available recordings of Mayakovsky reading his own poems. These were made by S. I. Bernshteyn in 1920 and thus predate the days of the *lesenka*. As Zhirmunsky reports, "This collection greatly suffered as a result of the low acoustic quality of the recordings of that time" (1975, 637). Three Soviet records made from this source have been released; they provide us with complete recitations of two poems, "Listen!" (1914) and "An Unusual Occurrence Which Happened to Vladimir Mayakovsky in Summer at his Dacha" (1920).[21] A number of other poems reportedly were recorded but have not been released, perhaps because of the above-mentioned poor quality.[22]

---

[21] *Govoryat pisateli*, I (D95592-05593), *V. Mayakovsky. Stikhi* (D012237-38), and *Revived Voices* (33M 40-39857-58[a]).

[22] The following other poems are listed as having been recorded in 1920: "A vy mogli by" (1913), "Gimn sude" (1915), and "Voennomorskaya lyubov" (1915) (PSS I, 429-33). According to Bernshteyn himself, recordings were made in 1920 and 1926 of nine poems on four phonographic cylinders. All the surviving recordings are from 1920 (what was recorded in 1926 is not mentioned). These were later re-recorded onto various media. Some were successful representations of the poet's voice, but

Mayakovsky's reading of "Listen!" recorded in 1920 is not exactly like either the first version (*First Journal*, 1914; fig. 182) or the final version (PSS I, 60-61; fig. 183) in text or posited layout, but is somewhere in between. The final version, with the exception of a few minor details of punctuation, was arrived at already in 1916 (*Simple as Mooing*, 17-18) before the *lesenka* took hold, and the recorded version is nearly the same in text. But if we place our own line divisions according to the pauses taken by the author on the recording, we arrive at a layout with long lines closer to the first version than the final, more subdivided version:

Послушайте!
Ведь если звёзды зажигают, значит это кому-нибудь нужно?
Значит кто-то хочет, чтобы они были?
Значит кто-то называет эти плевочки жемчужиной?
И надрываясь/ в метелях полуденной пыли
Врывается к богу
Боится, что опоздал
Плачет
И целует ему жилистую руку
И просит, чтоб обязательно была звезда
Клянётся/ что не перенесёт эту беззвёздную муку
А после ходит тревожный
Но спокойный наружно
И говорит кому-то/ "Ведь теперь тебе ничего? Не страшно? Да?"

---

others "which are occasionally broadcast on the radio" are not. To which category the two poems on the available phonograph records belong is not clear. The original cylinders perished in World War II (Artobolevsky 1959, 126-27).

Fig. 182. V. Mayakovsky, "Listen!"
First Journal of the Russian Futurists,
1914.

Fig. 183. V. Mayakovsky, "Listen!" PSS I, 1955.

Послушайте!
Ведь если звёзды зажигают/ значит это кому-нибудь нужно
Значит это необходимо
Чтобы каждый вечер над крышами
Загоралась хоть одна звезда.

A few more subdivisions occur here than at first but not as many as later. The slashes indicate very slight pauses not judged to be of line-breaking weight. These do, however, fall at places where subdivisions were later made. If the layout truly reflects Mayakovsky's pausing at the time the version was published, then we can see that he was in the process of increasing the number of pauses over the years.

Incidentally, to my ear Mayakovsky's reading of the end of the poem removes the question, "Are stars necessary?" with a cadence that conveys: "At least one star per evening is necessary." Note the lack of the question mark in the last line of fig. 182, which entered the final version by 1916.

With "An Unusual Occurrence" we have a different situation. The recording of 1920 was made before the poem was published in any form. Written in June-July 1920, it was first published in *Liren* (dated 1920, but not appearing until 1921; PSS II, 494). The text of the reading differs to some extent from the final version (PSS II, 35-38) in word choice, but the *stolbik* layout corresponds closely with the pausing of the reading. There are only a few cases of lines running together (enjambment), and even fewer cases of midline pauses. Clearly a relationship between desired reading and layout was worked out from experience and was part of the conception of the poem. There is, in other words, a definite layout system employed. The temporal proximity between the composition and recording of the poem facilitated this close relationship, but little evolution took place thereafter. The few departures in the author's reading from the given layout may be considered ephemeral interpretational additions, which, incidentally, Mayakovsky was willing to permit not only in himself, but also in other interpreters (PSS XII, 113).

Other reciters of Mayakovsky, if the record *V. Mayakovsky: Poems* (DO12237-38) is a representative sample (and it includes many of the more celebrated reciters), entirely ignore the *lesenka* layout and read the poems as if they were laid out in standard quatrains (V. Aksyonov, L. Kayranskaya). Pauses come wherever the syntax or punctuation, but not the steps, dictate them, and the old-fashioned automatic intonation that rises at the end of odd-numbered verses and falls at the end of even-numbered verses is the typical pattern. Some are better than others. Yakhontov, for instance, is oblivious to the given layout about half the time; Kachalov is even worse; Ilinsky is a little better; and Zhuravlyov, reading the striking seventh chapter of *Good!*, is remarkably close to the page most of the time. Zhuravlyov's reading, with the exception of a few places, can be taken as a model recitation of the text as printed. Thus, in such unusual lines as

```
No-                                          Knife-
    zhi-                                            let
        chkom                                           in
            na                                              the
                meste chik                                      place click
lyu-                                         of
    to-                                          a
        go                                           cru-
            po-                                          el
                meshchika.   (PSS VII, 268)          landowner,
```

he separates each descending syllable with a pause in a kind of staccato dance rhythm. Most of the other pauses indicated by the layout are taken as well.

Yakhovtov, on the other hand reads the lines,

```
Glaz
        kosya
                v pechati surgucha,
naprolyot
            boltal o Romke Yakobsone
i smeshno potel,
                    stikhi ucha.
Zasypal k utru.
            Kurok
                azh palets svyol . . .   (PSS VII, 163)
```

```
Eye
        askance
                in sealing-wax impression,
he constantly
                babbled about Romka Jakobson
and sweated funnily,
                    learning verses.
He fell asleep toward morning.
                            Trigger
                                finger cramped . . . ,
```

as if they had been laid out thus:

```
Glaz kosya
                v pechati surgucha,
naprolyot boltal
            o Romke Yakobsone
```

> i smesho potel,
>   stikhi ucha.
> Zasypal k utru.
>   Kurok azh
>   palets svyol . . .

Generally, where punctuation or syntagmatic divisions require pauses, they are made; but other pauses required only by the *lesenka* are ignored.

As with Bely's double dashes, Mayakovsky's *lesenka* causes (or ought to cause) a reading different from one without a *lesenka*. It intensifies pauses. "Line end" has always meant a pause was structurally provided for, sometimes in correspondence with a pause created by syntax and punctuation, sometimes in contradiction to the expected places for such pauses. As a good orator knows, spoken language, particularly when it is concentrated in style and content, requires frequent pauses to allow time for the listeners to absorb the orator's words. Mayakovsky's consummately oratorical poetry incorporates this principle into its layout by indicating the desired pauses by steps.

Artobolevsky's article, "Performing Mayakovsky's Poetry" (1959, 125-62), is the best single manual showing how to interpret Mayakovsky's layout for recitation. He provides us with several carefully analyzed examples. He quotes the lines:

> I v etu
>   tishinu
>   raskativshisya vslast
> bas,
>   okrepshi,
>   nad reyami reya:
> "Kotorye tut vremennye?
>   Slaz!
> Konchilos vashe vremya."   (PSS VIII, 261)

> And into this
>   silence
>   rolling out full-force
> a bass,
>   strengthened
>   soaring over yardarms:
> "Which are the temporaries here?
>   Get down!
> Your time is up."

He then requotes them without the steps (omitted here). Having just commented that "a line reformed into a *lesenka* is automatically pronounced more slowly than a solid line" (p. 136), he remarks:

If we compare what we get, we see how much we have impoverished the intonational expressiveness of the excerpt. Instead of the triumphant, monumental speech, there sounds a not quite convincing chatter. How magnificent is Mayakovsky's word *tishinu!* separated by pauses. The word is "proffered" by the author with all significance: after all this is not that "silence" into which we can sink in everyday life, but a "silence" which has resounded over the whole world after the roar of battle, when the rudder of history has come into the hands of the proletariat. And how Mayakovsky proffers the word *bas* to which, after a pause, is added an attribute full of proud love *okrepshi*, and finally it is explained that this bass became strong in the free elements: *nad reyami reya*. Could such a thought- and image-packed concept occur to a reader upon glancing at the neat line in which all these words are set up one after the other along a ruler? And Mayakovsky's pause after the question: "*Kotorye tut vremennye?*" You just feel the sharp, penetrating eye with which the sailor surveys the "thirty temporaries" before saying his powerful "Get down!"

In another example Artobolevsky demonstrates the significance of a pause that contradicts logical syntax. The lines are:

Tovarishch Lenin,   Comrade Lenin,
                rabota adovaya   the hellish work
budet   will be
        sdelana   done
        i delaetsya uzhe.   (PSS X, 18)   and is being done already.

He notes first of all that the inversion *delaetsya uzhe* serves to emphasize *uzhe* and weaken *delaetsya*, which is "deprived of its own independent stress." Then he turns to *budet*:

The word *budet* . . . , deprived of substantive meaning and expressing only the future tense, is brought onto a separate line and is strengthened vis-à-vis *sdelana*: it forms an antithesis to the word *uzhe*, which emphasizes the meaning of the present time, expressed by *delaetsya*; and what is more important, with its increased stress *budet* acquires an additional shade of meaning—a shade of persistence, of assurance that the action indicated by the participle *sdelana* (with which *budet* is grammatically joined) will occur. In regard to this example it is worth noting that in other and rather numerous instances, isolating a word on a separate line in Mayakovsky's verse evidently indicates an increased stress without a pause after it: a break between *budet* and *sdelana*, which form in essence one grammatical form (future tense of the passive participle), can scarcely be justified, whereas an increased stress on the first of these words as was just shown, substantially enriches the content of the statement.   (1959, 138-39)

However, such a subtlety escapes Kachalov in his reading of the poem (DO12237-38), and *budet* receives neither additional stress nor a pause after it. We might also note that the extra stress on *budet* turns into an independent stress phrase that may produce at least a slight pause (*budet/sdelana*, vs. *budet sdelana*). As a general rule, Artobolevsky advises: "One ought to be guided only by the free rhythm of speech which is defined by the thought and feeling of the reader who has analyzed the text from all sides with a critical account for the segmentation of the text marked by the author" (ibid., 157).

Paperny notes that Mayakovsky combines his orientation toward conversational style with an avoidance of cliché expressions. He accomplishes this by removing all unnecessary "filler" words and phrases. "His skill in finding his own inimitably personal words in the living element of conversational language is what is unique about his work" (1958, 268; see also Vinokur 1943, 111ff.). The resulting maximally compressed, telegraphic style requires a clear conveyance of the subtleties of syntagmatic segmentation, since misunderstandings seem to occur because readers (even good ones) are not sensitive enough to the layout.

Mayakovsky himself indicates one such mistaken reading by the renowned V. I. Kachalov:

V. I. reads:
      No ya emu—   But I to him—
           na samovar!   the samovar!
That is to say, take the samovar (from my "Sun").

But I read:
      No ya emu . . .
           (na samovar)
(pointing to the samovar). The word "pointing" is omitted for the sake of emphasizing the conversational speech.   (PSS XII, 163)

We might add here that perhaps it is not Kachalov who is at fault. The final layout and punctuation of the lines are:

      no ya emu—
      na samovar: (PSS II, 37)

Although the author's intended reading makes more sense, he is at fault for not making his intentions clear enough. The punctuation used above (PSS XII, 163) conveys his intentions better than the final version.[23] However, Kachalov's reading would have required a marked stress on *na* to indicate the conversational imperative "take!" In any case, such authorial lapses are relatively rare.

One can concede, of course, that no two performances of the same work, even by its own author, will be exactly the same; yet the performances would be likely to vary only within certain limits. The *lesenka* and other such devices were attempts by the author *as author* to fix the limits of allowable interpretation, taking into account the "averageness" of the reader's perceptiveness. Mayakovsky

---

[23] It should be noted that at least one version of the poem published during Mayakovsky's lifetime has a proper form for conveying the desired reading:
    No ya
      emu:
        (Na samovar):   (Mayakovsky, n.d., 6)

would hardly expect this guide to be ignored by the sophisticated critic or reciter. Certainly, as we have seen, there was a myriad of subtle features of his own recitation, such as gestures, foot tapping, intonation, and idiosyncratic pronunciation, that Mayakovsky chose not to convey (or attempt to convey) into print. What he did strive to convey must have been exactly what he considered essential. As Artobolevsky puts it, "Mayakovsky's pauses are always motivated and expressive" (1959, 134). And as Zhovtis further notes:

In verses of any structure the joining of several lines into one, or, on the other hand, the breaking of it into pieces immediately affects the intonation. The intonation changes, carrying along with it the sphere of content, for it is an inseparable part of content. (1966, 108)

We can generalize this to say that no change of layout is without its consequences, since layout is an inextricable part of literary expression. Luriya put it well when he said that pauses and intonation reveal the subtext of a statement. They can "change the meaning of a read text without changing its word composition" (1979, 249).

To summarize, when we combine the various factors involved in the *lesenka* as it appears on the page before a reader's eye, we get the following general picture: The verse appears as a unit ending in a rhyme at the right. This unity is maintained typographically by the smooth stepping-down that retains the normal pattern of reading from left to right, no matter how many steps are descended in the process. Unity is maintained in recitation at least conceptually by a potential intonational arch that rises at the beginning of the verse and forms a cadence at the end on the rhyme, followed usually by a pause. The falling diagonal graphic reinforces this concept, and the rhyme and pause are in most cases a reliable, audible sign of verse end. The verse forms a recitational phrase comparable to a musical phrase and up to this point is not unlike the traditional one-line verse. However, within the verse there are clearly marked subdivisions indicated typographically by a step down. Each step down is accompanied by a slight pause or intonational break that is usually placed naturally, as it would occur in emotive, highly expressive speech. Typically each step corresponds to the specific syntagmatic segmentation required to achieve a given expressive effect. The steps form pieces subordinated to the total intonational arch of the verse, just as note groupings separated by short rests can subdivide a musical phrase without causing it to fall apart. This is a conceptual framework based on what the reader clearly sees and may not have as clear a correspondent in what he may hear when a poem is only heard. Most of the features will be comparably audible, but even slight variations in pausing, intonation, or stress emphasis from line to line and from reciter to reciter will diminish the clarity of the verse structure that is so obvious on the printed page.

The *stolbik* differs from the *lesenka* in being deprived of the unifying intonational arch. While the verse end can be recognized by the rhyme scheme, individual lines are not subordinated to the verse. The line-end pause is equal to the verse-end pause, and the relationship of line to verse as part to whole is absent. But this is not to say that the *lesenka* is better as a structure than the *stolbik*; there are cases, such as "Left March," where the *stolbik* is obviously exactly right for the poem. In fact, it was unfortunate that Mayakovsky turned exclusively to the *lesenka* and slighted the use of the *stolbik*, since the *lesenka* has certain liabilities in terms of monotony and predictability. The constant subdivision of lines into two, three, or four steps can become self-defeating as a means of isolating words for emphasis and leads to its own automatic intonational melody.

MAYAKOVSKY'S LEGACY

Of all the major literary figures we have considered, Mayakovsky has left the most obvious visual legacy: the *lesenka*. It was an invention that caught on rather rapidly.

The journal *Lef* (1923-25), which was edited by Mayakovsky and whose first edition included a publication of *About This*, may have had only a slow effect on the use of the *lesenka* by other contributors.[24] By the time of *Novy Lef* (*New Lef*, 1927-28), however, the *lesenka* was commonly used by others. One should not assume that Mayakovsky, as editor, limited his selections to those that carried his banner; he was above that. Rather, it was simply a matter of others adopting a successful device. In the beginning, most of these were his close associates and friends, among them Semyon Kirsanov, who began publishing poetry in 1923, and included the *lesenka* in a variety of other layout designs to form elaborate visual rhythms.[25] The closest to Mayakovsky's pure use of the *lesenka* and the most regular contributor of such poems to *Novy Lef* was Nikolay Aseev.[26] Others were Sergey Tretyakov[27] and P. Neznamov,[28] though they, like Kirsanov, tended to use the *lesenka* as only one of several layout devices in the course of a poem. Nikolay Ushakov[29] used an elaborate combination of steps, columns, and indentations closer to Bely's later practice (for example, "Summer Murmur"), but without double dashes, than to Mayakovsky, who always remained faithful to

---

[24] Sporadic steps appear in S. Tretyakov's "Rychi Kitay," *Lef*, no. 1(5), 1924, 23-32, and S. Kirsanov's "Krestyanskaya-Budyonnovtsam," *Lef*, no. 3(7), 1925, 24; and even in two novel excerpts by Artem Vesyoly, "Volnitsa," *Lef*, no. 1(5), 1924, 36-47, and "Strana rodnaya," *Lef*, no. 3(7), 1925, 59-69. N. Aseev adopts a thorough *lesenka* in "Liricheskoe otstuplenie," *Lef*, no. 2(6), 1924, 5-15.

[25] *Novy Lef*, 1927, no. 1, 41-43; no. 8-9, 2-31; no. 11-12, 26-28.

[26] Ibid., no. 3, 11-15; 1928, no. 1, 4-7; no. 3, 17-19.

[27] Ibid., no. 2, 21-23; no. 10, 3-6.

[28] Ibid., no. 2, 30-31; no. 4, 22-23; no. 10, 24-27.

[29] Ibid., no. 3, 25-26.

an observable quatrain structure. Even a contemporary such as Kamensky made frequent use of the device in his poems. Half or more of his collection *Izbrannoe* (*Selected Poems*, 1948) is in *lesenka*. Ehrenburg, probably without much exaggeration, has said: "In 1940, nine-tenths of the aspiring poets were writing in 'stepped' lines" (1976, 239). Of course, Stalin's enshrinement of Mayakovsky may have had something to do with it.

One must be aware that although it takes talent (and work) to successfully imitate Mayakovsky's rhymes, images, and rhythms, it takes no genius to stepladder a line, even a line of prose. Though Zhovtis is able to cite poets among the younger generation who successfully applied Mayakovsky's legacy (Voznesensky, Sosnora, L. Martynov), he is also able to provide examples of the bad imitation of this legacy (1968b, 155-62). As Zhovtis warns, what was originally a device for expressing an individual poet's feelings better can become a sign of a certain orientation or style—a sign that the other poet wants to be like Mayakovsky, to be oratorical, or to be civic. The device then becomes a substitute for the feelings, and the poetry is a poor imitation of its model (ibid., 162-63).

Bely commented very favorably on Mayakovsky's layout:

At one time even strophic layout was an achievement. They worked hard on it. It still corresponded to the rhythm of not long ago. It flowed slowly and calmly, with a large scope.

Now its pulse beats wildly, breathing is intermittent. Mayakovsky speaks about this. Its appearance is not accidental. Try to fit him into the earlier stanzas. He is right. He wants to breathe freely, to move quickly. This is possible only in an internally found—"individual"—live shape. But—this is not a verse? Not poetry? No, this is a verse and this is poetry. Mayakovsky's verse layout is not a whim, not a vagary, not arbitrary. This is a necessity for living verse, which moves abreast with speeded-up time and which strives to express *its own intonation*. (Bugaeva 1971, 107)

Bely had found his own new style of layout by 1922 and Mayakovsky, building on Bely, developed his own more straightforward system. Neither converted the other to his own version, but each went his parallel way and both returned to some earlier works and updated the layouts. Mayakovsky was, luckily or unluckily, canonized in 1935 and his system thus became the enshrined model for future generations.

Even if all the other visual effects discussed in previous chapters were eliminated by Soviet literary politics, Mayakovsky's *lesenka* can be said to have transformed the look of Soviet poetry for several generations, and its traces are still visible today.

Appendixes

APPENDIX 1. RESOLUTIONS OF THE ORTHOGRAPHIC SUBCOMMISSION OF THE IMPERIAL ACADEMY OF SCIENCES, MAY 11, 1917

1. To exclude the letter ѣ with consequent replacement of it by е (колено, вера, семя, в избе, кроме).

2. To exclude the letter Ѳ with replacement of it by ф (Фома, Афанасий, фимиам, кафедра).

3. To exclude the letter ъ at the end of words and of parts of compound words (хлеб, посол, мел, пять куч, контр-адмирал) but retain it in the middle of words in the meaning of a separating sign (съемка, разъяснить, адъютант).

4. To exclude the letter i with replacement of it by и (учение, Россия, пиявка, Иоанн, высокий).

5. To consider desirable but not obligatory the use of the letter ё (нёс, вёл, всё).

6. To write the prefixes из, воз, вз, раз, роз, низ, без, чрез, через before the vowels and voiced consonants with з, but to replace з with the letter с before voiceless consonants including also с (извините, воззвание, взыскать, разумно, низвергать, безвольный, чрезвычайно, исправить, воспитать, всхожие семена, расстаться, роспись, ниспосланный, бесполезно чересполосица, чересседельник).

7. To write in the genitive case of adjectives, participles, and pronouns ого, его instead of аго, яго (доброго, пятого, которого, синего, свежего).

8. To write in the nominative and accusative case plural feminine and neuter gender of adjectives, participles, and pronouns ые, ие instead of ыя, ия (добрые, старые, синие, какие).

9. To write они instead of онѣ in the nominative case plural of the feminine gender.

10. To write in the feminine gender одни, одних, одним, одними instead of однѣ, однѣх, однѣм, однѣми.

11. To write in the genitive case singular of the feminine personal pronoun ее (or её) instead of ея.

12. To be guided in hyphenation by the following rules: A consonant (one or the last in a group of consonants) immediately before a vowel must not be separated from this vowel. Similarly, a group of consonants in the beginning of words is not to be separated from the vowel. The letter й before a consonant must not be separated from the preceding vowel. Also, a final consonant, final й, and a group of consonants at the end of words cannot be separated from the preceding vowel. In hyphenating words having prefixes, one is not allowed to carry over into the next line a consonant at the end of a prefix if that consonant occurs before a consonant, e.g., it is proper to divide: под-ходить but not по-дходить, раз-вязать but not ра-звязать.

13. To allow the joined and separated writing of adverbs composed of nouns, adjectives, or numerals with prepositions (встороне and в стороне, втечение and в течние, сверху and с верху, вдвое and в двое).

Note: Contrary to the suggestions of the Orthographic Subcommission published in 1912, the Conference resolved:

1. To retain without change the now existing rules for the use of the letters o and e after ч, ш, ж, щ, ц;

2. To retain the letter ь in all instances where this letter is used in contemporary orthography (for instance, to write: речь, вещь, прочь, режь, ходишь, настежь, etc.).

APPENDIX 2. TRANSLATIONS OF ILLUSTRATED FIGURES

Figures translated or discussed in detail in the text have been omitted here, as have, for reasons of space, figures 1-9, 14-19, 43, 44, 52, 53, 102, 104, 131-134, 150-153, 181. The translations aim, first, at literal accuracy; and second, to preserve the layout of the original by trying to keep corresponding words in corresponding positions if this can be done without great distortion of the English. All translations are by Janecek.

Fig. 10

the swan of sorrow, sadly crying out in the silence, caressing.
    10. From everywhere fell night shadows.

    1. The deceased king raised the marble lid of his coffin and went out into the moonlight.
    2. Sat on the coffin in red clothing trimmed in gold and in a multipointed crown.
    3. Saw the sadness poured over the city, and his face darkened from distress.
    4. He understood that his son had abandoned the country.
    5. And he threatened his son, who had fled, with his dead hand and sat long on the coffin, propping his old head on his tired hand.

    1. Meanwhile the young king and his queen were running through lonely fields. They were drenched by moonlight.
    2. The moon stood over a copse of sickly northern birches and they sighed in exitless wastelands.
    3. The king wept.
    4. His tears, like pearls, rolled down his pale cheeks.
    5. Rolled down his pale cheeks.

Fig. 11

    It could not strangle the child and so it carried the killer on its back across the endless ocean, the killer capable of anything . . .

    Child. Old man, who is it roaring so long, so sadly in the ocean? . . . I have never heard such a voice . . .

    Old Man. That is a sea citizen who has swum up out of the depths . . . Now he is shaking the water from his green beard and is trying his voice, because he considers himself a singer . . .

    Child. I know the voices of sea citizens and they do not sound so long, so strange.

    But the old man was silent. He trembled from the bad chill that had blown over them. He mumbled to himself: "No, you cannot save him . . . It must repeat itself . . . One of its unnecessary repetitions will occur . . .

    "The day of the Great Sunset is approaching."
    The distant past washed over them from the constellations shining in the sky . . .

    On the sandy promontory took place a vile consultation. The serpent, wound in a loathsome coil, stretched out its neck and dully moaned, while the reprobate who had been brought from beyond the misty ocean meekly listened to the orders of the commander . . .

Fig. 12a

Enough.
Soon she would sink into convent life, would tire.
She said to her friend: "It's time."
"Because all will pass."
"And all will resurrect."
Involuntarily—
at the blizzard she flashed her eyes, sparkled
because in the window from under the window
a flock of silver threads swished their wings; . . .

Fig. 12b

Involuntarily
the friend rustled her head in her lap, just as if
in a snowy hill of silver.
And she whispered: "It's time—
the blizzard is blowing, he's coming."

Fig. 13

pa-a-
a-a-a-a-
a-a-a-ainful to-o-o speak.

Hoo-
oo-ow muu-ch I waa-nt to beliee-eve aand loo-ove.

Fig. 20

Papa brings me an alphabet book.
And—the old men's whispering stands around me: and it seems to me that they are on the point of bowing down before me with gifts,—to be secretive, to be silent, to recall some sort of ancient truth which may not be touched upon, which you recall without a murmur, recall then—
—about Adam, paradise, Eve, the Tree, the ancient snake, and good and evil.
Papa, Fyodor Ivanych, and Sergei Alekseevich made up their own conception of Eve and the Tree; and they wait for my confirmation of their words; I subsequently imagine myself standing among them; and my gesture is visible to me:—
—I am standing, having lowered my eyelashes: and—with a beating heart; two palms—palm under palm!— all strive to raise up the word given to the heart: to my throat; in the throat something is tight; and a tear ripens brightly; but the word is—not raised; into my little half-opened mouth my sweet wind blew: the two palms raised only— empty air to my mouth: there was no word; I—am silent . . . —
—and I am sad: I will say nothing; even if I said something my words would deceive them, repudiating the gifts; because I know that I know: a little piece of rowan-berry pastil says nothing to me;

the pastil will be eaten; and nothing will happen because of it; if I say this,—I know—
my friend, Fyodor Ivanych Buslaev will be chagrined; and how can I tell Papa that the
alphabet book is entirely incomprehensible and alien to me.

Figs. 21, 22, 25, 27, 32

"Thou—art."

The first "thou—art" grips me in imageless deliria;
and—
    —as ancient kinds, familiar immemorially: inexpressibilities, nonhappenings of con-
    sciousness lying in the body, the mathematically exact sensation that you are both
    you and not you, but . . . a kind of swelling into nowhere and nothing, which all
    the same is not to overcome, and—
                —"What is this?" . . .
Thus would I condense in a word the inutterability of the advent of my infant
life:—
    —the pain of residing in organs; the sensations were horrible; and—objectless; none
the less—age-old: immemorially familiar—
                —there was no division into "I" and "not—I,"
    there was no space, no time . . .
    And instead of this there was:—
                —a condition of the tension of sensations; as if it
was all-all-all expanding: it was spreading out, it was smothering; and it began to dash
about in itself as wing-horned storm clouds.
    Later a semblance arose: a sphere experiencing itself; the sphere, many-eyed and
introspective, experiencing itself, sensed only—"inside"; sensed were invincible distances:
from the periphery to . . . the center.
    And consciousness was: a growing consciousness of the unembraceable; the invincible
distances of space created a sensation of horror; sensation slipped from the circumference
of the spherical semblance—to touch: inside itself . . . farther; as sensation, consciousness
crawled: inside itself . . . inside itself; a vague knowledge was attained: consciousness was
transferred; it dashed from the periphery to the center as a kind of wing-horned storm
cloud; and—it was tormented.
    —"Not allowed."
    —"Without end."
    —"I'm being drawn over . . ."
    —"Help . . ."
The center—was flashing:—
                —"I'm alone in the unembraceable."
                —"Nothing is inside: all is—outside . . ."
And it snuffed out again. Consciousness, expanding, ran back.
    —"Not allowed, not allowed: Help . . ."
"I'm—expanding . . ."—
                —this is what the little child would have said if he had been
able to speak, if he had been able to understand; and—speak he could not; and—understand
he could not; and—the little child cried: what for—they were not understanding, they did
not understand.

Figs. 23, 24

I think: Uncle Yorsh will now take his disks (the harmonies of the sphere) from his briefcase . . .

But hazily, biting on a piece of his beard, Uncle all of a sudden hops up on tiptoes on the black background of the piano; he begins to snort at Papa with his nose:

—"Ugh, ugh, ugh!"

—"I, I, I . . ."

—"Ugh, and he!"

—"And she!"

—"Ugh, and I!"

. . . .

Transfiguration by memory is—the reading: of the universe, not ours, standing behind what was previous:—

—I wait:—

—a beating, furry tail would squeeze out from under Uncle's yellow jacket; I think—there will be a dance; and I wait—by now they would be gripping candlesticks; having arranged their hands in a hilariously funny way, they would keep moving faster and faster, one after the other: jumping up, like . . .—

—the figures of the yellowish-brown uncles seen by me; flamelets would fly out from the candlesticks—

—and in the sparkling rhythms they would begin to beat the realm of rhythm, where the pulse rhythm of the sparkles is— my own, beating in the realm of the dances of rhythm . . .

Fig. 26

. . . for some reason I am embarrassed by them; they aren't embarrassed by—me . . .

And hiding my embarrassment, I shout:

—"Oh, what a bunch you all are . . ."

Recollections of Kasyanovo.

The recollections of Kasyanovo dissolve into themselves the recollections of the people living there at the time: the emerald foliage seethes; and off in that direction, into this foliage, go—the people for me; I am running toward the pond where the steely outflows are going off beneath the lindens and the willows; and into my forehead crunches the dry wing of a yoke; but a one-armed statue had risen up from the greenery—with an age-old face and shield: he looks at us . . .

Beneath it, preaching to Papa on a bench, where the bright-red roses are, is Kasyanov. Papa doesn't agree with him, he is shouting:

—"I would take all these speeches and . . ."

And in dispute he began to wave at him his *durandal* (a rooty cudgel which he used to walk)—

—subsequently Mama burnt durandal up—quietly when Papa wasn't around; he waved it in dispute; my Papa named his stick *durandal*, deriving the word from "Durandal"—the sword: (Roland fought with it)—

—Papa used to fly in the huge lanes for whole days waving his *durandal*; this was him getting upset: this was all—the *differing of opinions*; and he would stumble across Mrktich Avetovich; Mrktich Avetovich is a hunchback in a bright-red shirt; Mrktich Avetovich doesn't agree with Papa; pinning him to a tree-trunk, my Papa would start shouting:

    —"Permit me to . . ."

    —"No, sir . . ."

    —"What is it you're saying? . . ."

    —"And I'd like to take you and . . ."—

                       —Mrktich

    Avetovich—

            —many years later I read his fat volume: *Era*—

                       —is mordantly poking Papa, sparkling his teeth beneath Papa, with a huge hand—in the stomach:

    —"No, and all the same . . ."

    —"All the same . . ."

. . . .

    Often when seeing Papa Mrktich Avetovich retreats headlong under the lindens; taking a seat in the bushes, he reddens there with his humps; these are—*differences of opinion;* "they" retreat from Papa—into forest retreats; and persuading *"them all,"* shaking his *durandal,* my sweated-up Papa chased after them in the foliage of Kasyanovo.

Fig. 28

    The lacy days—in the night—repeat themselves in nights; the shadows have been blown down out of the corners; the shadows have been hung down from the ceilings; and appearing out of air,—the black-horned women were passing by in the air.

. . . .

A   In the evenings Raisa Ivanovna always reads to me—

                       —of kings, of swans; I

B   won't understand anything: good!

C   We are—under a lamp; the lamp is—a swan; and the raylets would widen—into the snow-white sparkles of unfolded, sunny wings, intersecting in my eyelashes; sticking in my hair, they would tickle my ear; half-drowsily I cuddle up to the raylets; head on knees: I cuddle up to my knees; everything has gushed away—into the shadowy, dark sea; the back of the armchair is—a cliff; it—is running over, growing: good!

D   From the cliff:—

    —(Reality had gone off into half-sleep: into half-sleep came fantasy)—an age-old king summons a faithful swan to swim through the waves, across the seas after his daughter in the land of forget-me-nots (when was this?)—

E   —the lamp is—a swan: I too am flying away with the swan:—

                   —we—rush into the waves; we dash through the air into the voice: forgotten and ancient:—

F   —. . . . .

G   "I wept in my sleep . . .
And dreamed: you had forgotten me.
I woke . . . And long, and bitterly
Then I wept . . ."

H   (This is—someone: singing from the living room) . . .

D′   Half-sleep mixes with fantasy in me, and into the fantasy pours the voice:—

I   —we
are—in the air: on outspread swan's wings, where harpists were playing on stretched strings of air and where swan feathers, like fingers, shiningly pass along them; the azure—

J   —(*soundlessly, as you were nodding to me earlier*: you were not there; I wept without you; having forgotten all, I wept; you returned to me—my swan queen)—

F′   — . . . .

G′   "I wept in my sleep.
And dreamed: you love me as before.
I awoke, but tears were still flowing . . .
And nothing will wipe them away . . ."—

E′   —We are dashing: all together. The red Preceptor is also dashing after us: as a millennium, flames and purple:—

C′   —I open my eyes: the swan is—a lamp.

A   Raisa Ivanovna will cut the swan out for me tomorrow . . .

Fig. 29

Snow flurries are being sprinkled about; unstrewn whistles are being sprinkled about; it smells of pipes in the air; multi-eyed time has by now run along the streets in a golden thread of lights: a pre-evening patrol; all in the sky is rifted; someone sparkles from there, from behind the crimson rifts; he turns yellow, grows gloomy; and passes over into dark.

     We—head homeward.

. . . .

     In the evening:—
                    —on the flying spirals from the wallpaper, the jambs of red dawns, burning, grow lacy: with a pale-rose-colored swarm, but—
                               —Raisa Ivanovna with a soft, agate glance mysteriously leads my glance over: leads it to where—
                                      —a crimson head, chuckling from the wall, had snapped with a grin.
     I don't have time to cry out: Raisa Ivanovna—
                          —dearest!—
                          —is by now playfully bowing her lock to my lock; and—she begins to laugh.

Fig. 30

     —one time they brought me a piece of fresh bread . . . to make a sinner out of it, that is, to dip it into tea; they broke the piece up, but right there—
                                —in that piece!—
                                   —bugs—
                                       —red
ones!—
     —were crawling!—

—Papa poked his nose into the matter, and propping up his glasses with two fingers he twitched his face and cried out:

—"Ekh! what a mess: bugs!"

At home, though, he himself bred all sorts of functions on leaflets (to Lagrange's function inclusive), and beings of other lives in everything: both in the buffet crannies, and in the spider-web under the curtains—

—I saw a belly-legged function there:—

—Papa speckles white leaflets with his *functions; functions* from the leaflets are crawling all over the house; he would throw the leaflets into a little basket; but I would pull them out; and Raisa Ivanovna would cut a raven out of them for me; all my ravens are special: they are speckled; and—they wear: many multitudes of x's dancing about; . . .

Fig. 31

. . . to take me to sleep: in her bed; I don't sleep; I—am silent: I hardly breathe; it is—

—dear and ancient, and hot, and threatening, and sad for me;—

—horribly pressing my chest, the horrible pressures sink into my chest as feelings: to puff up . . . And everything begins to shout at me in very loud stories again; through the dear, ancient, cross Tree it would cut:—

—clearly:—

—it is no longer Raisa Ivanovna breathing next to me, but a flame erupting here—

—"it!"—

—I am horrified and feel: the growing through, the swelling of "it"— into nowhere and nothing, which all the same is not to overcome; and—

—what is this?

. . . .

The "*it*"—was not mine; but to me it was as . . . in me, even though— "*outside*":—

—Why "*this!* . ." Where? is not "*it*" really Kotik Letaev? "Where is I?" How is it so? And why is it that for "it" "I" is not—"I"?—

—"You are not you because next to you is something: sort of searing . . ."

Figs. 34, 35

the pillows, because I am—

—dissatisfied; they told me after that I was sick at this time, that I was suffering from a fever; there's no fever; and—there are no events; that is, there is nothing anymore; but . . . the cereal . . . eaten up . . . by me; I ate— every day; ate up: also—all those same humdrum days: I feel like crying; time is overcome in the ticking: it is twilight already.

Nanny looked at me; and above a stocking bright knitting needles began to dart—

—The semolina cereal deceived me; my little stomach is weighted down and somnolence is invading; I try to get help; Nanny has bowed down toward me; instead of her head—

—above the collar of the vermilion dress, without a cap, sticking out, it licks me, sparkles at me and blinks at me with a little bluish fire, breathes through an opening: a lamp glass!—

—But Nana, with the bright knitting needles, only looks!

A Stroll.

Nanny Alexandra and I are making our way along the corridor—from the nursery; in the corridor stove—

Fig. 36

—a heavenly bird!—

—And then from fires and shadows will bubble up stripiness; and— will roar: or—a tigery beast, called a tiger by me for its play of shadows and fires forming its luminous shell: *"tiger"* . . . Look—

—arboreousness would rise upward as a wing-feather; and in the center would puff a Disk bending out two wings and falling down in a rain of light rose feathers forming its body:—

It will explode and — — — — — — — He will explode in his breast
will beat out a huge shining geyser which and will beat out as a Sword; will rush
had shot out in a column, like a Sword as love: with Fire, as a Sword, into the
into the universal universal
Nothing!— —All!

—I find out that this Sword is—
the Archangel; his name
is Raphael:
Raphael
Sound
of
ex-
plo-
sion!—

—Yes, Heaven is a sparkler!—

—Trees, they are seized by a weighty bottle, a clear transparent silver vessel in a thousand-branched Luminary pierced by the golden warmth of threads of precious metal and beautiful bright rooms;

Fig. 37

of Angels conveying with warmths the
Word
and
as
if—
—a
sphere

surpassing
in sparkle the
sun, in the presence
of these pict-
ures in
me
a-
-rose:—
—to
m
e—
—it seemed: wordless stares were piercing me by my
recognized
brothers:
They foresaw me
in the future; and that loud shame, impressing itself in the present
gave to the present a murky, prophetic meaning; and the sunsets,
shining at me, seemed to me clearer, more luminous, and—the air
cleaner. I felt that which was occurring—
—from—
—far
far
a-
way—I saw
through all things;
I—read about the incidents
of everyday life
not as if they had happened
to others: I knew
them from the be-
ginning; events
—began to lose
their incidental
character for me; and my
very muscles conducted me
down the street not incidentally—
—into our movements fate
is passionately poured; thus, wandering down Berlin boulevards, I—
—looked into the hap-
penings of the street; and these happenings spread out for me into a pattern of ex-
periences which reflected the pattern of my experiences; they became me;—

Fig. 38

WORLD SOUL

An eternal
Cloud it rushes,
A careless
Smile,

An unstable smile
It laughs.
A silvery ridge
It flies above the water—
—ray-like—
A wavy
Ridge.

Clean,
Like the world,
All ray-like—
The golden dawn,
The world soul.
After you you run,
All
Burning,
As to a banquet,
As to a banquet
Rushing.
You rustle as grass
"I am here,
Where the flowers are . . .
Peace
To you . . ."

And you run,
As to a banquet,
But you are—
There . . .
Dashing by
As the wind,
You scarcely touch the greenery,
You smell
Of cold,
And laughing
In a second
You'll drown in the azure,
You'll fly away on gossamer wings.
From raspberry
Carnations,
From pale-pink
Clover—
You drive away
Ruby
Insects.
                1902.

Fig. 39

    IN OPEN SPACE

Hail,—
      Desired
      Will—
      Free,
      Will
      Victorious,
      Illumined distance,—
                  Cold.
                  Pale.
The wind dashes by, moving the yellow grasses,—
Late flowers, white.
I fell to the cold earth.

Strange are the sweeps of the resilient stem,—
Free, bold.
I attend the sound of rustling.
      Quiet . . .
      Enough:
      Flowers
      Late, pale, white,—
      Flowers,
      Quiet . . .
           I weep: I'm in pain.
             1904. Serebryany-Kolodez.

Fig. 40

    No. 285
    TO ENEMIES.

In my soul space—
      The space of earth has gone.
      You the flow of my darknesses,
      To you is raised up from the earth,—
Pierced
By a cry . . .

Look, the shreds of mist—
      Crawl; shreds of anguish
      Bear swarms of darkness.
      And the distance snipes from the river—
Pierced
By a cry.

From the plain the sound of wind
      Into a single dream swept
      burned-out sorrows,
      the heat of muted passions,—

Of darkened
Distances . . .

Love in the breast—
   Freeze, cool!
   Rinse in a flow of clouds!
   Leave: depart into the night—
Of burned-out
Distances!

At this hour they crawl to you
   And as lightning pierce the eye
   Thunder massifs
   And the tale of winds wafts
With a prolonged
Groan:—

"You are treacherous . . ."
   Raising a cry in the distance,
   The languid darknesses
   Pierce, snipe—pierce
With a prolonged
Groan!

The languid darknesses
   languidly bowing
   I—avenger—have spilled!
   Do you hear me—
You
Treacherous ones?
      1908. Serebryany-Kolodez.

Fig. 41

     3.
Beyond the lilac seedlings threatens
     The old
     Jester:
Above it, like an infernal
     Flame,
   Flitted
 His
Rag . . .
Onto the sunny grasses
Fell a humped shadow:—
    —And
   Shadowy
  Arms—
Rocked
 Above
  The flower! . . .

Soundlessly heaves
The laughing
Breast;
The tiny bells
Sang out:
        "Forget,
            Forget,
                Forget!"
In the tower windows
            Sparkled
            Fires
            Like snakes,
There rustled
          In the heavy
        Heat
          Leaves.
The Humpbacked,
Gray
Castle
Above the meadow in broad daylight
With a wing—a noctule's
Wafted about
An evil
Shadow.
The princess awakened:
To all—
     —The end
      The end! . . .
      Break,—
          —O heart!—
The crackling
Bell . . .
You,—
    —Dandelion—
               Happiness:
        As fluff fly around!
She went off,
         Dropping
               Tears,
          On white ermine.
Waving away with a branch
The shining dragonflies,—
After her
The gray
Joker—
     Carried
     Her heavy
     Train.

The stems
Swayed
Of captivating
Verbena
     Between satiny
     Black
     Covered
     Knees.

Fig. 42

SPRING MELODY

Mandolin

1.

I hear in the mornings—
Calls
I . . .
See—fires:—
     —Days—
     Turquoise
     Full of meaning . . .

     Around me—
     Birch
     Stumps;
     And—
       —Mother-of-pearl stumps,
         And—
           —Mother-of-pearl
           Studded
           Rosy—
             —Dragonfly wings.

2.

A cloud—
Hung—
   —in the sky:—
       —Illuminated:—
          —Edges
          Of its shreds
          With fire
          And flights
       —Enveloped—
         —By a trembling
         Gold coin
Thus—
   —From time
    Immemorial—
       —Memorialized:—

—Holidays of nature, fulfilled
  By lights
  Of lost
  Meaning,—
      —As—
         —Bejeweled wings, in the shining
          Day
          Lightninged
          By the sun
          Of a dragonfly.

3.

I attend:—
      —With sensitive
      Ear
      The fearsome
      Flies—
      I do,—
         —The silver meters
         From the window
         Waft upon me:—
A little fly
Shining
Emerald,—
      —Spirit,
       Flight,
       Buzz—
         —And—
           —Cobweb
           From a silver stump,—
              —Lapped
              In the winds
              With light
              Of filament.

4.

Flying by, accidentally melting
Whiffs,—
      —Somewhere
      Breathing
      In silence,—
         —Splashes in silver winds
         Like meters,
         My—
        —Ear
        Spirit
        And
        Soul—
           —Singing . . .

Flying by, accidentally melting
Visions
Of light—
    —Pierces—
        —Firmaments, drylands
        Vision
        Of soul—
   —Pierces:—
    My heart
        —The secret—
            —Of inspiration . . .

5.

And of air—
    —Intertwining, wafting questions
    Of light
    Of words—
        —Howls
        Of winds—

    Pierce—
      —Birch
      Seedlings of words—
          —With calls
          Without answer!

And of rest—
    —Positing, ripening questions
    Of light
    Of words—
      —Sprays
      Of stanzas—
   Splash my heart—
        —Rosy
        Rose—
          —With dews!

6.

Yes,—
  —And—
    —My faithful
    A balance
    To hypocrisy,—
Yes,—
  —And—
    —To faithlessness
    Faithful
    Heart—
      —Ripens—
        —With eternal
        Tremblings
        Of the spirit . . .

Yes,—
   —And—
        —The weightlessness
        Of down
        From the pale undersky
        In flights—
             —Above the coming
             Murmurs
             Of leaves—
                  —Wafts
                  Lights . . .

Zossen. June 1922.

Fig. 45

As a coward, slave, man in stocks,
Be a devoted pimp to her—
    And don't bark!
Bury your hopes early,
So she can forget the wounds of heart—
    Help!
Let her curse and swear
Amuse herself with the look of a snake—
    Don't frighten!
And then in the years of joy
Expect from her a reward flunky—
    Don't wait!
You will capture a hot kiss,
A sole kiss, a pitiful one—
    And groan!
And then unhappy,
Don't dare to call her beautiful
    Don't torment! . . .—

Figs. 47, 66

If you want to be unhappy
Watch the beautiful girls go by
      And notice their figures!
Don't dare to catch an eye
Lightning sparks are hidden there
      You'll ignite pray!
For the eyes of a maiden-beauty
    Every man boldly sacrifices his life
        As if for heaven

If there's cowardess to be dragged
To pine over one's sad lot
      Choose!   1.

Fig. 54

> AKHMET
> hOlds a cup
> MIlitaRy   PoRtrait
>
>   GENeRaL
> * IN 5 YEARS
>   INn
>
>   An ANGEL FLeW
> * WILL Be a POET
>   IS WRITING A PLAY *

Fig. 56

Khlebnikov: "From the Songs of the Haidamaks"

From the overhang the gentleman would fly brightly
In overseas snouts flit legs,
And the gentlewoman seeing a knife above her,
Falls to earth, kisses his legs.
From the abyss a mustached man swims up like a walrus,
In order to moan out—"Santa Maria."
We, fellows, would merrily roar
And heat with stones in the depths of the chartoria
We float the gentlemen down the rivers,
But the daughters strolled on arms.
It was a merry time
And the stakes of the game were high.
"The gentlewoman serves us as hired washerwoman,
And the gentleman sails and on his face a gull sits down."
—No, old man, it's not good—
Brocade is far behind the bast mat.

Fig. 63

>   3 poems
> written in
> my own language
> different from others:
> its words do not have
> a definite meaning
>   *
>
> No. 1 Dir bul shchyl
>   ubesh shchur
>   skum
>   vy so bu
>   r   l   ez

Fig. 64

Giving hours to music
Or you watch the pure light of snow
In the heavenly gaze drowning
As a dream hurtling into the depths of years

Or as a quiet water nymph
You glance eyes flowers of anguish
Amid the night you wander in the darness [misspelling] of the park
Or suddenly you'll awaken the glass of the river

Fig. 65

Ah it's bitter, ah it's sweet
To live in the desert in the quiet!
The dawn will shine at us stealthily,
At us so soon in the depth!
From flowers of the distant earth
From the smiles of a bright-eyed girl
We have hid ourselves, we have buried ourselves
In a dark, stifling, eternal hiding place!
We live—around is a dark place—
In stifling nights there is no sleep,
Coffins full of dust
Ancient tsardoms here sleep!
    We have covered their tracks,
    Torn out the ore roots
    Thrown them in the water, burned them
    Down the stream of water—
    So they'd not bring us woe!

Attending to the directions of the elders,
The beasts circle the earth
From everywhere: from the endless blizzard,
And from the east, evil destiny,
They bring us on a silver tray
All crafts of swarthy slave girls
Frisky-eyed, wise of mouth,—
    Skillful in the bargain . . .
        And with the sunset
            Also payment,
        Fruits from the south
            The charm of the meadow . . .

We are like tsars in gold:
Thus on every patch of robe
We shine as a carbuncle
Or number known only
        To us and God! . . .

Our eyes, though they are ancient,
But they will hotly pierce like a true arrow:
  Tiger child and old man
  Each sleeps, head bowed ...
You take from the beast his fur
And another will not eat you! ...
  Strong are the signs
  Things in a fight,
Amid things and a dog's liberties,
We hold the country in disgrace!

If only the powerful found out!

Figs. 67, 68

  I
(From the letters of Natasha to Herzen.)

I come into a sacred tremble
Strolling beneath your umbrella,
I go off early to the lindens,
The blue copse draws me to the distance.

From a wellspring with your glass
I drink in consonance with the anthems of the birds,
And everything seems to me deception
I am far away ... O day of whirlwinds! ...

Now the bell rang measuredly,
The village sleeps ... I awoke
Kneeling on the earth ... God stared
Into the depths of being ...

Fig. 72

Without thoughts
it didn't become
so much
Everything was filling out
At one time rings
Poured in beasted (?)

Fig. 75

On 27 April at 3 o'clock in the afternoon
I instantaneously acquired
to perfection all
languages Such
is the poet of contemp
oraneity
I place my
verses in the

Japanese	
Spanish	IKE MINA NI
and	SINU KSI
Hebrew	YA MAKH ALIK
languages	ZEL

Fig. 77

and up flew
  a merry ace
and with a rustle fell
  a five
and twists his
  mousey whisker
the stern player
  watches carefully

and in torment the writhing
  cardsharp
asked the devil:
  feel sick, brother?
he started trembling . . . I
  wouldn't want to be swindled
knocking into a neighbor:
  my fault!

the old man was sure
  of himself
concealing in his face a
  foxy grin
  and he didn't believe
    in fate
he gazes cunningly evilly and like a lynx

Figs. 78, 79

Leaf 8: In horror he recalls personally seeing people crucified upside down by the Germans (excerpt from a newspaper account)

Leaf 9: During the shooting execution of peaceful citizens, they forced those about to be executed to dig their own graves . . . (excerpt from a newspaper account)

Fig. 83

A faucet of blue-gray velvet in my heart - place for me
And turn out [?] tenderness as from the guts
into a scroll of banknotes rustling like a woman

      A - choo!
Hey, I'd rather be catcalled again by the HERD
(looking buffalo-like at my automobile)
or again as a tossed-out lout to fall past the carriage

So that I'm quiet
Didn't turn out honey . . .
                    I don't want to! . . .
           I'd rather with a spoon
Me-lan-chol-ically
                    pick the nose
                         of
                         a cow
                    A - a - choo! -

                                   A. Kruchonykh

Fig. 90a

She dashed away . . .
The local stud—splenetic!
But all the same—I'm surviving
Already a third week
In slush and cold
—no matter, I'm getting used to it
I go to work
and even daily dine
  on something
                    fatty
with sauerkraut.
I don't say her name.
I live a quiet life.
Knitting my brows
I try to fulfill
my predeparture promise.
Yes . . . more calmly—
  than an anemic . . .
A doctor naphthalated
  by medicines

with twenty pincers
aborted my memory . . .
. . . .
_____
They tossed [?] me into a hatch
I somersault *without memory,*
I knock on a stone
I know—I won't come out!
On wet boards
  with a silence—
     FLOP! . . .
_____

REVOLT OF WISDOM.

The ancient motto,
The tablet of great-crumbly
romantics and novelists:
LOVE-MYSTERY-DEATH.

Fig. 90b

  BUT WE,
having conquered sickly sclerosis,
have inscribed on our pullovers:
CATCH - POPFOOD - LAUGHTER!
A soaped centaur,
     squeaky,
was replaced by an electrocart
of three thousand HP.*
_____
IDYLLIC LEECHES
Not as a wonder,
  not a firebird
  (not really! where!)

I terribly much
unbearably need
for verse production
a scrap
of mountain air! . . .

_____
In a comforting robe
     RUBYATKA -
like a big-hearted nurse
place on the top of my head the stamp
     the auburn leeches of your brows!

As a friend,
   with the edge of your ear
Love me just a little!

Let my wounds cool,
in horror
    my fever will be shaken off,
forever I will shed
   the hateful bed

---

*HP = eych-pee = horsepower.

Fig. 105a-c

LOCOMOTIVE AND TENDER.

1. A little locomotive like a bird
   Whistled and was gone
   Moon = quotation mark +
   exalted object
   The locomotive's short-windedness
   Ascent and bridge
   Damp armpit
   Thundering tail
2. The baby was too small
   day and night crying
   The poet ran away
   Life is a butcher
   A head crowded
   With others' words
   An outsider bride
   A one-sided catch
   The wheels began to turn.
O curls of railroad expectations
Bouquet of fires + flitting locomotive
Among the night willows (not flown past)
Like a snowdrift of cursing
O tendrils of darkness and gloom
Rolling a whimsical railroad car
Past windows
Of sparkling lacquer
Russia has thrown itself around like a hasty cat
Embroidered on shirts a concertina motif
One flatland soul turned
Stinking like an earthenware saucer.
Russia has no corner where there'd be no oblivion
Purity of feelings tidy speed
(when twining leaves of snowflakes
Die to fall from sheer enjoyment).
    I'm going third class
    The class for castoffs
    "OF ARISTOCRATIC (!!) RACES"
    —An empty custom
    "All are equal"
    Hung down

        The bird
        Of an empty country.
    Train = arrow
    and city = bow
    (the hour of departure = firm)
    Every victim faulty
    Streetlight = needle
    and heart = bundle.
The autumn Wind Weaved its oWn
                snares
Clouds cirCled around the musty Campfire
And the sky Ratted befoRe the fRail mountain
GRievances Ran con-ceRn
    All crowded around at the pitiful gorge:
    Leaves flowers glances of thin maidens
    (Over them) untwiNed the maNe of the
              furry wiNds
    (In a row) brushing against all.

O bloom   it isn't blooming
Perfume out   only a stench
He'll open his mouth   no white armors
Old old man   o bald old woman
A last cry   doesn't wound the ear
O go away   you are seen corpse
Shepherd of scab and sheep
O go away   I'm a renter
Newborn   Vat   r
    Words galloped like FLEAS
    In his brain
    They weren't unpleasing
    In the young meadow
    He has the soul of a poet
    They said of him
    But he has no summer
    = sick inside
    The words turned black as fleas
    On the whiteness of consciousness
    [They were fly specks =
    OF YOUR ACKNOWLEDGMENT].
Mourning impediments of kilometric
Pillars and strings of long scrapes
When a gown train of blizzard unstably rippling
And furry saddlecloths of cloud tear at the face
The child moans hoarse cradle
The broth of rays is nasty liquid
Rolling graphs of these thin threads
When full of glumness rent they Ate
Around the settlements a weak hiccup

(A Distant bell) whose voice is thinly sticky
Sparkling with the white of frosted footstraps
Near naked ICON CASE DISHONOR.

Fig. 106a-b

FROM HIEROGLYPHS TO A

On the ceiling of the soul there rocks
with a tail of a smile
an electric chandelier
a sister of morning-evening
rusty coachman zarathustra
betrothes brides
hundreds of poems
ferroconcrete ones
in dresses made of fabrics
XRAYS
of bubbling energy
WORLD MORNINGS = it will raise
a florid advertisement
on blue velvet of
lines of letters
trolley sparks
crystal thawing
RECORDS OF HEIGHTS
        + 3.15
            of oxygen
to carry up like yokes the fate
            of news
OF THE RADIOTELEGRAPH
        from the island of ravath
where for the sake of the count or lord
they destroyed the warring tribe
        OF PEOPLE-PLANTS
        with wings
of mountain-peak birds
    Hamatsu-havu
OF THE FIRST AVIATORS
        who have flown to
Solomon
for the building of a temple
of the first to have read
from above THE PATH OF THE EARTH ——————

Figs. 107, 114

A TANGO WITH COWS
              to Vl. Mayakovsky
LIFE is shorter than a sparrow tweet
is a dOg SwimminG THERE
on the Ice down a springtime RIVER
WITH PEWter MERRIment we lOOk
on FATE
[tied into a seaman's knot of loneliness]*
We Discoverers of COUNTRIES
beyond-rind WORMS
K I n G S of orange groveS [and]*
and C A T T l e D e A l E r S
Perhaps we will drink a goblet of WINE [to]*
the hEaltH of the pLants eLApsinG
              oR
              Better
              we'll wiNd up
              THE GRAMOPHo   NE NOW
Y O U G O T O H E L L
              H o R N l E S S and
              f L a T i R o N s
I want to dance ALONE
A T A N G O W I T H C O W s
to bUild
              B   I   G   S
                 r D e
              from TeARS
of bullish
——————————————————Jealousy
              to the TeArs
of a CRIMSON girl

*words added to version in fig. 114 (G.J.)

Figs. 108, 115

SUMMONS

CACoPHoNy of SOUL[s]
s y m p h o n y of MoTOrS
——————frrrrrrrr
It is I it is I
f u t u r i S t - S O N G W A R R I O R and
PILOT-AVIATOr*
V A S I L I K A M E N S K Y
      with eLaAsTic pRopelLer
SCREWED into THe CLouds

*Diploma from the IMPERIAL All-Russian Aeroclub No. 67, issued on 9 November 1911.

> for the visit
TO the FaT COURTESAN death
>> sewn from Pity
A TAngO MaNtLe and
>> STOCKINGS
>> with
>> PAnTIES

Fig. 109

GyPsY

FREEDOM-UNBRiDLED
HEART—without HARNESS
THOUGHTS—without HAT in a
REVELROUS souL
the BaNkS OVERFLOWED
FIREWOOD 2 armsful
RIFLE and AxE and
REINDEer HORNS
a TenT and a CampFiRE and
SHARP hARPOONS
DANCE with bells and Conjure
I AM A HUNTER————yOU to the CatcheR
>> the SheeP has gotten Lost
>>> kiss
GIve ME a holey shawl
TAKE mY BEARskin
COME aGain SPEND THE NIGHT
MIGRATE WITH SONGS
LIFE IS—RESURRECTION
YoUr EYES ARE—CHARRED LOGS
LIPS—CRUSHED CherrIEs
Breasts an EARTHquAKE

Fig. 110a-b

VASILI THE WANDERER

>>> to fanny ML
I am a Strange wanderer
>> OF STRANGE LANDS
I will put my VERSES
into a flour sack
will load it on my humped back
>> and with a crutch
I will go begging
>> I'll visit even YOU
>>> at your estate
to drink COFFeE to smoke a cigar

———

We'll drink our fill of tea
We'll go for a drive in the car
We'll stop in at the aErodome
   on airplanes I
   am an experienced pilot
if you want I'll take you lady
   as a passenger
We'll fly over the evening city
at exactly 6 o'clock
the electric streetlights will flicker
   O isn't it enchanting
    to feel the whirl of
    B E A U T Y
Below they'll ignite Bonfires
   this will be a sign to us
   wherE to land
After the flight
   By car to a CafE
   From there to the CircuS
   Then the VArietY Show
B U T I N T H E M O R N I N G
   I'll again be serious
I'll put my Verses
into a flour sack
will load it on my humped back and go away to beg
   I BElieve
   Sometime
in the mountains I will meet a GIRL
with a basket of ripE-red berries

Fig. 111

BA — KU — KU

They bring the black in tanks from bakU
from boundlessness of smoky thoughts
in the forest coos the cU-ckOO-cU
The EvenIng noise smellS of PeTroleuM
26 seats IN a ruby-red buS
 next to me is sHe over the trembling of the WindoW
No. 147
   the highway rocks
   pasT the dAYS
   tElEgRaPh poleS WITH
   WhitE cuPs
WiReS of brass hOpes
   March 4th (To HEr)
In my hEAd a geOgraphicAl maP
of VaiN docKs

circassians passEd on the way to the River
        a Village in the mountAins
           heart motor beaTs
tHey bring black in tanks from BakU
I sleeP
        — ku — ku ——
and I know somewHere in wandering
words of flying windily tossed up
on shouLders carRied soNgs
        OF TIGER SKINS
moved by aErowisdom
and the wAy mounTained
           TEMIR—KHAN—SHUR

Fig. 116a-b

barefoot through nettles
CHILDHOOD (the poem was written in Perm
           at the dock when I was
           11 years old)
1884 on the Kama

—————

    on the rock
     Vasya Kamensky
april 5 before EASTER
from the gold mines
to the barge dock
      of lyubimov
steamboat whistles
AT NIGHT
    splashes velveteen
    and on masts fires
    we alone
give out anchors
      from wonders
       three pressed close
under one blanket
    vasya alyosha and petya
on the dock
    in a megaphone they shouted
from some country
      they were docking
      with barges
we were tired
    along sacks and crates
      in red flour shops
EVERYTHING DROWNED
the smell of home remained

```
            and beckons
to fish beyond the Kama
I'm quiet t—t—cricket
let's set
a trap
tomorrow
sonday
we must
get up early
in the fog
suddenly
a steamer at the window
and MELONS
```

Fig. 119

host
sitiznz heerz tha akshun ov yanko king ov albania ov tha famus
albanian poet brbr kolum ov tha stokekschange dedikaetid to
olga lyashkova heer they dont no thee albanian langwidge and
a bludliss killing givz thee akshun willy-nilly without
tranzlayshun sints thee albanian langwidge from rushun comz from
it yu will notiss wordz similer to rushun wunz like dunkee
blokhed galoshez and suchlaik but bekauz tha wordz ar albanian
ther meening iz not rushun like dunkee meenz (nessessarily aye
woont giv tha meening) and suchlaik wy dont get upset remember
heer tha langwidge iz albanian
akts
yanko iz in pants from somewon elsez bak shood in nu taim
prins prenkbibdada

Fig. 128

                                        sitiznz   seen I
                                        host

tha wOr deekwAIrd by tha kIdz ov Olya lyashkOva
dAId laikthis
andAId her lidantYU aikonpEYntingz ovhizwAIf tafInish(?)
nottrYing apOrtrit ovmElnikova
      azaprEzen tuthasOrserer ovthabrAId
ilYA zdanEvich
tharEE tAImz gotsIk hEven hElpm
[etc.]

Fig. 137

My soul is sick with a bad sickness
in shameful tatters my elbows
and my guardian also:

yesterday he came in shining garments
today he'd burned out cold
Feet leathered in Havana! . . .
I'm about to croak—and the quoly[?] settlements will perish
From a word—the whole city
there walks a DIRTY-FACED PLAGUE! . . .
But if they hold out the black genius
forever they'll be solid—
like my laugh of jersey
like a lovers'
W   A   R !

Figs. 138, 140

In a purely feminine way tenderly and caressingly
She convinces me that I am a talent
That according to the menu they will put me on the table
And they will all like the best supper imbibing lap
A band of effete chewers
Will throw themselves on my veal leg
I'll toss them a packet of smiles of golden fishes
They'll amazed dance till morning tapping
                    in truth their spoons
Drinking up with the liqueur of my flowering shirt,
Where on the suspenders hangs a mahogany sofa
And I will stand in the corner and will weep from
                    exultation and gratitude
And after me
THE WHOLE CAFE-RESTAURANT . . .

Fig. 141

—18—

SURIA illuminates
With a gold sand fountain
BliNds the eyes . . .
you'll faIL completely fooled! . . .
            CONTRASTS
                From OL to SHI
a mole tarrEd
rollings
skullies wildly
fracturations
FRAMO-CHO-MANY-y
        SHLYK!
            HUBU
        COMPAREND! . . .

—19—

TO ILYA ZDANEVICH

How easy it is to read
                    EESTER
                    AILEND!
Manahinda!
The Easter Eve service is made easy . . .
As the bicycle was pinned to Eric! . . .
                    TEACHINGS
One must feed intuition
Tend it BY LONG SLEEP
BY SQUIRREL SABBADIL WASH IT OUT
Running away NUFFIN!
Don't drink kerosene at night!
Guzzle wine more reservedly! . . .

Fig. 145

2/3 of a vershok under heel
          POETRY MINE
BLOOM BITCH'S DAUGHTER
       Romulus and Remus
               sucked
                  tin

      From a uniform plate
CREATURNIPSHARPSIGON
WORDOWNTURNINGONE
          NONPABA
          NONBADA
          STAPAGA
          JANOGAH
     ONAGAHAAHA
             ready

Fig. 146

               to the leg
                  of illuck
       running behind me
turning around I'll cut the stretched-out vein
               Clock
I'll stop at the bed
                  of a friend
I'll sit on a fallen mare

And until then I'll jump over
       THE CORD
Until the earth becomes thick
       COFFEE
Then I'll sell the horse to a circus
And on an old-old bird
I'll fly to Havana money
       THERE I'LL DISMOUNT
And near the worked island
       I'LL HANG
THE SHIN-BONE

Fig. 147

       6.
       tool II
     to Break into pieces and
      to saturate
   This is done in a sieve
       by sifting
  the large it is shaken
    into fine grains
    before
       turning
    into
    a powder
    rustle
Or
    CONSTRAINS
Don't lose your common sense
for examples go around
       they are carrying an aspen stake
       they will kill living foreheads
          Kruchonykh

  bonZA
   NAbza
    ZaNba
     Feve
      Terentev
       demon head
        head less
         deadhead
          he is
Kobiev
     strange name
      son of a bitch
       Sarkisov
        still

7.
tool III

to get up and go to the city

OR

to fall asleep before breakfast

Fig. 148

12.
EIGHTH

TO DRINK WINE AFTER 11:00 PM.
IN SOLITUDE
IF YOU DON'T FALL ASLEEP

13.
NINTH

UNDIVIDED (IT IS I WHO POKED
MY FINGER INTO THE SKY
MAYAKOVSK.) PASSION TEACHES
LIVELY
CONVERSATION WITH ONESELF
PROVIDES A DRY HOT
STEADY PERPENDICULAR
    OF THOUGHT
THUS APPEARED MAYAKOVSKY

Fig. 149

16.
TWELFTH

REWRITE
REREAD
CROSS OUT
REARRANGE
ADOPT
JUMP OVER AND SKEEDADDLE

17.

Thirteenth Tool
IS NEVER
USED

Fig. 154a-b

FUNDAMENTAL DEVICES

ENANTOSEMIA. Enantosemia is a stylistic practice which submits the *expressive sign* to many polar, reserved interpretations.

An *expressive sign* is material organized to correspond to the needs of the constructivist.

AMPHIBOLIA. Amphibolia is a stylistic practice which places the *expressive sign* in a neutral or polysemantic position.

RUSSIAN RHYTHM. INTONATION. THE SYSTEM OF COORDINATES. ARCS. ACCOMMODATIVE DRAINAGE. THE TAUTOLOGICAL CIRCLE.

SIGNS USED.

1 or / —Main stress in the word

2 3 4 5 —Gradations of secondary stresses in the word.

+ —Central stress of the entire construeme.

1 2 3 4 5 —Secondary stresses in the construeme.

Quotation marks over a letter - a secondary stress in the word.

Horizontal line over a letter - a sign of sound length.

Dot over a letter - abruptness (staccato) of sound.

˙— —Abrupt (staccato) beginning of length.

Ӿ —Pause.

‖ —Sound (breathing) break.

Letters enclosed in □ mean a complex sound in Moscow pronunciation.

Ł and ł—Blunted Polish L.

dD —Transfer from hard to soft D.

Ш̆—Indicates soft Ш

"р̃d dazh . . ." etc.—Such a parenthesis means an uninterrupted sound equal in pronunciation time to two.

A bracket which unites a letter to a word ("lěny te ntilèn" etc.) is its phonetically organic unity with the word.

A bracket over a sound break ("d ‖ déti . . ." etc.) is unity of meaning in the broken rhythm.

"Brátshka . . ." "séstritsa ródnya . . ." - A conditioned rhythmic arrangement required by contextual plasticity of meaning.

> —The musical sign.

All the constructions found in the book were created and made in Moscow in the years 1921-23.

READ ALOUD USING MOSCOW DIALECT

For lack of typographical symbols, timbres and intonations could not be typeset in this book with the accuracy of the original.

Fig. 165

GYPSY WALTZ ON THE GUITAR

The nnight's saleepy. Cool? ness.
Here in the llanes of a mu?teted gaar-den
And only the moooans of a gii-ta-aar ree-zound.
Taratinna-Taratinna ten

"My deee-rest[man]—don' be ang-gree—
My bitter heaaart is not? for youuuu
In it Yaga has bbboiled with pep-perd poisonnn
The black? froth—ov-va—lllov."

"My deee-rest [woman]—I'm haaappeee
Suffocating with smo?thered paaashun
I'll second all your pain after youuuuu
    If only to bee—in tune wiiith yur heaart."

Ahhh, the nnight's saleepy cool?ness
Here in the llanes of a mu?teted gaaar-den
And only the moooans of a giitaarar reezound
    Taratin?na. Taratinna ten.

Fig. 166

SKI RUN
(Declamational poem for baritone)

The snows are deep
paths along the drifts
skis skis skis skis
—O-o-o-oh! . . .
The sky is blue and gloomy
and the snows—squint your eyes
are sparkling, sparkling, sparkling
—O-o-o-oh!
Skis—a pointed sagene [2.5 meters] . . .
No huts nor villages—
only empty empty empty . . .
—O-o-o-oh!

Fig. 167

SKI RUN

DECLAMATIONAL (simplified)

The entire poem has integral elements of rhythm and intonation which must be perceived from the voice and not from the paper. The doubled consonants are pronounced as long, their duration twice that of ordinary ones. The signs (ˉ) (˘ ˘) etc. indicate pauses one, two, etc. times the length of vowels. Letters in parentheses are pronounced as added sounds equal in length to one vowel but less clearly. The numbers "2" and "4" say that the "line" (verse) is read to the count of one—two or one—two—three—four, in which every stress always has four syllables. The question mark (?) over a vowel shows the rising of the voice, and the letters α, β, γ various levels of tone from low to high; the sign \ \ or / —the direction of the voice when reading the line—higher or lower. Lines without α, β, etc. are read in a normal voice. Stresses ''',",' go from strong to weak. The expressive curve is calm to the semantic turning point on the word "kompas" (p. 21); here it rises sharply and goes upward to the end.

SEMANTIC

The poem fixes on a definite period of time, e.g., from five to seven o'clock in the evening. The main event in this period is the victory of organized willpower (by means of an instrument—the compass) over fantasy (pp. 14-20) and consciousness-disorganizing endless wildness of our country. Correspondingly the work falls into two parts, "before the compass" and after. The verse, "Strelka, kak belka" [An arrow like a (white) squirrel] is transitional leading the two parts to the focal point of the compass dial [(white) squirrel, arrow]. The command "Attention" in gymnastics precedes (but here we are talking about military sports) every other command—a local device. Regardless of the period of real time, the poem can be looked at as a projection of the dialectical development of culture's organization pressure.

Figs. 169, 170, 171

Along the pavement of my soul
                    rutted
        the feet of madmen
pound hard phrases of heel
        Where
                cities
        are hanged
and in the noose of cloud have cooled
                towers' crooked
        Necks
I go alone to sob that by the crossroad
        Are crucified
        Police-
                    men

A few words about my wife
Along a distant beach of unknown seas
    Moves the moon
                    my wife
My lover auburn-haired
        Behind her carriage
Shoutingly drags love of con-
            stellations a vari-colored belt
She marries an automobile
                garage
She kisses newspaper stands
and the milky way of her train as a blinking pageboy
Is decorated with tinsel sparkles

Fig. 176

Come all to me WHO broke the silence
WHO HOWLED BECAUSE the nooses of half-days were tight
I'll show you with words simple as mooing
Our new souls humming LIKE streetlight arcs
I'll only touch YOUR HEAD with my fingers
And on you
Will grow out lips for HuGe kisses
and a TONGUE native to all peopleS
But I my soul hobbling will go off to MY throne
With holes of stars in the worn-out canopies

Fig. 177

Farther to the north
To
Where in the grip of eNdLeSs anguish
With fingers of waves
ETERNALLY
the fanatic ocean tears its breasT
I'll wander to there
and TIRED
In my last delirium
I'll toss your tear
To the old god of storms
At the source of animal beliefs
      Curtain

Epilog
Mayakovsky
      Kind sirs
      I wrote all this
      About you poor rats
      I don't have a breast
      I would have fed you like a Good wet-nurse
      But now I've dried up a little
      I'm blessed
      But even so by whom and where would a
      PERSON be given the space of oceanic thoughts
      It is I who poked my finger into the sky
      And shouted it was a THIEF

Fig. 178

THE *BOLSHEVIKS*
    ARE LOOKING FOR BOURGEOISIE.
THE *BOURGEOISIE* IS RUSHING
    A MILE A THOUSAND.

MENSHEVIKS
    ARE SUCH PEOPLE—
THEY COULD JUDASIZE
    DEAR *MOM*.

FOR A *COW* IT'S HARD TO
    RUN QUICKLY
KERENSKY WAS THE
    PRIME MINISTER

FLOWERS SMELL NICE
    TOWARD NIGHTTIME.
TSAR NIKOLAS LOVED THEM
    VERY MUCH.

Fig. 180

REMEMBER THE DAY OF THE RED BARRACKS

1) We beat the Russian Whiteguards.
    That's not enough:
2) The monster of world capitalism is still alive,
3) Which means we still need the Red Army,
4) Which means helping it is still necessary—it's clear.

Figs. 182, 183

    Listen!
After all if stars light up
This means someone needs it?
Means that someone wanted them to exist?
Means that someone called these spit blobs pearls
And anguishing in blizzards of noonday dust
Hurries to the sky fears he's late
Cries and kisses the veiny hand
And asks for there definitely to be a star
Swears he won't survive this starless torture
But afterwards walks worried and
Externally calm
And says to someone that after all now nothing is frightening to you.
    Yes?
    Listen?!
After all if stars light up
This means that someone needs it
Means that it's vital that every evening above the roofs
There lights up at least one star!

References

Listed are works referred to in parentheses in the body of the text, plus a number of other works relevant to this study but not directly referred to.

Adams, H. P.
  1935   *The Life and Writings of Giambattista Vico.* New York: Russell & Russell.
Afonnikov, G.
  1958   Szhatoe slovo. In *Poema Mayakovskogo "Khorosho!" Sbornik statey,* 93-103. Moscow: ANSSSR.
  1963   K voprosu o pauzakh v stikhakh Mayakovskogo. In *Problemy narodnosti, realizma i khudozhestvennogo masterstva,* 43-58. Charzhou.
Aksyonov, I.
  1921   Sto pyadesyat millionov: Poema. *Pechat i revolyutsiya* 2:205-206.
Alexandrov, V.
  1983   Belyj subtexts in Pil'njak's *Golyi god. Slavic and E. Eur. J.* 27(1): 81-90.
Apollonio, U., ed.
  1973   *Futurist Manifestoes.* New York: Viking Press.
Arnheim, R.
  1969   *Visual Thinking.* Berkeley: Univ. of California Press.
Artobolevsky, G.
  1940   Kak chitat Mayakovskogo. In *Mayakovsky, 1930-1940: Stati i materialy,* 272-92. Leningrad: Sovetsky pisatel.
  1959   *Ocherki po khudozhestvennomu chteniyu.* Moscow: Uchpedgiz.
Arutcheva, V.
  1958   Zapisnye knizhki Mayakovskogo. *Literaturnoe nasledstvo* 65:325-96.
Aseev, N.
  1914   *Zor.* Kharkov-Moscow: Liren.
  1969   Melody or intonation (1923). In *Pasternak: Modern Judgements,* edited by D. Davie and A. Livingstone, 73-84. Nashville: Aurora.
Autographs
  1921   *Avtografy.* Moscow.
Bailey, J.
  1979   The Russian linguistic statistical method for studying poetic rhythm: A review article. *Slavic and E. Eur. J.* 23(2): 251-61.
Bann, S.
  1974   *The Tradition of Constructivism.* New York: Viking Press.
Barr, A.
  1951   *Matisse. His Art and His Public.* New York: Museum of Modern Art.
Baudouin de Courtenay, I.
  1912   *Ob otnoshenii russkago pisma k russkomu yazyku.* Petersburg: Obnovlenie shkoly.
Belenson, A., ed.
  1915   *Strelets.* Vol. 1. Petrograd: Strelets. Reprint. Ann Arbor: Ardis, 1978.

Bely, A.
1902   *Simfoniya (2-ya, dramaticheskaya)*. Moscow: Skorpion.
1904a   *Severnaya simfoniya (1-ya, geroicheskaya)*. Moscow: Skorpion.
1904b   *Zoloto v lazuri*. Moscow: Skorpion.
1905   *Vozvrat: III simfoniya*. Moscow: Grif.
1908   *Kubok meteley: Chetvyortaya simfoniya*. Moscow: Skorpion.
1909a   *Pepel*. Petersburg: Shipovnik.
1909b   *Urna*. Moscow: Grif.
1910a   *Simvolizm*. Moscow: Musaget.
1910b   *Serebryany golub*. Moscow: Skorpion.
1913-14 *Peterburg*. Sirin, vols. 1-3.
1916   *Peterburg*. Moscow: Sirin.
1917   Zhezl Aarona. *Skify* 1:155-212.
1917-18 *Kotik Letaev*. Skifyk, vols. 1-2
1918   *Khristos voskres*. Petersburg: Alkonost.
1919   *Korolevna i rytsari*. Petersburg: Alkonost.
1921   Prestuplenie Nikolaya Letaeva. *Zapiski mechtateley* 4:21-165.
1922a   *Peterburg*. Berlin: Epokha.
1922b   *Glossaloliya*[sic]. Berlin: Epokha.
1922c   *Kotik Letaev*. Petrograd-Berlin: Epokha.
1922d   *Zapiski chudaka*. Moscow-Berlin: Gelikon.
1922e   *Zvezda*. Moscow: Altsion.
1922f   *Posle razluki*. Petersburg-Berlin. Epokha.
1923   *Stikhotvoreniya*. Berlin-Petersburg-Moscow: Izd. Grzhebina.
1926   *Moskovsky chudak; Moskva pod udarom*. Moscow: Krug.
1927   *Kreshchony kitaets*. Moscow: Nikitinskie subbotniki.
1928   *Peterburg*. Moscow: Nikitinskie subbotniki.
1929   *Ritm kak dialektika i "Medny vsadnik."* Moscow: Federatsiya.
1930   Andrey Bely. In *Kak my pishem*, 9-23. Leningrad: Izd. Pisateley.
1932   *Maski*. Moscow: GIKhL.
1966   *Stikhotvoreniya i poemy*. Moscow-Leningrad: Sovetsky pisatel.
1967   *Peterburg*. Letchworth: Bradda.
1971a   Zovy vremyon: Vmesto predisloviya. *Novy zhurnal* 102:90-99.
1971b   *Kotik Letaev*. Translated by G. Janecek. Ann Arbor: Ardis.
1978   *Petersburg*. Translated by R. Maguire and J. Malmstad. Bloomington: Indiana Univ. Press.
1979   *The First Encounter*. Translated by G. Janecek. Notes by N. Berberova. Princeton: Princeton Univ. Press.
Berkov, P. N.
1969   Kniga v poezii Simeona Polotskogo. In *Literatura i obshchestvennaya mysl drevney Rusi* (Trudy otdela drevnerusskoy lit., IRLI ANSSSR XXIV, Leningrad), 260-66.
Bernshteyn, S.
1926   Zvuchashchaya khudozhestvennaya rech i ego izuchenie. *Poetika* 1:41-53.
1936   "Mayakovsky-chtets." *Govorit SSSR* 4:47-52.
Blavatsky, H.
1877   *Isis Unveiled*. Reprint. Pasadena: Theosophical Univ. Press, 1972.
1888   *The Secret Doctrine*. Reprint. Pasadena: Theosophical Univ. Press, 1970.

Blok, A.
1960-63 *Sobranie sochineniy v 8 tt.* Moscow-Leningrad: GIKhL.
Bobrov, S.
1913 O novoy illyustratsii. *Vertogradari nad lozami*, 151-56. Moscow: Lirika.
Bojko, S.
1972 *New Graphic Design in Revolutionary Russia.* New York: Praeger.
Bolinger, D.
1946 Visual morphemes. *Language* 22(4): 333-40.
Bolshakov, K.
1913 *Le Futur.* Moscow?
Bowlt, J.
1974 Neo-Primitivism and Russian painting. *The Burlington Magazine* 116 (March): 133-40.
1980 *Journey into Non-objectivity.* Dallas Museum of Fine Arts.
Bowlt, J., ed.
1976 *Russian Art of the Avant-Garde: Theory and Criticism 1902-1934.* New York: Viking Press.
Bowlt, J., and Long, R.-C. Washton
1980 *The Life of Vasilii Kandinsky in Russian Art: A Study of "On the Spiritual in Art."* Newtonville, Mass.: Oriental Research Partners.
Bozhidar (B. Gordeev)
1914 *Buben.* Moscow: Liren.
Brandt, R.
1901 O lzhenauchnosti nashego pravopisaniya (publichnaya lektsiya), Otdelny ottisk iz *Filologicheskikh zapisok*, vols. 1-2. Voronezh.
Bravsky, R.
1913 Simultanizm. *Helios* (Paris) 1:35-37.
Brown, E.
1973 *Mayakovsky: A Poet in the Revolution.* Princeton: Princeton Univ. Press.
Bruns, G.
1969 Mallarmé: The transcendence of language and the aesthetics of the book. *J. of Typographical Research* 3(3): 219-34.
Bryusov, V.
1918 *Opyty po metrike i ritmike, po evfonii i sozvuchiyam, po strofike i formam (Stikhi 1912-1918 g.).* Moscow: Gelikon.
1973-75 *Sobranie sochineniy v semi tomakh.* Moscow: Khud. lit.
Bubrin, V.
1982 Mudhuts and airplanes: The futurism of Vasily Kamensky. Ph.D. dissertation, Univ. of Toronto.
Bugaeva, K.
1971 Stikhi: Ob Andree Belom. *Novy Zhurnal* 102:103-109.
Bugaeva, K., and Petrovsky, A.
1937 Literaturnoe nasledstvo Andreya Belogo. *Literaturnoe nasledstvo* 27-28:575-638.
Bung, The
1913 *Zatychka.* Kherson: Gileya.
Burliuk, D.
1930 *Entelekhizm-iskusstvo kak organichesky protsess.* New York: Izd. M. Burliuk.

Burliuk, N.
1914   Poeticheskie nachala. *Pervy zhurnal russkikh futuristov.* Moscow. (See also Markov 1967, 77-80.)

Calinescu, M.
1977   *Faces of Modernity: Avant-Garde, Decadence, Kitsch.* Bloomington: Indiana Univ. Press.

Cassedy, A.
1981   Mallarmé and Andrej Belyj: Mathematics and the phenomenality of the literary object. *Modern Language Notes* 96:1066-1083.

Cendrars, B.
1966   *La prose du Transsibérien et de la petite Jehanne de France.* Reprint in book form. Paris: Editions Pierre Seghers.

Chamot, M.
1972   *Gontcharova.* Paris: La Bibliothèque des Arts.
1973   Russian avant-garde graphics. *Apollo* 97(142): 494-501.

Chernyshov, V.
1947   F. F. Fortunatov i A. A. Shakhmatov: reformatory russkogo pravopisaniya. In *A. A. Shakhmatov: Sbornik statey i materialov,* 167-252. Moscow-Leningrad: ANSSSR.

Chicherin, A. N.
1926   *Kan-Fun.* Moscow: Tsekh Poetov.
1939   O Vladimire Mayakovskom. Vospominaniya; avtorizovannaya mashinopis, Moscow, TsGALI, fond 336, op. 7, ed. 63.

Chicherin, A. N., Zelinsky, K., and Selvinsky, I.
1924   *Mena vsekh.* Moscow.

Chudovsky, V.
1917   Za bukvu ѣ . *Apollon* 4-5: v-viii.

Chukovsky, K.
1963   Mayakovsky, V. *Mayakovsky v vospominaniyakh sovremennikov,* 119-36. Moscow: GIKhL.
1967   *Sovremenniki.* Moscow: Molodaya gvardiya.

Ciszkewycz, M.
1980   "Nova Generatsiia" (1927-1930) and the artistic avant-garde in the Ukraine. Ph.D. dissertation, Univ. of Texas, Austin.

Cohen, A.
1976   Futurism and constructivism: Russian and other. *Print Collector's Newsletter* 7(1): 2-3.

Compton, S.
1978   *The World Backwards: Russian Futurist Books, 1912-16.* London: The British Library.

Cooper, D.
1971   *The Cubist Epoch.* New York: Phaidon.

Croaked Moon
1913   *Dokhlaya luna.* 1st ed. Moscow: Gileya.
1914   *Dokhlaya luna.* 2d (expanded) ed. Moscow: Gileya.

Crushed Skulls
1913   *Razvorochennye cherepa.* Petersburg.

Delaunay, S.
   1980   *Sonia Delaunay: A Retrospective.* Buffalo, New York: Albright-Knox Art Gallery.
Desargues, P.
   1961   *The Hermitage Museum, Leningrad.* New York: Abrams.
Donkey's Tail and Target
   1913   *Osliny khvost i mishen.* Moscow: Ts. A. Myunster.
Doria, C.
   1979   Visual writing forms in antiquity: The *Versus intexti.* In Kostelanetz 1979, 63-92.
Duvakin, V.
   1952   "Okna Rosta" i ikh politicheskoe i literaturnoe znachenie. In *Tvorchestvo Mayakovskogo: Sbornik statey.* Moscow: ANSSSR.
Eagle, H.
   1976   The semantic significance of step-ladder and column forms in the poetry of Belyj, Majakovskij, Voznesenskij, and Rozhdestvenskij. *Forum at Iowa on Russian Literature* 1:1-19.
   1978   Typographical devices in the poetry of Andrey Bely. In Janecek 1978, 71-84.
Economic Plan for Literature
   1925   *Gosplan literatury.* Moscow-Leningrad: Krug.
Efros, A.
   1930   *Profili.* Moscow: Federatsiya.
Ehrenburg, I.
   1976   People, years, lives. Excerpt in *Vladimir Mayakovsky: Innovator.* Moscow: Progress.
Ermilova, E.
   1964   Mayakovsky i sovremenny russky stikh. In *Mayakovsky i sovetskaya literatura: Sbornik statey,* 231-56. Moscow: Nauka.
Eryomin, I.
   1966   *Literatura drevney Rusi,* 212-17. Leningrad: Nauka.
Eskova, N.
   1966   Kosnyomsya istorii. In *Orfografiya i russky yazyk,* 57-96. Moscow: Nauka.
Ex Libris Catalogue #6
   1977   *Constructivism and Futurism: Russian and Other.* New York: T J Art, Inc.
Fairbank, J.
   1979   *The United States and China.* 4th ed. Cambridge, Mass.: Harvard Univ. Press.
Fenollosa, E., and Pound, E.
   1936   *The Chinese Written Character as a Medium for Poetry.* New York: City Lights Books.
Finter, H.
   1980   *Semiotik des Avantgardetextes: Gesellschaftliche und poetische Erfahrung im italienischen Futurismus.* Stuttgart: J. B. Metzler.
Folejewski, Z.
   1963   Mayakovsky and futurism. *Comparative Literature Studies,* special advance issue, 71-77.
   1978   The place of futurism in West and South Slavic poetry. *Canadian Contribu-*

tions to the VIII International Congress of Slavists (Zagreb, 1978), 45-59. Ottawa: Canadian Association of Slavists.

1980   *Futurism and Its Place in the Development of Modern Poetry.* Ottawa: Univ. of Ottawa Press.

From Painting to Design

1981   *Russian Constructivist Art of the Twenties.* Cologne: Galerie Gmurzynska.

Fyodorov, N.

1904   O pismenakh. *Vesy* 6:1-5.

Gasparov, M.

1974   *Sovremenny russky stikh: Metrika i ritmika.* Moscow: Nauka.

Gelb, I.

1963   *A Study of Writing.* Chicago: Univ. of Chicago Press.

Ginsburg, M.

1973   Art collectors of Old Russia: The Morozovs and the Shchukins. *Apollo* 97 (142): 470-85.

Goncharov, B.

1970   O pauzakh v stikhe Mayakovskogo. *Russkaya literatura* 2:47-61.

1971   Ob izuchenii stikha Mayakovskogo. In *Poet i sotsializm: K estetike V. V. Mayakovskogo,* 233-66. Moscow: Nauka.

1972   Intonatsionnaya organizatsiya stikha Mayakovskogo. *Russkaya literatura* 2:77-97.

Goncharova, N.

1914   *Voyna: misticheskie obrazy voyny.* Moscow: N. V. Kashin.

Gould, A.

1966   Protest by design. *Typografica* 14 (Dec.): 41-56.

Gray, C.

1971   *The Russian Experiment in Art: 1863-1922.* New York: Abrams.

Grot, Ya.

1885   *Russkoe pravopisanie.* 4th ed. Petersburg: Tipografiya Imperatorskoy Akademii nauk.

Gruzinov, I.

1978   Literaturnye kafe 20-kh godov: Iz vospominaniy I. V. Gruzinova "Mayakovsky i literaturnaya Moskva." In *Vstrechi s proshlym,* issue 3:174-92. Moscow: Sovetskaya Rossiya.

Grygar, M.

1973   Kubizm i poeziya russkogo i cheshkogo avangarda. In *The Structure of Texts and the Semiotics of Culture,* edited by J. van der Eng and M. Grygar. The Hague: Mouton.

Gukovsky, G.

1927   *Russkaya poeziya XVIII v.* Leningrad: Academia.

Havelock, E.

1963   *Preface to Plato.* Cambridge, Mass: Harvard Univ. Press.

1976   *Origins of Western Literacy.* Ontario Institute for Studies in Education, Monograph series #14.

Higgins, Dick,

1977   *George Herbert's Pattern Poems: In Their Tradition.* West Glover, VT, and New York: Unpublished Editions.

1979   The strategy of visual poetry: Three aspects. In Kostelanetz 1979, 41-50.

Hippisley, A.
  1971   The emblem in the writings of Simeon Polockij. *Slavic and East European J.* 15(2): 167-83.
  1977   Cryptography in Simeon Polockij's Poetry. *Russian Literature* 5(4): 389-402.
Hughes, R.
  1978   Bely's musical aesthetics. In Janecek 1978, 137-45.
Ignatev, I.
  1913   Smert iskusstvu! In V. Gnedov, *Smert iskusstvu!*, 1-2. Petersburg.
Iliazd
  1978   Paris: Centre Georges Pompidou.
Jakobson, R.
  1969   *O cheshskom stikhe preimushchestvenno v sopostavlenii s russkim.* Brown University Slavic Reprint.
  1971   Visual and auditory signs. On the relation between visual and auditory signs. Quest for the essence of language. In *Selected writings.* Vol. 2, 334-59. The Hague: Mouton.
  1980   *The Framework of Language.* Ann Arbor: Michigan Studies in the Humanities.
Jakobson, R., and Halle, M.
  1956   *Fundamentals of Language.* The Hague: Mouton.
Jakobson, R., and Waugh, L.
  1979   *The Sound Shape of Language.* Bloomington: Indiana Univ. Press.
Janecek, G.
  1971   Poetic devices and structure in Andrej Belyj's "Kotik Letaev." Ph.D. dissertation, Univ. of Michigan.
  1980a   Intonation and layout in Belyj's poetry. In *Andrey Bely, Centenary Papers*, edited by B. Christa, 81-90. Amsterdam: Hakkert.
  1980b   The many faces of Voznesensky's *Oza. Canadian-American Slavic Studies* 14 (4): 449-65.
  1980c   Krucenych and Chlebnikov co-authoring a manifesto. *Russian Literature* 8:483-98.
  1981a   Baudouin de Courtenay vs. Krucenych. *Russian Literature* 10(1): 17-29.
  1981b   A. N. Chicherin, poet-constructor. *Benzene*, Summer-Fall, 48-49.
  1982   Kruchonykh's Minimal Books. *Lightworks* 14/15:48-49.
Janecek, G., ed.
  1978   *Andrey Bely: A Critical Review.* Lexington: Univ. Press of Kentucky.
Jansen, A.
  1973   *Validation of Graphological Judgements: An Experimental Study.* The Hague: Mouton.
Kalder, I.
  1969-70 The genesis of the Russian *Grazhdanskii shrift* or civil type. *J. of Typographical Research* 3(4): 315-44, 4(2): 111-38.
Kamensky, V.
  1910   *Zemlyanka.* Petersburg.
  1914a   *Nagoy sredi odetykh.* Moscow.
  1914b   *Tango s korovami.* Moscow: Izd. Pervogo zhurnala russkikh futuristov.
  1916   *Devushki bosikom.* Tiflis.
  1918a   *Ego-moya biografiya velikogo futurista.* Moscow: Kitovras.
  1918b   *Zvuchal vesneyanki.* Moscow.

Kamensky, V.
   1931   *Put entuziasta*. Moscow: Federatsiya.
   1948   *Izbrannoe*. Moscow: Sovetsky pisatel.
Karginov, G.
   1979   *Rodchenko*. London: Thames and Hudson.
Karlinsky, S.
   1966   *Marina Cvetaeva: Her Life and Art*. Berkeley: Univ. of California Press.
Karshan, D.
   1975   *Malevich: The Graphic Work 1913-1930, A Print Catalogue Raisonné*. Jeru-
           salem: The Israel Museum.
Karsky, E. F.
   1928   *Slavyanskaya kirillovskaya paleografiya*. Leningrad: ANSSSR.
Katanyan, V.
   1958   O nekotorykh istochnikakh poemy "Khorosho!" *Literaturnoe nasledstvo* 65:285-
           324.
   1963   *Khudozhnik Vladimir Mayakovsky*. Moscow.
Kennedy, G.
   1964   Fenollosa, Pound and the Chinese character. In *Selected Works by G. A. Ken-
           nedy*. New Haven: Far Eastern Publication, Yale University.
Kepes, G., ed.
   1949   *Graphic Forms: The Arts as Related to the Book*. Cambridge, Mass.: Harvard
           Univ. Press.
Keyes, R.
   1978   The Bely-Ivanov-Razumnik correspondence. In Janecek 1978, 193-204.
Khardzhiev, N.
   1962   El Lissitzky—konstructor knigi. In *Iskusstvo knigi*. Vol. 3, 145-62. Moscow:
           Iskusstvo.
   1968a   Pamyati Natalii Goncharovoy (1881-1962) i Mikhaila Larionova (1881-1964).
           In *Iskusstvo knigi*. Vol. 5, years 1963-64. Moscow: Kniga.
   1968b   Novoe o Mayakovskom-khudozhnike. *Iskusstvo* 11:36-41.
   1976   Poeziya i zhivopis. In *K istorii russkogo avangarda*. Stockholm: Hylaea Prints.
Khardzhiev, N., and Trenin, V.
   1970   *Poeticheskaya kultura Mayakovskogo*. Moscow: Iskusstvo.
Khlebnikov, V.
   1913   *Ryav! Perchatki*. Moscow: "euy."
   1914   *Izbornik*. Petersburg: Izd. "euy."
   1919   Khudozhniki mira. In Khlebnikov 1968-71, 3:216-21.
   1920a   Nasha osnova. In Khlebnikov 1968-71, 3:228-43.
   1920b   *Ladomir*. Kharkov.
   1930   *Neizdanny Khlebnikov*. Vol. 18, years 1912-14. Moscow: Izd. "Gruppy druzey
           Khlebnikova."
   1968-71 *Sobranie sochineniy*. Munich: Fink.
Khudakov, S.
   1913   Literatura, khudozhestvennaya kritika, disputy i doklady. In *Osliny khvost i
           mishen*, 126-51. Moscow: Myunster.
Klonsky, M.
   1975   *Speaking Pictures: A Gallery of Pictorial Poetry from the Sixteenth Century
           to the Present*. New York: Harmony Books.

Kogan, F.
1935   *Tekhnika ispolneniya stikha*. Moscow: GIKhL.
Kondratov, A.
1962   Evolyutsiya ritmiki V. V. Mayakovskogo. *Voprosy yazykoznaniya* 5:101-108.
Korolyova, N.
1978   Sto albomov (Kollektsiya A. E. Kruchonykh). In *Vstrechi s proshlym*. Vol. 3, 294-305. Moscow: Sovetskaya Rossiya.
Kostelanetz, R.
1970a   *Moholy-Nagy*. New York: Praeger.
1970b   Words and images artfully entwined. *Art International* 14/7 (Sept. 20): 44-56.
1974   After sentences. In *I Articulations/Short Fictions*. New York: Kulchur Foundation.
Kostelanetz, R., ed.
1979   *Visual Literature Criticism: A New Collection*. Reno: West Coast Poetry Review.
1981   *The Old Poetries and the New*. Ann Arbor: Univ. of Michigan Press.
Kostetsky, A. G.
1979   Materialnaya priroda poeticheskogo teksta i ego vospriyatie. In *Lingvistika i poetika*, 200-206. Moscow: Nauka.
Kovtun, E.
1970   Lithographed books by Russian futurists. *Projekt* 6:40-46.
1974   The beginning of suprematism, 32-49; Varvara Stepanova's anti-book, 57-63. In *Von der Fläche zum Raum*. Cologne: Galerie Gmurzynska.
1976   K. S. Malevich: Pisma k M. V. Matyushinu. *Ezhegodnik rukopisnogo otdela Pushkinskogo doma na 1974*, 177-95. Leningrad: Nauka.
1979   Iz istorii russkogo avangarda (P. N. Filonov). In *Ezhegodnik rukopisnogo otdela Pushkinskogo doma na 1977 god*, 216-35. Leningrad: Nauka.
Kruchonykh, A.
1912   *Starinnaya lyubov*. Moscow.
1913a   *Pomada*. Moscow: Izd. Kuzmina i Dolinskogo.
1913b   *Poluzhivoy*. Moscow: Izd. Kuzmina i Dolinskogo.
1913c   *Pustinniki*. Moscow: Izd. Kuzmina i Dolinskogo.
1913d   *Vozropshchem*. Petersburg: Izd. "euy."
1913e   *Porosyata*. Petersburg: Izd. "euy."
1913f   *Chort i rechetvortsy*. Petersburg: Izd. "euy."
1913g   *Pobeda nad solntsem*. Petersburg: Izd. "euy."
1913h   *Stikhi Mayakovskogo*. Petersburg: Izd. "euy."
1913i   *Utinoe gnezdyshko durnykh slov*. Petersburg: Izd. "euy."
1913j   *Bukh lesinny*. Petersburg: Izd. "euy."
1913k   *Vzorval*. Petersburg: Izd. "euy."
1914a   *Porosyata*. Petersburg: Izd. "euy."
1914b   *Vzorval*. Petersburg: Izd. "euy."
1914c   *Te li le*. Petersburg.
1915a   *Taynye poroki akademikov*. Moscow.
1915b   *Zaumnaya gniga*. Moscow.
1915c   *Voyna* (Linocuts by O. Rozanova).
1916   *Vselenskaya voyna*. Petersburg.
1917a   *1918*. Tiflis.

1917b	*Uchites khudogi.* Tiflis.
1917c	*Golubye yaytsa.*
1918a	*F/nagt.*
1918b	*Iz vsekh knig.*
1918c	*Ozhirenie roz.*
1919a	*Tsvetistye tortsy.*
1919b	*Lakirovannoe triko.*
1919c	*Lakirovannoe triko,* typeset version, cover by I. Zdanevich. Tiflis: 41°.
1919d	*Milliork,* cover by I. Zdanevich. Tiflis: 41°.
1921	*Zaum.*
1922	*Zaumniki* (with G. Petnikov and V. Khlebnikov, cover by Rodchenko).
1924	*500 novykh ostrot i kalamburov Pushkina.* Moscow: Izd. Avtora.
1925	*Zaumny yazyk u Seyfullinoy, Vs. Ivanova, Leonova, Babelya, I. Selvinskogo, A. Vesyologo i dr.* Moscow: Izd. VSP.
1928	*15 let russkogo futurizma, 1912-1927 g.* Moscow: Izd. VSP.
1930a	*Ironiada.* Moscow: Izdanie avtora.
1930b	*Rubiniada.* Moscow: Izdanie avtora.
1973	*Izbrannoe.* Edited by V. Markov. Munich: Fink.

Kruchonykh, A., and Khlebnikov, V.

1912a	*Igra v adu.* Moscow.
1912b	*Mirskontsa.* Moscow.
1913	*Igra v adu.* 2d ed. Moscow.

Kuzminsky, K.

1980   300 let futurizma (fragmenty). *Soviet Union,* pts. 1-2, 7:238-56.

Lapshin, V.

1963   "*Mayakovsky—khudozhnik.*" *Iskusstvo* 7:43-53.

Lapshina, N.

1977   *Mir iskusstva.* Moscow: Iskusstvo.

Larionov, M.

1913   *Luchism.* Moscow.

Lavrentiev, A.

1981-82 The graphics of visual poetry in the life work of Varvara Stepanova. *Grafik* (Budapest).

Leering-van Moorsel, L.

1968   The typography of El Lissitzky. *J. of Typographical Research* 2(4): 323-40.

Lemon, L., and Reis, M.

1965   *Russian Formalist Criticism, Four Essays.* Lincoln: Univ. of Nebraska Press.

Levinton, G.

1981   Kak naprimer na YU. *Russian Linguistics* 6:81-102.

Lissitzky-Küppers, S.

1968   *El Lissitzky: Life, Letters, Texts.* Greenwich, Conn.: N.Y. Graphic Society.

Litvinenko, I.

1970   Dvadtsat pyat let truda. *Vstrechi s proshlym.* Vol. 1, 197-202. Moscow: Sovetskaya Rossiya.

Livshits, B.

1933   *Polutoraglazy strelets.* Leningrad: Izd. pisateley v Leningrade.

1977   *The One and a Half-eyed Archer.* Translated by J. Bowlt. Newtonville, Mass.: Oriental Research Partners.

Lotman, Yu.
　1972　*Analiz poeticheskogo teksta.* Leningrad: Izd. Prosveshchenie.
　1976　*Analysis of the Poetic Text.* Translated by D. Barton Johnson. Ann Arbor:
　　　　Ardis.
Lotman, Yu., and Uspensky, B. A.
　1978　On the semiotic mechanism of culture. *New Literary History* 9(2): 211-32.
Lunacharsky, A.
　1963-67 *Sobranie sochineniy v 8 tt.* Moscow: Khud. Lit.
Luriya, A.
　1979　*Yazyk i soznanie.* Moscow: Izd. Moskovskogo universiteta.
McIntyre, J. L.
　1903　*Giordano Bruno.* London: Macmillan & Co.
McLuhan, M.
　1969　*The Gutenberg Galaxy.* New York: Mentor Books.
McVey, G.
　1975　Alexei Kruchenykh: The bogeyman of Russian literature. *Russian Literature
　　　　Triquarterly* 13:571-90.
Magarotto, L.; Marzaduri, M.; and Pagani Cesa, G.
　1982　*L'avanguardia a Tiflis.* Venice: Quaderni del Seminario di Iranistica, Uralo-
　　　　Altaistica e Caucasologia dell'Universita degli Studi di Venezia, no. 13.
Malevich, K.
　1919　*O novykh sistemakh v iskusstve.* Vitebsk: Vitsvomas.
　1920　*Suprematizm: 34 risunka.* Vitebsk: Unovis.
Malmstad, J. E.
　1968　The poetry of Andrej Belyj: A variorum edition. Ph.D. dissertation, Princeton
　　　　University.
Marcadé, V.
　1971　*Le Renouveau de l'art pictural russe 1863-1914.* Lausanne: Editions L'Age
　　　　d'homme.
Marcuse, I.
　1962　*The Key to Handwriting Analysis.* 3d ed. New York: Rolton House.
Mares' Milk
　1914　*Moloko kobylits.* Kherson: Gileya.
Markov, V.
　1962　*The Longer Poems of Velimir Khlebnikov.* Berkeley: Univ. of California Press.
　1968　*Russian Futurism: A History.* Berkeley: Univ. of California Press.
Markov, V., ed.
　1967　*Manifesty i programmy russkikh futuristov.* Munich: Fink.
Marshall, H.
　1977　*The Pictorial History of the Russian Theatre.* New York: Crown.
Maslenikov, O.
　1956　Ruskin, Bely, and the Solov'yovs. *Slavonic and E. Eur. Rev.* 35(84): 15-23.
Matejka, L.
　1977　The alphabet. In *Modern Encyclopedia of Russian and Soviet Literature.* Vol.
　　　　1, 129-37. Gulf Breeze, Fla.: Academic International Press.
Matejka, L., and Titunik, I., eds.
　1976　*The Semiotics of Art: Prague School of Art, Prague School Contributions.*
　　　　Cambridge, Mass.: MIT Press.

Mayakovsky, V.
1913   *Ja!* Moscow: Izd. Kuzmina i Dolinskogo.
1914   *Vladimir Mayakovsky, Tragediya.* Moscow: Izd. 1-go zhurnala russkikh fu-
        turistov.
1916   *Prostoe kak mychanie.* Petrograd: Parus.
1919   *Sovetskaya azbuka.* Moscow.
1923a   *Pro eto.* Moscow-Petrograd: Gosizdat.
1923b   *Mayakovskaya gallereya.* Moscow: Krasnaya nov.
1923c   *Dlya golosa.* Designed by El Lissitzky. Berlin: Gosizdat.
n.d.   *Solntse v gostyakh u Mayakovskogo.* New York.
1955-61 [PSS] *Polnoe sobranie sochineniy v 13 tt.* Moscow GIKhL.
Mead, G.R.S.
1949   *Thrice-great Hermes: Studies in Hellenistic Theosophy and Gnosis.* London:
        John M. Watkins.
Ménard, L.
1866   *Hermès trismégiste.* Paris: Didier. 2d ed., 1867.
Messing, G.
1951   Structuralism and literary tradition. *Language* 27:1-12.
Metchenko, A.
1940   Ranni Mayakovsky. In *Vladimir Mayakovsky,* 9-68. Moscow-Leningrad:
        ANSSSR.
Mitler, L.
1979   The Genoese in Galata: 1453-1682. *Int. J. of Middle East Studies* 10(1): 71-91.
Moorhouse, A.
1953   *The Triumph of the Alphabet: A History of Writing.* New York: Henry Schu-
        man.
Morris, C. W.
1946   *Signs, Language, and Behavior.* New York: Prentice-Hall.
Motherwell, R., ed.
1951   *The Dada Painters and Poets: An Anthology.* New York: Wittenborn.
Motsh, V.
1963   K voprosu ob otnoshenii mezhdu ustnym i pismennym yazykom. *Voprosy ya-
        zykoznaniya* 1:90-95.
Mueller, L., ed.
1877   *Publilii optatiani porfyrii carmina.* Leipzig: B. G. Teubner.
Nadal, A.
1964   *Le Lettrisme, école poetique d'extrême avant-garde.* Nîmes, France.
Nakov, A.
1976   Malevich as printmaker. *The Print Collector's Newsletter* 7(1): 4-9.
Nikolaeva, T.
1961   Pismennaya rech i spetsifika eyo izucheniya. *Voprosy yazykoznaniya* 3:78-86.
Nikolskaya, T.
1980   Russian writers in Georgia: 1917-1921. In *Ardis Anthology of Russian Futur-
        ism,* 295-326. Ann Arbor: Ardis.
Nikonov, Vl.
1928   *Stati o konstruktivistakh.* Ulyanovsk: Strezhen.
Nivat, G.
1974   Trois documents importants pour l'étude d'Andrej Belyj. *Cahiers du Monde*

Russe et Soviétique 15(1-2): 41-146.

Oginskaya, L.
1973   On byl odnim iz bolshikh khudozhnikov-poligrafistov. *Dekorativnoe iskusstvo* 6:29-37.

O'Grady, H.
1979   Sperry: A verbal/visual novel. In Kostelanetz 1979, 157-60.

Olson, D.
1977   From utterance to text: The bias of language in speech and writing. *Harvard Educational Review* 47:257-81.

Paperny, Z.
1957   *O masterstve Mayakovskogo.* 2d ed. Moscow: Sovetsky pisatel.
1958   Mayakovsky v rabote nad poemoy "Pro eto." *Literaturnoe nasledstvo* 65: 217-84.

Paris-Moscou
1979   Paris: Centre Georges Pompidou.

Paustovsky, K.
1966   *Povest o zhizni.* Moscow: Sovetskaya Rossiya.

Pechorov, G.
1969   *Stikh Mayakovskogo—kak ego ponimat.* Moscow: MOPI im. N. Krupskoy.
1970   O sintagmennoy ritmiki stikhov Mayakovskogo. In *Voprosy filologii* (Uch. zap. Kuybyshevskogo gos. ped. in-ta) 74:146-64.
1971   *Problema novatorstva v poezii dorevolyutsionnogo V. V. Mayakovskogo (sin-tagmennaya organizatsiya stikha).* Moscow: Ph.D. dissertation, Spets. no. 1 10,641 Sov. literatura.

Peshkovsky, A.
1925   Stikh i proza s lingvisticheskoy tochki zreniya. In his *Sbornik statey*, 153-66. Moscow: GIZ.

Phillpot, C.
1979   Visual language, visual literature, visual literacy. In Kostelanetz 1979, 179-84.

Plato
1953   *Dialogues.* Vol. 3. 4th ed. Translated and edited by B. Jowett. Oxford: Clarendon Press.

Plotinus
1956   *Enneads.* English translation by S. MacKenna. London.

Poggioli, R.
1968   *The Theory of the Avant Garde.* Cambridge, Mass.: Belknap Press.

Pomorska, K.
1968   *Russian Formalist Theory and Its Poetic Ambience.* The Hague: Mouton.

Potyomkin, Pyotr
1908   *Smeshnaya lyubov.* Petersburg: Popov.

Pravdina, I.
1965   Poet i khudozhnik. In *Mayakovsky i problemy novatorstva*, 211-30. Moscow: Nauka.

Prayerbook of Three
1913   *Trebnik troikh.* Moscow: Izd. Kuzmina i Dolinskogo.

Rayt, R.
1963   Tolko vospominaniya. In *V. Mayakovsky v vospominaniyakh sovremennikov*, 236-78. Moscow: GIKhL.

Reeder, R.
    1980   The interrelationship of codes in Maiakovskii's ROSTA posters. *Soviet Union*, 7 pts., 1-2:28-52.
Remizov, A.
    1927   *Olya*. Paris: Izd. Vol.
    1929   *Po karnizam*. Belgrad: Russkaya biblioteka.
Reynolds, L.
    1969   Comment: Marshall McLuhan and italic handwriting. *J. of Typographical Research*. 3(3): 293-97.
Richter, H.
    1965   *Dada Art and Anti-Art*. New York: Oxford Univ. Press.
Roaring Parnassus
    1914   *Rykayushchi parnas*. Petersburg: Zhuravl.
Roman, K.
    1968   Graphology. In *Encyclopedia of the Written Word*, 431-52. New York: Ungar.
Rosenblum, R.
    1966   *Cubism and Twentieth-Century Art*. New York: Abrams.
    1973   Picasso and the typography of Cubism. In *Picasso in Retrospect*. New York: Praeger.
Rowell, M., and Rudenstine, A., eds.
    1981   *Art of the Avant-Garde in Russia: Selections from the George Costakis Collection*. New York: Guggenheim Museum.
Rubakin, A.
    1920   *Gorod. Stikhi*. Paris.
Rubinger, K., ed.
    1979   *Russian Women-Artists of the Avantgarde, 1910-1930*. Cologne: Galerie Gmurzynska.
Rudenstine, A., ed.
    1981   *The George Costakis Collection: Russian Avant-Garde Art*. New York: Abrams.
Russian Epigram
    1958   *Russkaya epigramma (XVIII-XIX vv)*. Leningrad: Sovetsky pisatel.
Sapir, E.
    1949   *Language*. New York: Harcourt, Brace, World.
Saussure, F. de
    1959   *Course in General Linguistics*. New York: McGraw-Hill.
Schapiro, M.
    1973   *Words and Pictures: On the Literal and the Symbolic Meaning in the Illustration of a Text*. Approaches to Semiotics, no. 11. The Hague: Mouton.
Sechenov, I.
    1973   *Biographical Sketch and Essays*. New York: Arno Press.
Shaginyan, M.
    1917   Lyap da tyap. *Russkaya volya*, July 2, 2.
Shchepkin, V. N.
    1920   *Russkaya paleografiya*. Moscow: Gos. Izdat.
Shershenevich, V.
    1916   *Avtomobilya postup*. Moscow.
    1919   *Krematoriy*. Moscow.
    1920   *Loshad kak loshad*. Moscow: Pleyada.

Shklovsky, V.
1919   O poezii i zaumnom yazyke. *Poetika: Sborniki po teorii poeticheskogo yazyka.* Petrograd.

Shtokmar, M.
1952   O stikhovoy sisteme Mayakovskogo. *Tvorchestvo Mayakovskogo,* 258-312. Moscow: ANSSSR.

Silvestrov, D.
1968   Mezhdu poeziey i zhivopisyu. *Dekorativnoe iskusstvo* 3:10-17.

Skydiggers
1913   *Nebokopy.* Petersburg.

Slap in the Face of Public Taste, A
1912   *Poshchochina obshchestvennomu vkusu.* Moscow: Izd. G. L. Kuzmina.

"Slap in the Face of Public Taste, A"
1913   Poshchochina obshchestvennomu vkusu. Flyer.

Slutsky, B.
1977   O Vasilii Kamenskom. In Vasili Kamensky, *Stikhi,* 5-23. Moscow: Khud. lit.

Sobolevsky, A. I.
1906   *Novy sbornik paleograficheskikh snimkov s russkikh rukopisey XI-XVIII vv.* Petersburg: Tip. A. Pavlovoy.

Spassky, S.
1940   *Mayakovsky i ego sputniki.* Leningrad: Sovetsky pisatel.

Spencer, H.
1969   *The Visible Word.* 2d ed. New York: Hastings House.

Sreznevsky, I. I.
1882   *Drevnie pamyatniki russkogo pisma i yazyka.* 2d ed. Petersburg: Tip. Imp. Akademii nauk.

Stankiewicz, E.
1972   *A Baudouin de Courtenay Anthology.* Bloomington: Indiana Univ. Press.

Stapanian, J.
1980   *Cubist "Vision" in the Early Lyrics (1912-13) of V. V. Majakovskij: A Literary Interpretation through Artistic Analogies.* Madison: Univ. of Wisconsin Press.
1982   V. Majakovskij's "To Signs" (*Vyveskam*)—A Cubist "signboard" in verse. *Slavic and E. Eur. J.* 26 (2): 174-86.

Stepanova, Varvara
1919   *Gaust chaba.* Moscow.

Struve, G.
1978   Andrey Bely, Redivivus. In Janecek 1978, 21-43.

Stuckenschmidt, H.
1975   Kandinsky and music. In *Homage to Wassily Kandinsky,* 27-30. Special issue of *XXe siècle Review.* New York: Leon Amiel.

Stutterheim, C.F.P.
1961   Poetry and prose, their interrelations and transitional forms. In *Poetics. Poetyka. Poetika,* 225-37. The Hague-Warsaw: Mouton.

Suvorova, K.
1978   Rukoy Aleksandra Bloka. . . . In *Vstrechi s proshlym.* Vol. 3, 77-90. Moscow: Sovetskaya Rossiya.

Szilard, L.
1973   O vliyanii ritmiki prozy F. Nitsshe na ritmiku prozy A. Belogo. *Studia Slavica Hungarica* 19 (1-3): 289-313.

Tarasenkov, A.
1966   *Russkie poety XX veka, 1905-1955.* Moscow: Sovetsky pisatel.
Tatlin's Dream
1970   *Russian Suprematist and Constructivist Art, 1910-1923.* London: Fischer Fine Art, Ltd.
Terentev, I.
1919a   *Rekord nezhnosti.* Tiflis: 41°.
1919b   *Kheruvimy svistyat.* Tiflis: 41°.
1919c   *Fakt.* Tiflis: 41°.
1919d   *17 erundovykh orudiy.* Tiflis: 41°.
1919e   *Kruchonykh grandiozar.* Tiflis: 41°. Reprinted in Kruchonykh 1973, 503-20.
1920(?)   *Traktat o sploshnom neprilichii.* Tiflis: 41°.
Teryan, N.
1973   Andrey Bely: Pisma k A. M. Miskaryan. *Russkaya literatura* 1:155-58.
Themerson, S.
1965   A well-justified postscript: Typographical topography. *The Penrose Annual* 58:334-43.
1968   *Apollinaire's Lyrical Ideograms.* London: Gaberbocchus.
Three
1913   *Troe.* Petersburg: Zhuravl.
Timofeev, L.
1941   *Poetika Mayakovskogo.* Moscow: Sovetsky pisatel.
1952   Iz nablyudeniy nad poetikoy Mayakovskogo. In *Tvorchestvo Mayakovskogo,* 163-209. Moscow: ANSSSR.
1958   *Ocherki teorii i istorii russkogo stikha.* Moscow: Goslitizdat.
Tomashevsky, B.
1959   *Stilistika i stikhoslozhenie.* Leningrad: Gos. uch-ped. izd.
Tisdall, C., and Bozzolla, A.
1978   *Futurism.* New York: Viking Press.
Tolstoy, L.
1978   *Azbuka: Novaya azbuka.* Moscow: Prosveshchenie.
Trap for Judges 1
1910   *Sadok sudey* 1. Petersburg. Zhuravl.
Trap for Judges 2
1913   *Sadok sudey* 2. Petersburg. Zhuravl.
Tretyakov, S.
1919   *Zheleznaya pauza.* Vladivostok.
Tretyakov, S.; Burliuk, D.; Tolstaya, T.; and Rafalovich, S.
1923   *Buka russkoy literatury.* Moscow.
Tsvetaeva, M.
1922   *Razluka.* Moscow: Gelikon.
1927   *Versty.* Vol. 2. Paris.
1928   *Posle Rossii.* Paris.
Tugenkhold, Ya.
1914   Frantsuzskoe sobranie S. I. Shchukina. *Apollon* 1-2:5-46.
Turbayne, C.
1969   Visual language from the verbal model. *J. of Typographical Research* 3(4): 345-70.

Tynyanov, Yu.
    1963   *Problema stikhotvornogo yazyka*. Reprint. The Hague: Mouton.
Union of Youth 3
    1913   *Soyuz molodyozhi* 3. Petersburg: Gileya.
Upensky, L.
    1973   *Po zakonu bukvy*. Moscow: Molodaya gvardiya.
Uspensky, P. D.
    1911   *Tertium Organum*. English translation by Bessaraboff and C. Bragdon. New
            York: Vintage, 1970.
Uvarova, I.
    1968   Veshchi tyanut k sebe v noru. . . . *Dekorativnoe iskusstvo* 9:29-32.
Vinokur, G.
    1943   *Mayakovsky—novator yazyka*. Moscow: Sovetsky pisatel.
Vysheslavtseva, S.
    1927   O motornykh impulsakh stikha, *Poetika* (Leningrad) 3: 45-62.
Weber, G.
    1976   Constructivism and Soviet literature. *Soviet Union*, 3, pt. 2, 294-310.
West, J.
    1975   The poetic landscape of the Russian Symbolists. *Forum for Modern Language
            Studies* 11(4): 289-304.
White, J. J.
    1976   The argument for a semiotic approach to shaped writing: The case of Italian
            Futurist typography. *Visible Language* 10(1): 53-86.
Williams, R.
    1977   *Artists in Revolution: Portraits of the Russian Avant-Garde, 1905-1925*.
            Bloomington: Indiana Univ. Press.
Winner, T.
    1977   Roman Jakobson and avantgarde art. In *Roman Jakobson: Echoes of His Schol-
            arship*, edited by D. Armstrong and C. van Schooneveld, 503-14. Lisse, Neth.:
            Peter de Ridder Press.
Word as Such, The
    1913   *Slovo kak takovoe*. Moscow.
Yates, F.
    1969   *Giordano Bruno and the Hermetic Tradition*. New York: Vintage Books.
Zdanevich, Ilya
    1918   *Yanko krul albanskay*. Tiflis: Sindikat.
    1919a   Asyol naprakat, *Sbornik S. G. Melnikovoy*, 39-68. Tiflis: Fantastichesky ka-
            bachok.
    1919b   *Ostraf paskhi*. Tiflis: 41°.
    1920   *zgA YAkaby*. Tiflis: 41°.
    1923   *lidantYU fAram*. Paris: 41°.
Zdanevich, I. et al.
    1919   *Sbornik S. G. Melnikovoy*. Tiflis: Fantastichesky kabachok.
Zdanevich, I., and Larionov, M.
    1913   Pochemu my raskrashivaemsya. *Argus* (December), 114-18.
Zdanevich, K.
    1919   Kruchonykh kak khudozhnik. *Kuranty* 3-4:12-14.

Zemtsov, S.
1964   Iskusstvo pervopechatnika. *Dekorativnoe iskusstvo* 3:16-17.
Zhadova, L.
1975   Des Commencements sans fins: Sur le théâtre futuriste russe. *Europe,* April
          1975, 124-35.
Zhegin, L.
1963   Vospominaniya o Mayakovskom. In *V. Mayakovsky v vospominaniyakh so-
          vremennikov,* 99-102. Moscow: GIKhL.
Zheverzheev, L.
1940   K istorii teksta tragedii "Vladimir Mayakovsky." In *Vladimir Mayakovsky,*
          339-53. Moscow-Leningrad: ANSSSR.
Zhirmunsky, V.
1975   Stikhoslozhenie Mayakovskogo. In *Teoriya stikha.* Leningrad: Sovetsky pisa-
          tel.
Zhovtis, A.
1966   Granitsy svobodnogo stikha. *Voprosy literatury* 5:105-23.
1968a   V rassypannom stroyu . . . (Grafika sovremennogo russkogo stikha). *Russkaya
          literatura* 1:123-34.
1968b   *Stikhi nuzhny.* Alma-Ata: Zhazushy.
1971   Osvobozhdyonny stikh Mayakovskogo. *Russkaya literatura* 2:53-75.
Zhurov, P.
1923   Smysl slova. *Krasnaya nov* 7:277-83.
Ziegler, R.
1978   Aleksej Krucenych als Sprachkritiker. *Wiener slavistisches Jahrbuch* B.24: 286-
          310.
No author
1966   Figurnye stikhi. *Nauka i zhizn* 8:79.
No author
1966   *The Lubok: 17th-18th Century Russian Broadsides.* Moscow: Sovietsky Khu-
          dozhnik.

Index

Library of Congress Cataloging in Publication Data

Janecek, Gerald.
The look of Russian literature.

Bibliography: p.
Includes index.
1. Russian literature—20th century—History and criticism.
2. Visual literature—History and criticism. I. Title.

PG3020.5.V58J36 1984   891.7'09'003   84-42578
ISBN 0-691-06604-3